LIFE DEATH

THE SEMINARS OF JACQUES DERRIDA

Edited by Geoffrey Bennington and Peggy Kamuf

Life Death

Jacques Derrida

Edited by Pascale-Anne Brault and Peggy Kamuf

Translated by Pascale-Anne Brault and Michael Naas

The University of Chicago Press ‡ CHICAGO AND LONDON

The University of Chicago Press, Chicago 60637
The University of Chicago Press, Ltd., London
© 2020 by The University of Chicago
All rights reserved. No part of this book may be used or reproduced in any manner whatsoever without written permission, except in the case of brief quotations in critical articles and reviews. For more information, contact the University of Chicago Press, 1427 E. 60th St., Chicago, IL 60637.
Published 2020
Paperback edition 2023
Printed in the United States of America

32 31 30 29 28 27 26 25 24 23   1 2 3 4 5

ISBN-13: 978-0-226-69951-6 (cloth)
ISBN-13: 978-0-226-82644-8 (paper)
ISBN-13: 978-0-226-70114-1 (e-book)
DOI: https://doi.org/10.7208/chicago/9780226701141.001.0001

Originally published in French as *La vie la mort. Séminaire (1975–1976)*
© Éditions du Seuil, 2019

"Logic of the Living" was published in French as "Logique de la vivante" in Jacques Derrida, *Otobiographies. L'enseignement de Nietzsche et la politique du nom propre*
© Éditions Galilée, 1984

Published with the generous assistance of the France Chicago Center.

Cet ouvrage a bénéficié du soutien des programmes d'aide à la publication de l'Institut français. This work, published as part of a program of aid for publication, received support from the Institut Français.

Library of Congress Cataloging-in-Publication Data

Names: Derrida, Jacques, author. | Brault, Pascale-Anne, editor, translator. | Kamuf, Peggy, 1947– editor. | Naas, Michael, translator. | Derrida, Jacques. Works. Selections. English. 2009.
Title: Life death / Jacques Derrida ; edited by Pascale-Anne Brault and Peggy Kamuf ; translated by Pascale-Anne Brault and Michael Naas.
Other titles: La vie la mort. English (Brault and Naas)
Description: Chicago : University of Chicago Press, 2020. | Series: Seminars of Jacques Derrida | Includes bibliographical references and index.
Identifiers: LCCN 2019050021 | ISBN 9780226699516 (cloth) | ISBN 9780226701141 (e-book)
Subjects: LCSH: Life. | Death.
Classification: LCC B2430.D483 V5413 2020 | DDC 194—dc23
LC record available at https://lccn.loc.gov/2019050021

CONTENTS

Foreword to the English Edition : vii
General Introduction to the French Edition : ix
Editorial Note : xi
Translators' Note : xix

FIRST SESSION Programs : 1

SECOND SESSION Logic of the Living
(She the Living) : 25

THIRD SESSION Transition (Oedipus's Faux Pas) : 50

FOURTH SESSION The Logic of the Supplement:
The Supplement of the Other,
of Death, of Meaning, of Life : 77

FIFTH SESSION The Indefatigable : 96

SIXTH SESSION The "Limping" Model:
The Story of the Colossus : 115

SEVENTH SESSION : 138

EIGHTH SESSION Cause ("Nietzsche") : 156

NINTH SESSION Of Interpretation : 177

TENTH SESSION Thinking the Division
of Labor — and the Contagion
of the Proper Name : 198

ELEVENTH SESSION   The Escalade—of the
                    Devil in Person : 219

TWELFTH SESSION   Freud's Leg(acies) : 241

THIRTEENTH SESSION Sidestep Detour: Thesis,
                    Hypothesis, Prosthesis : 260

FOURTEENTH SESSION Tightenings : 283

Index of Proper Names : 301

FOREWORD TO THE ENGLISH EDITION

When the decision was made to edit and publish Jacques Derrida's teaching lectures, there was little question that they would and should be translated into English. From early in his career, in 1968, and annually thereafter until 2003, Derrida regularly taught at US universities. It was his custom to repeat for his American audience the lectures delivered to his students in France the same year. Teaching first at Johns Hopkins and then at Yale, he read the lectures in French as they had been written. But from 1987, when he began teaching at the University of California, Irvine, Derrida undertook to lecture in English, improvising on-the-spot translations of his lectures. Recognizing that the greater part of his audience outside of France depended on translation proved easier, however, than providing a satisfying ad libitum English version of his own elegant, complex, and idiomatic writing. In the circumstances, to his evident joy in teaching was often added a measure of suffering and regret for all that remained behind in the French original. It is to the memory of Derrida the teacher as well as to all his students past and still to come that we offer these English translations of "The Seminars of Jacques Derrida."

The volumes in this series are translations of the original French editions published by Éditions du Seuil, Paris, in the collection "Bibliothèque Derrida" under the direction of Katie Chenoweth. In each case they will follow shortly the publication of the corresponding French volume. The scope of the project, and the basic editorial principles followed in establishing the text, are outlined in the "General Introduction to the French Edition," translated here. Editorial issues and decisions relating more specifically to this volume are addressed in an "Editorial Note." Editors' footnotes and other editorial interventions are all translated without modification, except in the case of footnoted citations of quoted material, which refer to extant English translations of the sources as necessary. Additional translators' notes have been kept to a minimum. To facilitate scholarly reference, the page numbers of the French edition are printed in the margin on the line at which the new page begins.

Translating Derrida is a notoriously difficult enterprise, and while the translator of each volume assumes full responsibility for the integrity of the translation, as series editors we have also reviewed the translations and sought to ensure a standard of accuracy and consistency across the volumes. Toward this end, in the first phase of work on the series, we have called upon the advice of other experienced translators of Derrida's work into English and wish to thank them here: Pascale-Anne Brault, Michael Naas, Elizabeth Rottenberg, and David Wills, as well as all the other participants in the Derrida Seminars Translation Project workshops.

Geoffrey Bennington
Peggy Kamuf
MARCH 2019

GENERAL INTRODUCTION
TO THE FRENCH EDITION

Between 1960 and 2003, Jacques Derrida wrote some fourteen thousand printed pages for the courses and seminars he gave in Paris, first at the Sorbonne (1960–64), then at the École normale supérieure, rue d'Ulm (1964–84), and then, for the last twenty years of his life, at the École des hautes études en sciences sociales (EHESS, 1984–2003). The series "The Seminars of Jacques Derrida," in the collection "Bibliothèque Derrida," will make available, after this inaugural volume of a seminar from 1975–76, *Life Death*, the seminars that Derrida gave at EHESS, four of which have already appeared.[1] This corresponds to the period in Derrida's teaching career when he had the freedom to choose the topics he was going to treat, most often over two or even three years, in seminars that were themselves organized into the following thematic series: "Philosophical Nationality and Nationalism"

1. These four volumes were published by Éditions Galilée (Paris): *Séminaire La bête et le souverain. Volume I (2001–2002)*, ed. Michel Lisse, Marie-Louise Mallet, and Ginette Michaud (2008) [*The Beast and the Sovereign*, v. 1 (2001–2), trans. Geoffrey Bennington (Chicago: University of Chicago Press, 2009)]; *Séminaire La bête et le souverain. Volume II (2002–2003)*, ed. M. Lisse, M.-L. Mallet, and G. Michaud (2010) [*The Beast and the Sovereign*, v. 2 (2002–3), trans. Geoffrey Bennington (Chicago: University of Chicago Press, 2010)]; *Séminaire La peine de mort. Volume I (1999–2000)*, ed. Geoffrey Bennington, Marc Crépon, and Thomas Dutoit (2012) [*The Death Penalty*, v. 1 (1999–2000), trans. Peggy Kamuf (Chicago: University of Chicago Press, 2014)]; *Séminaire La peine de mort. Volume II (2000–2001)*, ed. G. Bennington and M. Crépon (2015) [*The Death Penalty*, v. 2 (2000–2001), trans. Elizabeth Rottenberg (Chicago: University of Chicago Press, 2017)]. In addition, two courses given prior to these seminars were also published by Éditions Galilée: *Heidegger: la question de l'Être et l'Histoire. Cours de l'ENS-Ulm 1964–1965*, ed. Thomas Dutoit, with the assistance of Marguerite Derrida (2013) [*Heidegger: The Question of Being and History* (1964–65), trans. Geoffrey Bennington (Chicago: University of Chicago Press, 2016)], and *Théorie et pratique. Cours de l'ENS-Ulm 1975–1976*, ed. Alexander García Düttmann (2017) [*Theory and Practice* (1976–77), trans. David Wills (Chicago: University of Chicago Press, 2019)].

(1984–88), "Politics of Friendship" (1988–91), followed by the long sequence "Questions of Responsibility" (1991–2003), focusing successively on the secret (1991–92), testimony (1992–95), hostility and hospitality (1995–97), perjury and pardon (1997–99), the death penalty (1999–2001), and, finally, questions of sovereignty and animality under the title "The Beast and the Sovereign" (2001–3). We will here follow the logic previously established for the final seminars of Jacques Derrida, namely, publishing in reverse chronological order all the seminars given at EHESS, all the while respecting the internal chronology of each thematic series. After the exceptional case of *Life Death*, we will return to publishing the seminars given at EHESS, starting with "Perjury and Pardon I" (1997–98), followed by "Perjury and Pardon II" (1998–99), and so on up through the fourth volume of the first series, titled "Philosophical Nationality and Nationalism."

We have tried in our editorial work to remain as faithful as possible to the text as Jacques Derrida wrote it, and we present it here with as few editorial interventions as possible. With very few exceptions (for example, improvised sessions), Derrida would prepare for each class session not notes but a continuous written text, sometimes punctuated by references to the texts he was quoting, didascalia (e.g., "comment") indicating a time for improvisation, and marginal or interlineal annotations. When we have been able to locate tape recordings of the seminars, we have also indicated in footnotes the oral comments that Derrida added to his text in the course of a seminar session. It is likely that if Derrida had himself published his seminars during his lifetime he would have reworked them. This practice of reworking was in fact rather common with Derrida, who frequently drew from the vast wealth of material of his courses for lectures and texts he intended for publication. This explains the fact that we sometimes find a partial reworking or adaptation of a seminar in an already published work, highlighting even further the dynamic and coherence that characterized Derrida's teaching, a laboratory where ideas were tested and then frequently developed elsewhere in a more or less modified form. That being said, most of the seminars that will appear in the "Bibliothèque Derrida" have not been previously published in any form: their publication can only greatly enrich the corpus of Derrida's thought by making available one of its essential resources.

Katie Chenoweth,
  Head of the Editorial Committee
Geoffrey Bennington
Pascale-Anne Brault
Peggy Kamuf

Ginette Michaud
Michael Naas
Elizabeth Rottenberg
Rodrigo Therezo
David Wills

EDITORIAL NOTE

The *Life Death* seminar was given by Jacques Derrida as part of his teaching responsibilities as maître-assistant of philosophy at the École normale supérieure (ENS), rue d'Ulm, in Paris, from fall 1975 through May or June 1976.[1] Though none of the seminar sessions are dated in the typescript, a few references to the calendar — "before Christmas" (third session), "in the few sessions remaining after the Easter break" (tenth session) — help us to follow the progression of a seminar that, with its fourteen sessions, is longer than most of the yearly courses given by Derrida at ENS. To understand some of the context for this seminar, it is important to know that during the previous academic year, in April 1974, the first steps were taken toward the creation of GREPH (Groupe de recherches sur l'enseignement philosophique), an organization for which Jacques Derrida would be the driving force and that would eventually lead to the Estates General of Philosophy (États généraux de la philosophie) in June 1979. It is thus a few months before giving the *Life Death* seminar, in January 1975, that GREPH was officially formed.[2] It is probably at that time that Derrida began a second series of ten sessions, which, in the catalogue of his courses and seminars, bears the title "GREPH (the concept of ideology in the French ideologues)."[3] In a published fragment from the first session of this series, Derrida qualifies

---

1. Though the French edition of Jacques Derrida's *Théorie et pratique* gives 1975–76 as the date of the course, it was in fact given in 1976–77. We would like to thank Alan Schrift for having pointed out this error.

2. Concerning the formation of GREPH and the role played by Jacques Derrida in it, see "*Avant-Projet*: For the Founding of a Research Group on the Teaching of Philosophy," in *Who's Afraid of Philosophy?: Right to Philosophy 1*, trans. Jan Plug and others (Stanford, CA: Stanford University Press, 2002), pp. 92–98 [*Du droit à la philosophie* (Paris: Éditions Galilée, 1990), pp. 146–53].

3. The catalogue can be found on the website of the Derrida Seminars Translation Project, http://derridaseminars.org/seminars.html.

the series as "a sort of counter-seminar,"⁴ a formulation that might lead one to think that *Life Death*, a seminar preparing students for the *agrégation* exam, was providing the prime example of that which needed to be countered. And, in some sense, that is not entirely false, inasmuch as Jacques Derrida, in his role as "caiman"⁵ at ENS, was not completely free to determine the themes or topics he was going to teach. On the contrary, he had to "follow the program," namely, the program for the *agrégation* in philosophy for that particular year. This programming of the teaching of philosophy in preparation for a competitive exam was one of the principal targets of the critiques and analyses of GREPH. For the competitive exam of 1976, therefore, the theme announced was "Life and Death," a title that Derrida retains but only after dropping the conjunction "and," a modification that he justifies at some length during the first session.

And yet, in a more general sense, this seminar can also be considered a sort of "counter-seminar" in the spirit of GREPH. Indeed, Derrida leaves no doubt on this score when, near the opening of the first session of *Life Death*, he writes:

> Every year for a number of years now, at the beginning of each seminar, as some of you know, I explain my uneasiness in trying to adapt my work here to the *agrégation* program and the strategic decision that I make, each time, all the while fighting against the institution of the *agrégation*, elsewhere and right here, to negotiate with it from within a given set of conditions. I am not going to repeat what I have already said and reproduce ad infinitum the same schema. I would rather, in analyzing the title of the *agrégation* program, not conform to it but make of it the object—to be deconstructed—of this seminar.⁶

It is thus indeed a question, "elsewhere and right here," of countering, or rather of deconstructing, what in the teaching of philosophy remained still too programmed and programmatic. This is clearly what was behind Derrida's thinking when he later gave as a title to this inaugural session, adding it by hand to the typescript, "Programs"—in the plural.

---

4. J. Derrida, "Where a Teaching Body Begins and How It Ends," in *Who's Afraid of Philosophy?*, pp. 67–98 ["Où commence et comment finit un corps enseignant," in *Du droit à la philosophie*, pp. 111–53].

5. In ENS slang, a "caiman" is an "agrégé-répétiteur," that is, a professor charged with preparing students for the *agrégation* exam, the notoriously competitive qualifying examination taken by prospective higher-level teachers in the secondary and university systems.

6. See below, first session, p. 7.

As he had done since nearly the beginning of his teaching career, Jacques Derrida wrote out the entirety of the *Life Death* seminar in order to read it aloud and comment on it in front of his audience.[7] Of course, this weekly practice of writing was usually taking place at the same time as numerous publication projects and public presentations. Sometimes, indeed rather often, these different facets of Derrida's intellectual activity overlapped, as it were, as when he selected pages previously written for his seminar for a later publication or lecture. In this respect, the *Life Death* seminar is exemplary, since it provides the first version of texts presented at several different conferences and published in two important books by Derrida.

The second session of the seminar was thus published, with minimal reworking, in *Otobiographies. L'enseignement de Nietzsche et la politique du nom propre*, a text first presented as a lecture, in an American translation, in 1976, before being presented again as a lecture in French in 1979.[8] The eighth session and part of the ninth form the basis of a lecture that was given in 1981 at the Goethe Institute in Paris, with Hans-Georg Gadamer in attendance, and subsequently published in German and in English.[9] But the most significant borrowing from the seminar is without a doubt that of the last four sessions in *The Post Card: From Socrates to Freud and Beyond*, in 1980.[10] In a long essay in the second part of that book, titled "To Speculate—On 'Freud,'" Derrida follows the general trajectory laid out in these

---

7. No tape recording of this seminar could be found in the archives.

8. See Jacques Derrida, "Otobiographies: The Teaching of Nietzsche and the Politics of the Proper Name," trans. Avital Ronell, in *The Ear of the Other: Otobiography, Transference, Translation*, ed. Christie V. McDonald (New York: Schocken Books, 1985), pp. 1–38 [*Otobiographies. L'enseignement de Nietzsche et la politique du nom propre* (Paris: Éditions Galilée, 1984), pp. 33–118. This text had been previously published in French under the title *L'oreille de l'autre, otobiographies. Transferts, traductions. Textes et débats avec Jacques Derrida*, ed. Claude Lévesque and Christie V. McDonald (dir.) (Montréal: VLB éditeur, 1982), pp. 11–56].

9. See Jacques Derrida, "Guter Wille zur Macht II. Die Unterschriften interpretieren (Nietzsche/Heidegger)," German translation by Friedrich Kittler in *Text und Interpretation*, ed. Philippe Forget (Munich: W. Fink, 1984), pp. 62–77; and Jacques Derrida, "Interpreting Signatures (Nietzsche/Heidegger): Two Questions," trans. Diane Michelfelder and Richard E. Palmer, *Philosophy and Literature* 10, no. 2 (October 1986): 246–62; reprinted in *Dialogue and Deconstruction: The Gadamer-Derrida Encounter*, ed. D. Michelfelder and R. E. Palmer (Albany: SUNY Press, 1989), pp. 58–74. This text was previously unpublished in French.

10. Jacques Derrida, *The Post Card: From Socrates to Freud and Beyond*, trans. Alan Bass (Chicago: University of Chicago Press, 1987), pp. 257–409 [*La carte postale. De Socrate à Freud et au-delà* (Paris: Aubier-Flammarion, 1980), pp. 275–437].

four sessions, but not without developing and complicating that trajectory in numerous ways.¹¹ In his introductory note to that essay in *The Post Card*, Derrida recalls the origin and ambitious itinerary of these sessions of his seminar, which, while themselves already complex, form just one of the seminar's three intertwined "rings":

> The text on whose borders this discourse would be attempting to maintain itself is Freud's *Beyond the Pleasure Principle*. In effect, I am extracting this material from a seminar which followed the itinerary of three rings. Proceeding each time from an explication with a given text of Nietzsche's, the seminar was first concerned with a "modern" problematic of biology, genetics, epistemology, or the history of the life sciences (readings of Jacob, Canguilhem, etc.). Second ring: return to Nietzsche, and then an explication with the Heideggerian reading of Nietzsche. Then, here, the third and last ring.¹²

For today's reader of this seminar, it is interesting to compare the first state of these texts, written for oral presentation, with their published version. We did so systematically, which allowed us not only to appreciate the care with which Derrida reread his own work but also to resolve several questions raised in our reading, most of these the result of Derrida's numerous handwritten additions on the typescript. It is well-known that Derrida's handwriting is often difficult to decipher, and never more so when, as here, he was writing for himself without other readers in mind. Despite our best efforts, we sometimes had no choice but to signal in footnotes our perplexity before certain "illegible" words.

But the interest of the *Life Death* seminar goes well beyond these "genetic" considerations regarding the work, since the majority of these seminar pages were not published in any form until now. That is especially the case of the four sessions (the third to the sixth) that treat the "life sciences" and, in particular, genetics, this time in the biological and not literary sense. In his patient and incisive analysis of the writings of Georges Canguilhem and, especially, of *The Logic of the Living* by the famous French biologist Fran-

---

11. The four sessions essentially correspond to the four chapters of "To Speculate—On 'Freud'": chap. 1 "Notices (Warnings)" (eleventh session); chap. 2 "Freud's Legacy" (twelfth session); chap. 3 "Paralysis" (thirteenth session); chap. 4 "Seven: Postscript" (fourteenth session). The twelfth session was also published in *Études freudiennes*, nos. 13–14 (1978): 87–125, under the title "Legs de Freud," that is, "Freud's Legacy."

12. J. Derrida, *Post Card*, p. 259n1 [*La carte postale*, 277n1]. Derrida also makes reference to these "rings" or "loops" throughout the seminar: see *infra*, pp. 48, 141, 218–20, 227, and 297.

çois Jacob, Jacques Derrida demonstrates how these scientific discourses are susceptible to be deconstructed right down to their conceptual foundations, there where they try to develop, without posing too many critical questions, such notions as *text, program, trace, code, supplement, language, metaphor,* or *analogy*—all notions that Derrida had himself been thoroughly rethinking for some time. Through this tightly focused discussion of biology and genetics, the *Life Death* seminar indisputably establishes, it seems to us, the pertinence of Derridean thought for treating some of the great scientific questions of our time, beginning with questions about life, living beings, and death—or, as he will write it, eliminating the conjunction and the space between words, "lifedeath."

This edition is based on digital copies of the original transcript of the seminar, which is housed in the Jacques Derrida papers at the Critical Theory Archive of the library at the University of California, Irvine.[13] We also consulted the *fonds* Derrida at the Institut Mémoires de l'édition contemporaine (IMEC).[14] The fourteen sessions of the typescript amount to some 264 pages typed by their author. It is interesting to note that Derrida typed these sessions on the backs of ENS letterhead, or of photocopies announcing a meeting of GREPH,[15] or of pages of an English translation of "White Mythology."[16] The archives at Irvine include carbon copies of all these pages, which we also had to check since Derrida sometimes added handwritten notes on these copies that are not to be found on the original. When such differences needed to be taken into account we have referred to "T1" for the typescript and "T2" for the carbon copy. As already noted, there are numerous handwritten additions, especially on the pages of the original typescript: they are sometimes interlineal, sometimes in the margins, sometimes marked by arrows indicating the place of insertion, and sometimes in an ambiguous relation with the typed text. In our editorial notes, we have

---

13. The original typescript is located in box 12, folders 10–19, of the Jacques Derrida archives at the University of California, Irvine.

14. The "Life Death" seminar is kept at IMEC in two boxes, 219 DRR 225.5 and 225.6.

15. This little material fact confirms our suggestion above that the activities of GREPH are hovering in the background of this seminar.

16. This is apparently the typescript of what would become the first publication of this translation, "White Mythology: Metaphor in the Text of Philosophy," trans. F. C. T. Moore, *New Literary History* 6, no. 1 (1974): 5–74. See Jacques Derrida, "La mythologie blanche. La métaphore dans le texte de la philosophie," in *Marges—de la philosophie* (Paris: Éditions de Minuit, 1972), pp. 247–324.

attempted to describe and decipher as best we could these additions, without however venturing too far when we were uncertain about our reading. Unless otherwise indicated in the notes, all of Derrida's additions are handwritten.

Several folders archived with the seminar contain photocopies of the texts quoted by Derrida during a session. The particular passages that Derrida wanted to quote are often indicated in the margins and the words he wanted to comment on are underscored. These photocopied pages do not represent, however, all the passages quoted in the course of the seminar. For the others, we consulted, whenever this was possible, the editions of the works that Derrida himself would have used, referring when necessary to Derrida's personal library housed at the Princeton University Library.

In addition to the insertion of handwritten words and phrases, several pages bear marks that were apparently made with an eye toward reworking the text of the seminar for various lectures and publications. Among these are vertical lines in the margins, passages or entire pages crossed out, and other similar indications of this textual "repurposing." Since such indications add nothing to the reading of the seminar itself, we have left out all mention of these in our editorial notes. For the same reason, we do not signal any handwritten additions to the typescript that were completely unreadable to us.

In his typescript, Derrida tended to abbreviate certain proper names, "FN" for Friedrich Nietzsche, "J" for Jacob, and "F" or "Fr" for Freud, as well as, for this latter, "PR" for "Principe de réalité" (Reality Principle) and "PP" for "Principe du plaisir" (Pleasure Principle). Derrida no doubt began by pronouncing these terms in full during the seminar but, toward the end of the eleventh session, while speaking of Freud and his grandson, he plays on the fact that "PP" is pronounced in French "Pépé," meaning "grandfather," while "PR" could be heard as "Père," "father." From that point on, we have retained these two abbreviations as they appear in the typescript. As for the [French] title of Freud's text, *Au-delà du principe du plaisir*, Derrida refers to it throughout as *Au-delà du principe de plaisir*. When he speaks of the concept, however, he goes back and forth between *du* and *de*.

Jacques Derrida typed up his seminars at a rate of about twenty-five pages a week. It is thus hardly surprising that one would find traces of that pace in the typescript: incomplete sentences, parentheses opened but not closed, and other little signs of inattention to established conventions. When necessary, we signal these problems to the reader in our notes, though we do not indicate corrections made to the typescript of obvious errors (typos, misspellings, etc.). Whenever we have had to restore words or parts of words that were missing in the typescript, we use angle brackets (< . . . >) to signal our intervention. When the typescript presents a more significant problem for reading, we signal this in the notes by: "As such in the typescript."

Although Derrida consulted the published translations of the works of Nietzsche, Heidegger, and Freud that he quotes, he very often modifies them and sometimes gives his own translation of the passages quoted. We note throughout when the translation has been modified or completely redone in this way. When words are in italics in quotations, we note only those instances where it is Derrida who has added the italics. As for the footnotes, they are all, without exception, ours.

We wish to express our deep gratitude to all those who helped us over the course of this long process. We would especially like to thank Brieuc Gérard, a doctoral student in French Studies at the University of Southern California, who was an absolutely ideal assistant, and Katie Chenoweth, Professor of French Studies at Princeton University, who graciously responded to all our requests for information about the works in Derrida's personal library. The help of Ginette Michaud, Michael Naas, Elizabeth Rottenberg, Rodrigo Therezo, David Farrell Krell, and the entire editorial team of the seminars of Jacques Derrida was invaluable to us as well. We also thank DePaul University for its support. But we would especially like to acknowledge and express our gratitude to Marguerite Derrida for all her help with this project from the very beginning.

Pascale-Anne Brault
Peggy Kamuf

TRANSLATORS' NOTE

In an envoi from *The Post Card* dated 29 August 1977 we read the following: "M., who has read the seminar on *Life Death* along with several friends, tells me that I should publish the notes without changing anything. This is impossible, of course, unless I just detach the sessions on Freud, or only the one on Freud's legacy, the story of the *fort/da* with little Ernst. Difficult and abstract without the context of the entire year. Perhaps . . ." (*PC* 41/47).

As we know, Derrida did detach those sessions on Freud, revising them significantly before publishing them in the second part of *The Post Card*. But now that we have "the context of the entire year," we can see just how right "M." was, that is, that the *Life Death* seminar was eminently worthy of being published on its own. What we have tried to translate here as faithfully as possible is thus not an essay or book prepared for publication by Derrida but a *seminar*. To that end, we have tried whenever possible to retain Derrida's original syntax, sentence length, and so on, in order to give a sense of the pace or rhythm of Derrida's seminar preparation, writing, and presentation. Whenever possible we have used extant English translations of all of Derrida's French and German texts. It was, however, sometimes necessary to modify these published translations, or abandon them altogether, in light of either Derrida's comments on these texts or his own retranslations or modifications of extant French translations of German texts.

This translation has benefited enormously from the help of all those who participated in the Derrida Seminar Translation Project workshops over the course of two successive summers (2017–18) at the IMEC archives in Normandy. We would like to thank all the doctoral student participants at the workshops, Alex Baron-Raiffe, Ernesto Blanes, Rachel Gardner, Brieuc Gérard, Andrew Kingston, David Maruzzella, Rich McLaughlin, Michael Peterson, Bradley Ramos, Brigitte Stepanov, and Rodrigo Therezo, as well as our fellow faculty members, Geoffrey Bennington, Ellen Burt, Katie Chenoweth, Peggy Kamuf, Kir Kuiken, and David Wills. Special thanks are due to our colleagues from DePaul University, David Farrell Krell, who gave us precious advice on the entire translation, and particularly on Derrida's readings of Nietzsche and Heidegger, and Elizabeth Rottenberg, who helped us enormously not only at IMEC but back in Chicago with every aspect of this work, including, and especially, with the sessions on Freud. Our heartfelt thanks, finally, to the staff at IMEC for its assistance and hospitality each summer at the Abbaye d'Ardenne and to DePaul University and its College of Liberal Arts and Social Sciences for its generous support of this project.

Pascale-Anne Brault
Michael Naas

FIRST SESSION

Programs[1]

What did I do when I announced this seminar under the title "life-death," that is, when I replaced with a hyphen [*trait d'union*] or a space without mark [*trait*] or a mark without word, with a marked silence, the *and* that generally posits death *with* life, the one juxtaposed with the other, or, more surely, opposed to the other? It is perhaps just such a relationship of juxtaposition or opposition, such a relationship of position, such a logic of position (dialectical or non-dialectical), that will come into question when it comes to life death. By doing away with the *and*, I was trying to intimate not that life death did not form two, or that the one was not the other of the other, but that this alterity or this difference was not of the order of what philosophy calls opposition (*Entgegensetzung*), the double positioning of two facing one another, in the sense in which, for example in Hegel, the concept of position and the position of the concept, self-positioning and opposition, are the driving schemas of the dialectic, a dialectic that essentially moves forward or puts itself forward as a very powerful thinking of life and death, of the relations, as one says, between life and death, and especially where the opposition, the contradiction (dialectical or not), is the process by which one opposite passes into the other, the process of identification whereby the one is sublated into the other.

If you were to follow the great syllogism of life at the end of Hegel's *Science of Logic* (perhaps we will do so later), you would see how life, which is essentially a position (*Setzung*), a position of the Idea that posits itself through its three oppositions, namely, "the living individual (*das lebendige*

---

1. In the typescript the word "Programs" is handwritten below the title "LIFE DEATH (1) [*LA VIE LA MORT (1)*]." Several sessions have a handwritten annotation in the same place. These were probably intended by Derrida to serve as the title for the session. In subsequent sessions we have simply inserted these session titles without any further indication.

Individuum), the life-process (*der Lebensprozess*), and the genus (*die Gattung*)," reappropriates itself as life through the opposition with death and is born as life of the spirit in natural death, following a movement that is everywhere marked in Hegel (let us call it the movement of the phoenix) and to which we will naturally have to return.² By simply alluding to it in this way in order to begin, I wished to note *three things*:

1. First of all, the *and* of juxta-position or of op-position must be questioned and thus suspended long enough to ask not only whether the relationships between being and death really are a matter of what is called opposition or contradiction, but also, more radically, whether what we think we understand by the concept of position, op-position or juxta-position, or even contradiction, was not constructed by a logic of "life death" that would itself be concealed—but with what interest in view, that is the question—beneath a positional (oppositional, juxtapositional, or dialectical) schema, *as if* (I can here use only the *as if*, since I neither want nor am able to oppose some other logic to the logic of opposition) the entire logic of opposition (logic of identity or dialectical logic, formal or dialectical logic) were a ruse put forward by "life death" in order to conceal, protect, shelter, harbor, or forget—something. But what? A what, in any event, that is no longer either *posited* or *opposed* and that would no longer be something in this sense of position.

You will surely find that I am beginning a course on life and death in a rather abstract manner. What is more concrete than life death, you will say? But what is more abstract as well? Is there a greater or another *power of abstraction*? By insisting on the necessity of beginning with questions of this type, questions of a logical type, if you will, by asking whether the entire positional and oppositional logic in which we have thought and continue to think the limit, the slash Life/death, is not only not powerful enough to think this limit but is itself produced as an effect of life death and so must be reread as logic in general from this point of view, I am indicating two textual markers that today seem to me indispensable. On the one hand,

---

2. G. W. F. Hegel, *Science of Logic*, trans. A. V. Miller (Atlantic Highlands, NJ: Humanities Press International, 1989), pp. 761–74 [*Wissenschaft der Logik*, in G. W. F. Hegel, *Werke in zwanzig Bänden* (Frankfurt am Main: Suhrkamp, 1969), v. 6, pp. 469–87]. [Translators' note:] Hegel refers to the phoenix myth several times in his works (see *Werke* v. 12, p. 98, v. 16, p. 408, v. 18, p. 11, and v. 9, p. 538). This last reference, near the end of Hegel's lectures on the philosophy of nature, is particularly striking: "The goal of nature is to kill itself and to shatter the crust of its immediacy and sensuousness, like the phoenix immolating itself in order to emerge from this externality rejuvenated as spirit."

Hegel—and especially Hegel's *Logic*, which says at the beginning of the chapter "Life" (*Das Leben*) that "The Idea of Life is concerned with [touches on, *betrifft*] a subject matter (*Gegenstand*) so concrete, and if you will so real (*einen so konkreten und, wenn man will, reellen Gegenstand*), that with it we may seem to have over-stepped (*überschritten*) the domain of logic as it is commonly conceived."[3] Now, the whole demonstration that follows tends, on the contrary—against this received view—to make of life, the idea of life, the living being (the living individual and its death), the life-process, the reproduction of the species, something that not only has to do with logic but also defines our access to knowledge. On the other hand, another textual marker, what I will call the *logic of the living*, to use the title of Jacob's book,[4] tends today, through the whole problematic of the *message*, the *code*, indeed the *genetic text*, to decode the living [*le vivant*] (not life, say these biologists, because of their skepticism regarding what they believe, a bit too quickly, to be the hypostasizing and substantialist compulsion of the philosopher, though they fail to mention, for example, that Hegel demonstrated the necessity of going by way of the living (the living individual) as a necessary position within the syllogism of life, that is, the judgment—*Ur-teil*—of life that originarily divides (*urteilen*) in order to produce itself and re-produce itself), a modernity, then, that tends to decipher the living as a language (a word I leave in all its indeterminacy for the moment) that itself partakes of a logic. We will restrict ourselves here to the field marked out between these two textual indicators in order to locate just a few points of reference.

2. I also wanted to underscore with this first reference to Hegel and to the logic of opposition that it is not a question for me of (1) *opposing* another logic to this logic of opposition (life *and* death): it goes without saying that if somewhere (when it comes to life death) the logic of opposition, opposition itself, is lacking in pertinence, the other logic to which we will then have recourse will not be *other* in the Hegelian sense, that is to say, it will not be *its* opposed other, it will not be another logic that has a relationship of opposition with the logic of opposition. It would therefore be a question of an *other alterity* in which the other that is qualifying alterity, the other alterity,

---

3. Hegel, *Science of Logic*, p. 761 [p. 469].

4. [Translators' note:] Derrida is referring here to François Jacob's *La logique du vivant. Une histoire de l'hérédité* (Paris: Gallimard, 1970). Jacob's work has been translated into English as *The Logic of Life: A History of Heredity*, trans. Betty E. Spillman (New York: Random House, 1973). Since both Jacob and Derrida distinguish between *la vie* (life) and *le vivant* (the living, living beings), Jacob's book will be referred to throughout as *The Logic of the Living*.

would no longer have anything to do with the alterity it would come to alter. But in saying "life death" in order to approach this other alterity, it is also not a question for me of (2) trying to identify life and death, to say life *is* death, a proposition that, as you know, can be supported in multiple ways, through numerous well-known paths. The blank [*trait blanc*] between life and death does not come in place of an *and* [*et*] or an *is* [*est*]. In Hegelian dialectical logic, the *is* of judgment here comes, as the place of contradiction and of its *Aufhebung*, to declare that life is death, that life is posited in its syllogism through the mediation of death, that *is* is, in the dynamic and productive sense of the word *is*, the process of death (the death of natural life as the birth of spiritual life), at the end of which the *is* itself becomes Life, the being of the is becomes Life once again in a dissymmetry that I tried to analyze elsewhere. In this dissymmetry, Life is marked twice, first as a moment in the process of the Idea or of being (where life is death through its opposition to death) and then, *without* death, which always remains natural, at the moment of the absolute idea, at the end of the Greater Logic, when Hegel writes: "the absolute Idea alone is being (*Sein*), imperishable life (*unvergängliches Leben*), self-knowing truth (*sich wissende Wahrheit*), and is all truth (*und ist alle Wahrheit*)."[5] At this moment, this ultimate moment, life no longer has any opposition, any opposite; the opposition has taken place within it so that it might reappropriate itself, but life no longer has any other facing it. The *is* of life is death is *of life*, being is life, death is unthinkable as something that is. That is where oppositional logic leads us when the greatest attention is paid to death (as in Hegel): to the suppression of opposition, to its sublation in the elevation of one of the terms and the process of its own reappropriation. Life is this *reappropriation* of being, it is being: only the absolute idea is being, it alone is imperishable life (nondeath). Between opposition (and [*et*]) and copulatory identification (is [*est*]) there is, therefore, no opposition; opposition is the process of identification or of reappropriation of being as life or of life as being.

At the moment when Heidegger once again asks the question of Nietzsche's biologism, Nietzsche's alleged biologism, that is, whether it is on the basis of a biological determination of life that he thinks (will to power, eternal return, etc.), he cites a particular passage from the fragments grouped together under the title "The Will to Power."[6] The passage says this: "'Being'

---

5. Hegel, *Science of Logic*, p. 824 [p. 549].

6. [Translators' note:] Derrida is referring here to Martin Heidegger's *Nietzsche*, a text he will return to in detail much later in the seminar. See n. 18 of the seventh session for the full bibliographical reference to this work.

(in quotation marks: das 'Sein')—we have no other representation (*Vorstellung*) of this than as '*living*' (als '*leben*': in quotation marks and italics).—How can anything dead 'be'?" (Nietzsche, fragment 582, 85–86).[7] If, in the "metaphorical" etymology of the word *being*, there is something that means *living*, if being equals *living*, being-dead is unthinkable. Or, rather than unthinkable, we should say, if we wish to follow rigorously the implications of this utterance of Nietzsche's, in its language and with its quotation marks, being-dead would be unrepresentable, unpresentable, unsayable. Unrepresentable because, Nietzsche says it quite precisely, we have no other representation (*Vorstellung*) of being than "living," in other words, living is or is only a representation of being, though we are still free to think being beyond representation. And one might pursue Nietzsche's thinking to the point of saying that, on the one hand, those who identify, in one way or another, as Hegel does, for example, at the end of the trajectory of the Idea, Being and Life, remain within representation and it is necessary to go *beyond* representation (or presence or presentation as standing up in front of: *Vorstellen*). Let me announce by way of anticipation that it is toward a certain other thinking of the beyond, of beyond, of the *Jenseits* of Nietzsche and of Freud, and especially of the *step (not) beyond* [*pas au-delà*] of Blanchot, that I would like to lead this seminar.[8] You will say to me that if I invited you to reconsider the question of death in order to speak to you of the beyond it was not worth the trouble, it is rather late, and such a step is not new [*pas nouveau*]. But it is this not new (step) [*le pas nouveau*] that must be, perhaps, attempted if we are to know whether it can be gotten over [*ça se franchit*] or not, and whether the beyond does not remain a completely new question. So, on the one hand, one might pursue Nietzsche's thinking to the point of saying: those who think being as living and who, therefore, cannot think being-dead remain at the level of representation, of being as representation, the example here being Hegel, whom Nietzsche would

---

7. Cited by Heidegger in his *Nietzsche*, this corresponds to fragment 582 of the English (and French) edition of Nietzsche's *The Will to Power* (hereafter abbreviated *WP*), trans. Walter Kaufmann and R. J. Hollingdale (New York: Random House, 1967), p. 312, where it is translated: "Being—we have no idea of it apart from the idea of 'living.'—How can anything dead 'be'?" *La Volonté de puissance*, v. 1, trans. Geneviève Bianquis (Paris: Éditions Gallimard, 1948). The original German, *Der Wille zur Macht*, can be found in volume 12 of Friedrich Nietzsche's *Sämtliche Werke, Kritische Studienausgabe* (hereafter abbreviated *KSA*), in 15 volumes, ed. Giorgio Colli and Mazzino Montinari (Berlin: Walter de Gruyter, 1980): *KSA* 12: 2[172], p. 153.

8. Maurice Blanchot, *The Step Not Beyond*, trans. Lycette Nelson (Albany: State University of New York Press, 1992); *Le Pas Au-Delà* (Paris: Éditions Gallimard, 1973).

therefore oppose. Or else, on the other hand, we cannot think being outside the representation (or the metaphorical trope) "living," and to try to do so is to forget that being is only a representation or a metaphor. To claim to be thinking beyond representation is a forgetting of language, of the origin of language, and even of the life at the origin of language. If language and logic are a language and a logic of the living, it is futile to try to say and to think within these something like the dead [*le mort*]. Whence, once again, two possible consequences—at least two: either give up thinking beyond logic and language, beyond logos, since this has never made any sense, had any possibility; or else think—the dead, for example—beyond language, logic, and metaphorics, the dead becoming then, in turn, the generic name for everything that exceeds, overflows, transgresses the limits of the sayable, the expressible. Whence Nietzsche's insistence on the quotation marks: "being" and "living" are words that he is quoting, utterances he is designating: being-dead is something we are unable to think because we are unable to say it, etc.

My intention today is not to broach this problem of Nietzsche's biologism or lack thereof, or of Heidegger's interpretation of it, of its relation to the Hegelian dialectic and to philosophy in general. We will come back to this, I think, at length.[9] Starting out from this Hegelian identification of life with death, from an opposition that proceeds in view of its cancellation in the final identification "being is life," where life is marked twice, once as death (the death process), once as immortal, imperishable, I simply wanted to indicate that the same logic could help to distinguish the various semantic registers of life *and* (*et*) death (where the *and* signifies position, juxtaposition or op-position) and life *is* (*est*) death, where death defines essence as the dialectical process of life keeping itself alive as life, producing itself and reproducing itself, etc. So that, by saying, with the blank of a pause or the invisible mark of a beyond, "life death," I am *neither* opposing *nor* identifying life and death (neither *and* [*et*] nor *is* [*est*]), I am neutralizing, as it were, both opposition and identification, in order to gesture not toward another logic, an opposite logic of life and death, but toward another topos, if you will, a topos from which it would be possible to read, at the very least, the entire *program* of the *and* and of the *is*, of the positionality and presence of being, both of these being effects of "life death." How to think position and presence as effects? That presupposes, obviously, another thinking of effect.

3. This leads me to my third point. I just spoke and emphasized the word *program*, the "program," I said, of the *and* and of the *is*.

---

9. See *infra*, eighth session and following.

The suspension of the *and* in my title, in the title of the seminar, constitutes a rather discreet, not terribly violent intervention, you will say, in the *agrégation* program, which this year bears, in a very traditional way, <the title> "life and death," life first, then death. Every year for a number of years now, at the beginning of each seminar, as some of you know, I explain my uneasiness in trying to adapt my work here to the *agrégation* program and the strategic decision that I make, each time, all the while fighting against the institution of the *agrégation*, elsewhere and right here, to negotiate with it from within a given set of conditions. I am not going to repeat what I have already said and reproduce ad infinitum the same schema. I would rather, in analyzing the title of the *agrégation* program, not conform to it but make of it the object—to be deconstructed—of this seminar.[10] Along with the "seminar" itself, in fact, that is, what is called, and not by chance, a program and a seminar. There is no need to underscore what the word and concept *seminar* owe to a bio-logical, seminal or spermatic, germinal metaphor. As for the program, the value of program, it is a little more complicated, but it leads us back to a metaphorical or topological effervescence where the institution, as the possibility of stable erection and reproduction, is often described by means of organicist or biologistic metaphors, and this is hardly fortuitous. The fact, for example, that the concept of program works just as well to define a system of academic prescriptions organizing the reproduction of an institutional organization as it does to define the schemas of the reproduction of living beings, such as modern biologists imagine it today, is something that must not be ignored.

How are we to explain that the biological or organicist metaphor—which I am not conflating here, for they are not exactly the same, but let's leave that aside, at least for now—that biological or organicist metaphors so often serve to describe institutions, the institution of the university in particular, and this just as much on the side of those who defend that institution as those who attack it? How are we to explain that the same concept or the same figure, for example, program or reproduction, can be so easily transposed from the language of life to that of the institution, and vice versa? And this is the case just as much for those who want to preserve as those who want to destroy. For the former, the necessity of the program and of reproduction is a condition of life, a condition of development and of production; for the

---

10. In the typescript this passage was crossed out after the first occurrence of the word "program." In addition, the words "the *agrégation* that this year bears" are crossed out with another line and replaced by "on, let us say, traditional questions." The second occurrence of the expression "*agrégation* program" was modified to read: "traditional program."

latter, the program and reproduction are bearers of death. And today, as you know, the political critique of the institution, the fight against the institution, draws the principal part of its argumentation and motivation from this value of re-production. The university is a system that, through its programs, assessments, and constraints, aims to ensure the re-production of its organization, which amounts not only to maintaining the system of forces but also to rigidifying the living being in death. And that is what should be prevented. How are we to explain that re-production and program are conditions of both life and death? And is this metaphoricity fortuitous? Is it one metaphorical structure among others?

Instead of developing for its own sake and in general this question of program and of this singular metaphorical exchange, I suggest that we analyze the concept of program as it is operating in the book of a modern biologist, one who could hardly be suspected of giving in to the old programs of philosophical speculation, namely, François Jacob's *The Logic of the Living*. Its introduction bears the title "The Program," and you know, if you have read it, that the concept of program plays a decisive role in that work, coming to resolve all the problems and all the antinomies that philosophy in general, the philosophy of life, and biological thought were themselves unable to resolve up until now: for example, the problem of finalism or of teleology. Up until now, says Jacob, the biologist refused to have explicit recourse to any finalism or teleologism, which contained all sorts of obscurantisms or occultisms, or at least all kinds of metaphysical speculations, and he claimed to be acting as a scientist only insofar as he broke with all finalism or teleology. And yet, Jacob thinks, this break never took place, could not take place, an implicit teleologism or finalism remaining persistent, unavowed, shameful. And the contradiction between the hidden finalism and the declared antifinalism, the necessity of having recourse to both, this *double bind*[11] of the biologist, remained unsolvable. Well, it is the notion of program, at least as it is determined today in biological discourse, that comes to take note of this *double bind* and, especially, resolve the contradiction. And reproduction, the essential characteristic of the living being, according to Jacob, "the principal operative factor of the living world," reconciles, through the program, through the new concept of program, the finality of each organism and the non-fatality of organisms, of the history of organisms; "it provides," he says [p. 8], "an aim [*but*] for each organism," and, at the same time, "it gives a direction to the aimless history of organisms." And here is the formulation: "For a long time, the biologist treated teleology as he would a woman he

---

11. In English in the original.

could not do without, but did not care to be seen with in public. The concept of program has given to this secret relationship a legal status."[12]

What is it, then, about this value of program that would finally provide the solution to all these problems, that would come to institutionalize, by giving it a *status*, the contradiction or the double postulation of the biological approach [*démarche*], giving a legal, that is, here, a scientific status, allowing it to be recognized as scientific, giving a legal status to a discourse that would have otherwise been taken as non-scientific, metaphorical, ideological, imaginary, or however else one might wish to characterize the non-scientific, that is, as that which does not have the right of entry into the scientific institution?[13]

Let us imagine that Jacob, in speaking of genetic programs, were speaking of the program in the institution of the university and let us see to what extent it works and why it works.

From the opening words of his introduction (entitled, as we said, "The Program"), Jacob recalls how science can lag behind, how biological science regularly lags behind the physical sciences. Without asking whether this lagging behind is essential or not, whether or not it has to do with the very structure of the object and of the relation to the object in what is called the biological domain, whether it has to do with the very constitution of the object "life," Jacob both notes the lagging behind and defines it from a place where, or at a moment when, the science of the living would finally be constituted as a science, even if it is not yet a "unified science,"[14] as he later says. Jacob thus remarks upon this lagging behind: "Even when the virtues of the scientific method had become solidly established for the study of the physical world, those who studied the living world continued for several generations to think the origin of beings . . ."[15] Let me interrupt for a moment my quotation for a digression: despite Jacob's putative emancipation with regard to philosophy, or at least the type of philosophy that is nowadays attributed to these modern biologists, as opposed to the one he would attribute to himself, for Jacob is more modest in his discourse than Monod and in the ambitions that might be attributed to him,[16] Jacob speaks

---

12. Jacob, *Logic of the Living*, pp. 8–9 [p. 17].

13. In the left margin of this paragraph in the typescript there is the handwritten word *concubinage*, that is, "living out of wedlock."

14. Jacob, *Logic of the Living*, p. 6 [p. 14].

15. Ibid., p. 1 [p. 9].

16. See Jacques Monod, *Chance and Necessity: An Essay on the Natural Philosophy of Modern Biology*, trans. Austryn Wainhouse (New York: Vintage Books, 1972) [*Le hasard et la nécessité. Essai sur la philosophie naturelle de la biologie moderne* (Paris: Seuil, 1970).]

regularly of *beings* in order to designate the living and of *things* to designate the non-living. He does this regularly, as you can confirm, when he writes, for example, in the final pages: "This applies equally to the formation of beings and things; to the constitution of a cell, an organism, or a population, as well as of a molecule, a stone, or a storm."[17] Hence a cell, an organism, and a population are beings, and a molecule, a stone, or a storm — all non-living — are simply things. Beneath this convenience of writing and this concession to everyday language that makes beings of the living and things of the non-living, there lies hidden a vast sedimentation that I do not wish to expose here, no more than I wish to give the impression of pestering a scientist who is simply expounding his discourse with a demand for rigor that might seem to come from a philosopher who knows nothing about the matter. But I think that indications of this type must be taken seriously and that they reveal in the scientist who writes a greater philosophical *and* scientific naïveté than one is generally willing to say. And, as we know, it is in biological science that the non-scientific (conveyed through ordinary language or, and this is often the same thing, philosophical language) contaminates the very posing of scientific problems from within. And for essential reasons. Jacob essentially acknowledges this when he admits that the lagging behind in scientificity is more common in the study of the living than in the study of the non-living. Just a few more words, then, regarding this opposition being/thing before returning to my interrupted quotation. Two remarks, one of which is essential. This attributing of the name *beings* to the living, which is common in an everyday language marked by a culture that is at once philosophical and Christian and that makes that which lives and speaks *be*, goes back to what we were saying earlier about the equivalence between being and living and to the whole problematic nexus that comes with it. The other remark is anecdotal: I knew someone (whose sex I will leave unspecified here) who, consumed by the problems of an undeclared homosexuality, often said "a being" or "beings" in everyday conversation where we would say him or her, he or she, a man or a woman, and this person would say "a being" or "beings" not with that somewhat incantatory affectation of the salon or the Sunday sermon but simply in order not to reveal the sex of the *being* of whom this person was speaking. I recount this story only to suggest or to recall that sexual difference (marked or erased, marked, which is

---

[Translators' note:] Monod (1910–76) was a French biochemist who shared the 1965 Nobel Prize in Medicine with François Jacob and André Lwoff.

17. Jacob, *Logic of the Living*, p. 323 [pp. 344–45].

to say, erased as sexual *opposition*) is perhaps at stake in the process by which the equivalence between being and living gets produced.

I return now to my quotation:

> Even when the virtues of the scientific method had become solidly established for the study of the physical world, those who studied the living world continued for several generations to think the origin of beings in terms of beliefs, anecdotes, and superstitions. Relatively simple experiments suffice to make short work of the notion of spontaneous generation and impossible hybridations. Nevertheless, some aspects of the ancient myths concerning the origin of man, of beasts, and of the earth persisted, in one form or another, until the nineteenth century.[18]

End of paragraph. The paragraph that follows says "today" (1971, the date of the book).[19] Having started upon the sure path of a science, biology, or more precisely genetics, today describes heredity, says Jacob, and I quote, "in terms of *information*, *messages*, and *code*."[20] It is starting from here that I propose we listen to what is said about genetic inheritance as if Jacob were speaking of inheritance (of inheritors, as one would say in Bourdieu's language of socio-analysis) as organized by an institution, or if not by it at least through it by those forces that have an interest in reproduction. Reproduction is the concept that is common to the two systems — life, or rather the living, and the institution — and it is this shared concept that ensures the unity of the metaphorical code that passes from one to the other. It is this unity of the metaphorical code that enables us to read "The Program," Jacob's introduction, as if it were about the University. That is what we are going to do, before then asking ourselves what such a metaphorical possibility presupposes, whether we are dealing with one metaphor among others or with a more fundamental metaphoricity.

Heredity, therefore, *today*, is described in terms of *information*, *message*, and *code*. These three words seem to have been borrowed from a vocabulary of semiotic or linguistic communication. Each message is emitted according to the constraints of a code, which is what allows for exchange and identification. The content of a genetic message, its information, what Jacob calls the *instructions* specifying molecular structures, would be like the signified that is taught through the very determined, invariable norms of the code. I am imposing neither the word "instruction" (which can be heard both in the sense of the instruction delivered in schools and the instructions

---

18. Ibid., p. 1 [p. 9].
19. The official date of publication is in fact 1970.
20. Jacob, *Logic of the Living*, p. 1 [p. 9]; Derrida's emphasis.

of the board of education that aim to ensure the proper conditions for reproduction), I am imposing neither the word "instruction" nor the word "teaching" on Jacob, who writes, for example: "What are transmitted from generation to generation are the 'instructions' specifying the molecular structures,"[21] or, "The rigidity of the program thus varies according to the operations. Certain instructions are carried out literally. Others are expressed by capacities or potentialities. However, in the end the program itself determines its degree of flexibility and the range of possible variations."[22] There is no need to insist on the ease with which one might, without changing a word, transpose these statements in order to describe the functioning of all institutional programs, in particular academic programs, and more precisely still those of competitive exams. We should not be astonished by this ease; it is not fortuitous if we consider that the code in which the modern biologist speaks is first of all that of language, of semiotics rather than linguistics, or even of grammatics (I will clarify this point in a moment), which itself comes from the region of either the institution in general or the academic in particular, or else that the two codes, the genetic and the academic, have a common provenance or appurtenance that will have to be questioned. As for the word "teaching," it is there as well. At issue is the old problem of the heredity of acquired characteristics. Jacob does not think that the word "teaching" is in itself inappropriate to designate the operation by which heredity is transmitted. The risk is that this word might lead one to think that the teaching done by heredity is absolutely identical to the teaching that is provided in schools through spoken language, the memory of the brain, etc. And here we are going to see just what, according to Jacob, the principle, as well as the explanation, is of these metaphorical possibilities. What does the paragraph in which we read the expression "teaching heredity" say exactly? It first notes that an organism is the transition between what was and what will be. An organism cannot be thought, as it were, in the present; it is not first of all the production of a present. It is first of all, in advance, what I will call an "effect of reproduction." It begins not with production but with reproduction. "Reproduction," says Jacob, "represents [for the organism] both the beginning and the end, the cause and the aim."[23] Now it was in order to think this reproduction that the classic problematic of biology or genetics came to be constituted, oscillating between finalism and mechanism, necessity and chance, fixity and trans-

---

21. Ibid., p. 1 [p. 10].
22. Ibid., p. 10 [p. 18].
23. Ibid., p. 2 [p. 10].

formation. It is precisely to the notion of program that Jacob attributes the power to erase the oppositions, even the contradictions, that constitute this classic problematic, the philosophy or the metaphysics of this classic problematic. "With the application to heredity of the concept of program, certain biological contradictions formerly summed up in a series of antitheses at last disappear: finality and mechanism, necessity and contingency, stability and variation."[24]

How does Jacob conceive of or construct this concept of program? He does not retain the reference that is found within it to inscription or to the graphic, either in the sense of phonetic writing or in the sense of non-phonetic writing. We will come back to this in a different way later. In order to construct or to analyze the concept of program as it functions in the field of genetics, Jacob retains two essential predicates, what he calls two *notions*: memory and project.[25] And it is within these two notions, each divided and articulated from within, that he determines both the analogy and the difference that, on the one hand, legitimates metaphor (the fact that one speaks, for example, of project and of memory) and causes confusion. But, you will have understood, this concept of program, when rightly understood and having been reworked by modern genetic science, must at once authorize one to speak of program (memory and project) and prohibit confusion. Let us first read this: "The concept of program blends two notions which had always been intuitively associated with living beings: memory and project."[26] Let's not quibble with Jacob here over what he calls the "intuition" that associates memory and project with living beings. Especially since Jacob is justified in calling this an "intuition," thereby implying that it is confused, and since his intention is to find within it the origin of a confusion between two types of memory and two types of project. He writes:

> By "memory" is implied the traits of the parents, which heredity brings out in a child. By "project" is implied the plan which controls the formation of an organism down to the last detail. Much controversy has surrounded these two themes. First, with respect to the inheritance of acquired characters. *The idea that the environment can teach* [enseigne] *heredity* represents an *intuitively* natural confusion between two kinds of memory, genetic and mental [*nerveuse*].[27]

---

24. Ibid.
25. The words "memory" and "project" are both circled in the typescript.
26. Jacob, *Logic of the Living*, p. 2 [p. 10].
27. Ibid.; Derrida's emphasis.

Before going any further, let me specify that the confusion, in Jacob's eyes, lies not in the expression "teach heredity" but in the concept that we are going to form of this teaching as soon as we confuse the two memories that must be distinguished, genetic and mental (cerebral). Each of these two memories corresponds to a certain stage of emergence, accompanied by a break. In both memories there is conservation (this is Jacob's word) of a past and transmission. But with the emergence of the living there is first constituted the genetic memory of heredity, which is absolutely rigid. There will later be, within the living, another break, the emergence of another memory, that of the "brain," says Jacob, which is much more flexible (with thought and language), which can transmit what is acquired, acquired characteristics, whereas genetic memory resists this. Now since there are certain "analogies," this again is Jacob's word, between the two systems, that of genetic memory and that of mental memory (brain, thought, language), the intuitive analogy—and thus all the genetico-institutional metaphorics—has some legitimacy. But it loses this legitimacy as soon as it transforms the analogy into identity and the two memories become assimilated, as do the two systems. Yet it is through analogy that the concept of program and even that of the teaching of heredity can cover the entire field of both systems and resolve the classical contradictions. It is just that we need to say that, within the program, within general programmaticity, there are two distinct types of programs, the rigid and the flexible. There is thus a rigid teaching and a flexible one, a transmission of invariants and a variable transmission of variables. Two types of schools, if you will, two systems of teaching and of programming. They are systems because they are closed in their own way and have their own logic, their immanence, their internal regulation or normativity. It is not that one of them, the flexible or liberal one, has to do with the outside and the other does not. The relation to the outside is more complex; and that is what I really want to insist on now. It is, seemingly, the flexible system (brain, thought, language), the one that would be more naturally compared to the pedagogical institution, that has a relation to its outside and registers its effects; it is porous, susceptible to the influences of history and of the politico-economic field. The other program, on the contrary, the genetic, is completely closed off to all this, repeating, like a parroting scholasticism, the internal prescription. That is what Jacob initially leads us to think. He writes this, which I read as a reminder:

> The two points of rupture in evolution—first the emergence of the living, later the emergence of thought and language—each correspond to the appearance of a mechanism of memory, that of heredity and that of the mind.

There are certain analogies between the two systems: both were selected for accumulating and transmitting past experience, and in both, the recorded information is maintained only as far as it is reproduced at each generation. However, the two systems differ with respect to their nature and to the logic of their performance. The flexibility of mental memory makes it particularly apt for the transmission of acquired characters. The rigidity of genetic memory prevents such transmission. The genetic program, indeed, is made up of a combination of essentially invariant elements. By its very structure, the message of heredity does not allow the slightest concerted intervention from the outside.[28]

Two remarks and two questions before moving on.

1. Jacob does not ask about the implications of such an analogy or about the very choice of its name. He determines it as a resemblance between two systems (accumulation, in both cases, of a "past experience" and the transmission, in both cases, of this experience). But one need only analyze Jacob's text to gain a better understanding of the necessity and problematicity of this word *analogy*. First, the analogy here is between two systems and two logics; it is a system of relations of proportionality among several terms with variables. Just as memory (we will speak later of project, the other characteristic of the program), just as mental memory (cerebral memory, thought and language in the traditional sense) accumulates and transmits information, so too does genetic memory accumulate and transmit information. This relation, and this relation of relations (among four terms), is what the Greeks called a *logos* and an *analogia*. Here the *analogia* between the two relations, between the two *logoi*, is a relation between a memory that includes language or logos in its everyday sense (the mental or cerebral memory corresponding to the second emergence) and a memory without language in the everyday sense (genetic memory). It is an analogy, in the logos of the geneticist (in his metalanguage or what is alleged to be a metalanguage), between a logos in the so-called proper sense of the term and an a-logos. But this general analogy became possible only at the moment when (today) we came to know, by means of what is called "scientific" knowledge, that the a-logos was also a logos in the broader sense, when we came to know, by means of a scientific knowledge, that genetic memory operated *like* a language, with a code, a message, and a possible translation of messages; and that it also operated with analogies, that is to say, with relations put into relation with one another, and more specifically with radical elements that

28. Ibid., pp. 2–3 [p. 11].

are four in number. Genetic reproduction is not a copy, says Jacob, it is not a *copie d'élève* (a student paper), but then the copy is not a copy either; it is a variation within a strictly regulated code. Jacob writes:

> Heredity is described today in terms of information, messages, and code. The reproduction of an organism has become that of its constituent molecules. This is not because each chemical species has the ability to produce copies of itself, but because the structure of macromolecules is determined down to the last detail by sequences of four chemical radicals contained in the genetic inheritance [*patrimoine*]. What are transmitted from generation to generation are the "instructions" [Jacob's quotation marks] specifying the molecular structures: the architectural plans of the future organism. [You see here that the institutional metaphor functions right down to the literalness of the edification of an instituting, upright being, upright in its most erect authority.] They are also the means of executing these plans and of coordinating the activities of the system. In the chromosomes received from its parents, each egg therefore contains its entire future: the stages of its development, the shape and the properties of the being which will emerge. The organism thus becomes the realization of a *program prescribed* [my emphasis] by its heredity. The intention of a Psyche has been replaced by the translation of a message. The living being does indeed represent the execution of a plan, but not one conceived in any mind. It strives towards a goal, but not one chosen by any will. The aim is to prepare an identical program for the following generation. The aim is to reproduce itself [*se reproduire*].[29]

First question or series of questions. Once this analogy is accepted, without any question regarding the nature of a logos, a message, and a code determined on the basis of their semiotic code, one might wonder whether it is enough to dispense with the subject, what Jacob calls "the intention of a Psyche," a formulation that caricatures all traditional theological notions of providence, in order to escape everything that the values of message, translation, design, and aim import from the system of logos, from traditional logocentrism. The analogy is that of logos returning always to *logos*. Instead of taking this rather easy and well-trodden path, I would like to ask in

---

29. Ibid., pp. 1–2 [pp. 9–10]; Derrida's emphasis. [Translators' note:] The French *se reproduire* is often best translated simply as "to reproduce," as the English translation of *The Logic of the Living* has it here and throughout. But since Derrida will question throughout his reading of Jacob what it means for something not just to produce or reproduce something other than itself but to reproduce *itself*, we have translated *se reproduire* as to "reproduce itself" or "reproduce oneself."

particular about the consequences or the implications of the fact that, at the very moment he opposes the genetic program to the "mental" program (of language or of thought, and so for us of the cultural institution), at the very moment he opposes the genetic program to the institutional program, the process, language, and *topos* of Jacob's discourse describing the genetic program are the very ones with which, today, a certain modernity marked by psychoanalysis, linguistics, and a certain Marxism describes the functioning of institutional programs, academic ones in particular. That is, we are talking about a planned program, but one whose subjects are effects and not authors, a program whose design is not structurally deliberate, conscious, and intentional but functions all the better as a program, an oriented program, as a result, a program in compliance with predetermined goals, corresponding to relations of production, of reproduction, to an entire agonistics where every force works to promote its own reproduction and modes of reproduction, etc. As a result, under these conditions, the difference between the two systems (the genetic and the institutional, the "mental," which opens the way for the institutional form) is no longer rigorous, even if it is quantitatively enormous. We are no longer dealing with two rigorously distinct types but with two tracks or two relays in the same economy. This explains, moreover, why the criteria used by Jacob to distinguish between the two analogous systems are economic, by which I mean quantitative, a difference in flexibility or rigidity: "The flexibility of mental memory makes it particularly apt for the transmission of acquired characters. The rigidity of genetic memory prevents such transmission."[30]

If, therefore, within the analogy, rigorous criteria are lacking to oppose the two systems, so that one can today also describe institutional memory, the institutional program — with every imaginable difference of degree in the relays, the mediations, the potentializations, etc. — in the same terms as the genetic program, then the analogy is no longer simply an analogy between different things but a resemblance within the element of homogeneity. For my part, I would see here nothing but progress in this suppression of a limit that often served the most obscurantist ideologies, whether humanist, spiritualist, or more generally metaphysical; I would see here nothing but progress were the question of the logos of the analogy to have been elucidated in a critical manner so as to avoid the full-fledged return — thereby validating a kind of clandestine metaphysics — of everything that got attached to the value of logos and analogy in the tradition. To say it in advance in a somewhat algebraic

---

30. Ibid., p. 3 [p. 11].

fashion: I would be in favor of a de-limitation that gets rid of limits or oppositions (for example, the two types of program wherein we recognize, on the one hand, the purely genetic, and, on the other hand, the great emergence of the cerebral, from standing upright to the *zōon logon ekhon* and everything that follows), a de-limitation that gets rid, therefore, of this opposition in order to make way not for the homogeneous but for a heterogeneity or a differentiality; for, as I suggested at the beginning, the functioning of oppositions always has the effect of erasing differentiality. What interests me under the rubric of the beyond or of the step (not) beyond is indeed this limit without opposition between opposition and difference.

We will see this problem return later, once again under the rubric of the logos of analogy.

Second remark, which I add without delay to the preceding one. Still in the course of an explication of memory — one of the two essential characteristics of the program, the other being project — Jacob, you will recall, distinguished between the two systems or the two programs in terms of their relations to the outside. One might then get the impression that, in contrast with the first distinguishing criterion (rigidity/flexibility), we are here going to be dealing with a more rigorous qualitative determination. Jacob indeed says that "by its very structure, the message of heredity does not allow the slightest concerted intervention from the outside," a formulation taken up again just a few lines further down: "The very nature of the genetic code prevents any deliberate change in program whether through its own action or as an effect of its environment. It prohibits any influence on the message by the products of its expression. The program [that is, the genetic program] does not learn from experience."[31] We should thus conclude from this that the mental (institutional) program has a relation to the outside, that it learns from experience, that it lets itself be transformed, whereas the genetic program forms a closed, deaf system, purely endogenous, impervious to the kind of change that Jacob calls, with this very suspect word, "deliberate." Such an opposition is in fact just as fragile as the previous one. When Jacob says that the genetic message does not allow the slightest intervention from the outside, he immediately has to clarify the meaning of that formulation. Of course there are interventions from the outside: it is just that, between the cause coming from the outside to transform the program and the effect in or on the program there is no relationship of resemblance, no conscious or knowing correlation. It is this heterogeneity and this relationship of non-

---

31. Ibid.

knowing or non-consciousness that Jacob calls contingency. I have to read the entire paragraph. Read p. 3 (Jacob):[32]

> The genetic program, indeed, is made up of a combination of essentially invariant elements. By its very structure, the message of heredity does not allow the slightest concerted intervention from the outside. Whether chemical or mechanical, all the phenomena which contribute to variation in organisms and populations occur without any awareness [*en toute ignorance*] of their effects; they are unconnected with the organism's need to adapt. In a mutation, there are "causes" which modify a chemical radical, break a chromosome, invert a segment of nucleic acid. But in no case can there be correlation between the cause and the effect of the mutation. Nor is this contingency limited to mutations alone. It applies to each stage in the formation of an individual's genetic inheritance, the segregation of the chromosomes, their recombination, the choice of the gametes which play a role in fertilization and even, to a large extent, to the choice of sexual partners. There is not the slightest connection between a particular fact and its consequences in any of these phenomena. Each individual program is the result of a cascade of contingent events. The very nature of the genetic code prevents any deliberate change in program whether through its own action or as an effect of its environment. It prohibits any influence on the message by the products of its expression. The program does not learn from experience.[33]

40

In order, then, for the genetic program, when described in this way, to be opposed in a pertinent fashion to the mental, cerebral-institutional program, one would need to be certain that the same thing cannot be said about this latter. But can't the same thing be said about it?

If there is one generally accepted tenet of a certain number of theoretical breaks in what I call, just to say it quickly for now, modernity, it is that causality in the order of, let us say, "cerebral-institutional" programs (psychical, social, cultural, institutional, politico-economic, and so on) has exactly the same style, in its laws, as the causality that Jacob seems to want to reserve for genetic programs, namely—I am this time quoting Jacob while applying his phrase to "institutional" programs—"all the phenomena which contribute to variation in organisms and populations occur without any awareness of their effects." Similarly, the heterogeneity between causes and effects, the non-deliberate character of changes in the program, in a

---

32. On the photocopy of Jacob's text that accompanies the seminar typescript there is a "C" written in the margin and the words "contingency" and "contingent" are underlined.

33. Jacob, *Logic of the Living*, p. 3 [p. 11].

word, everything that places subjects from within the system in a situation of being unconscious effects of causality, everything that produces effects of contingency between an action coming from the outside and the internal transformations of the system—all of this characterizes the non-genetic program as well as the genetic program. Where does Jacob get the notion that, outside the genetic system and the genetic programs, changes in program are deliberate, essentially deliberate? Where does he get this notion if not from an ideologico-metaphysical opposition that determines superior or symbolic programs (with humanity at the very summit of these) on the basis of meaning, consciousness, freedom, knowledge of the limit between the inside and the outside, objectivity and non-objectivity, etc.? The apparent paradox is to be found in the chiasm by which Jacob places contingency on the side of the greatest internal rigidity, on the side of the most constraining necessity of reproduction, whereas along the other line of the chiasm, contingency, the effect of contingency, is limited even though freedom and deliberation are there predominant. Now if anything has been learned from what are today called the structural sciences, it is the possibility of affirming that systems linked to language, to the symbolic, to cerebral memory, etc., also have an internal functioning, itself internally regulated, that escapes deliberation and consciousness and enables the effects that come from the outside to be perceived as contingencies, heterogeneous forces that need to be interpreted, translated, assimilated into the internal code in an attempt to master them. And it is when this attempt fails that "mutations" are produced, mutations that might take all kinds of forms but that signal in each case a violent intrusion from the outside, necessitating a general restructuring. Here again, as you see, the opposition between the two programs cannot be rigorous, and this seems to me to be due to the fact that, for lack of reelaborating both the general notion of program and the value of analogy, they remain marked by a logocentric teleology and a humanist semantics, by what I will call a philosophy of life, about which I would like to say a few words in order to conclude today.

"Philosophy of life" is a quotation, or at least I am using it here as a quotation. These are the last words of an article by Canguilhem titled "The Concept and Life," an article included in his 1968 *Études d'histoire et de philosophie des sciences*.[34] I recommend that you read this article, along with the entire volume, as well as *La connaissance de la vie*, an earlier work. All of this

---

34. Georges Canguilhem, "Le concept et la vie," in *Études d'histoire et de philosophie des sciences* (Paris: J. Vrin, 1968), pp. 335–64. [Translators' note:] Our translation of Canguilhem throughout.

will be very useful for you from the point of view of the *agrégation*. Philosophy of life—these are, then, Canguilhem's final words at the end of his article. They are not meant pejoratively, and if the entire article aims to demonstrate that contemporary biology is still deeply Aristotelian and Hegelian, this is not to its discredit, quite the contrary. Here, first, are the last lines of this article:

> Knowledge is thus a restless search for the greatest quantity and variety of information. As a result, to be a subject of knowledge—if the a priori is in things, and the concept is in life—is simply to be dissatisfied with the meaning that has been found. Subjectivity, then, is nothing but dissatisfaction. But that is perhaps life itself. Contemporary biology, read in a certain fashion, is, in a way, a philosophy of life.[35]

It is also for the sake of finding models of *agrégation* rhetoric that I recommended that you read Canguilhem in order to follow in his work, as in the works of all the epistemologists of the French school, some of the effects of the *agrégation*, the effects of French schooling. And it would not take much explaining to hear, through the whole context of the quotation I just read, "philosophy of life" as "school of life," contemporary biology as school of life.

But what interests me most here is a particular phase in the trajectory that leads Canguilhem to this conclusion. This phase intersects in a very specific place Jacob's argumentation—and even a reference by Jacob to Claude Bernard. Jacob's reference to Claude Bernard concerns the *project*, the other characteristic of the program, along with memory. The point here is to show that the program acts like a preestablished design, a plan, without any subjective psychical intention, and that the notion of program resolves the classical contradiction between, on the one hand, a mechanism without plan, without reflecting the effects of teleology, and, on the other, a finality that has always been attributed to some theological providence or intentional consciousness, etc. He quotes a long passage from *Lectures on the Phenomena of Life Common to Animals and Plants* (1878), p. 36 (p. 4 in Jacob), where Bernard speaks of a "predetermined plan and design." The passage concludes:

> There is a kind of pre-established design for each being and each organ, so that, considered in isolation, each phenomenon of the harmonious arrangement depends on the general forces of nature, but taken in relationship with the others, it reveals a special bond: some invisible guide seems to direct it along the path it follows, leading it to the place which it occupies.[36]

---

35. Ibid., p. 364.
36. Jacob, *Logic of the Living*, p. 4 [p. 12]. Claude Bernard, *Lectures on the Phenomena of Life Common to Animals and Plants*, trans. Hebbel E. Hoff, Roger Guillemin,

And Jacob then adds: "Not a word of these lines needs to be changed today: they contain nothing which modern biology cannot endorse. However, when heredity is described as a coded program in a sequence of chemical radicals, the paradox disappears."[37] And since—and this is a topic we will study next time—it is through reproduction that Jacob defines the living, which he wants to distinguish from life, a term he sets aside in order to avoid its hypostasis (though this gesture is perhaps not sufficient—we will return to this), he writes a bit further on: "the program is scrupulously recopied, sign by sign, from one generation to another."[38]

It is with regard to this semiotics that I would like to cross Jacob's text with Canguilhem's. Canguilhem too, after having quoted Claude Bernard, who speaks of "the manifestation here and now of a primitive impulse . . . and of an *instructional sign* [consigne: Canguilhem's emphasis] that nature repeats after having ordered it in advance," Canguilhem then adds: "Claude Bernard seems to have sensed that biological heredity consists in the transmission of something that is today called coded information."[39] But Canguilhem emphasizes that if an instructional sign [*consigne*] is not far from a code, at least semantically, one cannot conclude that the semantic analogy "corresponds to a real filiation of concepts." What follows is an analysis—we will read it closely next time—that is as interesting as it is labored, one that tries to show that although Claude Bernard does not have the concepts of modern biology at his disposal, he tries to make up for this [*y suppléer*] with metaphors (we will look at this more closely next time). And Canguilhem comes to the following conclusion, which I quote in anticipation of the problems we will discuss next time: (read Canguilhem p. 362 Z.)[40]

> When we say that biological heredity is a communication of information, we are coming back in a way to the Aristotelianism with which we started. In our exploration of the Hegelian theory of the relationship between the concept and life, we asked ourselves whether we would not find in a theory so closely aligned with Aristotelianism, rather than in some intuitivist theory, such as Bergson's, a means of interpretation that would be more reliable for the phenomena discovered by contemporary biologists and for the explanatory theories they offer for them. To say that biological heredity

---

Lucienne Guillemin (Springfield, IL: Charles C. Thomas, 1974), p. 36 [*Leçons sur les phénomènes de la vie* (Paris: Librairie J.-B. Baillière & Fils, 1878), pp. 50–51].

37. Jacob, *Logic of the Living*, p. 4 [p. 12].
38. Ibid., p. 8 [p. 16].
39. Canguilhem, "Le concept et la vie," p. 358.
40. As such in the typescript.

is a communication of information is, in a certain sense, a return to Aristotelianism, if that entails admitting that there is in the living being a *logos* that is inscribed, conserved, and transmitted. Life has forever accomplished without writing, that is, well before writing and without any relation to writing, what humanity has sought through drawing, engraving, writing and printing, namely, the transmission of messages. And from now on the knowledge of life no longer resembles a portrait of life, which it could have when the knowledge of life was the description and classification of species. It does not resemble architecture or mechanics, which it did when it was simply anatomy and macroscopic physiology. It resembles instead grammar, semantics, and syntax. In order to understand life, one must begin, before reading it, to decipher the message of life.[41]

Neither Canguilhem nor Jacob problematized what they meant by this semiotics or, rather, this graphics of life, this non-phonetic writing that they claim to be "without writing" and that they are so ready to reinvest with all the values linked to logos in its most enduring Platonic-Aristotelian-Hegelian tradition, which is itself reread as a telos in progress.

Some ten years ago, in *Of Grammatology*, in a chapter near the beginning that was titled (already, one might say, by coincidence, prescience, or an almost subjectless teleology) "The Program," I recalled that, and I quote, "the contemporary biologist speaks of writing and *pro-gram* in relation to the most elementary processes of information within the living cell."[42] The point there was not, however, to reinvest the notion or the word *program* with the entire conceptual machine of logos and its semantics but to try to show that the appeal to a non-phonetic writing in genetics had to or should involve and incite an entire deconstruction of the logocentric machine rather than a return to Aristotle.

That is the direction I wish to privilege by returning to the texts of Jacob and Canguilhem on these problems of metaphor and concept in the domain of the life sciences. And next time we will also take a detour, something I wanted to do today, through one of Nietzsche's first texts (we will read others later), the text titled *On the Future of Our Educational Institutions*:[43] we see at work there a critique of the State and its pedagogy, the "sad want of

---

41. Canguilhem, "Le concept et la vie," p. 362.

42. Jacques Derrida, *Of Grammatology*, trans. Gayatri Chakravorty Spivak (Baltimore: Johns Hopkins University Press, 1976), p. 9 [*De la grammatologie* (Paris: Les Éditions de Minuit, 1967), p. 19].

43. Friedrich Nietzsche, *On the Future of Our Educational Institutions*, trans. John McFarland Kennedy (Edinburgh: T. N. Foulis, 1909) [*Über die Zukunft unserer Bildungsanstalten*, KSA 1: 641–752]. Derrida is working throughout with the French

spirit among modern pedagogues,"[44] and a call for the destruction and rebirth of the Gymnasium,[45] where a kind of elitism, aristocratism, and anti-democratism, as well as a certain anti-Hegelianism, build a whole system of language upon a zoological conception of the mother tongue (logos: *zōon*), a certain philosophy of life and a vitalist metaphorics of language, which, drawing yet again from the most traditional Platonism (the logos is a *zōon*), is reactivated by the historical linguistics of the times (even if it is reacting to it), a historical linguistics that uses and abuses vitalist metaphors in order to describe the evolution and transformation of languages. The transformation of the university must, according to Nietzsche, happen not through linguistic science but through a linguistic training that alone would be suitable for a language conceived as a living organism rather than as an object of science, a living organism whose life, whose living character, must be assumed, whose life, which it gets from the mother in the mother tongue, must be accepted rather than killed off through an anatomy of it. Let me read the following as an exergue for the next session:

> Instead of that purely practical method of instruction by which the teacher accustoms his pupils to severe self-discipline in their own language, we find everywhere the rudiments of a historico-scholastic method of teaching the mother-tongue: that is to say, people deal with it as if it were a dead language and as if the present and future were under no obligations to it whatsoever. The historical method has become so universal in our time, that even the living body of the language is sacrificed for the sake of anatomical study. But this is precisely where culture[46] begins — namely, in understanding how to treat the living thing as something living, and it is here too that the mission of the cultured teacher begins: in suppressing the urgent claims of "historical interests" wherever it is above all necessary to *do* properly and not merely to *know* properly. Our mother-tongue, however, is a domain in which the pupil must learn how to *do* properly, and to this practical end, alone, the teaching of German is essential in our scholastic establishments.[47]

---

translation of Jean-Louis Backès, *Sur l'avenir de nos établissements d'enseignement* (Paris: Gallimard, 1973).

44. Ibid., p. 44 [*KSA* 1: 673].

45. A handwritten insertion in the left margin of T1 reads "a critique of the institution" and, on T2, "a critique of the institution, therefore."

46. [Translators' note:] The German word translated here as "culture," *Bildung*, also means education, development, formation.

47. Nietzsche, *On the Future of Our Educational Institutions*, 2nd lecture, pp. 49–50 [*KSA* 1: 677].

SECOND SESSION[1]

Logic of the Living (She the Living)

───────

I would like to spare you the tedium, the waste of time, and the kind of servility there always is in constantly recalling prior sessions, in justifying one's trajectory, one's method, one's system, in providing more or less smooth transitions, in reestablishing continuity, etc., so many imperatives of traditional pedagogy with which it is impossible to break completely but which would, very quickly, if one were intent on abiding by them rigorously, reduce one to silence, to tautology, or to endless repetition. I thus propose to you *my* compromise, and, as we all know, in the terms of what is called academic freedom, you can take it or leave it. Considering the time at my disposal, the tedium I also wish to spare myself, the freedom I am able to exercise and want to preserve, I will proceed in a way that some will deem aphoristic and unacceptable in the context of a course but that others will accept as such, and that others still will find not aphoristic enough, listening to me in such a way, with such ears (everything depends on the ear with which you heard me last time and hear me in general), that the coherence and continuity of my trajectory will have been quickly apparent to them, right from the first session, right from the first words, from the very title of that first session. In any case, it is understood that whoever wishes not to follow along can do so and that whoever wants and is able to say something can do that as well. It goes without saying today that, in teaching, I am not

---

1. Several words are written on the folder in which this session was kept: "Life // death (Freud) + ms (fragment) *To Speculate* Life Death." In the left margin of the typescript is the word "Exergue," followed by "Zarathustra, *Von der Erlösung*, p. 158," circled in red. [Derrida is referring here to a passage from Nietzsche's *Zarathustra* titled "On Redemption." A photocopy of the passage is included in the folder containing this session and was presumably read as an exergue to the session. The same passage is placed as an exergue to the version published in *The Ear of the Other*, p. 3. See *Otobiographies*, pp. 33–118). See editorial note, p. xiiin8.]

teaching the truth itself by turning myself into some transparent instrument of a perennial pedagogy. I am simply addressing as best I can a certain number of problems, addressing them with you and with myself and, through you and myself, with a certain number of other authorities [*instances*] represented here. Hence I do not intend to exclude from the exhibition or the scene either the place that I occupy here or what I will call, to say it in a word—one whose meaning I am proposing we displace a little and hear with another ear—the *auto-biographical* demonstration,[2] in which I would here like to take a certain pleasure, and propose that you learn *from me this pleasure*: considering the size of the room, it may be, though this is not yet certain, that had there been fewer of us there might have been more pleasure to go around. But that is not certain.

So-called "academic freedom," the ear and auto-biography, those are my objects for today.

A discourse on life death, as we were already able to verify rather amply last week, is located in a certain space, still quite indeterminate, between *logos* and *grammē*, analogy and program, that is, the different meanings of program. And since it is a question of life, this space between logic and graphics must also be situated somewhere between the bio-logical dimension and the bio-graphical, the thanato-logical and the thanato-graphical.

The biographical, the *autos* of the autobiographical, must today undergo—is today in the process of undergoing—a complete reevaluation. A philosopher's biography can no longer today be considered either as an empirical accident that leaves the philosopher's name and signature simply outside the system that then lends itself to a simply immanent philosophical reading and thereby makes it possible to write the lives of philosophers in the ornamental, traditional style that you well know, or <as> psycho-biographies that give an account of the genesis of the system on the basis of empirical mechanisms (of the psychologizing type—even when inflected by psychoanalysis—of the historicizing, sociologizing type, etc.). A new problematic of the biographical in general and of the biography of philosophers in particular must mobilize more than one new resource, including, at the very least, a new problematic of the proper name and the signature of the philosopher. Neither immanentist readings of philosophical systems, whether structural or not, nor (external) empirico-genetic readings of philosophy have ever, as such, questioned this dynamic border between the work

---

2. [Translators' note:] Note that auto-biography sounds like oto-biography, a biography of or by the ear (*ous*, *ōtos*, in Greek).

and the life, the system and the subject of the system, the dynamic border that, inasmuch as it is neither simply active nor simply passive, neither outside nor inside, is also not a thin, almost invisible line between the inside of philosophemes, for example, and the life of a nameable author, but something that traverses the two bodies (the body of work and the body itself) according to laws whose complexity we are only now beginning to recognize.

What we call life, the thing or object of bio-logy and bio-graphy, has not only the complication of not being simply opposed to—as to a contrary—something that would be for it an opposable ob-ject, namely, death, the thanato-logical or thanato-graphical over against the bio-logical or bio-graphical. It is also, as we have begun to verify, what *has trouble* [a du mal] (I wish to hang onto this expression), what has trouble becoming the object of a science, and for essential reasons, the object of a science in the sense that philosophy and traditional science have always given to this word, that is, with the legal status of scientificity. And this trouble that it has, along with the lagging behind that ensues, as we talked about last week, stems in particular not only from the fact that a philosophy of life always has its place, a place prepared in advance, in a science of life (something that is not the case for the other sciences, in other words, for all the sciences that are sciences of non-life, in other words that are sciences, in some sense, of the dead, which would amount to saying that all the sciences that achieve this scientificity without leaving something behind or without lagging behind are sciences of the dead, and that there is between the dead and the status of the scientific object, between death and scientific objectivity, a co-implication that *interests* us, that interests the desire of the scientist). Not only, then, I was saying, because a philosophy of life always has its place prepared in advance in a science of life whose scientificity it thus limits accordingly, but, and as a result, the trouble (as well as the irreducible lagging behind) stems from the fact that the so-called living subject of bio-logical discourse is always implicated in its own field, always either having a stake or being itself at stake, with its desire, its enormous philosophico-ideological and political gains, with all the forces at work in it, in a word, with everything that has its potential increased in the subjectivity and signature of a biologist and of a community of biologists and that constitutes the irreducible inscription of the biographical in the bio-logical.

Now, the name of Nietzsche is today for us in the West the name of the one who was the only one, along with Kierkegaard, perhaps, though in another way, to treat, I would say, philosophy and life, the science of life and the philosophy of life, *with his name*, in his name, by putting his name on the line, his names, his biography, with almost all the risks that this entails, for him, his life, his name, and the future of his name, especially the political future of what he signed.

One must take this into account when one reads him and one reads him only by taking this into account.

Putting one's name on the line (with everything that this involves and that cannot be reduced to an *I*), staging one's signature, turning everything one has said or written about life and death into an enormous bio-graphical paraph—that is what he did and that is what we need to take note of, not in order to grant him some benefit—first of all because he is dead, a trivial point that the genius of the name is always there to make us forget; first, then, because he is dead, and being-dead means at the very least that no benefit or harm, whether calculated or not, can any longer return to the bearer of the name, such that the name, insofar as it is not the bearer, is always a name of the dead and what returns to the name never returns to something living; nothing returns to something living. And then, we will not grant him any benefit from this because what he bequeathed, in his name, as a legacy, was, like any *legs* (you can hear this word with whichever ear you want), a poisoned milk that got mixed up in advance, as we will be reminded today, with the worst of our times. And got mixed up not by chance.

One must therefore read Nietzsche—and I recall this before turning to any one of his texts—neither as a philosopher (of being, of life or of death) nor as a scientist or a biologist, so long as these three types have in common an abstraction from the bio-graphical and the pretense not to be engaging their life and their name in their writings. One must thus read Nietzsche only on the basis of a gesture like that found in *Ecce Homo* where Nietzsche puts forward his name and his body, even if what he puts forward has the form of a mask or of pseudo-nyms without any proper name, plural masks or plural names that can be put forward, like every mask and every theory of the mask, only by always granting the benefit of some protection wherein the ruse of life can be seen at work. One must read him starting from the moment when he says (*starting* from the final moment when he says) Ecce Homo, "*Wie man wird, was man ist*, how one becomes what one is," and starting from the preface to *Ecce Homo*, which can be said to be coextensive with Nietzsche's entire oeuvre, such that his entire oeuvre is also the preface to *Ecce Homo* and is repeated in what is called, in the strict sense, the preface (a few pages long) to *Ecce Homo*.[3] Let me recall the first lines:

---

3. Friedrich Nietzsche, *Ecce Homo*, in *On the Genealogy of Morals* and *Ecce Homo*, trans. Walter Kaufmann and R. J. Hollingdale (New York: Vintage Books, 1989) [*KSA*

Seeing that before long I must confront humanity with the most difficult demand ever made of it, it seems indispensable to me to say *who I am* [*wer ich bin*—underscored]. One should really know this, for I have always given proof of my identity [I am citing here Vialatte's French translation of "denn ich habe mich nicht 'unbezeugt gelassen'": a phrase Nietzsche puts in quotation marks: left unattested, without-attestation.] But the disproportion between the greatness of my task and the *smallness* of my contemporaries has found expression in the fact that one has neither heard nor even seen me. I live on my own credit [I go on, living on the credit I accord myself: *Ich lebe auf meinen eignen Kredit hin*]; it is perhaps a mere prejudice (*vielleicht bloss ein Vorurteil*) that I live (*dass ich lebe*).[4]

In other words, his own identity, the one he declares, wants to declare, and that has nothing to do with, is out of proportion with, what his contemporaries know under this name, under his name, Friedrich Nietzsche, his own identity results not from a contract with his contemporaries but from the unheard-of contract [*contrat inouï*] he signed with himself, through which he indebted himself to himself (*auf meinen eignen Kredit*), an unlimited credit that is without comparison to the one his contemporaries opened up for him or refused him under this name Friedrich Nietzsche. Friedrich Nietzsche is thus already a false name, a homonymic pseudonym, the homonym coming to dissimulate, as would a pseudonym, the other Friedrich Nietzsche; and this pseudonymy, linked to this strange business of contract, debt, and credit, already compels us to be wary when it comes to reading the signature, or even the autograph, of Nietzsche, every time he says: I, the undersigned Friedrich Nietzsche. With regard to this credit, this great line of credit he opened for himself, in his name, but then necessarily in the name of an other, he never knows in the present, and not even in the present of *Ecce Homo*, if it will be honored. And that is why, if the life he lives and recounts to himself as his auto-biography is first of all *his* life only as the effect of a secret contract, an open credit, a debt that has been contracted or an alliance or an annulus, a ring, then he can say, so long as the contract will not have been honored—but it can be honored only by the other—that his life is perhaps only a prejudice: "*es ist vielleicht ein Vorurteil, dass ich lebe . . .*" A pre-judice, life, or rather than life, the "I live" (in the present), a pre-judgment, a precipitous sentence, an anticipation that can be verified, fulfilled, only at the moment the bearer of the name—the one who is called,

---

6: 255–374]. Derrida is using throughout—and modifying—the French translation of *Ecce Homo* by Alexandre Vialatte (Paris: Gallimard, 1942).

4. Nietzsche, *Ecce Homo*, p. 217 [KSA 6: 257].

by prejudice, a living being — is dead. And the life that returns will return to the name and not to the living being, to or in the name of the living as the name of the dead. That the "I live" is a prejudice linked to the name, to the structure of the name, he (but who?) says he has proof of this each time he questions the first *"Gebildeten"* (educated, cultured person) who comes to the Upper Engadine. As Nietzsche's name is unknown to him, Nietzsche — which thus needs to be put in quotation marks — has proof that he does not live:

> I live on my own credit; it is perhaps a mere prejudice that I live.
>
> I only need to speak with one of the "educated" who come to the Upper Engadine for the summer, and I am convinced that I do *not* live (*dass ich nicht lebe*).
>
> Under these circumstances I have a duty against which my habits, even more the pride of my instincts, revolt at bottom — namely, to say: *Hear me! For I am this one and that one* [literally: I am who and who: *ich bin der und der*]. *Above all, do not mistake me for someone else* [all of this is underscored].⁵

Ich bin der und der: he says this only reluctantly, then, out of debt or duty, it revolts him and runs counter to his habits and his proud instincts, which thus naturally push him to dissimulate, to dissimulate himself, for, as you know, he constantly affirms the value of dissimulation (life is dissimulation, he often says). It is against the natural instinct for dissimulation that he announces that he is going to say *Ich bin der und der*, which leads us to conclude, *on the one hand*, that the credit and the contract that he commits himself to honoring in the name of the name, in his name and in the name of the other, are not natural, that they go against his nature (his instinct and his habit), but also, *on the other hand*, that this exhibiting of the *Ich bin der und der* might very well still be a ruse of dissimulation and would mislead us again if we were to hear it as a simple presentation of identity, supposing in advance that we in fact already know what a self-presentation, a declaration of identity, etc., is. Everything he goes on to say about truth will have to be reevaluated on the basis of this questioning and this worry. And not only does Nietzsche distrust here every assurance regarding identity and everything we think we know about a proper name, but, very quickly, on the following page, he tells us that his experience and his wandering into forbidden areas (*Wanderung im Verbotenen*) have taught him to consider very differently the causes (*Ursache*) of idealization and moralization and that he saw

---

5. Ibid. In the left margin of the typescript is the handwritten notation "ver<ify> Ecce Homo."

coming to light the hidden history of philosophers (not of philosophy) and the "the psychology of their great names": "*die* verborgene *Geschichte der Philosophen, die Psychologie ihrer grossen Namen kam für mich an's Licht.*"⁶

That the *I live* should depend on a nominal contract whose coming due presupposes the death of the one who says "I live" in the present; that the relationship of a philosopher to his "great name," that is, to what borders the system with his signature, stems from a psychology, a psychology that is still too new to be readable either in the system of philosophy, that is, as one of its parts, or in psychology as a region or part of philosophy; that this should be stated in the preface signed Friedrich Nietzsche of a book titled *Ecce Homo* and whose last words are "Have I been understood? —*Dionysus versus the Crucified*,"⁷ versus, against, the crucified, *gegen den Gekreuzigten*, Nietzsche, Ecce Homo, Christ being not Christ but Dionysus or, rather, the name of the combat between the two names, that would be enough not only to pluralize in a singular fashion the proper names and homonymic masks but also to lose in a labyrinth (of the ear, of course) the threads [*fils*] of the name, the borders of the name. Between the preface (signed "Friedrich Nietzsche"), which comes after the title, and the first chapter, "Why I Am So Wise,"⁸ there is a page, an outwork, an hors d'œuvre (an exergue), like a loose page, whose time, whose temporality, strangely dislocates all our assurances with regard to what we typically understand as the time of life and the time of the narrative of life, of the writing of life by the living, the time of auto-biography. This page is, in a sense, dated: it is an anniversary, the date when the year turns back upon itself, forms a ring or annulus with itself, is annulled and begins anew. It is the year I turn forty-five, the day of the year when I turn forty-five years old. This day is like the noon of life, it is around this age, in fact, that we commonly locate the noon of life, or even the midlife crisis or noonday demon, noon being the midpoint of the day. The exergue begins in this way: "On this perfect day (*An diesem vollkommnen Tage*), when everything is ripening and not only the grape turns brown, the eye of the sun just fell upon my life [it fell upon me on my life, it has fallen to me, to my life, as if by chance: *fiel mir eben ein Sonnenblick auf mein Leben*]."⁹ It is a moment without shadow, consonant with all the noons of Zarathustra. It is the moment of affirmation when one can look forward and backward at the same time and when all negativity, all shadow, is

54

6. Ibid., p. 218 [*KSA* 6: 259].
7. Ibid., p. 335 [*KSA* 6: 374].
8. Ibid., p. 222 [*KSA* 6: 264].
9. Ibid., p. 221 [*KSA* 6: 263].

dispelled. The text continues: "I looked back, I looked forward, and never saw so many and such good things at once."¹⁰ This noon is nonetheless the moment of a burial, and when Nietzsche says immediately thereafter, playing on common parlance, that he has just buried his forty-four years, insisting on it two different times, it is to underscore that what he has buried is death, and that by burying death, the dead, he has saved life, saved the immortal:

> It was not for nothing that I buried (*begrub*) my forty-fourth year today; I had the *right* to bury it [underscored: *ich* durfte *es begraben*: I had the right to bury it]; whatever was life (*Leben*) in it [in the forty-fourth year] has been saved (*gerettet*), *ist unsterblich*, is immortal. The first book of the *Umwertung aller Werte*, the *Lieder* of *Zarathustra*, the *Twilight of the Idols*, my attempt to philosophize with a hammer—all gifts (*Geschenke*) of this year, indeed of its last quarter! *How could I fail to be grateful to my whole life?* [underscored: *Wie sollte ich nicht meinem ganzen Leben dankbar sein*]—and so I tell my life to *myself* [I recount myself to myself, I recite my life to myself: *Und so erzähle ich mir mein Leben*].¹¹

End of the exergue on the loose page, between the preface and the beginning of *Ecce Homo*.

To receive one's life as a gift calling for gratitude, or rather to be grateful to one's life for what it gives, namely, for the one who was able to write himself and sign himself with this name for which I opened up a line of credit and who will be what he became only on the basis of what was given by a year (the transvaluation of values, the songs of Zarathustra, *The Twilight of the Idols*, etc.), in the course of the event dated by a circuit of the sun and even just a part of its circuit, to reaffirm what has passed (the forty-four years) as good and as bound to return, eternally, as immortal, that is what constitutes the strange present of this auto-biographical narrative (*so erzähle ich mir mein Leben*), an auto-biographical narrative that buries the dead and saves what is saved as immortal, an auto-biographical narrative that is auto-biographical not only because the signatory recounts his life (the eternal return of his past life as life and not as death) but because he recounts himself, *erzähle ich mir*, recounts to himself,¹² recites to himself, his life. And since the *I* of this narrative is constituted only through the credit of the eternal return, it does not exist, it does not sign before the narrative as eternal return. It is, until then, a mere prejudice.

10. Ibid.
11. Ibid.
12. "Himself" is circled in the typescript.

One cannot therefore think the name or the names of Friedrich Nietzsche before the reaffirmation or the hymen or ring or alliance of the eternal return; one cannot think his life, or his life-his work, before this thinking of the "yes, yes" given to the gift (*Geschenk*) without shadow, when noon and the grape are at their fullest and the cup is overflowing with sun (and I refer you for all of this to the beginning of *Zarathustra*).

The difficulty we would then have in thinking the date of such an event, this event of the auto-biographical narrative—which requires, like the thought of eternal return, thinking otherwise the coming of any event—this difficulty cannot but crop up everywhere one seeks to date an event, to identify the beginning of a text, the origin of life or the first movement of a signature, its border. This structure of an exergue as a kind of bordering, or of a bordering as exergue, cannot fail to be reimprinted, to reverberate, everywhere it is a question of life, or of something like my-life. This exergue structure (between the title or the preface, on the one hand, and the book to come, on the other) situates the place from which life will be recounted, recited (yes, yes), that is to say, affirmed as having eternally to return, linked by the wedding ring to itself. The place of this affirmation or this exergue that is neither simply in the work nor simply in the life of the author, the place of this exergue that repeats the affirmation, that endorses, signs, subscribes (yes, yes, read and approved, and let it all begin again), the place-moment of this exergue that buries the negativity and thus buries even the shadow, is the place and the moment of noon, the noon of life. What the exergue I just read says will actually get taken up again in the chapter "Why I Write Such Good Books":[13] "My duty[14] to prepare a moment of the highest self-examination for humanity, a great noon when it looks back and far forward, when it emerges from the dominion of accidents and priests."[15] But the noon of life is neither a place nor a moment; it is not a place or a moment, first of all, because it is a limit that immediately vanishes, but then also because it returns daily, every day, each day, with each turn of the ring. If we are entitled to read Friedrich Nietzsche's signature only in this place and at this instant, in the place and at the instant he signs by saying yes, yes, I myself—and I myself recite my life to myself—you can begin to see the impossible protocol for reading and teaching that this constitutes; and how

---

13. Nietzsche, *Ecce Homo*, p. 259 [*KSA* 6: 298].
14. In the typescript the word "duty" is circled.
15. Nietzsche, *Ecce Homo*, p. 291 [*KSA* 6: 330]. In the left margin of the transcript, at the level of the quotation, are several handwritten words: "regeneration of hearing, p. 21, metaphor the proper <two illegible words> of the child."

pathetically naïve it can be to say Nietzsche wrote this, Nietzsche said that, Nietzsche thinks this or that about life, for example, life in the sense of human existence or biological life, etc.

I am not going to read *Ecce Homo* with you. I am going to have to make do with this foreword or forewarning [*avertissement*] about the place of the exergue, the place of the fold it makes along a barely apparent limit insofar as there is no longer any shadow, the place from which all the other utterances, before and after, left and right, are at once possible (Nietzsche said it all) and necessarily contradictory (he said the most contradictory things and he said that he said the most seemingly contradictory things). Just one indication of this contradictory duplicity before leaving *Ecce Homo*. Right after what I am calling the exergue and the point of view of the exergue, which does not hesitate to date (his birth, his birthday, the quarter of the year in which he received the gift of his last books, etc.), the beginning of the first chapter ("Why I Am So Wise") begins with the origins of my life, my father and my mother, and then immediately thereafter the principle of contradiction in my life (between the principle of death and the principle of life, the beginning and the end, the high and the low, the decadent or degenerate and the ascendant, and so on). This contradiction of my life—which is my destiny [*fatalité*]—has to do with my genealogy, with my father and my mother, with what I express in the form of an enigma as the identity of my father and the identity of my mother; in a word, my dead father and my living mother, my father as the dead man and as death, my mother as the living [*la vivante*] and as life. I am between the two and my truth takes after the two of them. You know this text that I am going to read and retranslate:

> The good fortune (*Glück*) of my existence (*Daseins*), its uniqueness perhaps [he says *perhaps* because he perhaps thinks this situation to be exemplary and paradigmatic], lies in its fatality: I am, to express it in the form of an enigma (*Rätselform*), already dead as my father, while as my mother I am still living and becoming old [the (French) translation by Vialatte is a disaster here: it says "in me my father is dead, but my mother is alive and is becoming old," but that's not it, the text says: I am as my father already dead (*als mein Vater bereits gestorben*), as my mother I am still living and becoming old (*als meine Mutter lebe ich noch und werde alt*)].[16]

So, insofar as I am and follow after [*suis*] my father, I am dead, the dead, death, insofar as I am and follow after my mother, I am the life that perseveres, the living, she the living [*la vivante*]. I am my father my mother and

---

16. Ibid., p. 222 [*KSA* 6: 264].

myself, my father my mother and therefore my son and myself, death and life, (he) the dead [*le mort*] and (she) the living [*la vivante*], and so on. That is who I am, *ich bin der und der*: this means all of that, and one cannot hear my name if one does not hear it as that of (he) the dead and (she) the living, that of the dead father and the mother who lives on, who will have outlived me and buried me, moreover, because it is living life [*la vie vivante*] that will have buried me, and the name of my living life is the name of the mother, the name of my dead life the name of my father. One must thus take this scene into account each time one claims to identify a statement by Friedrich Nietzsche. And the statement I just read is not auto-biographical in the usual sense of the term: this does not mean that it is incorrect to say that Nietzsche speaks, as we would say, of his real father or mother; it is just that he also speaks of them in "*Rätselform*," that is to say, symbolically, or, rather, enigmatically, the enigma being a story, a proverbial morality in the form of a narrative. What then follows in the text draws all the consequences of the double origin of my-life insofar as my life is born both from (he) the dead and (she) the living, from death and life, from the father and the mother. This double origin explains who and how I am: double and neuter, neutral [*neutre*]. Allow me to read:

> This double origin (*Diese doppelte Herkunft*), as it were, from both the highest and the lowest rungs on the ladder of life, at the same time a *décadent* and a beginning [*décadent* — in French — *zugleich und* Anfang] — this, if anything, explains that neutrality, that freedom from all partiality [from all taking sides] in relation to the total problem of life (*zum Gesammtprobleme des Lebens*), that perhaps distinguishes me. I have a subtler sense of smell [stay attentive to Nietzsche's nose and to what he says about his nostrils] for the signs of ascent and decline [literally, rising and setting, for example, of the sun: *für die Zeichen*, for the signs, *von Aufgang und Niedergang*, of what rises and what falls, upwards and downwards] than any other human being before me; I am the teacher (*Lehrer*) par excellence for this — I know both, I am both: *ich kenne beides, ich bin beides*.[17]

Ich kenne beides, ich bin beides, I know both, the two of them [*les deux*], or perhaps we should just say the two [*le deux*], I am the two, and the two here is life death (*beides*). When Friedrich Nietzsche says to us: do not be mistaken, know that I am "*der und der*," *der und der* is both of them, the two of them as death life, (he) the dead (she) the living. We have to read this in its letter, in the original language. Just as Vialatte earlier translated "I am as my father already dead" (*ich bin, als mein Vater bereits gestorben*) as "in

17. Ibid.

me my father is dead," so he translates "I know both, I am both" (*Ich kenne beides, ich bin beides*) as "I know them, I incarnate both of them."

It is this logic of (he) the dead as logic of (she) the living that we must endlessly decipher when Friedrich Nietzsche feigns signing by saying *Ich bin der und der*. I am not going to read *Ecce Homo* with you; I am simply citing before changing course, I am reciting, resituating by means of a few points of reference this affirmation of the demonic neutrality of midday, which is especially not negative (read Blanchot on this subject, regarding Nietzsche and the neuter as non-negative and non-dialectical),[18] a neutrality that is above all not negative or dialectical. I recite, therefore, without comment: "I am both. My father died at the age of thirty-six: he was delicate, kind, and morbid (*morbid*), as a being that is destined merely to pass by (*wie ein nur zum Vorübergehn bestimmtes Wesen*)—more a gracious memory of life than life itself (*eher eine gütige Erinnerung an das Leben als das Leben selbst*)."[19] Thus the father is not only dead when the son lives on; he, the father, was dead even while he was living; he was as the living father only the memory of life, of a prior, always prior life. This family structure—the father dead,[20] the mother living before all else and after all else, to the point of burying the son to whom she gave birth and attending his funeral, to the point of remaining a virgin in the face of everything that happens and everything she survives—this structure, which I elsewhere call the logic of obsequence,[21] is exemplified in the family of Christ (to whom Dionysus is here opposed, but as his double), in the Nietzsche family, if we consider that the mother survived what is called the "collapse," and in general in every family as family if we bracket all the facts. And Nietzsche will have first repeated the death of the father in his body before the recovery that he then also recounts in *Ecce Homo*:

> In the same year in which his life went downward, mine, too, went downward: at thirty-six [when I was thirty-six], I reached the lowest point of my vitality—I still lived, but without being able to see three steps ahead.

---

18. See Maurice Blanchot, "Reflections on Nihilism" and "The Narrative Voice (the 'he,' the neutral)," in *The Infinite Conversation*, trans. Susan Hanson (Minneapolis: University of Minnesota Press, 1993), pp. 136–70, 379–87.

19. Nietzsche, *Ecce Homo*, p. 222 [*KSA* 6: 264].

20. There is here in the typescript an interlineal handwritten addition—perhaps the word "absent."

21. See Derrida, *Glas*, trans. John P. Leavey Jr. and Richard Rand (Lincoln: University of Nebraska Press, 1986), for example, pp. 117bi, 122b, 174bi, and 255–56bi [*Glas* (Paris: Éditions Galilée, 1974), pp. 134bi, 140b, 196bi, and 283–84bi].

Then — it was 1879 — I retired from my professorship at Basel, spent the summer in St. Moritz like a shadow (*wie ein Schatten*),²² and the next winter (not one winter in my life has been poorer in sunshine) in Naumburg *as* a shadow ["as" is underscored, als *Schatten*; Vialatte has here: I became the shadow of myself]. This was my minimum: the *Wanderer and His Shadow* originated at this time. Doubtless, I then knew about shadows.²³

A bit further on: "My readers know perhaps in what way I consider dialectic as a symptom of décadence (*als Décadence-Symptom*); for example in the most famous case [and "case" here is *Fall*, case as indicating fall, *casus*, decadence, *im allerberühmtesten Fall: im Fall des Sokrates*]."²⁴ And further on still: "Apart from the fact that I am a décadent, I am also the opposite (*dass ich ein décadent bin, bin ich auch dessen Gegensatz*)."²⁵ Read the rest of the beginning of section 2 of the first chapter. Section 1 also began with the affirmation of this double provenance. And section 3 does as well: "*Diese doppelte Reihe von Erfahrungen*, this double series of experiences, this access to two apparently separate worlds, is repeated in my nature in every respect: I am a double (*ich bin ein Doppelgänger*), I have a 'second' sight [the gift of second sight] in addition to the first. And perhaps also a third."²⁶ (Elsewhere, as you know, he speaks of the third ear.)²⁷ Right before this, at the end of the preceding section, he had written: "Well then, I am the *opposite* of a *décadent* (*das* Gegenstück *eines* décadent), for I have just described *myself* (*denn ich beschrieb eben* mich)."²⁸ That is the end of section 2. Here is the end of section 3: "In order to understand anything at all of my *Zarathustra* one must perhaps be similarly conditioned as I am — with one foot *beyond* life [beyond, *jenseits* is the only word underscored: *mit einem Fusse jenseits des Lebens*]."²⁹ And so, rather than life or, and/or, death, it is the *step (not) beyond* [*pas-au-delà*] that counts. Read Blanchot again, and the strange syntax

---

22. In the left margin of the typescript are the words "Madness of the Day."
23. Nietzsche, *Ecce Homo*, p. 222 [*KSA* 6: 264–65].
24. Ibid., p. 223 [*KSA* 6: 265].
25. Ibid., p. 224 [*KSA* 6: 266].
26. Ibid., p. 225 [*KSA* 14: 472n3]. [Translators' note:] According to Colli and Montinari's commentary on *Ecce Homo*, this passage appears in the first version of this section but not in the version that Nietzsche eventually substituted for it.
27. See, for example, Friedrich Nietzsche, *Beyond Good and Evil*, trans. Walter Kaufmann (New York: Vintage Books, 1966), paragraph 246, p. 182 [*KSA* 5: 189]: "What torture books written in German are for anyone who has a *third ear!*"
28. Nietzsche, *Ecce Homo*, p. 225 [*KSA* 6: 267].
29. Ibid., p. 226 [*KSA* 14: 473n3]. [Translators' note:] According to Colli and Montinari's commentary on *Ecce Homo*, this line appears only in the first version of this section.

(without syntax) of the *pas au-delà* that approaches death in what I will call the step-by-step of an impossible overstepping or transgression.

The fact that the signature of the auto-biographer remains a credit open onto eternity, and that it refers back to one of the two I's contracting its name only through the ring of the eternal return, does not prevent—indeed it even allows—the one who says, "summer have I become entirely, and summer noon!" (in "Why I Am So Wise")[30] also to say: I am a double, and thus I am not to be confused—not yet—with my work. And it is in this *différance* in *Ecce Homo*, in this *différance* of the auto-biographical as allo-biographical or thanato-biographical, that what appears under a new guise is the question of the institution and of teaching to which I wanted to lead you back today.

By definition, the good news of the Eternal Return—which is a message and a teaching—cannot be heard in the present. But since this news, this message, is also that of a certain affirmative re-petition (yes, yes), a certain re-turn that recommences and reproduces in a certain way the affirmation of the Eternal Return, keeping this affirmation as the eternal return of the same, it is logical that it would give rise to a teaching and an institution. Zarathustra is a teacher (*Lehrer*), he has a doctrine and he intends to establish new institutions. How are these institutions of the "yes" [*oui*][31] related to the ear?

I will first read the beginning of the chapter of *Ecce Homo* titled "Why I Write Such Good Books":

> *Das Eine bin ich, das Andre sind meine Schriften*. I am one thing, my writings are another.—Before I discuss them, one by one, let me touch on the question of their being understood or *not* understood. I'll do it as casually as decency permits; for the time for this question certainly hasn't come yet. The time for me hasn't come yet: some are born posthumously.
>
> Some day institutions (*Institutionen*) will be needed in which one may live and teach as I conceive of living and teaching; it might even happen that a few professorial chairs will then be set aside for [chairs proper to, *eigene Lehrstühle*] the interpretation of *Zarathustra*. But it would contradict my character entirely if I expected ears *and hands* [note that "and hands," *und Hände*, is underscored—you will want to remember this later on] for *my* truths *already* today: that today one doesn't hear me and doesn't accept my ideas is not only understandable, it even seems right to me [it is just]. I

---

30. Ibid., p. 234 [*KSA* 6: 276].
31. [Translators' note:] Note that the French *oui*, "yes," is a homophone of *ouïe*, "hearing."

don't want to be confounded with others [exchanged for another, taken for another: *verwechselt werden*] — not even by myself.³²

This question of teaching and of the new institution is thus *also*, in some sense, a question of the ear. You know all that is coiled up in the figure or face [*figure*], so to speak, in the labyrinth, of Nietzsche's ear; I do not want to enter into that here. I will simply note the reappearance of this motif in the same chapter of *Ecce Homo*, and I will then immediately return — a labyrinth effect — to the exergue taken from Nietzsche's text (of 1872, all the way at the other end) titled *On the Future of Our Educational Institutions*. Here, first, is the reappearance of the ear in the same chapter of *Ecce Homo*:

> All of us know, some even from experience, which animal has long ears (*was ein Langohr ist*). Well then, I dare assert that I have the smallest ears. This is of no small interest to the little women (*Weiblein*) — it seems to me that they may feel I understand them better. — I am the *anti-ass* par excellence and thus a world-historical monster — I am, in Greek, and not only in Greek, the Antichrist.³³

How does this claim to having the smallest, keenest ears, along with this complexity of the "I am," I am the both, the double, I sign double, my writings and me make two, I am (he) the dead (she) the living, and so on — how does all this re-introduce us to the reading of *On the Future of Our Educational Institutions* and to politics, to all the politics at stake there?

Let me first reread what, at the end of last week's trajectory, I placed in exergue for today's session.³⁴

> Instead of that purely practical method of instruction by which the teacher accustoms his pupils to severe self-discipline in their own language, we find everywhere the rudiments of a historico-scholastic method of teaching the mother-tongue: that is to say, people deal with it as if it were a dead language and as if the present and future were under no obligations (*Verpflichtungen*) to it whatsoever. [Obligation, therefore: he is alluding to an obligation with regard to the life of the mother, the mother tongue, contract and alliance, against the dead, against death, with life, the life with her, the living: and since the contract, the alliance, the repeated affirmation is always of language or of the signature in language with language, the first contract of life is a contract of language with language — with the mother tongue, the

---

32. Nietzsche, *Ecce Homo*, p. 259 [*KSA* 6: 298].
33. Ibid., p. 263 [*KSA* 6: 302].
34. In the typescript a few words in this paragraph have been crossed out and others added. The result is: "Let me read first what I have given as an exergue."

maternal language, which is to say, the living language, living, which is to say, maternal and not paternal, and so on; our exergue is now becoming a bit clearer because of the detour through *Ecce Homo*: history, that is, here, the historical science that kills or that treats the dead with the dead, occupies the place of the father; and the institution must be revived against or despite the father. I continue reading.] . . . as if the present and future were under no obligations to it whatsoever. The historical method has become so universal in our time, that even the living body of the language (*der lebendige Leib der Sprache*) is sacrificed for the sake of anatomical study. But this is precisely where culture (*Bildung*) begins — namely, in understanding how to treat the living as something alive (*das Lebendige als lebendig*), and it is here too that the mission of the cultured teacher begins: in suppressing (*unterdrücken*) the urgent claims (*sich aufdrängende*) of "historical interests" wherever it is above all necessary to *do*[35] properly and not merely to *know* properly. Our mother-tongue, however, is a domain in which the pupil must learn how to *do* [treat: *handeln*] properly (*richtig*) . . .[36]

So we now come to this text that figures among Nietzsche's "juvenilia," as they say, on the future of our institutions of higher learning, in this place where the questions of life death, of (she) the living (he) the dead [*la vivante le mort*], of the contract of language, of signature and credit, of the biographical and the biological, intersect within the question of the teaching institution. The entire reading trajectory that I offered you by way of the detour through *Ecce Homo* was, I believe, indispensable for approaching this so-called early work and can tentatively serve as a protocol for it. It is not that one should teleologically and retrospectively shed light on the beginning by means of the end and say that Nietzsche was "already" saying this or that. But without giving to this retro-perspective the teleological significance it has in the Aristotelian-Hegelian tradition, one can appeal to what Nietzsche himself says regarding the "credit" opened with his signature, the delay in the coming due, the difference between what he is and his work, and the posthumous in general in order to complicate the protocols for reading this text *On the Future of Our Educational Institutions*. Let me tell you right away that I am not going to multiply these protocols in order to dissimulate, defuse, or neutralize this text with a view to clearing Nietzsche of everything in it that might be worrisome for a democratic pedagogy or a leftist politics — or of everything in it that provided the language for the most

---

35. In the left margin of the typescript, next to the word "do," which is circled, Derrida writes the German word *handeln*, "acting" or "doing," which invokes the hand, as in "handling."

36. Nietzsche, *On the Future of Our Educational Institutions*, pp. 49–50 [*KSA* 1: 677].

odious Nazi rallying cries. On the contrary, we will need to pose this question without the least concern for decency, and ask why it is not enough to say that Nietzsche did not think or want this, that he would have vomited [*vomi*] all this,[37] that there is here falsification and mystification in the interpretation and inheritance of his thinking, to ask why and how such a "falsification" (as we call it a bit naively) was possible, why the same words and the same statements can oftentimes be used in ways that are deemed incompatible, and so on. And why, in the end, has the only institutional initiative to which Nietzsche's teaching on teaching given rise been Nazi?

First protocol: not only does this text belong to the posthumousness of which *Ecce Homo* speaks; it is a text that Nietzsche would not have even wanted to be published after his death. Even more, it is not only a posthumous work that Nietzsche apparently never wanted to have published but also a discourse that Nietzsche actually interrupted along the way. That does not mean that he repudiated the whole thing, and Nietzsche would no doubt have subscribed to that which would be most scandalous to an anti-Nazi democrat of today. Nevertheless, let us not forget that he never wanted to publish these lectures and even interrupted the writing of them. On 25 July 1872, after the fifth lecture, he wrote to Wagner:

> At the beginning of next winter I will still give my Basel lectures, the sixth and seventh, "On the Future of Our Educational Institutions." I want to be *done* with it, at least in the diminished and inferior form in which I have treated this theme thus far. For the *higher* treatment, I must become even "riper" and seek to educate myself.[38]

As it turns out he will not give these final two lectures and will refuse to publish them. On 20 December he writes to Malwida von Meysenbug:

> By now you will have read the lectures and have been startled that the story should break off suddenly [narrative fiction, etc.], after such a long prelude, with the thirst for real new thoughts and proposals tending more and more to end up in mere *negativis* and prolixities. One gets parched while reading them, and then there is nothing to drink at the finish! What I had in mind

---

37. [Translators' note:] The French *vomir* would usually be translated in such a context as "to abhor," "to be repulsed," "to be revolted by," etc. But Derrida writes in a footnote appended to the passage corresponding to this one in *Otobiographies*: "I say 'vomit' deliberately. Nietzsche constantly draws our attention to the value of learning to vomit, forming in this way one's taste, distaste, and disgust . . ." (p. 23).

38. *Nietzsche Briefwechsel, Kritische Gesamtausgabe*, ed. Giorgio Colli and Mazzino Montinari (Berlin: Walter de Gruyter, 1978), v. 3, part 2, p. 39; hereafter abbreviated *KGB*. In the eight-volume paperback edition of the *Sämtliche Briefe*, see 4: 39.

> for the last lecture—a very droll and colorful scene of nocturnal illuminations—was not exactly suitable for my Basel public, and it was certainly a good thing that the words stuck in my throat.[39]

And at the end of February of the following year:

> You must believe me.... In a few years I will be able to do everything better, and I will want to do so. In the meantime, these lectures have for me the value of an exhortation: they remind me of a debt or of a task that has fallen precisely upon me.... These lectures are undeveloped and, in addition, somewhat improvised.... Fritsch was ready to publish them, but I swore not to publish any book with respect to which my conscience was not as pure as that of a seraph.[40]

Finally, some concluding protocols: it would be necessary to analyze in its own right the narrative and fictional form of these lectures and what, in these lectures of an academic to other academics on the topic of the university and high schools, already marks a break in academicism, in the academic scene. I will not analyze this for its own sake, for lack of time. It would also be necessary, following the invitation that is extended to us by Nietzsche himself in his foreword, to read slowly, as untimely readers who already escape the law of their time by taking the time to read, all the time it takes, indefinitely—and not to say, as I just did, "I will not do this for lack of time." It is only by means of this time of reading that one will be able not just to read between the lines, as Nietzsche invites us to do, and read not with a view to getting an overall "picture" of what we read, as is most often done, but to read in view of a *meditatio generis futuri*, a practical meditation that goes so far as to give itself the time for an effective destruction of high schools and the university. "And what," Nietzsche asks, "must happen in the meantime," between the time when new legislators of education, in the service of a totally new culture, will be born and the present time? Perhaps "between now and then all *Gymnasia*—yea, and perhaps all universities, may be destroyed, or have become so utterly transformed that their very regulations may, in the eyes of future generations, seem to be but the relics of the lake-dwellers' age."[41] And in the meantime, as he will do for *Zarathustra*, he advises us to forget and destroy <the> text, but to forget and destroy it *through action*.

---

39. *Selected Letters of Friedrich Nietzsche*, ed. and trans. Christopher Middleton (Chicago: University of Chicago Press, 1969), p. 112 [*KGB*, p. 104; paperback ed., 4: 104].
40. Nietzsche to Malwida von Meysenbug, *KGB*, p. 127; paperback ed., 4: 104.
41. Nietzsche, *On the Future of Our Educational Institutions*, p. 4 [*KSA* 1: 648–49].

Given the scene in which we find ourselves here, what am I, for my part, going to select from these lectures? First, what I called last time the traditional phoenix motif:[42] the destruction of life is first of all a destruction of what is already dead so that living life might be reborn and regenerated. The vitalist motif of de-generation/regeneration is powerfully active and central in this text. We have seen why this had to pass first of all through the question of language (maternal-living or scientific-formal-dead-paternal) and why this question of life as the life of language cannot be dissociated from the question of education or of linguistic training (we will see why it is a question of "training" in a moment). Thus when Nietzsche speaks of the destruction of the *Gymnasium*, it is with the hope of its "re-birth"; the annihilation (*Vernichtung*) of the *Gymnasium*, of which the university, whatever it may think, is simply the product or the pre-formed development, this *Vernichtung* of the high school must give rise to a *Neugeburt* (a re-birth). The destruction must be the destruction of what is already destroying itself, a destruction of the de-generate, the de-generated. The expression "de-generation" (a loss at once of the vital, genetic, or generic force and of the specificity of the type, of the species and of the genre, the *Entartung*) comes back regularly to characterize culture, and notably university culture, insofar as that culture becomes journalistic and influenced by the state. Now, this concept of degeneration already has the structure it will have in subsequent analyses, for example, in *Genealogy of Morals*: degeneration is not a mere loss of life through a regular and homogeneous exhaustion but an inversion of values by which a hostile and reactive principle becomes none other than the active enemy of life. The degenerate is hostile to life; it is a life principle that is hostile to life. And it is in the fifth lecture (the last one), the one in which the word degeneration is most often pronounced, that the essential condition of regeneration is defined. What must take the place of a democratic, leveling culture, of so-called academic freedom in the university, of the greatest possible extension of culture, is discipline, training (*Zucht*), selection under the direction of a guide, a *Führer*, even a *grosse Führer*, in order to save from its enemies "that earnest, manly (*männlich ernsten*), stern, and daring German spirit; that spirit of the miner's son, Luther, which has come down to us unbroken from the time of the Reformation."[43] For example, concerning the *Führer*, one must restore the German university as an institution of culture, and, to do that, bring about an "inward renovation and

68

---

42. The sentence was modified in the transcript so as to read: "what can be called the phoenix motif."
43. Nietzsche, *On the Future of Our Educational Institutions*, p. 138 [*KSA* 1: 749].

inspiration of the purest moral faculties. And this must always be repeated to the student's credit. He learned on the field of battle [1870]⁴⁴ what he could learn least of all in the sphere of *akademische Freiheit*: that *grosse Führer* (great leaders) are necessary, and that all culture (*Bildung*) begins with obedience (*Gehorsam*)."⁴⁵ A little further on, all the woes of today's students can be explained by the fact that they have not found a *Führer*, that they are "*führerlos.*"

> For I repeat it, my friends! All culture begins with the very opposite of that which is now so highly esteemed as "academic freedom": with obedience (*Gehorsam*), subordination (*Unterordnung*), discipline (*Zucht*), and service (*Dienstbarkeit*). And just as the *grosse Führer* must have followers so also must the followers have a *Führer* to lead them (*so bedürfen die zu Führenden der Führer*)—here a certain reciprocal predisposition prevails in the hierarchy of spirits: yea, a kind of pre-established harmony.⁴⁶

An "eternal order": that is what Nietzsche calls it, and it is this, he says, that the dominant, prevailing culture is trying to destroy.

While it would obviously be naïve and crude to extract the word *Führer*, to allow it to resonate all by itself with its Hitlerian echoes and with the use that was made of this Nietzschean reference, as if this word had no other linguistic context, no other occurrences in the German language, and to make of Nietzscheism-Nazism one and the same combat, it would be just as naïve and peremptory to deny that something is happening here that belongs to a same (a same what?—that is the question), to some same, from the Nietzschean *Führer*, who is not only a schoolmaster and master of doctrine, to the Hitlerian *Führer*, who also considered himself an intellectual leader, a guide in doctrine and in schools, a teacher of regeneration; just as peremptory, therefore, and just as politically somnolent as being satisfied with saying: Nietzsche never wanted this, Nietzsche never thought that, he would have vomited this, that is not what was in his head, and so on. Even if this were true—a hypothesis we would be right to reject out of hand, first because Nietzsche is dead, and it is not a question of knowing what he, Nietzsche, would have thought; next, because we have good reason to believe that what he would have thought or done would have been very complicated, in any case, and the example of Heidegger in this regard would give plenty of reason to pause; and finally, because the effects of a text

---

44. In *Ear of the Other*, Jacques Derrida corrected this date: 1813 and not 1870 (p. 27).
45. Nietzsche, *On the Future of Our Educational Institutions*, p. 139 [*KSA* 1: 749].
46. Ibid., p. 140 [*KSA* 1: 750].

and the structure of a text, as we know in part thanks to Nietzsche, cannot be reduced to its truth or to the intentions of the presumed author—thus even if it were simply true that Nietzsche did not think or want this, that he would have vomited this, and that Nazism, far from being the regeneration called for by him, is only a symptom of the accelerated decomposition of culture and of European society diagnosed by Nietzsche, even in this case, it remains to be explained how reactive degeneration is able to make use of the same language, the same words, the same statements, the same rallying cries, as the active forces of which it is the real enemy. Must there not be, in some sense, a powerful, logical, statement-producing machine that programs at once, within a certain set (and it is this set that would have to be defined, a set that seems to be neither simply linguistic nor simply historico-politico-economic, neither simply ideological nor psychical, a set for which these regional determinations no longer suffice, not even that of the "last instance," which belongs to philosophy or to theory as such, which is itself a subset of this set, and so on), must there not be a powerful, programming "logic" with which neither of the two camps, neither of the antagonistic forces, can break, simply decide to break, since they draw their energies from it, exchange their statements within it, letting them pass into one another through it, however opposed or antagonistic they might at first appear? It is this machine (which is obviously no longer a machine, since it has life as one of its factors and it plays with the opposition life/death), it is this program (which, however, is no longer a program in the metaphysical or mechanistic sense), this program that interests me and that would have to be not only deciphered (in a theoretical manner) but transformed and re-written practically (in a practical manner) in accordance with a theory/practice relationship that is not part of the program. It goes without saying that this transformative re-writing of the vast program is not a re-writing that takes place in books—I explained long ago now what I understood by such a practice of general writing—or through readings or courses on the texts of Nietzsche or of Hitler and Nazi ideologues. It is a question of the entire politico-economic and ideological history of Europe, and not only of Europe, the entire history of this century, and not only of this century, including the present in which we take or occupy a position.

And if one were to say: be careful here, Nietzsche's own statements and those of Nazi ideologues are not the same, not only insofar as these latter are infinitely more crude than the former, of which they are a caricature, but because, so long as one does not just pick out a short phrase here and there, so long as one reconstitutes the entire syntax of the system with all the subtlety of its articulations and its paradoxical reversals, etc., one will clearly see that the "same" statement (or what passes for the same) says exactly the contrary, corresponds exactly to the inverse, to the reactive inversion, for example, of what it mimes. But one would still have to account for this possibility of inversion or of perversion that can make the same statement be taken for another, or another for the same. The possibility of this perverting simplification is to be found—so long as one refrains from distinguishing between unconscious programs and deliberate ones (recall what was said last week),[47] so long as one no longer takes into account only intention in reading a text—in the very structure of the text, and this must be something we are able to read. There is nothing fortuitous in the fact—even if Nietzsche's intention had nothing to do with it—that his discourse should have served as a reference for Nazi ideologues and that the only politics that *actually* privileged it as a major reference should have been Nazi. I do not mean to suggest that this is forever the only possibility, or that it corresponds to the best reading of Nietzsche, or that those who did not refer to it had read Nietzsche well. The future of Nietzsche's text is not closed. I simply wish to say that the fact that, during a determined and limited period of time, the only actually self-styled Nietzschean politics (the only politics to call itself Nietzschean) was Nazi is itself necessarily significant and must be questioned as such. When I say this, I do not mean to say that, knowing what Nazism is, we should begin to reread Nietzsche from a politico-historical point of view. I do not believe that we know yet what Nazism is; that task too is still before us, and a political reading of Nietzsche is a part of that. Has Nietzsche's grand politics already run its course or is it still to come in the wake of the seism of which Nazism would have been but an episode? There is a passage from *Ecce Homo* that I earlier left in reserve. It is the passage "Why I Am a Fatality (*Schicksal*)" and it suggests that we will read the name Nietzsche only when a grand politics will have in fact come on the scene, and that, consequently, the question of knowing whether this or that lesser politics is or is not Nietzschean is irrelevant insofar as the name Nietzsche is not yet read there. This name still has its entire future before it. Here is the passage:

> I know my fate. One day my name will be associated with the memory of something tremendous (*Ungeheures*)—a crisis without equal on earth, the most profound collision of consciences (*Gewissens-Collision*), a decision (*Entscheidung*) that was conjured up *against* everything that had been believed, demanded, hallowed so far. I am no man, I am dynamite.—Yet for all that, there is nothing in me of a founder of a religion—religions are affairs of the rabble; I find it necessary to wash my hands after I have come

---

47. See supra p. 18 ff.

into contact with religious people.—I *want* no "believers"; I think I am too malicious to believe in myself; I never speak to masses. . . . The concept of politics will have merged entirely with a war of spirits (*Geisterkrieg*); all power structures of the old society will have been exploded—all of them are based on lies: there will be wars the likes of which have never yet been seen on earth. It is only beginning with me that the earth knows *grosse Politik*.[48]

We have no need, I believe, to decide; the interpretative decision does not need to decide between two political contents or intentions of these texts. Interpretations are not hermeneutics of reading but political interventions in the political rewriting of the text. This has always been the case, but especially so since what is called the end of philosophy, since the textual indicator named Hegel. It is not an accident but an effect of the structure of all post-Hegelian texts that there can always be a right and a left Hegelianism, a right and a left Heideggerianism, a right and a left Nietzscheism, and even, we must not forget, a Marxism of the right and a Marxism of the left. Is there something in Nietzsche that can help us—and help us in a specific way—to understand this political structure of the text and of interpretation? That is the question that would need to be elaborated. Does Nietzsche offer us anything to understand the double interpretation and perversion of his text? He says that there must be something *unheimlich* (that is, frightening, as the French translator of this fifth lecture has it) in the suppression (*Unterdrückung*) by force of the least degenerate needs. Why is it *unheimlich*? That is another form of the same question.

To conclude today, I will say just a word more about what I announced at the beginning under the title of "academic freedom" and the ear.

When Nietzsche recommends linguistic training as opposed to the "academic freedom" that leaves teachers and students free in their thinking, in their programs, in their choice of subjects, and so on, it is not because he thinks that constraint has to be opposed to freedom but because he diagnoses behind this so-called "academic freedom" a fierce constraint that is all the more effective for being dissimulated. And this constraint is exercised by the state, which, through this supposed academic freedom, controls everything. The state stands as the great target of the accusation in these lectures and Hegel, the thinker of the state, the great culprit. The autonomy of universities, teachers, and students is in fact a ruse of the state, the "absolutely complete ethical organism."[49] The state wants to attract, says Nietzsche,

---

48. Nietzsche, *Ecce Homo*, pp. 326–27 [*KSA* 6: 365–66].
49. Nietzsche, *On the Future of Our Educational Institutions*, p. 90 [*KSA* 1: 711]; Nietzsche is here quoting Hegel.

docile and wholly dedicated public servants through controls and rigorous constraints. And, in fact, these lectures can also be read as a modern, critical analysis of the state's cultural apparatuses and, particularly, of that fundamental cultural apparatus that, in a modern state, is the state's academic cultural apparatus. There is little doubt that this critique would be carried out from a point of view that quite probably—though we would here need to examine things more closely and proceed more slowly—would make of a Marxist analysis of state apparatuses, of the Marxist concept of ideology, and so on, a symptom of degeneration and a new form of servitude to the Hegelian state. But one would have to look a lot more closely, on the one side and the other, beneath everything that appears to make of Nietzsche an unquestionable adversary of socialism in general.[50] It would be necessary to see how, elsewhere, the critique of the state—one of Nietzsche's most constant preoccupations—will be developed right up to the fragments of *The Will to Power* and *Zarathustra* (see the chapters "On the New Idol"—"the state, where the slow suicide of all is called 'life' "—and "On Great Events," where "the state is a hypocritical hound" that talks and tries to make one believe that its voice "is talking out of the belly of reality" [Hegel]).[51]

The state—this hypocritical hound—whispers in your ear through its educational apparatuses, which are in fact acoustic or acroamatic apparatuses. You are long-eared beasts (*Langohre*) inasmuch as, rather than being obedient (*Gehorsam*), rather than obeying with your small ears the best of masters and the best of leaders, you believe yourselves to be free and autonomous while all you do is turn your big ears toward the discourse of the state, controlled as it is by reactive and degenerate forces. Hanging on every word of the state, you have transformed yourselves into one big ear, the ear coming to occupy a disproportionate place on your body (as in that appearance of a body almost totally reduced to an ear in *Zarathustra*).[52]

And here is my last question—for this session. Next time, we will return, by means of another loop, to Jacob and Canguilhem, on the question of the program, which we have not abandoned. My last question would be

---

50. There is here in the typescript an insertion mark and this handwritten insertion at the bottom of the page: "and of democracy ('Science is a part of democracy,' *Twilight* [*Crépuscule*], p. 139), → science/ideology."

51. Friedrich Nietzsche, *Thus Spoke Zarathustra*, trans. Walter Kaufmann (New York: Penguin, 1966), pp. 50, 132 [*KSA* 4: 62, 170].

52. In the typescript there is in the left margin of this paragraph this handwritten notation: "long-eared / *Ecce Homo* / 76 / + <illegible word>." Derrida is referring here to the monstrous ear that confronts Zarathustra in "On Redemption," *Thus Spoke Zarathustra*, *KSA* 4: 178–79.

this. Is it our scene, our pedagogical scene, that Nietzsche is describing in the passage I am about to read? Is it a question of the same ear? Is it the same ear that you lend me or that I myself lend in speaking? Or are we hearing all of this already with another ear? I do not believe there to be a simple answer to this question, which I prefer to let do its work all by itself. Here is the ear passage, in the fifth lecture (p. 125). (Read the fifth lecture, p. 125 and following; it is the philosopher who speaks while laughing):

> Permit me, however, to measure this independence of yours by the standard of this culture, and to consider your university as an educational institution and nothing else. If a foreigner desires to know something of the methods of our universities, he asks first of all with emphasis: "How is the student connected with the university?" We answer: "By the ear, as a hearer." The foreigner is astonished. "Only by the ear?" he repeats. "Only by the ear," we again reply. The student hears. When he speaks, when he sees, when he is in the company of his companions, when he takes up some branch of art, in short, when he *lives* he is independent, *i.e.*, not dependent upon the educational institution. The student very often writes down something while he hears; and it is only at these rare moments that he hangs to the umbilical cord of his alma mater. He himself may choose what he is to listen to; he is not bound to believe what is said; he may close his ears if he does not care to hear. This is the "acroamatic" method of teaching.
>
> The teacher, however, speaks to these listening students. Whatever else he may think and do is cut off from the student's perception by an immense gap. The professor often reads when he is speaking. As a rule he wishes to have as many hearers as possible; he is not content to have a few, and he is never satisfied with one only. One speaking mouth, with many ears, and half as many writing hands—there you have, to all appearances, the external academic apparatus, the university engine of culture set in motion. Moreover, the proprietor of this one mouth is severed from and independent of the owners of the many ears; and this double independence is enthusiastically designated as "academic freedom." And again, that this freedom may be broadened still more, the one may speak what he likes and the other may hear what he likes; except that, behind both of them, at a modest distance, stands the state, with all the intentness of a supervisor, to remind the professors and students from time to time that *it* is the aim, the goal, the be-all and end-all, of this curious speaking and hearing procedure.[53]

---

53. Nietzsche, *On the Future of Our Educational Institutions*, pp. 125–26 [*KSA* 1: 739–40]. On the photocopy of the text of Nietzsche that accompanies the typescript of this session, Derrida added by hand: "I leave you to read what follows."

THIRD SESSION

Transition (Oedipus's Faux Pas)

I am two, he said. (He) the dead and (she) the living, my father and my mother. And I became almost blind when I reached the age of my father when he died. He said this in *Ecce Homo*, around 1888. From there we returned — so to speak — to that discourse on the mother tongue, that is, the text of 1872 on the future of our educational institutions. Nietzsche is all the time in [*en*] Oedipus, I mean that, in writing *in* [*en*] Oedipus, he explains Oedipus, and since he knows that one never explains anything except by explaining oneself with or *engaging oneself* in the explanation, he described and explained Oedipus by saying, in his own way, which is at once exhibitionist and dissimulating, I, my father, my mother, my son and me (am . . .). I am not going to run through all of Nietzsche's explicit references to Oedipus.[1]

Oedipus is for me a tranition. Oedipus is today, for me, a transition. How can Oedipus provide a transition? Toward what can he be the passage?

He is doubly a passage,[2] he is a double *pas* [step/not], doubly *pas*.

In *The Future* (I will say from now on *The Future* to refer in an abbreviated way to *On the Future of Our Educational Institutions*, not to be confused with *The Future* — also *Zukunft* — *of an Illusion*), Nietzsche is very critical of the way the pedagogues and teaching philologists of his time use Oedipus. It is just one example cited in passing in the course of a marvelous description of

---

1. There is a handwritten addition at this point in the transcript that reads "in order to show that Nietzsche is not locked *into* a problematic," and, in the left margin of the typescript, a long handwritten addition that is difficult to decipher: "<two illegible words> that he *treats* this <illegible word> poorly, knowing that it can be treated only by treating oneself, without the naiveté of believing that one can get out of it <several illegible words> without some <unreadable word> effect."

2. [Translators' note:] The French *passage* can also be heard as *pas sage*, that is, as "not well-behaved" or "not wise."

how the swarm of young university philologists of the time, armed with their science and their historical erudition (read this double page), wander about in a Greek culture to which they are complete strangers, like tourists or anachronistic policemen who project their problems or their morality onto Greek culture, appropriate it, take all the taste out of it, and reduce it to their own size. And what do they do when they encounter Oedipus, a malevolent miscreant through whom a pre-Christian Sophocles wants to give a lesson in Christian morality to anyone who will listen: do not be Oedipus, or else . . . ! Here is an excerpt from this double page: these new philologists are so barbaric that "they dispose of these [Greek] relics to suit themselves: all their modern conveniences and fancies are brought with them . . . and there is great rejoicing when somebody finds, among the dust and cobwebs of antiquity, something that he himself had slyly hidden there not so very long before."[3] A series of very funny examples follows and then, finally, this:

> What a deep breath he draws when he succeeds in raising yet another dark corner of antiquity to the level of his own intelligence! — when, for example, he discovers in Pythagoras a colleague who is as enthusiastic as himself in arguing about politics. Another racks his brains as to why Oedipus was condemned by fate to perform such abominable deeds — killing his father, marrying his mother. Where lies the blame! Where the poetic justice! Suddenly it occurs to him: Oedipus was a passionate fellow [a fervent fellow, *leidenschaftlicher Gesell, un drôle*, says J. C. Hemery, the French translator, who translates this well. I think that this text is well translated, a lot better than many others. *Un drôle* for *ein Gesell*, that is to say, a fellow, a guy, a buddy, a more or less ruseful companion], lacking all Christian gentleness — he even fell into an unbecoming rage [a fever, a hot flash] when Tiresias called him a monster and the curse (*Fluch*) of the whole country. Be humble and meek (*Seid sanftmütig*)! was what Sophocles tried to teach, otherwise you will have to marry your mothers and kill your fathers! Others, again, pass their lives in counting the number of verses written by Greek and Roman poets, and are delighted with the proportion 7:13 = 14:26. Finally, one of them brings forward his solution of a question, such as the Homeric poems considered from the standpoint of prepositions, and thinks he has drawn the truth from the bottom of a well with *ana* and *kata*.[4]

---

3. Nietzsche, *On the Future of Our Educational Institutions*, p. 78 [*KSA* 1: 701].
4. Ibid., pp. 79–80 [*KSA* 1: 702].

In other words, these academics made of Greece and of Oedipus, of Oedipus's *faux pas*, a transition to Christianity and to themselves. They took Oedipus like a train, like the last train.⁵

The year of these lectures (1872) is the very same year as the *Philosophenbuch*. Autumn/winter 1872. Exactly contemporary with these lectures, this book has as its subtitle, as you know, *Der letzte Philosoph. Der Philosoph. Betrachtungen über den Kampf von Kunst und Erkenntnis*.⁶ What do we read there?

By way of transition, first of all, and in particular from what I was saying last time about auto-biography in *Ecce Homo*, by way of transition, I take from this text a fragment on the fragment, on myself as the last philosopher. And this fragment is called Oedipus: that is its title (*Ödipus*). In this fragment, the last, the last man, the last philosopher is named Ödipus, and he thinks of himself as the last, and he says I, and Nietzsche says "I Oedipus," and we must say it and reread it by saying "I Oedipus." But in saying I Oedipus, I the last philosopher and the last man, giving myself all these names, I, I Oedipus, I Friedrich Nietzsche, I the last, the last man, the last philosopher, and so on, by referring to myself in this way, I affirm myself and re-cite myself as a *transition*, a passage and a descent (*Übergang und Untergang*, as will be said of man at the beginning of *Zarathustra*). I the undersigned so-and-so (Nietzsche, Oedipus, last man, last philosopher, and so on, with all these names that are the same), I am passing by [*je passe*], I say

---

5. In the left margin of the typescript there is this handwritten addition: "or like a bus, rather, transporting, moving between 2 university stations the whole neo-Christian, modern-style apparatus."

6. Derrida is referring here to *Le livre du philosophe/Das Philosophenbuch* (Paris: Aubier-Flammarion, 1969), a bilingual French-German edition that has no English equivalent. The volume, which is divided into four chapters, collects many of Nietzsche's writings from 1872, just after *The Birth of Tragedy*, 1873, and 1875. The subtitle Derrida refers to, "The Philosopher. *Observations on the Struggle Between Art and Knowledge*," is actually the title of chapter 1 of the collection. Most of the fragments Derrida quotes from this work can be found in Friedrich Nietzsche, *Unpublished Writings from the Period of Unfashionable Observations*, trans. Richard T. Gray (Stanford, CA: Stanford University Press, 1995). It should also be noted that chapter 3 of *Le livre du philosophe/Das Philosophenbuch* contains the essay "On Truth and Lie in an Extra-moral Sense," as well as a number of fragments from the same period (summer 1873). An English translation of this essay can be found in *Writings from the Early Notebooks*, ed. Raymond Geuss and Alexander Nehamas, trans. Ladislaus Löb (Cambridge: Cambridge University Press, 2009), pp. 253–64. Finally, while *Das Philosophenbuch* does not exist as such in the *KSA* edition, most of the fragments included in that work can be found in *KSA* 1 and 7. We have thus provided the corresponding *KSA* references whenever possible.

to men, thus I say to myself, I say to the philosophers, thus I say to myself, I am passing by: I am thus passing by beyond myself, and it is in this word of transition, this voice of passage, that I hear myself and call myself.

I call myself Oedipus. Here is the fragment (which I here re-translate):

Oedipus.
Soliloquies of the Last Philosopher
(Reden des letzten Philosophen mit sich selbst).
A Fragment (*Ein Fragment*) from the History of Posterity (*Nachwelt*).

I call myself [*nenne ich mich*: in the present] the last philosopher because I am the last man. I myself am the only one who speaks with me, and my voice comes to me as the voice of someone who is dying. [In this soliloquy, as you are going to hear, Oedipus (with all of his synonyms) is not *only alone* [*seulement seul*]; he is not *only alone* because he speaks with no one else and no one else speaks with him. If it is a soliloquy this is not because he speaks alone or speaks only to himself but because he *only* speaks, does nothing but hear himself speaking to himself, and, blind and dying as he is, he no longer has any other relation than to the voice, to his voice. He is no longer anything but mouth and ear, his mouth and his ear. Soliloquy should here mean not the speaking of a single person to himself but speaking alone, speaking only]. Let me commune with you for just one hour, beloved voice, with you, the last trace of the memory of all human happiness; with your help I will deceive myself about my loneliness and lie my way into community and love; for my heart refuses to believe that love is dead; it cannot bear the shudder of the loneliest loneliness and it forces me to speak as if I were two persons (*als ob ich Zwei wäre*).[7]

Do I still hear you, my voice? You whisper when you curse. (*Höre ich dich noch, meine Stimme? Du flüsterst, indem du fluchst.*) And yet your curse should cause the bowels of this world to burst! But it [this world] continues to live and merely stares at me all the more brilliantly and coldly with its pitiless stars; it continues to live (*sie lebt*), as dumb and blind (*so dumm und blind*) as ever, and the *only thing* that dies is — man [*und nur* Eines stirbt — *der Mensch*; Oedipus, the last man-philosopher-dying, is blind, he does not see, but he is seen dying, he is stared at by that which survives him, the world and its icy, fixed, pitiless stars, which are, they as well, blind. There is only blindness at the moment of the last man. One can be only blind with Oedipus and at the moment of the last, at the last moment. No one sees anyone any longer. There is no more point of view, that is, no point to view and no point of view. But in this night without borders where the very thing

---

7. In the typescript there is, at the end of the paragraph, this handwritten addition between parentheses and in quotation marks: ("*Ich bin beides*").

that gives light [the stars] is without life and does not see, where the source of light is cold like death (*noch glänzender und kälter*) and blind like that which is going to die, there is someone who at least has an ear for dying, who hears himself dying [*s'entend (à) mourir*]: and only one dies, man].[8]

The final paragraph is even more enigmatic. There is still one, someone (*Einer*), who dies outside the one who says I, I Oedipus, and who also dies, to make the transition. We do not know if this additional someone who dies is an other, or if it is the same, if it is the voice of the same that hears itself speaking to itself, that has an ear for dying. It is perhaps quite simply the voice that dies, the voice of Oedipus that dies, Oedipus who dies as voice or who dies to his voice, renouncing his voice. Let me first re-translate this final paragraph:

> And yet! I still hear you, beloved voice (*geliebte Stimme*)! *Someone* outside of me, the last man, is dying in this universe [there dies (*il meurt*) — an impersonal construction — yet another *one*: one more outside of me]: the last sigh, *your* sigh, dies with me, the drawn out Woe! Woe! sighing around me, Oedipus, the last of the woeful men.[9]

Literally, "woe, woe, *Wehe, Wehe*, sighing upon me, the last of the *Wehemenschen*: the last woe-man, the last woeful man, the last to say woe, the last to lament, Oedipus." But the structure of what Blanchot would call the *narrative voice* is such that we do not know if the one who dies outside of me (Oedipus) is someone else whose voice or whose sighs we hear, or if it is the voice itself, that of the one who alone dies and speaks to himself. It is as much to the other as to the voice as other that he says: the last sigh, *your* (*dein*, underscored) sigh dies with me. Reread this fragment and you will see that one cannot and thus does not have to distinguish between this other who dies always *with* me, in addition to me, in addition to me as an other endowed with a voice, and my voice endowed, I would say, with the other. It is a question of the voice as other, which always also dies with Oedipus, thereby constituting him in his terrible soliloquizing solitude — or else of the other as *my voice*. And what dies with the last (Man, Oedipus-philosopher — so many synonyms) is the other *as* voice or as my voice. It is the last word of the auto-biography as auto-thanatography, which would then no longer designate just the writing of my own death but also the writing of the death of the myself, of the *autos* as Oedipus-man-philosopher, as the voice

---

8. Nietzsche, *Unpublished Writings from the Period of Unfashionable Observations*, pp. 43–44 [*KSA* 7: 19[131], pp. 460–61].

9. Ibid., p. 44 [*KSA* 7: 19[131], p. 461].

of the hearing-oneself-speak, at the very moment when he says to it, as to the other beloved voice, "you are beautiful," and so on.

If it were not a little ridiculous to dole out praise in this way, I would say to you that, in this case, the best reading or, rather, as is appropriate, the best re-writing of the fragment I just read is Blanchot's narrative titled *The Last Man* (1957). Let me pull out just a few lines near the beginning, though you should read everything, of course, since this selection is a bit crude:

> He wasn't addressing anyone. I don't mean he wasn't speaking to me, but someone other than me was listening to him.... The happiness of saying yes, of endlessly affirming.... He needed to be one too many: one more, only one more.... The thought which is spared me at each moment: that he, the last man, is nevertheless not the last.... But slowly—abruptly—the thought occurred to me that this story had no witness: I was there—the "I" was already no more than a Who?, a whole crowd of Who?s—so that there would be no one between him and his destiny, so that his face would remain bare and his gaze undivided. I was there, not in order to see him, but so that he wouldn't see himself, so that it would be me he saw in the mirror, someone other than him—another, a stranger, nearby, gone, the shadow of the other shore, no one—and that in this way he would remain a man until the very end. He wasn't to split in two. This is the great temptation of those who are approaching their end: they look at themselves and talk to themselves; they turn themselves into a solitude peopled by themselves—the emptiest, the most false. But if I was present, he would be the most alone of all men, without even himself, without that last man which he was—and thus he would be the very last.[10]

The one who seems to be speaking here—the narrative voice—ensures, by his presence (I present, he would be the loneliest of men, without even himself: thus without I, without his I), the keeping [*la garde*] of the last man who must be alone without even this last one who he was, and it is in keeping him without him, without the last who he was, it is in this way that he assures that he is "the very last." For if the last were with himself (still able to hear himself), he would not be alone and thus would not be the last. To keep himself as last he must lose himself as last, and to lose himself as last he must still keep himself as last. This might be said of this last—(step) not-beyond [*pas-au-delà*] the last (philosopher, man, Oedipus). This necessarily has to do with a structure of forgetting that no longer has any relation

---

10. Maurice Blanchot, *The Last Man*, trans. Lydia Davis (New York: Columbia University Press, 1987), pp. 2, 4, 8, 10, 10–11; *Le dernier homme* (Paris: Éditions Gallimard, 1957), pp. 9, 11, 18, 21, 22–23.

to what psychology, philosophy, and even a certain psychoanalysis teach us with this word, which we must relearn to read, for example in Nietzsche or in Blanchot. The last man must forget in order to be the last man, he must no longer even see himself [*se voir*], have himself [*s'avoir*], or have any knowledge as to who he is [*savoir comme ce qu'il est*], no longer even keep himself [*se garder*] *as* last, no longer have any relation to himself, no relation of keeping [*rapport de garde*], even in the form of a forgetting that is kept, for example, in the form of something repressed. This implies, between the last and his beyond, a step/not of transition whose structure is unique, unheard-of, neither dialectical nor anti-dialectical, which neither keeps nor suppresses what it keeps and suppresses, and so on. The necessity of this rethinking of forgetting is often mentioned in *Le livre du philosophe*, as well as in Blanchot's *The Last Man*. Let me read, for example, two fragments before Oedipus, from *Le livre du philosophe*:

> Terrible loneliness of the last philosopher! All around, nature stands glaring at him [*méduse*, says the French translation for *umstarrt*: un-does him by rigidifying him, by turning him to stone, transforming him into a stiffened body, like a cadaver or a phallus erected in stone], vultures hover above his head. And so he calls out to nature: Grant forgetting! Forgetting! *Gib Vergessen! Vergessen!*—No, he endures his suffering like a Titan—until he is offered appeasement [*Versöhnung*—also forgiveness] in the supreme tragic art.[11]

And, for example, in *The Last Man*: "He seems to me completely forgotten. This forgetting is the element I breathe when I go down the hall. . . . We were seeing the face of forgetting. It can certainly be forgotten, in fact it asks to be forgotten, and yet it concerns us all."[12] The figure of Blanchot's Last Man is also—this is one of the very rare and thus very significant determinations it receives—that of the Professor (with a capital P: I leave you to read these texts, which are foreign to every class or classification).

What is this transition—in the philosophy whose course is here taking its course (for "it takes its course," as Blanchot says, and as the title of a recent book puts it)[13]— what is this transition in Oedipus leading up to? In

---

11. Nietzsche, *Unpublished Writings from the Period of Unfashionable Observations*, p. 42 [*KSA* 7: 19[126], p. 459].

12. Blanchot, *Last Man*, pp. 11–12 [p. 24].

13. The book in question here is Edmond Jabès, *Ça suit son cours* (Montpellier: Fata Morgana, 1975). For the Blanchot quotation, see Maurice Blanchot, "Le 'discours philosophique,'" *L'Arc* 46 (1971): 4: "Philosophical discourse always gets lost at a certain moment. It is perhaps nothing but an inexorable way of losing and losing oneself. This is also what is recalled by the dismissive murmur: "It's following its course [*Ça suit son cours*]."

order to allow—here and there—the Oedipean transition to be read (the phase of Oedipus and its resolution as a step (not) beyond Oedipus), you will have noticed that I selected what I was reproducing of the Nietzschean discourse; and I even had you take note that I was selecting as I was reproducing. And that there is no interpretative and active or productive reading without selection in the reproduction.

Selection and reproduction form a pair of concepts whose association is for us as enigmatic as it is necessary and at which we will necessarily have to pause. You *already* know that the Eternal Return (you already know, I keep saying, and that must imply in what is called the pedagogical scene that is being played out here that you already know everything I am talking about, or at least that I am making as if you already know everything I am talking about, such that the nature of what we receive here from one another remains very uncertain), you already know that the Eternal Return—or at least this is one of its certain and clear determinations—is both a repetition of becoming and a selection of active-becoming [*devenir-actif*]: it is a selective re-production. How can a reproduction be selective? This is as difficult to think as the contrary: how can a reproduction not be selective? I leave this question as it is for the moment. These two concepts, *reproduction* and *selection*, are interesting for us insofar as they assure the metaphorical passage, the metaphorical back and forth, between bio-logical discourse and peda-gogical discourse. One speaks just as naturally, or at least as necessarily, of reproduction and selection in the field of genetics as in the field of the academic institution. This is no accident, of course, and we can ask ourselves where all this is going, this double metaphorical transit, which is today so easy and so well established, between the bio-logical and the pedagogical. What about this metaphoricity and what do we understand by this word when we use it here?

Well, it is toward just this question of metaphor that I wanted to lead you back by way of this Oedipean transition. I say lead back because we had already come across this question in the course of the first session when reading Jacob and Canguilhem. It happens that, just as my Oedipean transition was a discourse on transition, on Oedipus as a transition, to come to metaphor here is to come to another transition, another vehicle. It is often said that metaphor is a vehicle (this is a *topos*: the metaphor as vehicle or transport) or that there is in the structure of all metaphor an element that modern rhetoricians call the vehicle. And modern Greeks, as you well know, since you know everything, call their transit system *metaphora*. Hence each time I try here to turn my pedagogical discourse into metalanguage, taking off from the one, going toward the other, managing the transitions, explaining to you the language of an other, and so on, well, I always fail, and for essential reasons. I was not able to make a transition out of Oedipus because he was himself the transition and a transition without any simple beyond, a transition toward the transition, and the moment I believe I am coming to a new object, bio-logico-pedagogical metaphor, it is still the transition that itself tells me in advance something about my pedagogical approach, that prevents it from becoming a mastering approach, that says more about it than I myself can say, that explains to me without explaining to me, and even before I have said a word, the very thing I would like to say.

Hence I never fail to be surprised when I give a course. Surprise is that structure that draws metalanguage back, that always surprises it in its naiveté, surprises it at the moment of its withdrawal, shows it that it is no longer virginal, that it is already violated—by the ear, at least, as you will have heard, and the smaller the ear the better, and it procures, so long as this surprise is affirmed and reaffirmed by the one who has the force to give in to it in the end, pleasure, a pleasure that, in keeping with the essence of pleasure or of desire, must be and remain *dubious*, entrusted to the other to take or to leave. One never knows where a course will go. That of which one speaks and those to whom one speaks always have in reserve something to say in advance not only about the course but about pedagogical theory.

The bus named pleasure, therefore. How is it going to continue to work? I am not going to talk to you about metaphor in Nietzsche. Others have done this before me—and done it better—in the last few years. I refer you to the excellent works of Sarah Kofman, and especially *Nietzsche and Metaphor*.[14] For my part, I am going to reproduce and select in this very place of the failing of metalanguage, this place of a specific failing where metaphorical language, far from being a rhetorical means of dominating a field or of passing from one field to another, far from being only a transitional object between two discourses—to put it metaphorically—is itself explained, in its possibility, as an effect of selection-reproduction as it is operating in several fields. What I just said is not so clear. Let me say it in another way: the schema reproduction/selection, for example, is not a schema that some metaphor would transport from one determinate field to another, from the bio-logical to the politico-institutional or to the academic, or vice versa. It is not primarily in this sense that it is metaphorical. It is metaphorical in the sense that it is the origin of metaphor in general. Metaphor does not

---

14. Sarah Kofman, *Nietzsche and Metaphor*, trans. Duncan Large (Stanford, CA: Stanford University Press, 1993); *Nietzsche et la métaphore* (Paris: Payot, 1972).

transport selection-reproduction like a bee or a bus from one place to another; metaphor is an effect of reproduction/selection; it is itself subjected to the genetico-institutional law of reproduction/selection. In his discourse on metaphor—and not only in the metaphoricity of his discourse—Nietzsche himself has recourse to the schema of reproduction/selection. He does not just explain life or school with metaphors; he also explains metaphor with the laws of life and of school. Let me take an example that will make this clearer to you. It comes once again from the *Philosophenbuch*, which contains, as you already know, a whole theory of metaphor, of the relations between metaphor and concept. This theory of metaphor claims to return to some of the bio-physiological foundations of perception, of knowledge, to a whole structure of neural activity in the constitution of sensory images, etc. Well, in the description of the image in general, and then in the description of thought in images, that is to say, through metaphors, etc., the schema reproduction/selection is explicitly at work. See, for example, fragments 65–67 [in *Le livre du philosophe/Das Philosophenbuch*]. I select first of all this:

> Dreaming as the selective extension [the elective prolongation, *als die auswählende Fortsetzung*] of visual images (*Augenbilder*).
> In the realm of the intellect, everything qualitative is merely *quantitative*. We are led to qualities by the concept, the word. [In other words, the beyond of the quantitative, of the economic, etc., is an impression produced by language (concepts and words).]¹⁵

Here is the following fragment, number 66:

> Perhaps the human being is incapable of *forgetting* anything. The operations of seeing and knowing are much too complicated for it to be possible completely to efface them again (*völlig wieder zu verwischen*); which means that from this point on, all forms that once have been produced (*erzeugt*) by the brain and the nervous system are repeated (*wiederholt*) frequently in the same way. An identical neural activity generates the same image once again (*Eine gleiche Nerventätigkeit erzeugt das gleiche Bild wieder*).¹⁶

End of quotation: according to this hypothesis (for Nietzsche says "perhaps," "frequently," and so on), insofar as forgetting—which we said earlier was called for by the affirmation of the last man—is acknowledged to be

---

15. Nietzsche, *Unpublished Writings from the Period of Unfashionable Observations*, p. 31 [*KSA* 7: 19[81], p. 447].

16. Ibid., p. 31 [*KSA* 7: 19[82], p. 447].

impossible, total forgetting being impossible,[17] like an absolutely complete memory or a total reproduction, reproduction will be selective and selection reproductive. It is in the process of this reproduction/selection, which is a process of inscription or pathbreaking along a surface, that the image, as reproduction/selection of sensation, is also a phenomenon of pleasure/displeasure (*Lust/Unlust*). This phenomenon of pleasure/displeasure can give rise to selection only insofar as it is a battlefield, an agonistics, between different forces, differences of forces, the stronger eliminating the weaker. And knowledge, insofar as it has its origin in these processes of inscription on neural surfaces, is inseparable from this selectivity of images and, as we will soon see, of metaphors. I spoke earlier of pleasure and of displeasure, of dubious pleasure, and here it is, as if by accident, the question of pleasure; I leave the dubious for later. Let me read on, fragment 67 [in *Le livre du philosophe/ Das Philosophenbuch*]:

> The most delicate sensations of pleasure and displeasure (*Lust- und Unlustempfindungen*) constitute the true raw material of all knowledge: the true mystery is that surface onto which the activity of the nerves, in pleasure and pain, inscribes its forms (*auf jener Fläche, in die die Nerventätigkeit in Lust und Schmerz Formen hinzeichnet, ist das eigentliche Geheimniss*): sensation (*Empfindung*) immediately projects *forms*, which in turn generate new sensations (*die dann wieder neue Empfindungen erzeugen*).
>
> It belongs to the very nature of sensations of pleasure and displeasure to express themselves in adequate motions: the sensation of the *image* (*Empfindung des* Bildes) is created (*entsteht*) due to the fact that these adequate motions cause other nerves to experience sensations.[18]

Let me clarify, for this is not very clear: the pleasure/displeasure associated with every impression is what attracts, brings together, gathers together other nerves, what interests them, as it were, in the impression and in reproduction. And this interest of pleasure, within agonistics and within the economic, is at the origin of images, which are themselves selective reproductions always already invested with pleasure or displeasure. Knowledge will never be unaffected by it.

And here, now, is the passage to which I most wanted to attract your attention; it follows right after what I just commented on: "Darwinism is right even with regard to thought in images (*Auch bei dem Bilderdenken*):

---

17. In the left margin of the typescript is the handwritten notation: "repression [*refoulement*]."

18. Nietzsche, *Unpublished Writings from the Period of Unfashionable Observations*, pp. 31–32 [*KSA* 7: 19[84], p. 448].

the stronger image (*das kräftigere Bild*) devours the weaker ones [*geringeren*, light, futile, or of low social standing: *image* of little importance]."[19] And Nietzsche immediately adds, after a space:[20]

> Whether thinking occurs with pleasure or displeasure is an absolutely essential distinction: anyone who finds it difficult will be less inclined toward it and will probably also not get as far [he will advance less far, not wanting to accept that thought advances according to the principle of pleasure/displeasure]: he *forces* himself (*er* zwingt *sich*), and in this realm that is useless.[21]

There would thus be, to follow this line of thought, a natural selection of metaphors, obeying the reason of the strongest. There would be a sociobiological, politico-biological system of images in a state of war — and one might imagine every type of war and weapon, every type of territorial occupation, diplomatic alliance, annexation, war of attrition, and so on, and it is not only the images that would be more or less forceful but also the representatives of forces, that is to say, as always, differences of force. And, let me recall, since this is important for what we are talking about here, this politico-biological selection of images is inseparable from the re-productive process that is at the origin of the image and that links its genesis to the principle of pleasure/displeasure.

A supplementary complication comes, as it were, to illustrate and confirm in Nietzsche's very writing the thesis he seems to advance: it is apparently by metaphor that he invokes here natural selection and the law of the strongest. He imports this metaphor from a genetic field and applies it to a psychorhetorical field. And he takes a certain pleasure in this expatriation and this violent extension; and he knows he is doing it since he says: "*Auch bei dem Bilderdenken hat der Darwinismus Recht* [Darwinism is right even with regard to thought in images]." In other words, Nietzsche demonstrates that conceptual thought, its rule of comprehension and extension, proceeds by metaphor, and he states this not as a statement but through the act of stating. He says in a metaphor that the concept is metaphorical; he forces the limits between distinct fields by saying that thought consists in doing just this, etc. I am not going to insist as one could on this text or head in this direction.

---

19. Ibid., p. 32 [*KSA* 7: 19[87], p. 448].

20. [Translators' note:] In the English edition of this work the two passages are separated by two other fragments. See *Unpublished Writings from the Period of Unfashionable Observations*, pp. 32–33.

21. Ibid., p. 33 [*KSA* 7: 19[90], p. 449].

Another supplementary complication. If, in 1872, Nietzsche says Darwin is right beyond even what Darwin could believe, it is for the same reason that he will soon no longer assert that Darwin is right. Nietzsche will then come to reproach Darwin, under the title of the anti-Darwin (this will be the title of several fragments collected in *The Will to Power*), with having conceived of this selection or this law of the strongest in a simple way, that is, without taking into account the enigmatic possibility of inversion that constitutes it, namely, the regular domination not of the strongest but of the weakest, the elimination of strokes of luck, the neutralization by the average of all excesses in force, and so on. It is a very enigmatic possibility since it leads to a form of the statement of the law of the strongest that contradicts itself and immediately reverses itself. How can force be less strong or forceful than itself? How can the weak be stronger than the strongest? And how can such a statement even be intelligible? And if we allow this, will we not have to reconsider all its premises, everything that concerns, for example, the process of re-production and the principle of pleasure? Does not this inversion in the process of life forces imply that, somewhere in life itself, as life itself, a force of death is at work, and something like a beyond of the pleasure principle? I leave these questions suspended for the time being . . .

. . . in order to make just a few remarks before returning to Canguilhem and to Jacob.

1. The *lucidity* with which Nietzsche credits Darwin in 1872 with regard to thinking in images gets its payback from what Nietzsche in 1888 defines as Darwin's *blindness*. How can one be so blind?, he will ask. To what was Darwin blind? Well, to nothing other than this transgression by life of its own law, this strange logic of the will to power that selects to the advantage of the weakest, this transgression of the law by law itself, this transgression of the law being the law, dictating the law. We are only beginning to investigate this type of logic: the step (not) beyond of the law.[22] I will simply mention the two texts of 1888 titled *Anti-Darwin*. They are part of the collection titled — with all the reservations that this might rightly inspire — *The Will to Power*. In the first, Nietzsche writes:

> What surprises me most when I *survey* the broad destinies of man is that I always *see* before me the opposite of that which Darwin and his school *see* or *want* [Nietzsche underscores *want*] to see today [from the beginning, Nietzsche locates his debate in a sort of struggle for vision: he sees the contrary of what Darwin and his school see or *want* to see, the implication being that seeing itself is directed by an interest or a desire that selects what the will

---

22. In the left margin of the typescript is this handwritten notation: "do not read me."

(to power) wants or does not want, wants without wanting, to see, the denegation being always inscribed somewhere in the optical and in an already selective putting into perspective.] What surprises me most when I *survey* the broad destinies of man is that I always *see* before me the opposite of that which Darwin and his school *see* or *want*: selection in favor of the stronger, better-constituted, and the progress of the species. Precisely the opposite is palpable: the elimination of the lucky strokes, the uselessness of the more highly developed types, the inevitable dominion of the average, even the *sub-average* types. If we are not shown why man should be an exception among creatures, I incline to the prejudice that the school of Darwin has been deluded everywhere.

That will to power in which I recognize the ultimate ground and character of all change provides us with the reason why selection is not in favor of the exceptions and lucky strokes: the strongest and most fortunate are weak when opposed by organized herd instincts, by the timidity of the weak, by the vast majority. My *general view* [my emphasis] of the world of values shows that it is not the lucky strokes, the select types, that have the upper hand in the supreme values that are today placed over mankind; rather it is the *décadent types*—perhaps there is nothing in the world more interesting than this *little desired* spectacle.²³

"*Little desired*" is here underscored. This spectacle of selection in reverse, which makes of decadence something elite, a form of election, is very intriguing—nothing is more interesting, says Nietzsche—but it is also, by essence, a little-desired spectacle, one that is contrary to desire; it is the spectacle of the inversion of desire, of the beyond of desire or of the principle of desire. This is also what makes it interesting, not very natural. Desire is interested by non-desire as the very thing that provokes it most. How can one not desire or not be desired? That is what is most exciting—for vision [*la vue*] and for life [*la vie*]. And by the same token, what is most intriguing for whoever sees is the one who does not see. And by the same token, it is not only the spectacle of selection in reverse that excites vision but the spectacle of a theory that is blind to this inversion, for example Darwin's theory, insofar as it blinds itself to this inversion, to this law of the inversion of law. How can one be so blind?, Nietzsche asks a little further down:

> I see all philosophers, I see science kneeling before a reality that is the *reverse* of the struggle for existence as taught by Darwin's school—that is to say, I see on top and surviving everywhere those who compromise life and

---

23. Nietzsche, *WP*, fragment 685, p. 364 [*KSA* 13: 14[123], pp. 303–4]. Derrida underlines "survey," "see," and "general view."

the value of life. — The error of the school of Darwin becomes a problem to me: how can one be so blind as to see so badly at *this* point?[24]

This blindness, which, you will recall, belongs to the event of the dead father (it is at the age his father died, according to the *Rätselform* of *Ecce Homo*, that Nietzsche, as it were, lost his vision while waiting for the process of regeneration to kick in), this blindness of Darwinian theory, astonishing as it may be, is an effect of the law and, astonishing as it may be, it is not fortuitous, or at least it corresponds to the elimination of the fortuitous, of chance, an elimination that is programmed by the law. In this sense, Darwinian theory, in its very blindness, is a symptom of degeneration. Blindness to the inverse transgression, to the trans-regression of the law of selection, is an effect of the law. And, finally, of the law of the Eternal Return, inasmuch as it is blinding. Blinding by clarity, but by a clarity such that one can only blind oneself, want to blind oneself, before it. The enigma to which the seemingly Oedipean *Rätselform* of *Ecce Homo* refers us is the enigma of the Eternal Return; the Eternal Return can announce itself only in the form of the enigma. This affinity between blinding oneself and the enigmatic form is essential. Here it is on display in a fragment from 1885 that speaks of this will to blindness, this desire to lose one's vision, as the very experience of lucidity with regard to the Eternal Return. Read *The Will to Power*, v. 1, p. 216, fragment 51 [in the French edition]:

And do you know what "the world" is to me? Shall I show it to you in my mirror? This world: a monster of energy, without beginning, without end; a firm, iron magnitude of force that does not grow bigger or smaller, that does not expend itself but only transforms itself; as a whole, of unalterable size, a household without expenses or losses, but likewise without increase or income; enclosed by "nothingness" as by a boundary; not something blurry or wasted, not something endlessly extended, but set in a definite space as a definite force, and not a space that might be "empty" here or there, but rather as force throughout, as a play of forces and waves of forces, at the same time one and many, increasing here and at the same time decreasing there; a sea of forces flowing and rushing together, eternally changing, eternally flooding back, with tremendous years of recurrence, with an ebb and a flood of its forms; out of the simplest forms striving toward the most complex, out of the stillest, most rigid, coldest forms toward the hottest, most turbulent, most self-contradictory, and then again returning home to the simple out of this abundance, out of the play of contradictions back to the joy of concord, still affirming itself in this uniformity of its

---

24. Ibid., fragment 685, p. 365 [*KSA* 13:14[123], p. 304].

courses and its years, blessing itself as that which must return eternally, as a becoming that knows no satiety, no disgust, no weariness: this, my *Dionysian* world of the eternally self-creating, the eternally self-destroying, this mystery world of the twofold *voluptuous* [my emphasis] delight, my "beyond good and evil," without goal, unless the joy of the circle is itself a goal; without will, unless a *ring* [my emphasis] {has the good will to turn eternally on itself and on nothing but itself, in its own orbit. This universe that is *mine*—who is lucid enough to see it without *wanting to lose his sight* [my emphasis]? Strong enough to expose his soul to this mirror? To oppose his own mirror to the mirror of Dionysus? To propose his own solution to the enigma of Dionysus? And should not the one who is capable of this do *even more*? Pledge himself to the "ring of rings"? Promise his own *return*? Accept the ring where he will eternally bless himself, affirm himself? With the will to wanting everything once again? To see return all the things that once were? To want to meet everything that must ever be? Do you know at present what *the world* is for me? And what I want when I want *this world*?}[25]—do you want a *name* for this world? A *solution* for all its riddles? A light for you, too, you best-concealed, strongest, most intrepid, most midnightly men?—*This world is the will to power*—*and nothing besides!* And you yourselves are also this will to power—and nothing besides![26]

That chance works toward the elimination of strokes of luck is also recalled in the other fragment entitled "Anti-Darwin": "We have convinced ourselves, conversely, that in the struggle for existence chance serves the weak as well as the strong; that cunning often substitutes advantageously for force; that the *fruitfulness* of the species stands in a notable relation to its chances for destruction."[27] It is indeed all the more surprising that the cunning that can substitute for [*suppléer*] force in this way, coming therefore, as weakness, in the place of force, is also defined elsewhere, just as dissimulation is, as what is proper to superior force. And this relation of substitution [*suppléance*] of the less strong for the stronger, of the dead for the living, as

---

25. [Translators' note:] The passage in curly brackets, which is included in the French edition of *La Volonté de puissance* that Derrida is quoting, is not part of either Kaufmann's English edition of *The Will to Power* or Colli and Montinari's German edition of *Der Wille zur Macht*. This latter does, however, include the passage in its commentary on this fragment (see *KSA* 14: 727), noting that it is an earlier form of the fragment, one that Nietzsche himself altered.

26. Nietzsche, *WP*, fragment 1067, pp. 549–50 [*KSA* 11: 38[12], pp. 610–11]. On the photocopy of this passage inserted into the typescript Derrida has underlined the words "voluptuous," "ring," and "wanting to lose his sight."

27. Ibid., fragment 684, p. 362 [*KSA* 13:14[133], p. 315].

well as this relation between the greatest fruitfulness and the greatest morality or destructibility, are relations for which the usual logic of relations between life and death will have difficulty providing an explanation. It is this logic that is of interest here.

Finally, a third remark.[28] Everything that, beginning in 1872, calls into question the usual relations between concept and metaphor, truth and metaphor, etc., and that reconstructs this problematic as one of selective reproduction, all that is very consistent and, indeed, literally consistent with what is said in the "Lectures on the Future": the extension of culture and, as we would say, equal opportunity, are condemned by Nietzsche as the greatest risk for the highest forces of culture. Hence Nietzsche does not just speak metaphorically or speak about metaphor; he defines genius, the very thing that culture must produce or facilitate and to which education must itself conform, as a living metaphor. A living metaphor of what? Well, of life, or again, another name for life, of the mother, or of this mother that the unconscious of a people is. Whether this is to be taken metaphorically or properly one can no longer say. It is this life, this unconscious, this genius, this mother that must be saved from the expansion of science, from the number of institutions, from death, therefore, from science, consciousness, fathers, and so on. Here is the passage (p. 75):

> The education of the masses cannot, therefore, be our aim: but rather the education of a few select men for great and lasting works. We well know that a just posterity judges the collective cultural achievement of a time only by those few great and lonely figures of the period, and it casts its vote in accordance with the manner in which these figures are recognized, encouraged, and honored, or else snubbed, elbowed aside, and destroyed. What is called the "education of the masses" cannot be accomplished directly; and even if a system of universal elementary compulsory education is applied, it can succeed only extrinsically.[29]

And after having shown that the unconscious of the people in all its depth cannot be reached by these direct paths but by respecting a certain healthy slumber, he continues:

> We know, however, what the aspiration is of those who would disturb the healthy slumber of the people (*die jenen heilenden Gesundheitsschlaf des Volkes*), and continually call out to them: "Keep your eyes open! Be sensible! Be wise!" We know the aim of those who profess to satisfy excessive educa-

---

28. For the first remark, see p. 62; there is no second remark.
29. Nietzsche, *On the Future of Our Educational Institutions*, p. 75 [KSA 1: 698–99].

tional requirements by means of an extraordinary increase in the number of educational institutions and the conceited tribe of teachers produced by the system. These very people, using these very means, are fighting against the natural hierarchy in the realm of the intellect (*die natürliche Rangordnung im Reiche des Intellekts*),³⁰ and destroying the roots of all those noble and sublime plastic forces which have their maternal origin in the unconsciousness of the people (*Unbewusstsein des Volkes*), and which fittingly terminate in the procreation of genius and its due guidance and proper training. It is only in the simile (*Gleichnisse*) of the mother that we can grasp the meaning and the responsibility of the true education of the people in respect to genius: its real origin is not to be found in such education [that is, in the mother]; it has, so to speak, only a metaphysical source, a metaphysical home (*Heimat*). But for the genius to make his appearance; for him to emerge from among the people; to portray the reflected picture (*das zurückgeworfne Bild*), as it were, the dazzling brilliance of the peculiar colors of this people, to depict the noble destiny of a people in the similitude of an individual (*in dem gleichnissartigen Wesen eines Individuums*) in a work which will last for all time, thereby making his nation itself eternal, and redeeming it from the ever-shifting element of transient things: all this is possible for the genius only when he has been brought up and come to maturity in the mother's lap of the culture of a people (*im Mutterschoosse der Bildung eines Volkes*): while, on the other hand, without this sheltering home (*Heimat*), the genius will not, generally speaking, be able to rise to the height of his eternal flight, but will at an early moment, like a stranger, weather-driven, upon a bleak, snow-covered desert, slink away from the inhospitable land.

"You astonish me with such a metaphysics of genius," said the teacher's companion, "and I have only a hazy conception of the accuracy of your simile. On the other hand, I fully understand what you have said about the surplus of public schools and the corresponding surplus of high level teachers..."³¹

Life, the mother, and genius are here—through the unconscious of a culture of the people—situated metaphorically, each being the metaphor of the other. And genius is always unique, the singular metaphorical representative of the unconscious or the mother or the life that is most living. This unicity counts and everything must work with the unique in view. Let me mention to you—not knowing exactly how to treat this biographical reference, which, to my knowledge, <neither> Nietzsche nor his biographers

---

30. At the top of the page of the transcript is a handwritten notation that appears to be: "explain."
31. Nietzsche, *On the Future of Our Educational Institutions*, pp. 75–77 [*KSA* 1: 699–700].

ever evoke—that not only was Nietzsche a unique son [*un fils unique*] but, in the year following the death of his father, his brother, four years younger than he, also died. It would be hard to maintain, however one interprets it, that when Nietzsche says I am two, (he) the dead and (she) the living, the dead father and the living mother, I am a double, it would be hard to maintain that the figure of the brother is not silently at work in this mise-en-scène, in a real way and according to the "form of the enigma."[32]

We will have to return, of course, to this entire problematic of metaphor, in its relation to reproduction-selection, in its relation to knowledge, concepts, and truth. What is nonetheless already certain is that on the basis of such a problematic one should no longer be able, or should no longer have been able, to consider as certain the limit, the rigorous cut, between a metaphor and a concept, and singularly so in the domain of life or biological science.

Now what first strikes me when I read philosophers or epistemologists of life such as Canguilhem is that when they get around—inevitably—to questioning the introduction of metaphors in the field in which they work, it is in order to maintain at all costs the rigorous and reassuring border between the conceptual and the metaphorical. What also strikes me is that, to my knowledge, they never cite Nietzsche and do not take him into account. What strikes me as well, and this is intriguing and interesting, is that they implicitly think that to meddle with the rigorous border between concept and metaphor is to compromise scientific objectivity, something that no self-respecting scientism should be willing to do since that is what actually turns science into scientism. What strikes me as well, and what seems to me intriguing and interesting, is that, in order to avoid meddling, one refrains from any question regarding the metaphoricity of metaphor and the conceptuality of the concept, and one forbids oneself from tampering in any way with their respective order, without suspecting that science, far from suffering from an erasure of the limit, might, on the contrary, demand a recasting of this division and of the law of this division. Finally, what strikes me, and seems to me intriguing, interesting, is that by keeping intact, by wanting to preserve at all costs, the traditional opposition between metaphor and concept, one prevents oneself not just from understanding anything about the actual history of science but also, and this needs no demonstration, from making the slightest contribution to it. In "White My-

---

32. In the left margin of the transcript, above a long line, is the handwritten word "end." Beneath this line is a word that could be the abbreviation "Genea<logy>."

thology" I tried to explain myself on this point with regard to Bachelard.³³ Let's see how things stand with Canguilhem in the text that we began to read last time. Let me pick it up at the point where he mentions Claude Bernard (whose work, I note in passing, Nietzsche knew—which is not insignificant—and quoted, for example in *The Will to Power*, p. 364 [of the French translation], at the moment he was underscoring that "health and sickness are not essentially different," that they are not distinct entities that would fight over the living organism as on a battlefield. To say this would be "silly nonsense and chatter."³⁴ Between sickness and health there are only differences of degree: it is the exaggeration, disproportion, and disharmony of normal phenomena that constitute the morbid state—see Claude Bernard, says Nietzsche). Thus I pick up Canguilhem's "The Concept and Life" at the point where it is discussing Claude Bernard and metaphor. I wish to highlight right from the start the opposition that Canguilhem seems to consider assured, founded, and untouchable. It is the opposition between what he calls, therefore, metaphor and what he calls an "adequate concept." Here are two quotations to underscore an opposition that is never questioned by him, much less put into doubt, that is not even subject to the most tentative re-elaboration.

First, p. 358:

> If genetic information is defined as the coded program of the synthesis of proteins, then can we not maintain that the following terms, all coming from Claude Bernard, and which are used not just once and by chance but constantly throughout his work, *instructional sign* [consigne], *guiding idea, vital design, vital preordination, vital plan, meaning of phenomena* . . . are so many attempts to define, in the absence of the adequate concept, and through the convergence of metaphors, a biological fact that is in some sense designated before being attained?³⁵

In other words, the convergence of metaphors comes in the place where the adequate concept is lacking, "in the absence of the adequate concept." What Canguilhem here implies is not that the adequate concept is always lacking and that concepts are never anything but metaphors or that concepts

---

33. See Derrida, "White Mythology: Metaphor in the Text of Philosophy," in *Margins of Philosophy*, trans. Alan Bass (Chicago: University of Chicago Press, 1982), pp. 207–71 ["La mythologie blanche: La métaphore dans le texte philosophique," in *Marges de la philosophie* (Paris: Éditions de Minuit, 1972), pp. 247–324].

34. Nietzsche, *WP*, fragment 47, p. 29 [*KSA* 13: 14|65|, p. 250].

35. Canguilhem, "Le concept et la vie," p. 358.

are already metaphors but that we have today an adequate concept where Bernard had to make do with metaphors.

Second quotation, p. 360:

> Message, information, program, code, instruction, decoding—such are the new concepts of the knowledge of life. But, one will object, are not these concepts ultimately imported metaphors, reminiscent of the way Claude Bernard, through a convergence of metaphors, sought to make up for [*suppléer*] the lack of an adequate concept? Apparently yes, but in fact no. For what guarantees the theoretical effectiveness or the cognitive value of a concept is its operational function.[36]

Before going any further in our reading, one must, one can, already acknowledge that, for Canguilhem, the adequation of a concept is not, as it is traditionally understood, a value that is measured against the more or less contemplative awareness of a correlation between a thought and an object in a judgment, in an *adaequatio intellectus ad rem*. What he calls with these more or less well chosen words "adequate concept" must be understood in its working context—and that is its practical function—in theoretical practice. And that is why Canguilhem also speaks of "theoretical effectiveness" or of "operational function." An adequate concept is, for him, an effective concept, one that facilitates scientific work, that causes this work to advance and does not hinder it. After having said "operational function," he adds and clarifies, "and thus the possibility it offers for the development and progress of knowledge."

Have we, by means of this practicist, operational definition of the adequate concept or of adequation, made any real progress in the problem that concerns us? Let me first remark—and this cannot be just a formal question of vocabulary—that it is odd to speak of an adequate concept in order to designate a concept that has a value of practical mobilization in the movement and progress of knowledge. Inadequation is just as mobilizing as adequation—as Canguilhem, in fact, would no doubt be willing to acknowledge in other contexts—and adequation, when taken literally, can be rather static and immobilizing. What Canguilhem seems to want to say—if we are to do everything possible here to validate his claim—is that the adequation of which he speaks is no longer that of a concept to a thing or object but the adequation, the right relation, between a conceptual system or network and a theoretical situation within a given field at a given moment of the scientific process. But even with this clarification, the problem remains, it

---

36. Ibid., p. 360.

seems to me, completely intact. Canguilhem wants to hold onto this distinction between adequate concept and metaphor. It is not my intention to remain at the level of a formal critique that would simply note, for example, that adequation to a movement or to a process, adequation as what allows for the progress of knowledge, is, like all adequation to a movement, inadequate, and that it can be productive only to the extent that there is a certain inadequate adequation; or else that this inadequate adequation is also what is proper—if one can still say this—to every metaphor, which makes the limit between concepts and metaphors very uncertain; or else that this opposition between the adequate concept—whatever transformation it might undergo—and metaphor presupposes at the very least a horizon of propriety, or of proper knowledge, one that belongs to a very determinate field and to an earlier stage of philosophical discourse, and particularly the discourse of philosophy with regard to science. Instead of simply remaining at this level of argumentation—which would be sufficient, I believe, but remains formal—I would like to put it to the test of the content itself of Canguilhem's text, the material he is treating.

How does Canguilhem operate? He begins, at a certain point, with what Claude Bernard calls his "fundamental conception of life," which can be summed up in two aphorisms: (1) Life is death; (2) Life is creation. Canguilhem notes that Claude Bernard had been "conscripted" into the antimaterialist camp in biology and philosophy because, indifferent as to which side he was furnishing arguments, "he was possessed by an idea," namely, that "the organized living being is the temporarily perpetuated manifestation of a *guiding idea* of its evolution." He had a guiding idea, which was that there was a guiding idea, and that physio-chemical conditions cannot account for the specific form of their composition in this or that organism.

> In *Lectures on the Phenomena of Life Common to Animals and Plants*, Claude Bernard writes: "In the living being there are necessarily two orders of phenomena: 1. The phenomena of *vital creation* or *organizing synthesis*. 2. The phenomena of death or *organic destruction*. . . . The first of these two orders of phenomena is alone without direct analogy; it is peculiar, special to the living being; this developmental synthesis is what is truly vital."[37]

The phenomena of death, of organic destruction linked to physio-chemical functioning and expenditure, are, to be sure, a part of life, life is life plus death, but in accordance with a dissymmetry that, Claude Bernard insists,

---

37. Claude Bernard, *Lectures on the Phenomena of Life Common to Animals and Plants*, pp. 28–29; cited by Canguilhem, "Le concept et la vie," p. 356.

makes of organizing synthesis alone irreplaceable life, without analogy; it alone is what is truly vital. In the life that includes death, there is only one true representative of life that thus gets marked twice, remarked upon twice, once in a living way and once in a dead way, etc. Let us go a little farther: in what is truly vital, organic creation, there are still two syntheses: the one, the chemical synthesis, constitutes the protoplasm; the other, the morphological synthesis, gives form to and molds (Buffon) living matter.[38] These two syntheses, which contemporary biology has brought together, demonstrate that cytoplasm is a matter that has already been informed, already been structured, and so is not a figureless matter. Now despite what certain statements seem to suggest, Claude Bernard, Canguilhem tells us while citing him (p. 357), suspected that a morphological synthesis was already operating in the chemical synthesis, that matter was already structured. It is with regard to this pre-structure of cytoplasm, in order to define it, in fact, that Claude Bernard writes the phrase I recalled two weeks ago and that Canguilhem cites: "the manifestation here and now of a primitive impulse, of a primitive action, and of an *instructional sign* [consigne: Canguilhem's emphasis] that nature repeats after having ordered it in advance."[39]

This is the beginning in Canguilhem's text of a movement that I will describe, for lack of a better image, as a hesitation waltz. Reread it closely and you will understand to the point of hearing the violins what I mean by this. Nietzsche, as you know, appealed to dance, but he would have been wary of a dialectical way of dancing the waltz, of *walzen*, which means turning round or in a circle. You know, or in any case you will find in your music dictionary, the definition of the waltz in three-quarter time:

> The step of the waltz is made up of three parts, a gliding step, then a coming together, a second gliding step, or, better, the step that glided first is detached from the other, which then glides in turn; these movements are done while turning, and in this turning round the dancers move along a circle or an ellipse depending on the shape of the room. The waltz originated in Germany. (Fétis)[40]

38. Derrida is here paraphrasing the following passage of Canguilhem's "Le concept et la vie": "This organic creation is chemical synthesis, constitution of the protoplasm, and morphological synthesis, a gathering of the immediate principles of living matter in a particular mold. Mold was the term used by Buffon ('the internal mold') to explain that through the perpetual maelstrom that is life a particular form persists" (p. 357).

39. Canguilhem, "Le concept et la vie," p. 358.

40. Derrida appears to be quoting here from the entry on *waltz* in the Littré *Dictionary of the French Language*, where both François-Joseph Fétis's *Dictionary of Musical Terms* and the line from Castil-Blaze that follows are cited.

But a Frenchman, Castil-Blaze, writes: "The waltz that we took back from the Germans in 1795 had been for four hundred years a French dance."

So Canguilhem wants to show that Claude Bernard was still in metaphor but already in the concept, that the concept in which he already was was only a metaphor but that the metaphor in which he still was was already a concept that nonetheless remained a metaphor in which one could see the beginnings of a concept that nonetheless retained within itself a preconceptual, metaphorical element that prefigured a quasi-metaphorical concept that retained within itself a metaphor, finally, wherein one could have retrospectively deciphered the precursory message of a concept that is, in the end, adequate, that is to say, that works and that makes science work, as one can see it working today, if one is well placed, not too close and not too far from the laboratories on rue St. Jacques. The violins stop here. Now let us watch the film again in slow motion.

First time, first step: "Claude Bernard seems to have sensed that biological heredity consists in the transmission of something that is today called coded information. Semantically, an instructional sign [*consigne*] is not far from a code."[41]

Second time, second step: "It would, however, be incorrect to conclude from this that the analogy—the semantic analogy—corresponds to a real filiation of concepts."[42] What follows is a historical reference to the fact that the contexts were totally different and that Claude Bernard could not have had access to the modern concept of heredity, which is completely new.

Third time, third step: "And yet it can be argued that there exists between the Bernardian concept of an instructional sign [*consigne*] of evolution and current concepts of genetic code and genetic message a functional affinity."[43] It is at this point, with this functional affinity (is it analogical, metaphorical because of the affinity, or conceptual because of the function?—we do not know), that the metaphorical borders on the conceptual. It is at this point that Canguilhem asks the question, which I quote again:

> This affinity is based on their shared relation to the concept of information. If genetic information is defined as the coded program of the synthesis of proteins, then can we not maintain that the following terms, all coming from Claude Bernard, and which are used not just once and by chance but constantly throughout his work, *instructional sign* [consigne], *guiding idea, vital design, vital preordination, vital plan, meaning of phenomena* . . . are

41. Canguilhem, "Le concept et la vie," p. 358.
42. Ibid.
43. Ibid.

so many attempts to define, in the absence of the adequate concept, and through the convergence of metaphors, a biological fact that is in some sense designated before being attained?[44]

Those are the three times or steps of the first movement. It is left suspended at a hesitation-question between metaphor and concept, one step taking over for [*suppléant*] the other; and then it starts up again. Note that neither in this first cycle of three times nor in the cycle that follows will Canguilhem, who nonetheless asks lots of questions — which always come down to the same one, namely, whether something is a concept or a metaphor — ever ask, from one step to the next, just what a step [*pas*] into metaphor is or is not [*pas*], just what a step into concepts is or is not, just what a concept or a metaphor is. This he knows. The only hint of a definition he gives regards the concept, namely, that it is effective and operational and helps us move forward. But what would he say if one were to point out to him that, according to his own description in this text, and those of Bachelard elsewhere, there are also operational metaphors, as we well know, metaphors that help us to advance? There are obstructive metaphors and operational metaphors, obstructive concepts and operational concepts. The distinguishing criterion is not between concept and metaphor but between the useful and the detrimental in science, and this is very Nietzschean; and Canguilhem, who also makes of the concept a production of life, should have come around to recognizing this. What is certain is that the distinction that he wants to save at all costs, that between concept and metaphor, is pre-critical, never problematized, and therefore remains, as such, an antioperational obstacle. It prevents the reelaboration or recasting of this entire problem from taking place.[45]

After this first movement in three times or steps that has just been suspended, we start up again with another movement in three times or steps.

First time, first step: to answer the question left suspended, Canguilhem notes that Claude Bernard remained within the metaphor of what contemporary biology knows in the proper sense because he stated in psychological terms (guiding idea, design, and so on) what the science of today, which is now on a sure path, understands by the word *information* in the physical sense (a notion Canguilhem is a bit too quick to accept, though we will return to this point). Thus (1) he remains in the psychical metaphor of the physical.

---

44. Ibid.

45. In the typescript there is this handwritten notation at the end of the paragraph: "(concept of metaphor to be set aside) in B<ernard>."

But, *second time, second step*, Claude Bernard, who never ceases to surprise us, also ventured to speak of "the law of order and succession that gives the meaning or the relation of phenomena,"[46] a Leibnizian expression that is very close to the modern logic of the hereditary form, which can be, I quote, "related to the fundamental discovery in molecular biology of the structure of the deoxyribonucleic acid molecule, the essential constituent of chromosomes, the vehicles of genetic inheritance, vehicles whose very number is a specific hereditary characteristic."[47]

Third time, third step: it is starting from this order of succession of a finite number of bases along a double helix of sugars-phosphates, from this order that constitutes the instructional code, the language of the program, etc., that modern biology (at least since 1954) has moved on to language itself, that is, has changed languages in order to use the code of language, in order to replace by the code of language (information, etc.) the language of physics or chemistry or even mathematics, or at least a mathematics governed by two geometric models. It is here that Canguilhem writes, and I quote again what I quoted earlier:

> Message, information, program, code, instruction, decoding—such are the new concepts of the knowledge of life. But, one will object, are not these concepts ultimately imported metaphors, reminiscent of the way Claude Bernard, through a convergence of metaphors, sought to make up for the lack of an adequate concept? Apparently yes, but in fact no. For what guarantees the theoretical effectiveness or the cognitive value of a concept is its operational function, and thus the possibility it offers for the development and progress of knowledge.[48]

To all this it would be easy, too easy, to respond that what we have here is a putting into perspective or into retrospective through a privileging of the now that can quickly seem naïve. What is denounced today as a metaphor was once operational, and what is today operational, if one follows this line of argumentation, is sure to appear metaphorical tomorrow. And from where do we today get the assurance that the concepts of code (etc.) are adequate? Adequate to what? To the progress of science? That notion is a little vague and homogeneous. And what if they also limited, when interpreted in a certain way, the progress of science? And what if these concepts

---

46. Quoted in Canguilhem, "Le concept et la vie," p. 359; the phrase is taken from Claude Bernard, *Rapport sur le progrès et la marche de la physiologie générale en France* (Paris: Imprimerie Impériale, 1867).
47. Canguilhem, "Le concept et la vie," p. 360.
48. Ibid.

107 were to be interpreted as a *logos* that resembles Aristotle's? And what if, conversely, one were to show that Claude Bernard's guiding idea, about which, you will recall, Jacob said that the modern biologist would not have to change a word, had also been operational, etc.?

There is yet a third movement in three times or three steps to show that the terrain upon which Claude Bernard had formed the concept of internal secretion prevented him from conceiving of chemical messengers, what came to be called chemical messages and <unreadable word>, which is what led to the informational code. Here it is not a metaphor that poses an obstacle to the concept but a certain concept, a state of the concept, that poses an obstacle to another concept, to another network or terrain. Claude Bernard anticipated without anticipating, between still and already. And the fact that we are speaking here of terrain and of network, not of one particular metaphor hindering the concept that it announces but of what I will call one metaphorico-conceptual system actively interpreting another, this fact should have required or will require a general reinterpretation with regard to life death, because of life death, because of a metaphor-concept relation that would be understood neither in terms of a continuous teleology nor in terms of an epistemological break. Canguilhem, as you saw, wanted to save both at the same time.[49] Which perhaps means, and that will be the lesson for today, that they are more indissociable than one believes and that it is perhaps necessary, as with life death, to save them or to lose them at the same time, in a single stroke. This is, of course, impossible. At least before Christmas.

---

49. In the typescript there is an insertion mark here that is repeated in the left margin along with this handwritten notation: "teleology and rupture."

FOURTH SESSION[1]
The Logic of the Supplement
The Supplement of the Other, of Death, of Meaning, of Life

What is apparently most readable in the text of the "modern" biologist regarding his own science, in the text that the "modern" biologist writes, at once as scientist, as epistemologist of his science, as historian of his science, as philosopher of his science, what is apparently most readable in this text of the modern biologist or geneticist is that he does not write a text on something that would be outside the text [*hors texte*], something that would be a-textual, that would form a referent whose nature would be to be foreign, in its being or in its structure, to textuality, but, quite to the contrary, he writes a text on a text, a text on text, in order to demonstrate, recall, or write that his object has the structure of a text, and that there is no longer anything in the object of his science or of his research, nothing as scientific object, that is meta-textual. My point in saying this is not, to recall this mundane fact, that the biologist or the geneticist has to refer—as he does indeed have to refer,

---

1. On a sheet of paper attached to the first page of the typescript are the following handwritten words: "Life / supplement / death // Read Brisset {Frog / form and / meaning. is and. We will speak especially today of bacteria. Here, as an epigraph, are a few lines from Jacob, p. 307–308." Derrida appears to be referring here to Jean-Pierre Brisset, author of *La grammaire logique*, followed by *La Science de Dieu*, preface by Michel Foucault (Paris: Tchou, 1970); see Derrida's seminar *Theory and Practice: Course at the ENS d'Ulm, 1976–1977*, trans. David Wills (Chicago: University of Chicago Press, 2019), pp. 37–38 [*Théorie et pratique* (Paris: Éditions Galilée, 2017), pp. 58–60]. As for the "few lines" from Jacob used as an epigraph, Derrida no doubt read the following: "In the genetic program, therefore, is written the result of all past reproductions, the collection of successes, since all traces of failures have disappeared. The genetic message, the program of the present-day organism, therefore, resembles a text without an author, that a proof-reader has been correcting for more than two billion years, continually improving, refining and completing it, gradually eliminating all imperfections. What is copied and transmitted today to ensure the stability of the species is this text, ceaselessly modified by time." Jacob, *Logic of the Living*, p. 287 [pp. 307–8].

for this is indispensable — to scientific writings, to an archive of genetic science that is either out-of-date or current, an archive without which science would not be possible, but also, more radically, that his ultimate referent, the living, along with the productive-reproductive structure of the living, is now analyzed as text. Its constitution is that of a text. And the emergence of scientific modernity in the genetico-biological domain consists, it seems, in this mutation by which science, by which knowledge, is no longer the production of a text on the subject of an object that in itself would be, as the referent of this knowledge, meta-textual, but that is itself textual in its structure. What could have appeared, more or less naively, to be the limited condition of philology, of literary criticism, of the science of documents and archives, etc., namely, having as its ultimate referent something that we used to call text and that we believed we understood under this name, this condition is now shared by genetics or the science of the living in general; and if the science of the living is not a science among others but the science that is presupposed [*impliquée*] by all the sciences that determine their objects in fields involving [*impliquant*] the living (psychoanalysis, history, sociology — all the human sciences but also all the sciences inasmuch as they involve the activity of a living being — thus all the sciences, all discourses and all productions in general), if, then, the science of the living is not a science among others, its textualization, the textualization of its object and of its subject, leaves nothing outside it. This obviously does not lead to the claim, as one might be able to assert with a more or less interested or interesting naiveté, that everything is now going to be, as a result of this textualization, restricted to the safe confines of a book, of a notebook, or of a more or less specialized library. It leads, on the contrary, to an extremely violent reinterpretation of the limit between this inside and its outside.

Before situating the problems that follow from this, let me clarify through a few references what I understand here by the textualization of the biological object or referent. As announced earlier, I will return for this to Jacob's *The Logic of the Living*. Quite apart from all the questions that might be raised by the manner in which Jacob determines this genetic textuality, it is incontestable that he constitutes the genetic as text and that he is only describing — and this is what gives one the right to treat him as a representative or spokesperson for all of modern genetics — a consensus and an approach that is today common in the field of genetics. We confirmed this with regard to Jacob's notion of program and the word "program." Here, more broadly, is what Jacob says about the general concept of the text, of which the program is a specification. "When heredity is described as a coded program in a sequence of chemical radicals," says Jacob, "the contradiction [between teleology and mechanism] disappears."² Later he writes, p. 254:

> Organs, cells, and molecules are thus united by a communication network. They constantly exchange signals and messages in the form of specific interactions between constituents. The flexibility of behavior depends on feedback loops; the rigidity of structures on the execution of a program rigorously prescribed. Heredity becomes the transfer of a message repeated from one generation to the next. The programs of the structures to be produced are recorded in the nucleus of the egg.³

There is more than just messages, communication, and a transfer of information—one might in fact be tempted <to say> that such communication, such a language determined as communication, does not make a text. There is text only to the extent that there are instructional signs, an archive, codes and deciphering. Now, that is what was discovered in the course of what Jacob calls the fourth structure of order (fourth-order structure) to which modern genetics corresponds: the first-order structure, at the beginning of the seventeenth century, corresponds to an arrangement of visible surfaces; the second-order structure, at the end of the eighteenth century, to the organization that underlies organs and functions and that was finally broken down into cells; the third-order structure, at the beginning of the twentieth century, corresponds to the discovery of chromosomes and genes; finally, the fourth-order structure, in the middle of the twentieth century, which is the discovery upon which modern genetics lives, corresponds to the nucleic acid molecule. These four structures shelter one another, inhabit one another, are nested in one another like Russian dolls, to use the comparison that comes up frequently in this book, it being understood—as Jacob clearly notes—that the discovery of each new structure, to which Jacob devotes each time a chapter of his book, is not only an extension or a deepening of our knowledge but a structural transformation of knowledge itself, "a new way of considering objects."⁴ Moreover, for each order structure, one model, what Jacob calls a model—we will perhaps pose questions about this word later—dominates, "as if, in order to last," says Jacob, "a biological theory had to be based on a concrete model."⁵ What was discovered with the fourth-order structure, and the model corresponding to this discovery, is the text, the fact that reproduction, an essential structure of the

2. Jacob, *Logic of the Living*, p. 4 [p. 12].
3. Ibid., p. 254 [p. 274].
4. Ibid., p. 17 [p. 25].
5. Ibid., p. 14 [p. 22].

living, functions like a text. The text is the model. It is, rather, the model of models. Indeed Jacob mobilizes several analogies to describe the object of this discovery, but all of them involve regulation by something like a recorded [*consigné*] and deciphered program (writing, reading, code, copies, etc.). There is, for example, the analogy of the computer and the analogy of the factory. The analogy of the factory, in the case of bacteria, is eventually cast aside, and we will see why later. As for the analogy of the computer, it is dependent on the analogy of the text. This latter does not depend on the discovery of a substance such as deoxyribonucleic acid (DNA). The existence of this acid had been known for nearly a century. It was known to exist in the nucleus of cells, even its overall composition was known, but its role and its molecular structure remained unknown. It was the discovery of its role and its structure that led us to speak of a text. It was chemical and crystallographic analysis that allowed us to know this structure and this role, to know that we were dealing here with a long polymer formed by the alignment of four sub-units. These are "repeated by millions and permutated along the chain, like," says Jacob,

> the letters of the alphabet in a text. It is the order of these four sub-units that directs the order of the twenty sub-units in proteins. Everything then leads one to regard the sequence contained in genetic material as a series of instructions specifying molecular structures, and hence the properties of the cell; to consider the plan of an organism as a message transmitted from generation to generation; to see the combinative system of the four chemical radicals as a system of numeration to the base four. In short, everything urges one to compare the logic of heredity to that of a computer. Rarely has a model suggested by a particular epoch proved to be more faithful.[6]

Let me note in passing that this last little sentence seems to suggest that this accord is a stroke of chance, that this faithfulness in the application of a model imposed by an epoch to a given reality, this faithfulness or this adequation, has something surprising about it, even though everything demonstrates—and Jacob's book itself does as well—that there is nothing fortuitous here. There is a relationship of essential necessity between the possibility of constructing or of using computers and the possibility of attaining knowledge of this fourth-order structure.

The text is thus this time the dominant model. But can we blithely accept this so seemingly straightforward claim? Jacob speaks often of model, of image, of analogy, of comparison—these are all his words. But before refining

---

6. Ibid., pp. 264–65 [pp. 284–85].

my question and coming a bit closer to Jacob's discourse, let me indicate the general form of the problem I would like to pose: is the text or is textual language—the silent text, since it is always a matter here of a gram (an engram or a program) that is voiceless—something, something determinate that can provide a model for some objective knowledge (so, is it something, on the one hand, and is it something that can provide a model, on the other) *without* entailing a transformation in the structure of knowledge, in the objectivity of knowledge, in the referentiality of scientific discourse, in the very concept of model, a transformation so complete that the very axiomatic that subtends all these statements would have to be structurally altered? If the object, the referent of a scientific text (and science is a text), if the object, the referent, of a scientific discourse (and science is a discourse), if this object and this referent are no longer meta-textual or meta-discursive realities, if their very reality has a structure that is analogous to or fundamentally homogeneous with the structure of scientific textuality, if the object (the living, which is to say, reproducibility), the model, and scientific subjectivity (the knower, etc.) have an analogous structure, namely, that of the text, one can no longer speak as one does elsewhere of a knowing subject, of a known object, and of an analogical model. What is more, and for the same reason, what we human beings claim to take from culture as a model, namely, discursive texts or computers and everything we believe we know and are familiar with under the name *text*, what we then claim to take as a model, comparison, or analogy in order to understand the living at its most elementary level is itself a complex product of life, of the living, and the alleged model is external neither to the knowing subject nor to the known object. There is nothing fortuitous or external about the living being that we are producing things (texts) that might seem to serve as a model for the knowledge of the living, nothing fortuitous about this analogy of structure. The text is not a third term in the relation between the biologist and the living; it is the very structure of the living as the structure common to the biologist, as a living being, to science, as a production of life, and to the living itself. Since this cannot be said about every region of knowledge or about every model or every appeal to models, should we not admit that we are no longer dealing with just a model, that the science of the living or the logic of the living is not one region among others in the scientific field, and that there must, therefore, follow from this powers and risks that are absolutely unique? And that one can no longer speak of this without re-elaborating, as I announced last time when reading Canguilhem, everything that one takes up without any hesitation under the words metaphor (opposed to the concept), image, model, analogy, etc.

114

Having stated these generalities, and recalled these things, I propose not that we reread *The Logic of the Living* but that we construct with this book (or this discourse or this discursive set, of which this book is today an eminent representative, and one that is, as it were, highly distilled), to reconstruct the machine that governs it, quite obviously unbeknownst to it, where unbeknownst means not only unbeknownst to its author — which <is> more than evident on every page — but unbeknownst to the system, by which I mean not that the system should be conscious or not (I do not know what that would mean) but that it does not exhibit and does not put to work certain relations between statements or textual functions, and, as a result, is not constructed with maximal power and effectiveness, that is, with the power and effectiveness that seem to me possible today. Possible where and how and why? — it is to this that I would like my response to respond.

To construct this machine, one must bring into communication, plug into one another, concepts and statements that are detached from one another, and which the force of Jacob's discourse is incapable of bringing together and relating to one another, as if the presence of certain conceptual elements were perceived though one did not yet know how to make them function, or rather how to analyze them in their functioning, a bit like that deoxyribonucleic acid whose existence had long been detected without anyone being able in the beginning to understand and master its functioning, something that could be done only after progress had been made on all fronts (theoretical, technical, etc.). When everything has been plugged in, assuming this works, perhaps we will make some progress in the overall restructuring of the problems that we have been running into from the beginning of this seminar, in particular those of reproduction/selection, metaphor/concept, this latter problem being localized today in the problem of the model or analogy named *text*.

To put it briefly and in the most economical way possible, and in order to give to today's trajectory — and no doubt that of next week — a relative coherence, let me state right away that the two conceptual threads — the two conductive wires — that I am going to link together (and these are never linked by Jacob in his book, nor anywhere else, to my knowledge, except perhaps virtually in Nietzsche in fact) — are, on the one hand, the thread or wire that holds together the series "image," "analogy," "comparison," "model" (when Jacob says that the computer or the chemical factory or the alphabet and the text are analogies, models, etc.) and, on the other hand, the thread or wire that holds together the series "reproduction," "copy," "duplication" (when, for example, Jacob refers to these as the very essence of the living). These are the two conceptual threads or wires that I am going to try

THE LOGIC OF THE SUPPLEMENT ‡ 83

to plug into one another to see if any current passes between them. Death, sexuality, selection will all be part of the program but, as you will see, as supplements, following the logic of the supplement.

Let us begin with the concept of re-production. It is the ultimate conceptual criterion, Jacob tells us, the only criterion, the sole and unique criterion, by which to recognize that one is dealing with the living. Only the living—and it is by this that one recognizes the living—has the power to reproduce *itself* [*se* reproduire]. Before asking what "reproduce itself" means here, and notice I am saying reproduce-itself (for Jacob always says re-production whenever he is clearly describing self-reproduction: there are non-living things that re-produce without re-producing themselves, and this bending back upon the self, this auto-affection, is an essential fold of the structure), I would like to draw your attention to a gesture that recurs regularly in Jacob. You know why he titles his book *The Logic of the Living* and not "the logic of life": it is because, he maintains, the biologist is no longer interested in life, in the essence of life as some entity hidden behind phenomena, like some mysterious *grande dame* of metaphysics whom philosophers are prone to invoke. It is with just this metaphysical obscurantism that the scientist intends to break by speaking of the living rather than of life. Vitalism is one name for this metaphysical obscurantism. With the discovery of the fourth-order structure, one is led to speak of living beings and not of life. Pp. 299–300:

> Recognition of the unity of physical and chemical processes at the molecular level has deprived vitalism of its *raison d'être*. In fact, since the appearance of thermodynamics, the operational value of the concept of life has continually dwindled and its power of abstraction has declined. Biologists no longer study life today in their laboratories. They no longer attempt to define it. Instead, they investigate the structure of living systems, their functions, their history. Yet at the same time, recognition of the purpose of living systems means that biology can no longer be studied without constant reference to the "plan" of organisms, to the "sense" which their very existence gives to structures and functions, an attitude obviously very different from the reductionism that was long dominant.[7]

And p. 306, in the same chapter:

> And yet biology has demonstrated that there is no metaphysical entity hidden behind the word "life." The power of assembling, of producing increasingly complex structures, even of reproducing oneself, belongs to the

---

7. Ibid., pp. 299–300 [pp. 320–21].

elements that constitute matter. From particles to man, there is a whole series of integrations, of levels, of discontinuities. But there is no breach either in the composition of the objects or in the reactions that take place in them; no change in "essence."[8]

One cannot but agree with Jacob if, or when, he is going after a caricatural metaphysical vitalism that introduces Life as some abstract entity or occult power so as to dispense with scientific investigation. It would be necessary to look more closely at which scientist and which metaphysician did that. On the other hand, Jacob cannot himself refrain from making reference to the essence of the living—indeed he does so everywhere. It is not enough simply to replace life by the living to escape the philosophico-Socratic question: what is it that makes the living being a living being? You speak of living: so you must know or must be seeking to know what you understand by that, by the being-living of the living, by the livingness [*la vivance*] of the living, in other words, the life of the living, the difference between the living and the non-living. And if you are right not to want to make of life an abstract and separate entity or essence, you cannot avoid the implication that living means something and that there is a being-living of the living, a livingness or a life, which is the very thing that you study. What modern science has *perhaps* transformed is the concept of this essence of life or of being-living but not at all the reference to an essence of the living as such. And in fact Jacob posits this essence and defines it very frequently—it is a leitmotif of his book: a living living being [*un vivant vivant*] is recognized by its capacity to reproduce itself. It thus just so happens that the essential definition Jacob gives of livingness, of what determines an existing thing (a system or an individual living being) as living, is literally the definition given it by the most metaphysical of metaphysicians, the metaphysician par excellence, that is, Hegel, namely, that the individual living being is living insofar as it can reproduce itself. In the last section of the *Science of Logic*, for example, in subchapter A of chapter 1, Life (I am not going to reconstitute all the syllogisms), Hegel writes: "The first two moments, sensibility and irritability, are abstract determinations; in reproduction (*in der Reproduktion*) life is concrete and is vitality [*vivance*]: *in der Reproduktion ist das Leben* Konkretes *und Lebendigkeit*."[9] Let me now quote a few of Jacob's statements on this subject. When, in the passage I just read, Jacob said that the power of "reproducing oneself belongs to the elements that constitute matter," he did not mean by this that these elements form

---

8. Ibid., p. 306 [p. 327].
9. Hegel, *Science of Logic*, p. 769 [p. 479].

on their own a system of reproduction, reproducing themselves; he merely meant that these are elements which, insofar as they are present in a living system — which alone has the capacity to reproduce itself — play a role there and are integrated into it. He in fact added immediately afterward, I pick up the quotation:

> ... no change in "essence." So much so, that investigation of molecules and cellular organelles has now become the concern of physicists. Details of structure are now defined by crystallography, ultracentrifugation, nuclear magnetic resonance, fluorescence and other physical techniques. This does not at all mean that biology has become an annex of physics, that it represents, as it were, a junior branch concerned with complex systems. At each level of organization, novelties appear in both properties and logic. *It is not within the power of any single molecule by itself to reproduce itself*. This faculty appears only with the simplest integron deserving to be called a living organism, that is, the cell.... The various levels of biological organization are united by the logic proper to reproduction.[10]

The introduction, "The Program," spoke of "'reproduction,' the intrinsic property of all living systems."[11] The aim of the program, what Jacob calls its "sense," its "plan," with or without quotation marks (for the quotation marks are not enough to neutralize the problem; the semantics and the teleology that form the content of this entire book end up breaking, thanks to what these quotation marks signal, only with a semantics of consciousness or of freedom, of the individual psyche, of deliberate intentionality, but not with either intentionality or sense in general), the aim, then, of the program, its sense or its plan, is to "reproduce itself": "The intention of a Psyche has been replaced by the translation of a message. The living being does indeed represent the execution of a plan, but not one conceived in any mind. It strives towards a goal, but not one chosen by any will. The aim is to prepare an identical program for the following generation. The aim is to reproduce itself."[12] Pp. 4–5:

> Everything in a living being is centered on reproduction. A bacterium, an amoeba, a fern — what destiny can they dream of other than forming two bacteria, two amoeba, or several more ferns? If there are living beings on earth today, it is because other beings have reproduced themselves with desperate eagerness for two thousand million years or more. Let us imagine an uninhabited world. We can conceive the establishment of systems possessing

10. Jacob, *Logic of the Living*, pp. 306–7 [pp. 327–28]; Derrida's emphasis.
11. Ibid., p. 17 [p. 25].
12. Ibid., p. 2 [p. 10].

certain properties of life, such as the ability to react to certain stimuli, to assimilate, to breathe, or even to grow—but not to reproduce themselves. Can they be called living systems? Each represents the fruit of long and laborious elaboration. Each birth is a unique event, without a morrow. Each occasion is an eternal recommencement. Always at the mercy of some local cataclysm, such organizations can have only an ephemeral existence. Moreover, their structure is rigidly fixed at the outset, incapable of change. If, on the contrary, there emerges a system capable of reproducing itself, even if only badly, slowly, and at great cost, that is a living system without any doubt. It will spread wherever conditions permit. The more it is disseminated, the greater its protection from catastrophe [that is the convoluted *apotropos* and the *double bind* of dissemination]. Once the long period of incubation is over, the system becomes established by the repetition of identical events. The first step is taken once and for all. In such a system, however, reproduction, which is the very cause of existence, also becomes its purpose. It is doomed to reproduce itself or disappear.[13]

This last sentence, pleonastic in its very form, indeed confirms that reproduction is being defined as the very essence or the essential property of the living, what is proper to the living, livingness itself, its *ousia* and its *aitia*, its being-living, its essence-existence, the efficient and final cause, the final outcome of the efficient cause: "in such a system, reproduction, which is the very cause of existence, also becomes its purpose."

When Jacob says that there is "no change in 'essence'" when we come to the living, this has to be read with the greatest circumspection. First, because he puts quotation marks around the word "essence," which implies that he is speaking only of a metaphysico-vitalist, essentialist, and caricatural code, one he is citing from a certain distance as a foil (this does not mean that there have not been historical examples of such a vitalism, though simply going after caricatures is not going to solve the problem). One must also read this "no change in 'essence'" with circumspection because Jacob does nothing if not show that there is a change in essence, that there is an essence of the living. To be sure, this essence is not some substance hidden behind phenomena or represented by that Psyche that Jacob sometimes writes with a capital letter, but it does mark what Jacob calls an "intrinsic property" of the living, and that is the re-production of the self, the capacity to re-produce oneself. The fact that this capacity or this property is not some hidden power but a logic of integration of prior structures (integration or the integron is, I would say, the major operational concept of this whole discourse, each organiza-

---

13. Ibid., pp. 4–5 [pp. 12–13].

tion or order structure emerging, in discontinuous fashion, only to integrate the preceding one, which orders at once the "real" history "of beings and of things," as Jacob says, of the living and of the non-living, and the history of the sciences, which also proceeds by successive integration and inclusion. The concept of the integron provides the title for the conclusion of the work, while that of the program provides the title for the introduction. The construction of Jacob's book is very interesting and very reflective; it invites reflection on all of the content and on the entire orientation of the content. The introduction, before the first part, "The Program" (at once the genetic concept of the program and the program of the book), then the five chapters that describe the first-, second-, third-, and fourth-order structures, along with the current state of affairs from which everything is put into perspective, and, finally, the conclusion, "The Integron," which describes integration as both the law of the actual process of biological science and the epistemological or historical law of that science, that which makes intelligible the different phases of bio-genetic discovery or knowledge, this whole logic being very dialectical and very Hegelian, which we should not be too quick to treat with suspicion—I close my parenthesis), the fact that this intrinsic property of the living (the capacity to reproduce oneself) is not some hidden power [*vertu*] but a logic of integration does not necessarily mean that it cannot be considered as an essence: not only *ousia* (way of being, being in such a way [*d'être tel*], beingness [*étantité*]), not only essence as causality (*aitia*: efficient and final, as Jacob himself says: the reproduction that constitutes the very cause of existence becomes, in turn, the end) but also essence as *energeia*: Jacob regularly resorts to principles of energy in order to explain reproduction (free energy, bound energy, binding energy, tendency toward binding and "a decrease of free energy,"[14] which we will soon put into relation with what Freud says of free energy and bound energy in *Jenseits*). In other words, not only does Jacob not break purely and simply with the philosophical discourse on essence but he ends up returning, with this essence of life as tendency and capacity for reproduction, not only, I would say, to essence but also to the essentiality of essence, the origin and end of essence as a dynamics and energy of being, that which gives the power and actuality of being, maximal being, and which assures—from the inside, and that is the essence of essence, namely, to have one's principle of being in oneself and not in some accident coming from outside—assures from the inside its own production, that is, its re-production. From this point of view, it is not just difficult to claim that, for Jacob, there is no

---

14. Ibid., p. 301 [p. 322].

essence of life; indeed, quite to the contrary, he seems to be saying, in a traditional way, that life is the essence, the capacity to produce-reproduce oneself from the inside (an intrinsic property), that it is, in this sense, more essential than the non-living that it integrates into it, into its being living. If life had no essence, that would be because it is the essentiality of essence, being more essence than the rest. And this "more" brings in, as we saw earlier, the value of the maximal. It links these claims to a very classical discourse on essence, the one that, in Aristotle, relates *dynamis* to *energeia* (through efficient and final causes), or that of Spinoza's *conatus* or Leibniz's *appetitus*; but it is obviously Hegel's discourse, insofar as it develops the whole logic of essence based on the value of life (natural life and the life of spirit) that here seems the closest. And, especially, it is the economic dimension of this energetics (the reference to maximal and minimal) that is going to bring this discourse into proximity to Nietzsche's discourse insofar as it associates reproduction with selection. Time and again, Jacob shows how the logic of the living, as the logic of reproduction, precisely, is, by this very fact, selective, a logic of selectivity. Jacob writes (pp. 292–93):

> The very concept of selection is inherent in the nature of living beings, in the fact that they exist only to the extent they reproduce themselves. Each new individual, which by mutation, recombination, and addition becomes the carrier of a new program, is immediately put to the test of reproduction. If this organism is unable to reproduce itself, it disappears. If it is able to reproduce itself better and faster than its congeners, this advantage, however minor, immediately favors its multiplication and hence the propagation of this particular program. If in the long run the nucleic-acid text seems to be molded by environment, if the lessons of past experience are eventually written into it, this occurs in a roundabout way through success in reproduction. But only what exists reproduces itself. Selection operates not on possible living organisms but existent ones.[15]

That there is no reproduction without selection or selection without reproduction does not mean that these two "forces" cooperate peacefully—on the contrary. Their relation can only be one of tension and contradiction with effects of compromise. The deviation [*écart*] of a mutation can be reproduced—and so not remain unique and thus ephemeral—only to the extent that it limits itself and conforms to certain conditions of reproduction, of reproducibility. An absolute deviation—an absolute monstrosity—does not even relate enough to itself to reproduce itself, to divide itself and resemble itself in another copy [*exemplaire*] of itself. The relation to self of

---

15. Ibid., pp. 292–93 [p. 313].

self-reproduction [*auto-reproduction*] is the general form of what comes to limit the deviation or the mutant by giving it, at the same time, the chance for reproduction. Whence a strategy and endless compromises in the logic of the living in its tendency to integrate the novelty of programs, a novelty that must be new enough, disseminating enough, to ensure maximal propagation and reproduction but close enough to itself and repetitive enough to ensure that the dissemination is not a pure dissemination, that is, a loss without return in the unique. Later we will come across this same economy of dissemination in relation to viruses. For the moment, I am attempting to clarify the relationship of the geneticist's or modern biologist-scientist's discourse to the philosophical tradition: debt and unrecognized dependence, denegation, simplification, caricature, submission to the constraints of a code, of a program, precisely, of a calculating machinery from which he believes himself to be free even while he is reproducing its functioning, etc. In referring very rapidly, and one right after another, to Aristotle, Leibniz, Spinoza, Hegel, and Nietzsche, it was not my intention to conflate all these systems and make of them some confused amalgam, but simply to note, very quickly, that the discourse of modern genetics was making less of a break with these classical philosophemes than it appeared or than was claimed. And that not confronting them head-on was not only not justified but actually risked making one blind to the repetition of a very powerful code, itself the effect at some level of the logic of the living. Another example we could have taken, besides that of essence, is the example of truth.[16] In one of those statements that almost sounds like an advertising slogan for theory from the 1960s (it is true that there are fewer of these in Jacob than in Monod, this latter being at once less discreet and less advanced from this point of view), in one of these slogans, then, Jacob writes, still under the rubric of the program, "biology is . . . no longer seeking for truth. It is building its own truth." "Like the other natural sciences, biology today has lost many of its illusions. It is no longer seeking for truth. It is building its own truth."[17] The implication here is that, (1) inasmuch as Truth is no longer being sought, this value has been discarded and suspicion cast upon all those who once believed that Truth was this exalted thing [*hypostasis*] after which one ran or before which one bowed down. While this caricature is acknowledged to be a simplification, what we just read with regard to essence, with regard to the history of the integron, and so on, should be enough to convince us that biology still seeks the truth—of life and as life, as livingness in the

124

---

16. Handwritten note in the left margin of the typescript: "*Jenseits*."
17. Jacob, *Logic of the Living*, p. 16 [p. 24].

reproducibility of the self. As for the formulation "it is building its own truth," this implies (2) that truth can be appropriated, which is not new, and that it is specific, in its model, to each field. But we have never had more reason to doubt this specificity than after reading and even approving Jacob, who insists on the necessary and integrative cooperation between biology and the other natural sciences (first of all), on the fact that, I quote, "Contrary to what is often imagined, biology is not a unified science. The heterogeneity of its objects, the variety of its techniques and the divergent interests of its practitioners, all lead to a multiplication of disciplines."[18] Of course, one would be able to respond that the appeal (which is indispensable, as we saw) to the physico-chemical sciences is not necessarily in contradiction with the specificity of biology. As Jacob recalls in this regard, "This does not at all mean that biology has become an annex of physics, that it represents, as it were, a junior branch concerned with complex systems."[19] And, indeed, the value of complexity is not the only thing that distinguishes biology from physics: what also comes into play here is a new structure of the field of objectivity. But (secondly) even if in what Jacob still calls the natural sciences (when he says: "Like the other natural sciences, biology today has lost many of its illusions. It is no longer seeking for truth. It is building its own truth"), even if, then, in what Jacob still calls the natural sciences, among which he still locates biology, this latter had a specificity and *its* truth, one wonders how, once one has recognized the text, programming, information, the factory, and so on, as concrete models of the logic of the living, how, then, can one still oppose natural science, the science of nature, to—to what? the science of culture, of society, of man, of spirit? If there is some kind of homogeneity (differentiated but of the same type) between these productions of the living being called man (texts, in the narrow sense, computers, programs, and so on) and the functioning of genetic reproduction, the opposition between sciences of nature and other sciences loses its pertinence and its rigor, and one wonders whether biology can still claim to construct its truth, a truth of its specific field.

I said at the beginning that I wanted to put into some kind of organized relation the logic of reproduction and the question of the model (the textual model, which is not one model among others and requires, it seems to me, rethinking the entire logic of models). This will lead us—though perhaps not today—to appeal once again to what I elsewhere called the graphics of

---

18. Ibid., p. 6 [p. 14].
19. Ibid., p. 306 [p. 328].

the supplement.[20] Supplement, the word "supplement," is not something I am imposing on Jacob; it comes up repeatedly in his book, and not by chance, to define the acquisition, in the course of reproduction, of new genetic programs or new programming powers, and among these—and this is not by chance either, even though chance is on the program—are sexuality and death. In the history of genetic programs and of reproduction, sexuality and death have supervened; that is to say, they have happened, they have come to be added on unforeseeably, contrary to what we would tend spontaneously to believe. Note that Freud in *Beyond the Pleasure Principle* recalls this same fact, and we will have to read him from this point of view. In other words, we can think that the essence of the living, its reproducibility, its structure of self-reproduction, does not necessarily imply either sexuality or death. How do sexuality and death supervene upon it? How are these accidents, these accessories, integrated into the essence of certain living beings, that is, as internal properties? How do these supplements become essential functions? We will have to wait until next time to take on these questions. Today, in order to conclude, I simply want to note, by way of anticipation, *two things*:

1. Jacob does indeed identify sexuality and death as supplements, accidents, superfluous auxiliaries. He writes, for example (p. 309):

> But the two most important inventions are sex and death. Sexuality seems to have supervened early on in evolution. At first it was a kind of auxiliary of reproduction, a superfluous gadget, so to speak: nothing obliges a bacterium to make use of sexuality in order to multiply. It is the necessity of resorting to sex as a reproductive device that radically transforms the genetic system and the possibilities of variations. As soon as sexuality becomes obligatory, each genetic program is no longer formed by exactly copying a single program, but by reassorting two different programs.[21]

In other words, reduced to its minimal definition, what is here being called sexuality is not a passage from the one to the two, from the one dividing itself in two (which is what a bacterium does, reproducing itself without sexuality by dividing itself and copying itself by itself), but the passage from the copy of one by two to the copy of two by one (you will see later on the role played by this notion of copy, at the juncture of text and life). This surnumbering, this super-numeration, has an essential relation to the sexualization of self-reproduction. And it was with regard to just this that Jacob,

---

20. See Derrida, *Of Grammatology*, p. 141 sq. [p. 203 sq.].
21. Jacob, *Logic of the Living*, p. 309 [p. 330].

some twenty pages earlier, had evoked the supernumerary. I read p. 292 (in the chapter "Copy and Error"):

> Recombination only reassorts the genetic programs in populations; it does not add to them. Certain genetic elements are, however, transmitted from cell to cell and simply added to the genetic material already present. These elements constitute, as it were, supernumerary chromosomes. The instructions they contain are indispensable neither for growth nor for reproduction. But this supplement to the genetic text allows the cell to acquire new structures and perform new functions. It is an element of this type that determines sexual differentiation in certain species of bacteria, for instance. Furthermore, as it is not indispensable, the nucleic-acid sequence contained in such supernumerary elements is not subject to the constraints of stability that natural selection exercises on the bacterial chromosome. These elements represent a free supplement for the cell, a sort of reserve of nucleic-acid text that can vary freely over the course of generations.[22]

Jacob recalled that one used to believe, wrongly, in a necessary link between sexual reproduction and heredity. Bacteria, for example, have been reproducing themselves without any sexual relation, by means of simple self-division, and with great speed, for two billion years, identical to themselves. The bacterium's only goal, its only plan or project, says Jacob, is to produce two bacteria. And this is accomplished with an extraordinary fidelity, an extraordinary virtuosity. But the process is not infallible. There are errors that can always be interpreted as errors of transcription or translation, errors that are then faithfully, interminably, recopied. "There is a mutation," says Jacob,

> when the meaning of the text is altered, when a modification occurs in the nucleic-acid sequence prescribing a protein sequence, and therefore a structure fulfilling a function. Mutations result from errors *similar* [my emphasis] to those which a copyist or a printer inserts into a text. *Like a text* [my emphasis], a nucleic-acid message can be modified by the change of one sign into another, by the deletion or addition of one or more signs, by the transposition of signs from one sentence to another, by the inversion of a group of signs—in short, by anything that disturbs the pre-established order.[23]

These mutations, which are most often qualitative, transform the order of the genetic text, but they do not add to it; they reorder it without enriching

---

22. Ibid., p. 292 [p. 312].
23. Ibid., p. 289 [p. 309].

it. For example, the same segment can be recopied twice in the reproduction of a chromosome, an error that is *"similar,"* says Jacob, to that of a typographer who sets the same word or the same line twice. But there is something else. "Some bacteria," says Jacob, "have another way of supplementing their genetic program."[24] Indeed, since they are protected by a wall and do not communicate with each other, they are able to bring about transfers of genetic material either through the intermediary of viruses or through processes analogous to those involved in sexuality in so-called higher organizations. This might suggest, let it be said in passing, an analogy in function between viruses and sexuality. What is analogous to the sexual operation in this case, though Jacob does not describe this in great detail, is, for example, the fact that a segment of chromosome coming from a second individual can be substituted for a homologous segment in a first individual. This is obviously already sexuality inasmuch as two individuals are cooperating in the formation of a third; but it is not yet "real" sexuality because it is the communication of a homologous segment of chromosome, etc. But this already casts some doubt upon what is believed to be thought in a rigorous fashion as sexuality or a-sexuality. And when Jacob says real [*véritable*] (and this is the case every time one says real), one can assume that the rigor of the definition and of the criterion is lacking. Jacob writes, for example:

> Through recombination, the elements of genetic texts, genes from different individuals, can be reassorted in new combinations that sometimes offer advantages for reproduction. Even though sexuality is not really [*véritablement*] a method of reproduction for bacteria, which usually multiply by fission, it nevertheless allows the different genetic programs of the species to be mixed with the resultant appearance of new genetic types.[25]

The question of the "really" is not simple, however. It does not go so far as to undermine our statistical knowledge regarding the frequency or the probability of sexualized reproduction in bacteria, inasmuch as sexualized reproduction presupposes the transfer of something between two individuals, something that in fact happens only rarely. Yet the question of the *really* does go so far as to challenge our determination of reproduction as a-sexual when it happens through fission within a single individual that relates to itself in order to divide itself and produce a copy, so that supplementarity is perhaps intervening already here, with this auto-reproductive auto-affection of the most immured bacterium. If one is to link sexuality to

24. Ibid., p. 291 [p. 311].
25. Ibid., pp. 291–92 [p. 312].

supernumerary supplementarity, as Jacob does in the following passage, where is one to locate a beginning for all of this? This is the question that will preoccupy us next time—with regard to both sexual supplementarity and lethal or lethiferous supplementarity. Here, as I had indicated earlier, are a few other occurrences of (at least) the word supernumerary supplement. This passage immediately follows the one I just read. (Read *The Logic of the Living*, pp. 292–93):

> Recombination only reassorts the genetic programs in populations; it does not add to them. Certain genetic elements are, however, transmitted from cell to cell and simply added to the genetic material already present. These elements constitute, as it were, supernumerary chromosomes. The instructions they contain are indispensable neither for growth nor for reproduction. But this supplement to the genetic text allows the cell to acquire new structures and perform new functions. It is an element of this type that determines sexual differentiation in certain species of bacteria, for instance. Furthermore, as it is not indispensable, the nucleic-acid sequence contained in such supernumerary elements is not subject to the constraints of stability that natural selection exercises on the bacterial chromosome. These elements represent a free supplement for the cell, a sort of reserve of nucleic-acid text that can vary freely over the course of generations.
>
> Two apparently opposed properties of living beings, stability and variability, are based on the very nature of the genetic text. At the level of the individual—the bacterial cell—one observes the recopying, with extreme rigor, of a program which prescribes not only the detailed plan of each molecular structure, but the means of executing the plan and of coordinating the activities of the structures. On the other hand, at the level of the bacterial population, or of the species as a whole, the nucleic-acid text appears to be perpetually disorganized by copying errors, by recombinational spoonerisms, by additions or omissions. In the end, the text is always rectified. But it is rectified neither by a mysterious will seeking to impose its design, nor by an environmentally determined reordering of the sequence: the nucleic-acid message does not learn from experience. The message is rectified automatically by a process of selection exerted, not on the genetic text itself, but on whole organisms, or rather populations of organisms, to eliminate any irregularity. The very concept of selection is inherent in the nature of living organisms, in the fact that they exist only to the extent that they reproduce themselves. Each new individual, which by mutation, recombination, and addition becomes the carrier of a new program, is immediately put to the test of reproduction. If this organism is unable to reproduce itself, it disappears. If it is able to reproduce itself better and faster than its congeners, this advantage, however minor, immediately favors its multiplication and hence the propagation of this particular program. If in the long run the

nucleic-acid text seems to be molded by the environment, if the lessons of past experience are eventually written into it, this occurs in a roundabout way through success in reproduction. But only what exists reproduces itself. Selection operates not on possible living organisms but existent ones.[26]

Textuality, supplementarity, reproduction, and selection—those are the sites on the conceptual chain, on the same conceptual chain, that we have yet to analyze and displace.

2. The second point that I simply wanted to raise before concluding brings us back on this side of the sexual supplement, this side of the kind of reproduction that Jacob determines as sexual. If we return not only to bacteria in their simplest, a-sexual reproductive functioning, but also to the cell, and to every chemical substance within the cell, it can be said that each chemical species *is reproduced* from one generation to the next as exactly identical to itself. "But," Jacob clarifies, "each chemical species does not form copies of itself. A protein is not born of an identical protein. Proteins do not [therefore] reproduce *themselves*."[27] They depend in their organization and in their reproduction on something else that reproduces itself, spontaneously, by producing a copy of itself, and that is deoxyribonucleic acid. It is the only element in the cell capable of reproducing itself by producing "copies," says Jacob, of itself. This power to produce copies of itself stems from the fact that this acid is made up of two chains, each of them double (sugar and phosphate), and <it is> on the basis of this duplicity and the resulting internal duplication that the first textualization is produced as reproducibility. What is the relationship between this duplicity and the supplementarity we just mentioned? Jacob does not speak here of supplementarity, for it is obviously not a question here of either death or sexuality. It is right here, in this very primitive, monotonous, and archaic place that we will take up next time all these questions, in particular the question of the textual model.

---

26. Ibid., pp. 292–93 [pp. 312–13].
27. Ibid., p. 273 [p. 293].

FIFTH SESSION[1]

The Indefatigable

The concept of re-production is barely conceivable. A fortiori the concept of the reproduction of the self, of self-reproduction, of reproducing-oneself. Especially if one claims to find here an origin and an essence, the origin and the essence of the living, the internal property of the living. Especially, therefore, if reproduction of the self is not a particular capability, just one among other things, that is also compatible with life, but if one says, as we saw last week, that only the living is endowed with this capability and that the living would not be living without it. Self-reproducibility is the living itself [*le vivant*], insofar as (1) there is no living being that is not capable of it, and (2) there is no self-reproducibility that is not qualified as living. Self-reproducibility belongs only to the living.

Now this logic of self-reproducibility is, I said, barely conceivable, first of all as abstract logic. It is not one logic or concept among others, an example of logic or of a concept, for the reason, first of all, that it requires us to transform our current logic of logic and our current concept of the concept, and then, for a reason that comes before this first reason, because it is before reason, that on the basis of which logic and the concept are produced in general.

Reproducing oneself presupposes that one *already* is. As Jacob says in passing, "But only what exists reproduces itself. Selection operates not on possible living organisms but existent ones."[2] Hence the reproduction of self reproduces that which (itself) already exists. But, here, what already exists

---

1. Handwritten at the top right of the page in the typescript: "quote and comment on Ponge's Fable." Derrida is referring here to Francis Ponge's "Fable," in *Proêmes, I: Natare piscem doces* (Paris: Gallimard, 1948); quoted by Jacques Derrida in *Psyche: Inventions of the Other*, v. 1, ed. Peggy Kamuf and Elizabeth Rottenberg (Stanford, CA: Stanford University Press, 2007), p. 8.

2. Jacob, *Logic of the Living*, p. 293 [p. 313].

is the effect of a reproduction of the self. Of another self, the same. No matter how far one goes back, one will not find a reproduction that does not reproduce a re-production. An absolute production of self produces a self that is a (living) self only to the extent that and only insofar as this originary and living production is produced—produces itself—as reproducibility. The self of "producing itself" is already, in its identity, reproducibility; without this, it would have no identity. The identity of the self or of the self with itself [*de soi à soi*] is a certain reproducibility. One might say: but the non-living, that which is usually represented as non-living—the stone, for example—has an identity, and it could potentially be reproduced but it cannot reproduce *itself*. But it is precisely there that the definition of the logic of the living or of the essence of life as self-reproducibility makes of the relation to self, of the self to itself, of the self as relation to self, the essential fold of the living, the fold that makes it so that producing itself [*se produire*]—in other words, as living (only the living can produce itself)—is reproducing itself [*se reproduire*]. The *itself* [*se*] erases, as it were, the difference between producing and reproducing. In the reproducing itself [*le se-reproduire*], neither the *itself* [*se*] nor the *re-* comes to affect from without, neither of these supervenes upon, a producing that precedes them, a product that pre-exists them. That which seems to pre-exist is already a re-production [*un re-produit*] as re-production of self, a self-reproduction. And when Jacob says "only what exists reproduces itself," what exists is already a product as the effect of a self-reproduction [*un se-reproduit*]. One must therefore think the re-production of self otherwise, other than as that which comes after the fact to complicate a simple production. Producibility is from the very start reproducibility, and re-producibility is reproducibility of the self. But since the self is not before this capacity to reproduce itself, before its own reproducibility, there is no self-sufficiency or pure spontaneity before its production *as* reproduction, before its reproducibility as re-producibility. It is its reproducibility. As a result, production—the core meaning that one would want to isolate, the producing of production, the semantic core hidden within re-production and the reproduction of the self—production, therefore, the producing of production is neither thinkable nor possible before re-producibility as re-producibility of the self. The self (which is here produced as reproductive production) is obviously neither an I nor a consciousness nor a substance, not even a same [*ni même un même*], identical to itself, but rather a *selbst*. And the Hegelian work on the *selbst* would not be unhelpful for approaching the self as re-production.

All this—which I will keep from refining any further—is not an algebra or an alchemy next to which the positivity of genetic science would cut a good figure, a scientific figure, to be precise, concerned with the thing itself, a text, no doubt, but, in the end, the text as deoxyribonucleic acid, the program of bacteria, etc. Indeed you can readily see that things are not so simple. Jacob's discourse — like that of an entire modernity — takes up the concept of production or of re-production as if it were transparent, univocal, self-evident, as if there were also a clear distinction or opposition between producing and reproducing, reproducing and reproducing oneself. At no time does Jacob wonder what this means; never does he subject this concept or this word (self) production/reproduction to even the slightest critical question. And yet it is the major, the ultimate operative concept of his entire discourse. The logic of the living, the structure of the living, and so the essence of the living, are determined as productivity (re-productivity-of-self). And it is not only the re- and the *self* that are taken to be clear, the re- and the *self* that apparently qualify the producing but that in truth predetermine it; it is also the very meaning of *producing* that is taken to be clear. And one does not even question the fact that one cannot even (according to the logic of the living) lead this semantic question back to *producing*, following a classical philosophical approach that leads back to the originary act (a question of the type or of the form: what is the producing of production or what is the production of the produced?). For inasmuch as everything begins with re-production, production or producing are themselves products, that is, as a result, effects, the originary is an effect, something that complicates things in a rather singular way. Hence Jacob does not problematize, any more than anyone else, the meaning of the product of production or of production as produced. What are we saying, what do we mean to say, what do we hear when we hear the word "producing" [*produire*]? Is such a question some sort of hermeneutic alchemy from the standpoint of *The Logic of the Living*? Or does it touch upon the keystone of the entire edifice?

If all the productions of the living — what are called the productions of the living and, especially, the productions of the living being called man (culture, institutions, technē, science, biology, texts in the narrow sense of the term) — somehow have as their condition the production of the living as the reproduction of the self, and if, in addition, the supposed "models" needed to understand or to know the living are always themselves products or productions of the living, you can see not only the convoluted nature of this logic but also the urgency of asking about production and about the reproduction of the self. What does "product" mean?

The historical or historial urgency (I say "historial" because this is not a historical question, one of the questions of history or in history, but a question concerning the historical as such, inasmuch as it is itself determined on the basis of what is here put in question, history itself having a relation, in its very historicity, to the question of producing), the historial urgency of this question is signaled in particular by the fact that the notion of production everywhere comes to fill in the voids of modern discourse. These voids are not deficiencies; they mark, in their outline, the fact that we can no longer, in decisive places, use outdated values, values that are no longer fit for the times, and so we replace them regularly by production, this notion becoming the general surrogate [*vicaire*] for the determination of being. Where one can no longer say create (because only God is supposed to create and we are done with the theological), one says produce; where one can no longer say engender, express, think, and so on, where some concept is seen — and rightly so — to be importing too much from some dubious metaphysics, theology, or ideology, one calls upon producing to replace or neutralize it. You know that today one does not form a system or a theory or a concept, one does not conceive a concept, one does not express something; one produces a system of knowledge, one produces an utterance, one produces a theory, one produces an effect (one does not provoke or engender or even cause an effect, one produces an effect, one does not speak in order to say something, one does not publish a piece of writing in order to express an idea, one intervenes in order to produce a text or an utterance — and one would also have to reflect seriously upon "intervening"). I am not saying this in order to produce an effect of mockery but, on the contrary, convinced as I am of the historial necessity of this filtering and this selection, which is made first of all in order to eliminate a whole set of values implied by the notions that are excluded or replaced in this way, I am wondering what this surrogacy [*vicariance*] means. When selection or filtering is carried out in this way, an entire set of values (acting, creating, engendering, thinking, speaking, and so on, with their entire system, which is enormous) comes to be marked as irrelevant, excluded — everything except producing. What is it that one wants to keep and re-produce here? Well, it just so happens that:

1.[3] This word and this concept of production mark everything that, in this epoch, receives, whether directly or indirectly, in one mode or another, Marxist discourse or that which the general discourse reflects and calls Marxist. When I say epoch, I am designating a grouping that I do not know how to name otherwise, that I will continue to consider other names for, and that I am not offering as simply derivative of the Heideggerian discourse

---

3. This numbering does not continue.

on the epoch and epochs of being. Why, then, Marxist discourse and everything it gathers together or reflects? Well, first of all because the concept of production is undeniably a fundamental operator of Marxist discourse. Without pursuing here an analysis of how this concept functions in Marxist discourse (whether that of Marx or of other Marxists), one can at least note that even if Marx does not leave the concept of production in the state of some abstract essence, even if the fundamental concept is not simply "production" but already the complex "relations of production," even if, in his *Introduction to the Critique of Political Economy*, Marx insists on the fact that there is no production in general or general production, he deems it necessary, and it is indeed necessary, to refer to a concept or to a general meaning of "production" (even if he thinks, as he says, that we obtain it by means of a comparison, that is to say, by empirical induction, something that poses all kinds of problems: how is one to make this "comparison" without being guided in advance by some general sense of what "producing" means, etc.), it is nonetheless the case that the whole theory of historical materialism is a theory of production (of the forces of production, of the relations of production, of labor as a process of production, etc.), and it is material production, as *The German Ideology* has it, that produces, in the last instance, what Marx also calls "the production of ideas, of conceptions, of consciousness."[4] Production, productivity, is thus indeed the essence or—if this word is problematic—the general structure of human relations, of relations insofar as they are human, of humanity. And even of the living in general, for if Marx, in *Capital*, categorically opposes human productivity to animal productivity based on the fact that the latter does not first have the representation of its end "in its head," it is nonetheless the case that productivity in general is the structure of the living in general. We read in *Capital*:

> Darwin [says *Capital*] has directed attention to the history of natural technology, i.e., the formation of the organs of plants and animals, which serve as the instruments of production (*Produktionsinstrumente*) for sustaining their life. Does not the history of the productive organs (*produktiven Organe*) of man in society, of organs that are the material basis of every particular organization of society, deserve equal attention? And would not such a history be easier to compile, since, as Vico says, human history differs from natural history in that we have made the former, but not the latter?

---

4. Karl Marx and Friedrich Engels, *The German Ideology: Including Theses on Feuerbach and Introduction to the Critique of Political Economy* (Amherst, NY: Prometheus Books, 1998), p. 42 [*Deutsche Ideologie*, Karl Marx, Friedrich Engels, *Werke*, v. 3 (Berlin: Dietz Verlag, 1962), p. 26].

Technology reveals (*enthüllt*) the active relation of man to nature, the direct process of the production of his life (*den unmittelbaren Produktionsprozess seines Lebens*) . . .⁵

I will come back in a moment to this point, but I first want to go to the end of this note, where Marx criticizes, in a way that might interest and concern us today, the tenets of the abstract materialism of scientists in the natural sciences, who, as soon as they venture beyond their specialization—and because they do not have enough of a historical sense—begin to speak in an "abstract and ideological" language. One can retain at least the principle of this critique and apply it to the discourses of scientists—biologists, for example—who, when they speak in a general philosophical or epistemological register, are not vigilant enough with regard to the philosophy or the ideology that is implicit in their claims and do not sufficiently question the system and the history of the operative concepts they are using. And they turn out to be more abstract than the "philosophers," even though . . . One example, among others, would be the concept of production or of reproduction in Jacob. But perhaps also in Marx, whom I continue to quote: we are still in the same note from part 4, the chapter on "Machinery and Large-Scale Industry," section 1:

> Technology reveals the active relation of man to nature, the direct process of the production of his life, and thereby it also lays bare the process of the production of the social relations of his life, and of the mental conceptions that flow from those relations. Even a history of religion that is written in abstraction from this material basis is uncritical. It is, in reality, much easier to discover by analysis the earthly kernel of the misty creations of religion than to do the opposite (*als umgekehrt*), i.e., to develop from the actual, given relations of life (*Lebensverhältnissen*) the forms in which these have been apotheosized (*verhimmelten*). The latter method is the only materialist, and therefore the only scientific one. The weaknesses of the abstract materialism of natural science, a materialism which excludes the historical process, are immediately evident from the abstract and ideological conceptions expressed by its spokesmen whenever they venture beyond the bounds of their own specialty.⁶

That said, when Marx says that it is easier to write the history of the human process of production because it is a history that we have made, this argument, which is not entirely convincing, relies in any case upon a recurrent

---

5. Karl Marx, *Capital: A Critique of Political Economy*, v. 1, trans. Ben Fowkes (New York: Vintage Books, 1977), pp. 493–94n4 [*Das Kapital: Kritik der politischen Ökonomie*, in Karl Marx, Friedrich Engels, *Werke*, v. 23 (Berlin: Dietz Verlag, 1968), pp. 392–93n89].
6. Ibid.

distinction in Marx concerning the so-called natural and animal process of production and the human process of production. Not only, as I recalled earlier, is human production distinct from animal or natural production, inasmuch as it first has a representation of its end, but also, especially, and this is more interesting, human production produces not only products but productions and means of production. Man, unlike animals, produces his means of existence and his means of production. And in this way he produces re-production. But this production of re-production or of reproducibility, this producibility as re-producibility, is rigorously distinguished by Marx from biological or natural reproducibility. His distinction is thus multipronged: it runs first of all between human production and animal production, insofar as the former produces its means of production and (technical, technological) reproduction; it then runs between this reproducibility and what is commonly called the reproduction of life or the biological conditions of life. We read this in *The German Ideology*, and we could find confirmation for it in *Capital*:

> The first premise [presupposition: *Voraussetzung*] of all human history is, of course, the existence of living human individuals. Thus the first fact to be established is the physical organization of these individuals and their consequent relation to the rest of nature. Of course, we cannot here go into the actual physical nature of man. . . .
> Men can be distinguished from animals by consciousness, by religion or anything else you like. They themselves begin to distinguish themselves from animals as soon as they begin to *produce* [underscored by Marx: *zu produzieren*] their *Lebensmittel*, a step which is conditioned by their physical organization. By producing their means of subsistence (*Lebensmittel*) men are indirectly producing their material life.
> The way in which men produce their means of subsistence depends first of all on the nature of the means of subsistence they actually find in existence and have to reproduce.
> This mode of production must not be considered simply as being the reproduction (*Reproduktion*) of the physical existence of the individuals. Rather it is a definite form of activity of these individuals, a definite form of expressing their life [of exteriorizing it, rather, *äussern*: I insist on this production as exteriorization; the translations often say to manifest, to express, and that is not wrong: the important thing here is this pro-ducing as conducting to the light of day, putting forward, making come forth, a traditional determination that is present not only in the Latin *pro-ducere* but in the Greek and Aristotelian determination of technē (see Heidegger: technē, truth, *physis*, and so on)], a definite *mode of life* (*eine bestimmte Lebensweise*) on their part. As individuals express (*äussern*) their life [the French transla-

tion of the Éditions Sociales has here *"manifestent"* their life], so they are. [The German text says the following: *"Wie die Individuen ihr Leben äussern, so sind sie"*: As individuals express or manifest their life, so they are; in other words, they are their production as manifestation, being, the production and manifestation of life are equivalent, Marx insists. Thus:] What they are, therefore, coincides with their production (*Was sie sind, fällt also zusammen mit ihrer Produktion*), both with *what* they produce [*was*, underscored, *sie produzieren*] and with *how* they produce [*wie*, underscored, *sie produzieren*]. Hence what individuals are depends on the material conditions of their production.[7]

One is thus what one produces and how one produces, and the mode of being is the mode of production as manifestation of self or as exteriorization. Within this general determination of being as life and as production, Marx therefore distinguishes the production of animal life from the production of human life, biological re-production from the re-production of the conditions of production in human technology. Another remarkable feature, therefore, is that production in its essential determination as being, life, or manifestation is immediately defined as linked to the condition of re-production. Once again re-producibility is not an accident that supervenes upon production but the very essence of production. This is also very clear in the passages from *Capital* that we read together last year concerning ideology.[8] At the beginning of the seventh section, chapter 23, on "Simple Reproduction," Marx posits the following as essential premises for the entire analysis of the modes of capitalist production and reproduction in general — and this is a general law: "The conditions of production are at the same time the conditions of reproduction. No society can go on producing, in other words no society can reproduce, unless it constantly reconverts a part of its products into means of production, or elements of fresh products."[9] I leave aside the question of non-simple — or expanded — reproduction, since we spoke about this last year, but you can well imagine the interest it might have for us here from the perspective of what we said earlier about the program "supplements" of genetic production. In any case, we can see from this last passage that, on the one hand, there is no production that is not re-production, no producibility that is not in its very structure

---

7. Marx, *German Ideology*, p. 37 [pp. 20–21].

8. Derrida appears to be referring to his 1974–75 seminar "GREPH (the concept of ideology in the French ideologues)."

9. Marx, *Capital*, p. 711 [p. 591]; [Translators' note:] This is chapter 21 (not 23) in the English translation cited.

re-producibility, the *re-* of re-petition being neither simply secondary nor supervening nor simply re-petitive, a repetition of the identical, since it is the re- of a production that is perpetual and constantly in the process of transforming and generating structural supplements. And we can also see, on the other hand, that linked to this predicate of manifestation, of bringing to the light of day, to the light of the outside, a predicate that characterized all production, is the predicate of transformation, of putting matter into form, of transformative-information, which brings us back again to the function of *technē* in its relations with form (*morphē, eidos*, etc.) in Aristotle. As the essence of being as life (*physis*), production is at once manifestation and in-formation.

No more in Marx than in Jacob is there a question—I will not say a philosophical question but a question bearing on the philosophical—concerning the philosophical tradition or philosophical program working with, or let us say again producing, the general concept of production to which they nonetheless resort. Whatever the concrete determinations that both of them bring to this productivity (biological and animal or technical and human, natural or historical), they both imply that we understand one another when we say or write "production." But what is it that we understand? How does this supposed obviousness of everyday meaning function? And there is no question either about this strange logic that, through the unusual play of the *re*, places both identity and difference in the very structure of a concept or of an operation that begins only with its own re-production, with the re-production of production. No question either about the fact that, even if one distinguishes, by means of traditional oppositions, between nature and technics, nature and history, natural life and the life of history, or spirit, or society, or human society, between animal and man, etc., one still has to have some idea of the common semantic horizon that allows one to speak of production and re-production, of production as re-production in both cases, on both sides of the opposition.[10]

Once again, these are not the questions of a philologist, or even of a philosopher (since it is a matter of philosophemes that philosophy does not problematize any more than science does), but questions about the functioning of a certain number of discourses—even discourses that, within a certain field at least, are dominant—discourses that, as scientific as they may be up to a certain point, and up to that point their scientificity is not in question, none-

---

10. There is here in the transcript an arrow followed by the handwritten notation: "ANALOGY."

theless need an uncriticized, unquestioned operational support, the notion of production in this case, in order to ground all their scientificity. And this support is obviously a philosopheme (the determination of being as *physis-technē-alētheia*-life, manifestation-information: production of essentiality as maximal re-production of self, presentation of self—for what does to produce mean if not to present—etc.). And this philosopheme, which, at a certain moment, takes hold of the entire foundation, supports the selection necessary for the progress of science, the exclusion of the non-scientific, etc., this dominating philosopheme serves science, of course, but it is also through the body of this philosopheme that all the non-critical operations are going to pass—and right along with them, and thanks to them, all the impositions that are called, in Marxist language, a Marxist language linked to the philosopheme "production," *ideology*.

Suffice it to say that we will not be able to give questions of this type the ultimate form, the ultimate critical form, of a "what is production-reproduction?" "what is it in the end to produce or reproduce?" or "what is the meaning of producing/re-producing or producing-reproducing-oneself?" The kind of being [*être*] involved in the "What is?" ("What is it?" or "What does it mean?") has a now all-too-obvious relation of synonymy with this producing-reproducing-oneself (through the information, the manifestation, the presentation of one's own essence, truth, etc., etc.) for this question not to be what I will call a tautological question, that is, a question dominated by its object, a question that takes the form of its object. The question "What is being?" to which it amounts is not itself a question; it is a contract with the self whereby the self divides and augments itself at the same time, produces-reproduces itself in dividing itself.

Like bacteria.

Between what bacteria do—with or without sex, dividing themselves in order to multiply and return to themselves, in order to reproduce themselves by losing themselves, etc.—and what gets done through the question "What is being?" (with or without copulation), there is a—a what? I will certainly not say a continuity or a homogeneity, or an opposition, since opposition amounts to the same thing—there is the greatest difference in the world, they are worlds apart, as they say, but there is a world if we are to call *world* this unity without totality or homogeneity that nonetheless allows us to think together, according to a logic that is neither that of the *is* [est] nor that of the *and* [et], neither that of identity nor that of opposition, *différance* (for example, between the contract of the bacterium with itself and the contract of science or philosophy in its own operations).

Does the emergence within this world of the question *what is?* (and everything that follows upon it) have an essential relation, in some way, with this "invention," to take up again Jacob's term, of sexuality and death, a joint invention that calls forth numerous times the word "supplement" on Jacob's part without the logic or the graphic of the supplement ever being questioned or "produced" for itself, assuming it can ever be produced for itself?

Sexuality and death—this is a single "supplement," according to Jacob. Hence the bacterium, insofar as it is without sexual reproduction (we saw last time that it was more complicated than that, but let us put that aside for the moment and consider the hypothesis of a bacterium completely without sexuality, without sexual encounters or transfers of viruses or of homogeneous chromosomal segments from one individual to another), this bacterium without sex (without sex appeal,[11] Jacob also says) does not die, says Jacob. What is he saying here, what does he mean? The bacterium's only "plan," its only "ambition"—these are Jacob's parodic words—is "continually to strive to produce two bacteria."[12] Or again:

> Structure, function, and chemistry of the bacterial cell, all have been refined for this end: to produce two organisms identical to itself, as well as possible, as quickly as possible, and under the most varied of circumstances. If the bacterial cell is to be considered as a factory, it must be a factory of a special kind. The products of human technology are totally different [?][13] from the machines that produce them, and therefore totally different from the factory itself [?]. The bacterial cell, on the other hand, makes its own [?] constituents; the ultimate product is identical with itself. The factory produces; the cell reproduces itself.[14]

I will not pause here on all the elegant approximations contained in each of these formulations. There is not a single rigorous word in any of these statements. But that is not what I wanted to insist on today. This description leads Jacob to posit that in this system of simple reproduction of the

---

11. Jacob, *Logic of the Living*, 318 [p. 339]. [Translators' note:] "Sex appeal" in English in the original.

12. Ibid., pp. 270–71 [pp. 290–91].

13. The three question marks between brackets in this quotation were added by Derrida in the typescript.

14. Jacob, *Logic of the Living*, p. 271 [p. 291].

bacterium neither sexuality nor, *as a result*, death are essential constituents, and that, therefore, as a result, they both come as supplements, as if from the outside. It is this link between sexuality and death, on the one hand, and this value of the outside, <on the other,> that I wish to insist on for a moment. For Jacob, there is no bacterial sexuality because fission is produced within an organic individual and such fission excludes or does not need the intervention of another individual, another individual system, another program. For the same reason, there is no death because death does not come from inside; it consists in a dilution of identity, of the entity, says Jacob, through the simple disappearance and exhaustion of the reproductive capacity. I spoke last time about how confused and barely coherent the concept of sexuality that led to all these analyses appeared. Could we not say the same thing about the concept of death?

Here is what Jacob writes on p. 297:

> The little bacterial cell is so arranged that the whole system can reproduce itself as often as once every twenty minutes. With bacteria, unlike organisms which reproduce only sexually, birth is not *compensated* [my emphasis] by death. When bacterial cultures grow, the individual bacteria do not die. They disappear as individual entities: where there was only one, suddenly there are two. The molecules of the "mother" [quotation marks: no more a mother than a father] are distributed equally among her "daughters."[15]

"Daughters" is in quotation marks. But is it because *"la bactérie"* is, in French, a feminine noun or because bacteria have no sex that Jacob says mother and daughter rather than father and son or mother and son or father and daughter, or because in some systems of sexual reproduction it is the mother who seems to engender by dividing herself—I leave all these questions suspended . . . on Jacob's ladder, perhaps, the top of which, in the dream of the same, reached into the heavens above the angels, of whom it is not said whether they had a sex, these angels constantly ascending and descending while God, from over the top of the ladder, promised the dreamer that he would reproduce and that his offspring would spread across the earth like dust. The day before, I believe, Yahweh had said to him: "You shall not take a wife from the daughters of Canaan" (Genesis 28:1). I return to my quotation:

> When bacterial cultures grow, the individual bacteria do not die. They disappear as individual entities: where there was only one, suddenly there are two. The molecules of the "mother" are distributed equally among her

15. Ibid., p. 297 [p. 317].

"daughters." For instance, the mother contained a long duplex of deoxyribonucleic acid that splits into two before cell division. Each daughter [no longer in quotation marks] receives one of these identical duplexes, each of which is formed by an "old" chain and a "new" one. One of the criteria that a bacterium is no longer alive is its inability to reproduce itself. If this non-life is to be seen as death, it is a contingent death. It often depends on the milieu and on the conditions of the culture. When a small part of a culture is continuously replaced by a new milieu, such a culture remains in a state of perpetual growth: bacteria go on reproducing eternally.

What makes an individual ephemeral in a bacterial population is not, therefore, death in the usual sense, but dilution entailed by growth and multiplication.[16]

What is this passage saying, then, about the death of an organism whose reproduction is said to be a-sexual? It says, if I may paraphrase, that in reproduction without sexuality (through the internal fission of a single individual), there is no death. If we look more closely at this "there is no death," what do we see? There is no explicit death in "there is no death *in the usual sense*." That is, the passage from life to non-life is not a death in this usual sense, which is thus taken as the rigorous sense. And why is that? Because the passage of the bacterium to non-life through the inability to reproduce itself is a "contingent" death. Let me recall the phrase: ". . . its inability to reproduce itself. If this non-life is to be seen as death, it is a contingent death," and then a bit further on, it is "not, therefore, death in the usual sense."

What Jacob thus calls death in the usual sense, and thus, according to him, the only death worthy of the name *death*, is a death that is not limited to a non-life, a death that is not contingent, contingent meaning here "coming from the outside," affecting from the outside. Indeed, as you have seen, this contingency, which restricts death to a simple non-life, which prevents the bacterium from having a right to death, to its own death, this contingency stems from the fact that death depends on the outside, depends on the milieu. Let me reread so that things can become clear: "If this non-life is to be seen as death, it is a contingent death. It often depends [I have to say that this "often" introduces into a discourse that considers itself to be scientific with regard to the distinction between inside and outside, death and non-life, a murkiness that I would call *cultural*] on the milieu and on the conditions of the culture." And Jacob does not hesitate to speak of eternity in the hypothetical case of a milieu that would be constantly renewed. Notice that he does not say — another problem with these statements, which I find

16. Ibid., p. 297 [pp. 317–18].

to be extremely imprecise wherever we are in the vicinity of questions of death and sexuality — that a particular bacterium would reproduce itself eternally if the external milieu were always new; he says: "bacteria go on reproducing themselves eternally," which is something totally different from saying that death does not happen to a bacterium.

Let us consider a bit more the claim that has just been advanced.

1. A death coming from the outside (determined here as milieu) is not death (in the proper sense of the term, determined here on the basis of the "usual sense"). This non-life is a non-death, this non-life is not a death. The non-life that comes from the outside to the bacterium is not a death. A strange statement, whose formal, logical consequence is double, bifid. Saying that the non-life that happens to the bacterium is a non-death can be inverted into "life is death": real life is real death [*la vraie vie est la vraie mort*]. It seems to me that this consequence is not absent from Jacob's text, which will go on to show that death must be internal and essential to life in order really [*vraiment*] to be death (a double consequence: for the bacterium and for man). But another, just as logical a consequence can be drawn from this same statement, namely, that insofar as real death never touches the bacterium, and insofar as the bacterium is alive inasmuch as it reproduces itself (for that is the criterion), the life of the bacterium (the a-sexual life multiplying itself by the simple division of the one) is invulnerable, it is a life that is pure and immune from all negativity. Death does not touch it, it passes over it as its outside, etc. . . .

2. There is a death in the proper sense of the term — that is to say, in the usual sense — and Jacob asserts that it must be neither contingent (coming from the outside rather than from some internal process of the organic individual) nor, therefore, external. It must not come to be added on from the outside as an accidental fact but must be governed by an internal law of being, of essence, of reproducibility, and thus of life, of livingness. It must thus not have the status of an addition or a supplement.

And yet, and here is the paradox of the graphics of the supplement, something to which Jacob pays absolutely no attention: this death as an internal prescription within those living beings that reproduce sexually, this non-supplementary death intervenes in the chain of non-sexual reproduction like a supplement. You will recall the passages I quoted last time linking sexuality and death through the words "supplement," "superfluous," "supernumerary," etc. One would thus have to admit, for sexuality as well as for death, that these two "inventions," supervening from the outside, quasi-accidentally, consist in bringing inside, in inscribing as an internal law, the very thing that comes from the outside. What the supplement brings in

149

from the outside is an internal supplement, such that all these oppositions that Jacob takes up with such confidence (necessary/contingent, internal/external, organism/milieu, etc., and as a result non-sexuality/sexuality, life/non-life) break down, and this forces him, without him ever reflecting upon this law, to make either formally contradictory statements or empirical approximations in which the conceptual sharpness of certain claims gives way, dissipates, or loses its edge. Let me try to give some examples of this by reading the page that concerns death, the invention of death, which comes immediately after the passage concerning the invention of sexuality. Read *The Logic of the Living*, pp. 309–12], and comment, in particular on "error/event":

> The other necessary condition for the very possibility of evolution is death. Not death from the outside, as the result of some accident; but death imposed from within, as a necessity prescribed from the egg onward by the genetic program itself. For evolution is the result of a struggle between what was and what is to be, between the conservative and the revolutionary, between the sameness of reproduction and the newness of variation. In organisms reproducing by fission, the dilution of an individual caused by the rapidity of growth is sufficient to erase the past. But in multicellular organisms, with differentiation into somatic and germ lines, with sexual reproduction, individuals have to disappear. This is the resultant of two opposite forces: an equilibrium between sexual effectiveness on one hand, with its cortège of gestation, care and training; and the disappearance of the generation that has completed its role in reproduction on the other. The adjustment of these two parameters by the effect of natural selection determines the maximum duration of life of a species. The whole system of evolution, at least in animals, is based on such an equilibrium. The limits of life cannot be left to chance. They are prescribed by the program which, from the moment the ovule is fertilized, fixes the genetic destiny of the individual. The mechanism of ageing is not yet known. The theory at present most favored considers senescence as the result of accumulated errors, either in the genetic programs contained in somatic cells or in the way these programs are expressed, that is, in the proteins produced by the cells. According to this theory, the cell might cope with a certain number of errors, but once beyond this point, it would be doomed to die. In time, errors accumulated in an increasing number of cells would cause the inevitable extinction of the organism. The very way the program is executed would, therefore, determine the length of life. However this may be, death is an integral part of the system selected in the animal world and its evolution. Much may be hoped from what today is called "biological engineering [*le génie biologique*]": the cures for many scourges, cancer, heart disease, men-

tal illness; the replacement of various organs with grafts or artificial parts; a cure for some failings of old age; the correction of certain genetic defects; even the temporary interruption of active life to be resumed at will later. But there is very little chance that it will ever be possible to prolong life beyond a certain limit. The constraints of evolution can hardly be reconciled with the old dream of immortality.

The arsenal of genetics favors mainly changes in quality of the program, not in its quantity. In fact, evolution is first expressed by increased complexity. A bacterium is the translation of a nucleic-acid sequence about one millimeter long and containing some twenty million signs. Man is the result of another nucleic-acid sequence, about two meters long and containing several thousand million signs. The more complicated the organization, the longer the program. Evolution became possible, through the relationship established between the structure of the organism in space and the linear sequence of the genetic message. The complexity in integration is then expressed by the simplicity of an addition. The known mechanisms of genetics, however, favor variations of the program but hardly ever provide it with any supplement. There are, to be sure, copying errors that repeat certain segments of the message, genetic fragments that viruses can transfer, or even supernumerary chromosomes. But these processes are not very effective. It is hard to see how they could be sufficient to cause some of the major stages in evolution: the change in cellular organization from the simple or "procaryotic" form of bacteria to the complex or "eucaryotic" form of yeasts and higher organisms; or the transition from the unicellular to the multicellular state; or the appearance of vertebrates. Each of these stages, in fact, corresponds to a rather important increase in nucleic acid. These sudden increases can have occurred only by making the most of some exceptional chance event, such as an error in reproduction providing extra chromosomes, or even some exceptional process, such as a symbiosis of organisms or the fusion of genetic programs from distinct species. The fact that symbioses can indeed take part in evolution is now proved by the nature of "mitochondria," these organelles responsible for producing energy in complex cells; by all biochemical criteria, they bear the stamp of bacteria. They even have their own nucleic-acid sequence independent of the chromosomes of the host cell. In all likelihood, they are vestiges of bacteria that once associated with another organism to form the ancestor of our cells. As to fusions of genetic programs, they are known in plants, but not in animals, which are protected by a safety mechanism from the effects of the "abominable couplings" dear to antiquity and the Middle Ages. Cells from different species, however, have recently been fused in laboratory cultures, human and mouse cells, for example. Each possessing both the human and mouse programs, these hybrid cells multiply perfectly. What abnormal couplings between different species cannot achieve may nevertheless be accomplished in other ways. Were such encounters able, even exceptionally, to have consequences, this is enough to provide an opportunity for very profound changes. In practice, nothing proves that such accidents occur in nature; but in theory they are not impossible. There is no regularity in the expansions of program. There are sudden changes, unexpected increases, unexplained decreases, with no relation to the complexity of the organism. Very unusual events are required to fit enlargements of program into the rhythm of evolution. This shows how illusory any hope of estimating the duration or evaluating the probabilities of evolution is today. One day perhaps, computers will calculate what the chances were of man appearing on earth.[17]

152   Recourse on the part of the scientist to "death in the usual sense" in order to sustain a discourse on death in the proper sense, recourse on the part of the scientist to "real sexuality" in order to sustain a discourse on sexuality in the proper sense — that is what fails, and for reasons that are no longer essential or necessary but supplementary, necessarily supplementary. We thus witness here a heroic,[18] properly philosophical effort on the part of the scientist (for I am not reading here a scientist from a philosophical point of view but a philosopher still from the point of view of a science that would no longer be philosophical, perhaps no longer scientific either, and so, perhaps, more in conformity with the philosophical representation of science), a philosophical effort, then, to reconstitute conceptual oppositions or essentialities wherever the logic of opposition (whether dialectical or not) or the logic of essence is no longer pertinent. This effort attempts always to isolate or to purify certain models (pure models, therefore) that would allow one to use with confidence a binary or dialectical logic, that is, that would facilitate the mastery of certain programs that are impervious, in the end, to the supplement, or in which the supplement itself is incorporated into the program.

This purification of the model, taken to the ideal limit, already constructs the whole fable of *the* bacterium [la *bactérie*] as pure and purely a-sexual reproducibility. We know — and Jacob knows better than anyone else — that there is not in this sense *the* bacterium. There is a certain unstable quantity (even if it is very large, indeed a majority) of bacteria reproducing themselves in this way — more or less. But there are also mutations, which geneticists describe as sudden and "spontaneous" at the same time as they acknowledge the influence of the milieu, which is in contradiction with the

---

17. Ibid., pp. 309–12 [pp. 331–33].
18. The word "heroic" is crossed out by hand in the typescript.

idea of spontaneity. There are especially genetic recombinations, very recently discovered, in bacteria, two organisms combining their genetic material in order to give birth to a different individual. Reproduction of a sexual kind, therefore, according to Jacob's definition. And Wollmann emphasized — as early as 1925 — the existence and the importance of what he called "paraheredity."[19] One should thus already be speaking here of sexuality and of death for such bacteria (it takes two to reproduce sexually and thus two to die). There are especially the phenomena of "conjugation" — which Jacob discusses very little; they were discovered by Lederberg and Tatum and are described as an "equivalent of sexual reproduction": but what is an equivalent in this domain? In these phenomena of "conjugation" we see the insertion of genetic material from one cell into another. Naturally the cell that does the inserting is called the "male" cell and the cell that receives the "female." The donating (male) bacterium also comes to be characterized as "male" based on the fact that there is a transmittable sexual factor located within it, the episome. In other words, sexuality, properly speaking, would be present in such cases only in the male cell (the donating, inserting, transmitting cell). There are also what are called phenomena of transformation, which Jacob does not mention, if I recall correctly. According to a 1944 discovery (by Avery) concerning pneumococci, when one of two microbial strains is, as they say within quotation marks, "killed," the other, which is called "receptive," and living, appropriates the DNA-remains [*extraits*] of death, of the dead one, remains that then float in the ambient milieu. In the course of this ceremony whereby the receiver (female, therefore!) appropriates what might be called the sperm of the dead, it is only a tiny fragment that penetrates and gets integrated into the chromosome of the receptress. There are also phenomena of transduction through the intermediary of a bacteriophage, etc. No matter the frequency or rarity of these phenomena, no matter their partial character (without cellular fusion, etc.), they nonetheless signal, simply by being possible, that such things can always happen to the "pure" bacterium as a model of reproduction without sexuality and without death, pure inside or pure outside, pure inside of living reproducibility or pure surface able to receive death only from the outside as contingent.

I do not want to conclude from all this that there has always already been sexuality or death or that, according to the simple reversal, there will never

---

19. The reference here is to Eugène and Elisabeth Wollmann's research at the Institut Pasteur, in particular their 1925 study "Sur la transmission 'parahéréditaire' de caractères chez les bactéries."

yet have been sexuality or death, but rather that if "science" or "philosophy" must speak of sexuality or of death, the oppositions positive/negative, more/less, inside/outside, along with the logic of the either/or, of the *and* [*et*] or of the *is* [*est*], no longer suffice.

What I mean to say is that the concept of *model* is always there to mask the fact that such a logic no longer suffices.

I was not able to come back today to this question of model—and to the question of the text as model—as I had formulated or announced it last time. I will do so next week. You are perhaps already better able to see the stakes of the question. If the text, the word "text," functions as a model to reappropriate the graphic of the supplement for a traditional logic (which it sometimes does), then it will have to be subjected to the same kinds of questions as those I tried to begin asking today. Or else, another hypothesis, "text" names that which resists, that is, the structure that the text imposes on the concept of model designates that which resists that old and indefatigable [*increvable*] logic of opposition. When I say it is indefatigable, I do not mean that one might, in the end, heroically defeat it or destroy it, but only that one can try to think the indefatigable as such.

I will take up this question of the text again next time, and I will let myself be led to it by two sentences from Jacob that I will simply quote today in order to conclude: p. 305, "The genetic message can be translated only by the products of its own translation."[20] And, p. 316, "since Gödel we know that a logical system is not sufficient for its own description."[21]

---

20. Jacob, *Logic of the Living*, p. 305 [p. 326].
21. Ibid., p. 316 [p. 337].

SIXTH SESSION[1]

The "Limping" Model[2]
The Story of the Colossus

As for the question under discussion—the text and the model, the text as model, the model as text, the model-text—let me recall the statements from Jacob that I left you with last week:

1. "The genetic message can be translated only by the products of its own translation."[3]
2. "Since Gödel we know that a logical system is not sufficient for its own description."[4]

What is the common implication of these two propositions? Well, first of all, a paradoxical necessity: one can comprehend a set only with the help of one of its elements (products or parts), which amounts to the impossibility *both* of comprehending it or translating it within a larger set *and* of it

---

1. On a piece of letterhead from the École Normale Supérieure that precedes this session, there are several handwritten words. In the left margin, "The indefatigable [*L'increvable*]"; at the top of the page is a list of words that was subsequently crossed out: "a priori synthetic judgment / dialectic / Hegel / Nietzsche / aphorism / fragment." Then there is the poem by Francis Ponge, "Fable": "Par le mot *par* commence donc ce texte / Dont la première ligne dit la vérité / Mais ce tain sous l'une et l'autre / peut-il être toléré / Cher lecteur déjà tu juges / Là de nos difficultés / (Après *sept ans de malheur* / *Elle brisa le mirroir*)." (The italics are Ponge's.)

[By the word *by* begins thus this text / Of which the first line says the truth, / But this tain under the one and the other / Can it be tolerated? / Dear reader already you judge / As to our difficulties there. / (After *seven years of misfortune* / *She broke the mirror*.)]

2. [Translators' note:] The French here, "Le modèle 'boite,'" "The 'limping' model," could—with the addition of an accent—be read as "The 'box [*boîte*]' model," a reference, perhaps, to the Russian dolls with which this session concludes.

3. Jacob, *Logic of the Living*, p. 305 [p. 326].

4. Ibid., p. 316 [p. 337].

comprehending or comprising *itself* [se *comprendre*], at least according to a common logic of comprehension whereby the part is comprised by the whole, a set by a larger set. That said, the two propositions, at this level of formality, amount to the same, strangely, albeit by saying two apparently contradictory things. The first posits a possibility: a message can be translated (analyzed, described, transmitted, understood) on the sole condition of its being translated by itself, that is, by its products. The other proposition says: if a system is described on the basis of one of its elements (products or effects), it is not described, it is not sufficient for its own description. If I return to the example of the fable "By the word *by* [*par le mot* par] begins thus this text," this set describes itself well, it translates itself, it says the truth about itself, and it says it with the help of (by) one of its internal elements (by). It is in deciphering this message, in translating it with the help of what it translates, that I can at once produce the message and translate it. Its translation is its production. The word *by* (in italics) is an element that functions outside the system (metalinguistically, if you will) to describe the system, but it is borrowed from within the system. And there is no referent external to the system. At the same time, the second occurrence of the word *by* has descriptive or translational pertinence only to the extent that it repeats the first occurrence, though this first occurrence is not the occurrence of a translation or description translated or described but one that is already translating or describing. The text does not begin by the word by but by the word by begins thus this text. The logic of the *thus* presupposes here that the text begins by its translation or its description or its reproduction; and this syntactical order, which begins by the translation and not by the translated, by the translating and not the translated, has as its simultaneous effect—the effect of an irreducible syntax and not of simple semantics—that the text is a whole [*ensemble*] that can be translated or comprehended and at the same time a whole that cannot be translated or comprehended. It says everything about itself but says nothing about itself since what it says about itself is always a part of itself and not the whole. Without the translating event there would be nothing to translate. Without the event of trans-lation [*tra-duction*] or of re-production there would be no product and no production. This whole comprehends or comprises itself and does not comprehend or comprise itself. For that to happen, what is needed is a double occurrence of the same, such that the second is a part of the first whole [*ensemble*] (the second *by* is a segment of the whole sequence "by the word by," by the word X, but this segment must reproduce identically, with only a numerical difference, the origin of the entire sequence): this works only if the word is the same and if one can substitute the second for the first. The tain that is mentioned just after is what makes the very structure of the fabulous event at once opaque and specular. Opacity is the condition of specularity inasmuch as this opacity is produced at the limit, as the limit between one part and the other, one part and the other part of the same *par*. The *tain* is this strange limit that blocks the transparency of the system to itself and yet allows it to be reflected, to reflect itself without comprehending itself.

This fabulous event is not what is usually called an event, that is, what is called a real event that can become the referent of a narrative, of a narration, of a history, in short, of a language or a writing that has an object, that has to do with something. Here the event is a text: "by the word by begins thus this text"; it is a text-event that reproduces itself, that is to say, that takes itself as a referent, that has as a reference a text, and that not only reproduces itself but also induces itself as reproduction, begins by its reproduction, its *repro-traduction*.[5] When the first event, the real origin, etc., is a text, has the structure of a text, this fabulous adventure can always be reproduced. That is what happens with the living if it has the structure of a text. Note that I say a text and not a spoken word, not a verbal, a-textual language. It goes without saying that the genetic text is not verbal, that it is aphonic, so I will not insist on that. Let me insist instead on the fact that the textuality of an event of the type "by the word by begins thus this text" is constituted as textuality (whence its analogy with the structure of the living) by the fact that it is dominated neither by words nor by a semantic content, neither by an intention nor by a meaning. We have seen that the same semantic content arranged in a different order (this text begins by the word by) can yield an utterance that might well describe or translate or reproduce the first (utterance B translating utterance A) but that would fail to translate or reproduce itself. The reading of the other does not read itself, does not comprehend itself. It is only within a larger textual system, using a part or a product of itself to decipher itself, that one will be able to say that the utterance "this text begins by the word by" can be translated and reproduced. But the largest system, the general code, has the structure of the utterance "by the word by begins thus this text" insofar as it can be translated only by the products of its translation, insofar as the structure, the syntax, or the order comes first and determines the effects of meaning or intention, insofar as this syntactical structure is, by definition, dominated or determined not by nouns, that is, by referential terms that have a reference outside the text or outside the utterance, but by syntactical articulations that are directed, in the final

158

---

5. In the left margin of the typescript is this handwritten addition: "translation, its deciphering is part of it, and even constitutes it, institutes it."

analysis, at elements that are a part of the text, that remark the text. That the consistency or the remaining [*restance*] of an event, even if it is made up of words and even if it is vocal, has to do with a system of markings as re-markings, double markings, etc.—that is what imposes on us the necessity of speaking here of text or of writing rather than of speech. And that is why the notion of the text imposes itself on the science of the living, and not only imposes itself more than the notion of spoken language (that goes without saying, since there is no voice or words in genetic programs) but (and this goes less without saying for biologists such as Jacob and others) imposes itself even more than the notion of message, information, or communication. There are, to be sure, message, information, and communication effects, but only on the condition that these are, in the final analysis, textual, that is to say, that the message, the communication, or the information never transmits, never emits, never communicates, never informs any content that is not itself of the order of message, information, or communication, that is not itself, therefore, a trace or a gramme. Information does not inform one of something, communication does not communicate something, the message does not emit something that is not in itself already a message, a communication, or a piece of information. The message emits a message: that seems to be a tautology, but it nonetheless runs contrary to what seems to be common sense. The message does not transmit something, it says nothing, it communicates nothing: what it transmits has the same structure as itself, that is to say, it is a message, and it is this transmitted message that is going to allow one to decipher or to translate the emitting message, which thus implies the absence of anything at all outside the message, outside information, outside communication. It is because of this that we must specify here that the words *communication*, *information*, and *message* are intratextual and operate only on the condition of the text, contrary to what they ordinarily lead us to think, namely, that they communicate, inform, or emit something. Naturally, this textual self-reference, this closing upon itself of a text that refers only to text, has nothing tautological or autistic about it. On the contrary. It is because alterity is there irreducible that there is only text; it is because no term, no element, is itself sufficient or even has an effect, referring as it always does to the other and never to itself, that there is text; and it is because the whole that text is cannot close upon itself that there is only text, and that what is called the "general" text (an obviously dangerous and merely polemical expression) is neither a whole nor a totality: it can neither comprehend itself nor be itself comprehended. But it can be written and read, which is something else.

Is this not the situation — a text without external reference, completely outside because without any other reference than a text remarking a text — is this not, in the end, the situation of the text of biogenetics, which is written about a text of which it is a part or of which it is the product, which is written about an object or a referent that is itself not only already a text but a text without which the scientific text — itself a product of the living — would not be able to be written? The scientific text is indeed in the situation that Jacob describes within and with regard to its object, that is, the living cell: it is one of those translators that are to the genetic message the product, as it were, of its translation. The activity of the scientist, science, the text of genetic science taken as a whole are all determined as products of their object, if you will, products of the life that they study, textual products of the text that they translate or decipher or whose procedures of deciphering they decipher. And that which appears as a limit to objectivity is also, by virtue of the structural law according to which a message can be translated only by the very products of its own translation, the condition of scientificity in this domain, the condition of the effectuation of science (and of all the sciences). It is on this condition that translation or deciphering (a deciphering that is neither objective, in the traditional sense of this term, nor subjective, neither a hermeneutics of meaning nor an unveiling of truth), it is on this condition that intra-textual deciphering is possible in this textual science without extra-textual reference, etc.

If this is the case — and here is where I come back to the question of the model as I had begun treating it two sessions ago — the text can no longer be a model, a determinate model, something to which one can compare something else. Or if there is here some model or analogy, it cannot be one model or analogy among others. This has to do with both the structure of the living and the structure of the text, which can no longer play the roles of compared and comparing with regard to one another. If the text in the narrow sense of the term (let us just call this, crudely, the text as a human production) is in some way a production of the living, it cannot be the model to which to compare the living of which it is an effect. But the same is true if one extends the concept of textuality to the point of making it coextensive with the living. There is then no longer any sense or use in speaking of a model. We are dealing instead with a sort of synonymy or equivalency or redundancy.

What is the use, then, in speaking of text? Well, I believe that the necessity of doing so has, and this should be clear, nothing absolute about it, nothing that is not linked to and motivated by a certain historico-theoretical

160

situation and the politico-scientific strategy linked to that situation. Referring the living to the structure of a text is clearly a sign of conceptual progress in bio-genetics, progress in the knowledge, if you like, of the living, it being understood that this progress of knowledge is at the same time a transformation of the status of knowledge, which no longer has to do, as I was saying last week, with some meta-textual reality but with text and so consists in writing text upon text. We are going beyond this or that stage of biological knowledge. It was not recourse to the textual "model" that made this progress possible but the reverse: a certain transformation of knowledge imposed what is called the model of the text. Conversely, what is called the model allows for new hypotheses, new constructions, and it is then in turn determined by that for which it serves as the model: one understands a text—what a text *is*—differently once the so-called model-function has operated. It is here that we see—regardless of how inadequate this concept and this word "model" may be—the necessity of the theoretico-political strategy I just mentioned. There is no such thing as *the* living and *the* text. Not only are there structures typical of the living and structures typical of the text but, even if one is dissatisfied with the empiricist take on this multiplicity, there are many possible ways to define the textuality and the structure of the living. It is clear that if one determines textuality on the basis, this time, of a certain model of text (for example, the phonetic-logocentric text, oriented by a present intention, etc.), one is immediately caught up in a system of interpretation of the living that is different from, and even opposed to, the one that would subordinate this type of text to another (non-phonocentric, non-teleological, etc.). The question of the model then shifts and becomes: what type of text is going to serve as a model for the science of general textuality? Is there a model text for general textuality, etc.? This is a question that can be applied to the living: is the reproduction of the bacterium the (purified) model from which one will evaluate the supplements, the deviations (sexuality, death, for example), or is the re-production of the living being that "we" are the model, etc.?

That is why the question of the model is so important. Since we are taking it up again here, I would like to be as precise as possible about the use of this word. It appears in Jacob's book, though not very often, in a chain of substitutions where it has equivalents such as analogy, image, or comparison, or syntactical turns of phrase of the sort "just as, so." This suggests that the model of which he speaks is always a descriptive model, highlighting a resemblance or a natural affinity, and not a mathematical model, a model in the mathematical sense of the term. (I recommend that you read about the different uses of the word or concept of model in Alain Badiou's *Le concept de modèle* (Maspero, 1969),⁶ and I make this recommendation even though I am not sure that I subscribe to all the propositions in this book,⁷ or whether I understand them all, though I am sure that very important questions are broached everywhere along the way.) The models of which Jacob speaks are thus concrete, intuitive, descriptive models, perceptions of resemblances. Here is, for example, one occurrence of the word "model" (from p. 14, in "The Program"). Jacob has just noted that in the history of biology there have been many generalizations but very few theories. The theory of evolution is, in his eyes, if not the only one at least the most important. A generalization, a law, is not a theory, and apart from the great theory of evolution, the other theories of biology hardly deserve the name considering how poor in abstraction and how simple they are. That is the case, for example, with the theory of nervous conduction or theories of heredity. These theories, says Jacob, are "generally extremely simple and involve only a very minor degree of abstraction. Even when an abstract entity such as the gene appears, the biologist will not rest until he has replaced it by material elements, particles or molecules, as if, in order to last, a biological theory had to be based on a concrete model."⁸

This concrete (descriptive, analogical) model can be not only natural but technical—and it is precisely this opposition between the natural and the technical that here comes into question. When one says that the concrete model of the gene is the material element, "particles or molecules," this element is considered to be natural. But when molecular biology has recourse to the concept of information, the model is no longer considered to be natural or only natural. What follows from this? Well, the model begins to circulate—and note that I say "circulate"—in such a way that one no longer knows what is the model for what: that for which one is seeking and finds a model becomes, in turn, a model for the model or for something else altogether. Let us look more closely at what is at work in this circulation of the model.

---

6. Alain Badiou, *The Concept of Model: An Introduction to the Materialist Epistemology of Mathematics*, trans. and ed. Zachery Luke Fraser and Tzuchien Tho (Melbourne: re.press, 2007) [*Le concept de modèle* (Paris: Maspero, 1969)].

7. There is here an insertion mark in the typescript that is repeated in the margin, followed by this notation: "those that concern, for ex., the opposition science/ideology or that presuppose some clarity (<illegible word>) regarding what production (the production of knowledge) means."

8. Jacob, *Logic of the Living*, p. 14 [p. 22].

Let us consider, for example, what Szilard and Brillouin say about Maxwell's demon.[9] For Maxwell, the demon in his gas-filled tank could, freely, at no cost, as it were, evaluate the quality of the molecules and sort them, select them. The information was free. Szilard and Brillouin demonstrate, to the contrary, that the information is not free, that is, that the demon can "see" (in quotation marks) the molecules only on the condition that he has some connection to them — radiation, for example — that is, only if some energy, say in the form of light, is supplied to the system from without. It is the combination of the gas and the demon that thus tends toward equilibrium, and when light is introduced from the outside the demon sorts and selects, acquires information and lowers the entropy of the system. Without this, without this energy coming from outside the system, the demon would become "blind" in its gas. But when everything is taken into account, and this contribution from the outside has been accounted for, the total entropy of the system is increased. The link between information and entropy, this "isomorphism" of the two, says Jacob, allows one to say that in an organized system (this is the most general and indispensable concept), "whether living or not," Jacob specifies, the elements are united by exchanges, and these exchanges are just as much exchanges of information as they are exchanges of matter and energy. Information — inasmuch as it is always linked to the exchange of matter or of energy within a system — becomes the most general place where different types of order, whether living or non-living, intersect and interconnect. Jacob writes: "Every interaction between the members of an organization can accordingly be considered as a problem of communication. This applies just as much to a human society as to a living organism or an automatic device. In each of these objects, cybernetics finds a model that can be applied to the others."[10] In other words, between, for example, the order of human society, the order of the living organism, and the order of the machine (of the automatic device), the model will not function in only one direction: each order will serve as a model or will provide models for the others. One may then wonder about the epistemological value, or even the heuristic value, of the model as soon as it serves as a model for an object that is also its own model, or rather the model of its model, so that the model that is modeling it is part of the structure of each object. And you may have perhaps noticed, in the course of the argumentation I just went through, the surreptitious displacement that has just taken place:

---

9. In this paragraph Derrida is paraphrasing a passage from Jacob in *The Logic of the Living* (p. 250 [p. 270]).

10. Ibid., p. 251 [p. 271].

since information is inseparable from entropy, since there is just as much an exchange of matter and of energy as there is of information, there is only exchange. And with the concept of exchange taking the leading position as the most general concept, we go from exchange to communication and we privilege exchange as exchange of information over the exchange of matter and energy. That is how the circulation of the model operates: once exchange has been privileged over the content that is exchanged (matter, energy, or information, that is, selection/discrimination/election), it is easy to privilege, from among the contents exchanged, that content without content that information is, since information consists first of all in a selection, a discrimination. It is then said that everything in a system is information and thus communication: "Every interaction between the members of an organization can accordingly be considered as a problem of communication. This applies just as much to a human society as to a living organism or an automatic device. In each of these objects, cybernetics finds a model that can be applied to the others." This last sentence is going to be immediately illustrated, exemplified, typified. The model is going to be diversified into different types of models. We are going to have words such as "type," "the very type," "example," and, a little more vaguely, "defines." Jacob says that society is going to serve as a model for the other two (the living organism and the automatic device) because, I quote, "language represents the very type of a system of interaction between elements of an integrated whole."[11] Which is perhaps said a bit too quickly: we think we know what language is, and we determine society as language. Then, the living organism, the second model of that for which society can serve as a model, can itself be a model for the society that is its model or for the automatic device: the organism is a model because homeostasis serves as "an example of all the phenomena working against the general trend towards disorder."[12] The living, the living organism, is the only one to follow not the tendency to go from order to disorder but the tendency to maintain the existing order. Finally, third, the device is the model of its models because the combination of its circuits "defines" — the formulation is a bit vague — "the requirements of integration."[13]

The fact remains that if information, the emission or the reception of messages, is itself inseparable from an activity of sorting, of selection, that is to say, of force or of differences of force, etc., and if information is not

11. Ibid.
12. Ibid.
13. Ibid.

simply some neutral communication or language or knowledge, one will be unable to isolate a pure linguistic or semiotic model from, let us say, a dynamic or energetic or economic model. The circulating, circular model is at once informatic [*informatique*] (if information is only a formal message) and energetic. That which one might have wanted—and can always still want—to eliminate surreptitiously by privileging the message or communication or form, namely, the energetic, does not let itself be reduced. It does not let itself be reduced and it will not simply allow itself to be added onto or coupled with the message; it instead structures—as, for example, selection or a principle of selection—the message, the informational activity itself. And given this, whenever one speaks of textuality, the value of relations of force, of a difference of force, an economic agonistics, will be just as irreducible. Just like the opening to the outside of every textual system at the very moment it re-marks itself and re-inscribes itself. Re-production itself implies this agonistics.

Thus, after having defined the circulation of the model among three objects (social, animal, mechanical: and you can see that once the model starts circulating there is no longer any reason to say three rather than one or 3 + n; all sorts of different systems can then be added to these three, whose delimitations are, in sum, traditional, dogmatic, and in any case put in question by the circulation of the model, etc.), thus, after having defined the circulation of the model among the three types of object (social, living/animal, mechanical), Jacob writes, distinguishing in a traditional way between, let us say, form and force (information and energy regulation): "In the end, any organized system can be analyzed by means of two concepts: message and feedback regulation."[14]

Are we dealing here with two concepts? And can one separate them, even if only in the course of analysis, in the *ordo cognoscendi*, if you like? Jacob separates them, but when he begins analyzing them separately he has to introduce into the very concept of message (the first concept), into its very analysis, into its explicitation, a principle of choice or of selectivity (no message without discrimination), which already implies the regulation of energy that is to be taken up in the analysis of the second concept.

What is a message?, he asks: a succession of what he calls with this general and, here, rather conventional name "symbols." But that does not really matter. What matters is that these symbols, this succession of symbols, are "sampled," that is his word, from a repertory. No message without some sampling and, thus, without some selective screening. These symbols

14. Ibid.

can be, he says, signs (a very general word that seems to cover all kinds of marks) or else letters, sounds, phonemes. Jacob does not stop to define these notions (signs, letters, sounds, phonemes), and for what interests him this does not indeed really matter, since what is important is not the type of mark but the fact that there is an identifiable whole and a sampling from that whole. Neither the type of mark nor even the content of the message is of interest here, only the operation of the message and the fact that it implies a choice, a limit of probability or of improbability in a combinatory system.

> A given message thus represents a particular selection among all the arrangements possible. It is a particular order among all those permitted by the combinative system of symbols. Information measures the freedom of choice, and thus the improbability of the message; but it is unaware of the semantic content. Any material structure can therefore be *compared* [my emphasis] to a message, since the nature and position of its components, atoms or molecules, are the result of a choice made from a series of possible combinations. By isomorphous transformation according to a code, such a structure can be *translated* [my emphasis] into another series of symbols. It can be communicated by a transmitter to any point on the globe where a receiver reconstitutes the message by reverse transformation. This is how radio, television, and the secret service work. According to Norbert Wiener (*The Human Use of Human Beings*, 1954, p. 95), there is no obstacle to using a metaphor "in which the organism is seen as a message."[15]

The possibility of modeling that allows one to say, for example, "compared" (any material structure can be compared to a message) has to do not only, if you look closely here, with the fact that there is information or message in every system, for example, in the three types of systems already mentioned, but also with the very functioning of the message, its internal functioning, which entails the translatability of one "series of symbols" into another, a translatability internal to one code and to one type of symbol but from one code to the other and from one type of symbol to the other. That is where we first get the possibility of the analogical *as*, the *as* that allows one to say "compared to" or "the organism as a message."

Once the message or the "as" of the message has been defined, it is not another concept, not even another closely related concept, that is then taken up when one takes up feedback or the principle of regulation. As I said earlier, we do not have two concepts here (message plus energy regulation): in the message there was selection or sorting, and the principle of this selection that

---

15. Ibid., pp. 251–52 [pp. 271–72]. Derrida is referring here to Norbert Wiener, *The Human Use of Human Beings: Cybernetics and Society* (Boston: Houghton Mifflin, 1954).

is constitutive of the very operation of the message had to obey certain economic laws. And so when Jacob changes paragraphs as well as objects in order to examine what he calls the second concept — "As for feedback"[16] — he simply explains the same concept of message, just as, conversely, when he was analyzing the message, he implied feedback. Feedback consists in reintroducing into the system the results of the system's past action (already, in one form or another, a memory or an archive of messages) in order to be able to oversee and redress the mechanism's tendency toward disorganization. Such oversight thus provokes in a local and temporary way, and it is important to insist on this, a reversal in the tendency or the direction of entropy. This direction — this, let us call it, natural direction — of any system, living or not, leads to wearing out, deterioration, and an increase in entropy. Regulation thus consists in compensating for each local deterioration by means of a certain work or energy that comes from elsewhere within the organism or from outside the organism. This work or this local supplementary energy is itself then subjected to the same law, the same tendency, as will each one that follows, each loss being compensated by a gain, though in such a way that, if the system were closed, and according to the second law of thermodynamics, the disorder and the deterioration would go on increasing. The living being, insofar as it tends to reestablish the prior order or maintain the preexisting order, can thus never be a closed system, says Jacob:

> It cannot stop absorbing food, ejecting waste-matter, or being constantly traversed by a current of matter and energy from outside. Without a constant flow of order, the organism disintegrates. Isolated, it dies. Every living being remains in a sense permanently plugged into [note the technological metaphor . . .] the general current which carries the universe towards disorder. It is a sort of local and transitory eddy which maintains organization and allows it to reproduce itself.[17]

All this might appear somewhat trivial, but I am quoting Jacob here only in order to underscore that this structural opening of every living system makes untenable those statements about bacteria not dying because death comes to them from the outside or about death in the proper sense of the term having to be inscribed in the organism, etc. It also makes untenable all the simple oppositions between inside and outside that subtend what the book says both about sexuality and mortality as accidents come from the

---

16. Jacob, *Logic of the Living*, p. 252 [p. 272].
17. Ibid., p. 253 [p. 273].

THE "LIMPING" MODEL ‡ 127

outside that come to be inscribed within. Supplementarity is inscribed in the very definition of every system, every living or non-living system.

At this point, the feedback or regulatory structure of the message that is to be found in every system, a structure that is common to every system, living or non-living, allows the old animal/machine problem to be displaced. Jacob acknowledges this but it seems to me that he constantly wants, on the one hand, to take this displacement into account and to erase the traditional limit that is drawn there, and, on the other, to underscore firmly that we are dealing here with just a partial analogy and that, in fact, the living retains a capacity (for example the capacity to reproduce itself) that the non-living and the machine both lack. And this is where the circulation of the model allows for this double register or double play. On the one hand, the fact that the animal and the machine are models for one another, and reciprocally so, erases the opposition. On the other hand, insofar as the machine is produced by the living and cannot (it is said) reproduce itself, the model is teleologically oriented, irreversible, an imperfection separates it from itself, etc.[18] The circulation or the reversibility of the model is clearly posited in the passage that I have been following on information, messages, and feedback. For example, on p. 252:

169

> With the possibility of carrying out mechanically a series of operations laid down in a program, the old problem of the relations between animal and machine was posed in new terms. "Both systems are precisely parallel in their analogous attempts to control entropy through feedback," said Wiener. Both succeed by disorganizing the external environment, "by consuming negative entropy," to use the expression of Schrödinger and Brillouin. Both have special equipment, in fact, for collecting at a low energy-level the information coming from the outside world and for transforming it for their own purposes.[19]

And then, a bit further down, after describing this economy of entropy: "Animal and machine, each system then becomes a model for the other."[20]

Each of the systems becomes a model for the other; the animal and the machine are going to become, respectively, the model of their model, which annuls — and I say this while also thinking of the circular ring or annulus — the function of the model, assuming that this function has ever existed and that this circulation does not reveal in some way the very logic of

---

18. In the typescript there is the handwritten interlineal insertion ←→, which Derrida uses to indicate "develop" or "comment."
19. Jacob, *Logic of the Living*, p. 252 [p. 272].
20. Ibid., p. 253 [p. 273].

every appeal to a model, which, perhaps always and everywhere, has tended to take this circular form whereby the model must itself become the model of its model, the teleological or final meaning of the model coming to guide the mechanical or technical meaning of the constructed model, which itself becomes in turn the miniaturized or gigantic model of the finalized model, the one with a natural finality. And this whole circulation is an effect of the inconceivable logic of re-production about which we spoke last week,[21] the inconceivable logic of a production that is initiated in reproduction.

In the example we have been considering, namely, the specular reciprocity of the animal/machine models, the machine, on the one hand, is described as an animal; it has an anatomy, a physiology, executive organs activated by a source of energy, sense organs that respond to sonorous, tactile, luminous, and thermic stimuli; it investigates its environment, controls its food, is equipped with centers of automatic control for its activities and its performances, with a memory or a stock of archives and a nervous system that connects the senses to the brain or transmits orders to the limbs. The machine executes a program, but it can also correct it, even interrupt it upon the reception of particular messages, etc.

And "conversely"—this is Jacob's word—the animal can be described *as* a machine: organs, cells, and molecules form a communication network, with signals and messages, with the flexibility and rigidity of a machine, the flexibility of behavior being regulated by feedback loops and the rigidity regulated by a program. Heredity is then described as the transfer of a message, the program of the structures to be produced being recorded in the nucleus of the egg. Jacob again quotes Schrödinger (*What Is Life?*, pp. 18–19):[22]

> the chromosomes contain in some kind of code-script the entire pattern of the individual's future development and of its functioning in the mature state.... The chromosome structures are at the same time instrumental in bringing about the development they foreshadow. They are law-code and executive power—or, to use another simile, they are architect's plan and builder's craft all in one.[23]

In this paragraph where he is explaining that the animal can be described in terms of a machine, Jacob goes ahead and quotes—without paying any

---

21. See the beginning of the previous session, p. 96 and following.
22. Erwin Schrödinger, *What Is Life? The Physical Aspect of the Living Cell* (Cambridge: Cambridge University Press, 1944).
23. Jacob, *Logic of the Living*, p. 254 [p. 274].

attention to this or drawing any attention to it—someone who, in order himself to describe the fact that animal heredity functions like a textual machine, describes the textual or programmatic machine *as* a socio-political or socio-technical phenomenon (legislative power/executive power, architecture and construction, etc.). This last analogy, which allows one to describe the living being as a machine, rests, in the end, upon another even more general analogy between the living and the non-living, namely, the analogy between the chromosome and the crystal. The structure of the molecule is that upon which the order of the living rests. Now, for reasons of stability, the organization of the chromosome is "comparable," says Jacob, to that of a crystal, more specifically, the kind of crystal that physicists call "aperiodic," a crystal that breaks the monotony by putting together several patterns, though in very small numbers. For a very small number is sufficient for great variety. "The combination of two signs in the Morse code enables any text whatsoever to be coded." And Jacob concludes this line of argumentation by saying: "The plan of the organism is mapped out by a combinative system of chemical symbols. Heredity functions *like* the memory of a computer."[24]

The reference to writing in *Morse code*—that is to say, in principle, the simplest form of writing, since it is made up of only two elements (dots/dashes) and is able to re-code or translate-over [*surtraduire*] every other form of writing—the appeal to Morse code is obviously very significant and supports, better than any other, the textual or grammatical analogy in this domain. It is this reference that allows Jacob, some twenty pages later,[25] to multiply the words "image," "just as . . . so"; and this happens right at the moment he is also recalling the analogy between the living molecule and the aperiodic crystal that resembles it. It will be better for me to quote here directly; you will see appear here the motif of linearity, which I will talk about later and which will prove to be very important for us. Even crucial. "In the living world," Jacob will say, "the order of order is linear."[26] Here is the passage on Morse code and the analogy or the image:

> The representation of the genes envisaged by classical genetics as individual structures arranged like a string of beads has, therefore, been replaced by that of a linear sequence of chemical symbols, the aperiodic crystal predicted by physicists. The *image* that best describes our knowledge of heredity is indeed that of a chemical message. Not a message written in ideograms

24. Ibid., Derrida's emphasis.
25. Ibid., p. 275 [p. 295].
26. Ibid., p. 286 [p. 306].

like Chinese, but with an alphabet like that of the Morse code [comment]. *Just as* a sentence represents a segment of text, so a gene corresponds to a segment of nucleic acid. In both cases, an isolated symbol means nothing; only a combination of symbols has any "sense." In both cases, a given sequence, sentence or gene, begins and ends with special "punctuation" marks [quotation marks on "sense" and "punctuation"]. The transformation of a nucleic-acid sequence into a protein sequence is *like* a translation of a message received in Morse that does not make sense until it is translated, into French, for example. This is done by means of a "code" that provides the equivalence of signs between the two "alphabets."[27]

Jacob, who is keen on the circularity of the model, is also keen on limiting it. Whence the double gesture I spoke of earlier. If he acknowledges that animal and machine, living system and non-living system, are each the model for the other, he also limits the analogy at the point where the capacity to reproduce oneself comes into play. How is this possible and is it altogether coherent? As soon as the model is no longer circular-specular, the mechanical-technical model produced by the living, which alone is able to reproduce itself, can itself no longer be a model: every mechanical model, as the non-living product of life, or as the natural and non-living product (the aperiodic crystal, for example), is no longer a good model if it does not reproduce-itself. But conversely, if it were a good model, one would have to admit the circularity that would, in turn, annul the pertinence or the usefulness of the model. In both cases, and this is what my demonstration has been aiming at, the notion of model is at once inevitable and without any interest, without any pertinence, as soon as it is a question of something like the living—which is not something—something like the living defined as the faculty to reproduce-oneself. Self-reproducibility entertains a relation to the model such that it both constantly requires the model and, just as constantly, does without it. That is what I wanted to emphasize in order to conclude.

I was saying, then, that Jacob also wants to limit the analogy or the analogical circularity that he at the same time acknowledges. And what disrupts the analogy is always this *reproducing-oneself* that is found or that is supposedly found on one side and not the other. The power of reproducing-oneself represents an emergence and a superiority of life with regard to the machine, which is only able—or is supposedly able—to produce. But to say that the machine or the factory produces, and that to produce is inferior to reproducing oneself, implies that originary production is in fact on

---

27. Ibid., p. 275 [pp. 295–96]; Derrida's emphasis.

the side of living re-production and that the factory does not in fact even produce: it only re-produces without producing or re-producing itself in an originary way, whereas the living being produces and reproduces itself.

Here, first, is the passage concerning this limit of the analogy. Read *Logic of the Living*, pp. 270–71:[28]

> If analogy is to be used, the bacterial cell is obviously best described by the model of a miniaturized chemical factory. Factory and bacterium function only by means of energy received from the exterior. Both transform the raw material taken from the milieu by a series of operations into finished products. Both excrete waste products into their surroundings. But the very idea of a factory implies a purpose, a direction, a will to produce — in other words, an aim for which the structure is arranged and the activities are coordinated. What, then, could be the aim of the bacterium? What does it want to produce that justifies its existence, determines its organization, and underlies its work? There is apparently only one answer to this question. A bacterium continually strives to produce two bacteria. This seems to be its one project, its sole ambition. The little bacterial cell performs at top speed the two thousand or so reactions which constitute its metabolism. It grows. It gradually elongates. And when the time is ripe, it divides. Where there was one individual, suddenly there are two. Each of these individuals then becomes the center of all chemical reactions. Each manufactures all its molecular structures. Each grows anew. A few minutes later, each divides in turn to produce two individuals. And so on, for as long as conditions permit. For two billion years or more, bacteria — or something like them — have been reproducing themselves. Structure, function, and chemistry of the bacterial, all have been refined for this end: to produce two organisms identical to itself, as well as possible, as quickly as possible, and under the most varied of circumstances. If the bacterial cell is to be considered as a factory, it must be a factory of a special kind. The products of human technology are totally different from the machines that produce them, and therefore totally different from the factory itself. The bacterial cell, on the other hand, makes its own constituents; the ultimate product is identical with itself. Whereas the factory produces, the cell reproduces itself.[29]

I do not think that the most interesting thing here is to question these oppositions between the production of the factory and the self-reproduction of the cell. Can we say, for example, will we always be able to say, that a factory

---

28. In the typescript is this handwritten addition: "life," followed by a double line, with one line leading to the word "machine" and the other to "crystal" and to the reference "p. 324–325."

29. Jacob, *Logic of the Living*, pp. 270–71 [pp. 290–91].

does not reproduce itself? And if one points to the fact that the apparent self-reproduction of a factory is at once programmed and fueled from outside itself, by human technology and by the energy that is provided to it, is there not—and this is also acknowledged by Jacob—a structural outside of the cell without which it would not reproduce itself and which thus makes of the *itself*, of the relation to self of re-production, an always fissured and open structure, a system that functions only insofar as it is in relation to the other or to the outside, such that the identity of the itself and of the *re-* is and functions only in its difference with itself, and this just as much in the living as in the non-living? Jacob's way of taking up this entire conceptuality aims only to order the integration, what he calls integration and integrons, from the inferior to the superior. But, once again, it is perhaps not here that the strategic lever of the critical question is most effective. Perhaps it would be better to bring the question of the logic or of the rhetoric of analogy—which subtends this entire problematic of the model—back to the interior itself, to what Jacob ultimately calls the interior of the internal property of the living, namely, the ability to reproduce oneself. What I mean by this is that rather than asking about the role or the value of analogy, of models, resemblances, images, comparisons, assimilations, and so on, between the living and the non-living, perhaps we must first ask whether the schemas of this problematic are not already at work in the structure of the living, in the definition of the proper—the so-called proper—structure of the living. And if that is the case, then not only is the question of the analogical model not posed outside the living, that is, between the living and its outside (assuming that one can still *oppose* its outside to it); it is posed "in" the living itself, as the structure of reproducibility. It is posed there and, in fact, nowhere else.

There is, of course, between the concept of model and the concept of reproducibility an essential link. A model is what is used to reproduce, it is that on the basis of which one reproduces, and it is itself the effect of a reproduction. And when reproduction reproduces reproduction or reproducibility, one is caught up in the circularity of the model and the reflection of reproducing-*oneself*. There is thus nothing surprising about finding the vocabulary and the syntax of model and analogy in the description Jacob gives not of the relations living-non-living but of the living to itself in reproduction. The word "copy," for example, is one of the words most frequently used (see, for example, p. 273 and following). While proteins do not reproduce themselves ("A protein is not born of an identical protein"), the compound that organizes them, "another substance" called deoxyribonucleic acid, the constituent of chromosomes, does; in the cell, it alone is able to reproduce itself by "copying itself," says Jacob.

Read pp. 273–74 (emphasize "copy"), "the order of order is linear." See also pp. 275–76:

> The permanence of living organisms through successive generations is therefore observed not only in their shapes, but even in the fine chemical details of the substances that compose them. Each chemical species is reproduced exactly from one generation to another. Each chemical species does not, however, form copies of itself. A protein is not born of an identical protein. Proteins do not reproduce themselves. They are organized from another substance, deoxyribonucleic acid, the constituent of chromosomes. This compound is the only one in the cell that can be reproduced by copying itself. This is a consequence of its unique structure. Deoxyribonucleic acid is, in fact, a long polymer formed not of one, but two chains, helically twisted around each other. Each chain contains a skeleton formed of alternating sugar and phosphate groups. Each sugar molecule is linked to only one chemical residue—an organic base—of which there are four different kinds. These four sub-units are repeated by the millions in infinitely varied combinations and permutations along the chain. By analogy, this linear sequence is often compared to the arrangement of the letters of the alphabet in a text. Whether in a book or a chromosome, the specificity comes from the order in which the sub-units, letters or organic bases, are arranged. But what gives this polymer a unique role in reproduction is the nature of the relations that unite the two chains. Each organic base in one chain is associated with one in the other, but not just any one. The system of chemical bonding is such that each sub-unit on one chain can correspond to only one of the other three sub-units in the second chain. If the four sub-units are indicated by A, B, C, and D, A in one chain is always opposite B in the other, and D is always opposite C. The symbols go in pairs; the two chains are complementary. The sequence in one chain imposes the sequence in the other.[30]

176

> The activity of the genes, the ordering of the sub-units in the protein chains, therefore represent a far more subtle operation than their reproduction, the ordering of the nucleic-acid sub-units. To translate and form the chemical bonds in protein, the bacterial cell deploys a piece of extremely complex equipment. The synthesis of proteins is a two-stage process, since the protein sub-units are assembled and polymerized, not directly on the gene, but on small particles in the cytoplasm which serve as assembly lines. The

---

30. Ibid., pp. 273–74 [pp. 293–94].

deoxyribonucleic acid text of the gene is therefore first transcribed into another species of nucleic acid, the so-called ribonucleic acid, by means of the same four-sign alphabet. This copy, called the "messenger," associates with the particles in the cytoplasm and brings them the instructions for assembling the protein sub-units in the order dictated by the nucleic-acid sequence. The translation of the genetic text re-copied in the message takes place through the intervention of other molecules called "adapters." These adapters bring the appropriate protein sub-units into juxtaposition with the nucleic-acid sub-units and thus establish a univocal correspondence between the two alphabets. Carrying suitable adapters, the particles move from end to end of the messenger nucleic acid, like the reading head of a tape-recorder passing over the tape. The protein sub-units are thus aligned in the order prescribed by the gene. Each sub-unit is successively attached to the preceding one by an identical chemical bond. The protein chain is thus synthesized step-wise, from one end to the other.[31]

There is thus no model for reproduction, except for the model of the model or reproduction itself. If the genetic message seems to "resemble," says Jacob, "a text without an author, [one] that a proof-reader has been correcting for more than a billion years,"[32] the concept of text is here not a model or an analogy: first, because what we understand by "text without an author" (in the everyday sense, imagined as an unsigned book or manuscript in nature or in the library) is already a product [*produit*]—and thus something re-produced [*re-produit*]—an effect of the living as genetic message and thus something that has a structure that is inseparable from the structure of the living; next, because the text—which is today that which most resembles the genetic message or the structure of the living—cannot simply have the status of a model inasmuch as there has never been a model for the living. It is this, as it were, internal deconstruction (internal and supplementary) of the concept of model that intervenes whenever one appeals to the concept of text and whenever one acknowledges that "the genetic message can be translated only by the products of its own translation" (which comes down to saying there is no possible translation in the final analysis: textuality cannot be absolutely translated, despite all the effects of translation it induces), a claim that resonates with the appeal to Gödel and, in particular, the notion that "a logical system is not sufficient for its own description."

31. Ibid., pp. 275–76 [p. 296].
32. Ibid., p. 287 [pp. 307–8].

If one continues to think reproducibility as a complication that supervenes upon producibility, and self-reproducibility as a complication of reproducibility, then one runs back into all these questions, which are indeed difficult to avoid: where did it all begin, where and when was the first reproduction, the production of reproduction, the question of the chicken and the egg (which Jacob in fact mentions), the question of the origin of life (or of the text) now translated, in conformity with a model of the text governed, in Jacob, by an old but very enduring linguistic model (the oppositions code/message, on the one hand, signifier/signified, on the other), the question of the origin of life translated into the form: "what is the origin of the genetic code?"

At issue here is a pure event, the absolute event that would have been produced just once but whose single production would have consisted in reproducing itself, in dividing itself in order to reproduce itself, in folding back upon itself in order to multiply itself and thus disappear as an event in the usual sense of this word, which is linked to production and not reproduction.

It is with regard to this event that modern biology still reserves a place for chance, for what it calls chance and what it reinterprets, this time, in its relation to the text, but a text that, once again, is determined on the basis of a certain philosophical linguistics or semiotics and the oppositions code/message, signifier/signified. The scientist would like to eliminate or reduce chance and he admits that he cannot do so for essential reasons. We will return to these questions in two weeks, but I would like to read you one more passage before concluding. Read pp. 305–6.

> For want of vestiges to examine, biology is reduced to making conjectures. It tries to arrange the problems in series, to individualize the objects and formulate questions that can be answered by experiments. Which of the polymers, nucleic acid or protein, came first? What is the origin of the genetic code? The first question leads one to speculate whether anything vaguely like a living organism would be conceivable without both types of polymer. The second raises problems both of evolution and of logic. Of evolution, because univocal correspondence between each group of three nucleic-acid sub-units and each protein sub-unit cannot have arisen at a single stroke. Of logic, because it is difficult to perceive why this particular correspondence was adopted rather than another; why one nucleic-acid triplet "signifies" a certain protein sub-unit and not another. Perhaps primitive organizations had some constraints of structure we know nothing about: it would then be the adjustment of molecular conformations

that would have imposed, if not the whole system, then at least some of its equivalences. But again perhaps there was no constraint at all: then it would have been purely by chance that the equivalences were produced and persisted afterwards. For once a system of relations has been established, the relations cannot be changed without the risk of the whole meaning of the system being lost and all its value as a message destroyed. A genetic code is like a language: even if they are only due to chance, once the relations between "signifier" and "signified" are established, they cannot be changed. These, then, are the questions molecular biology is trying to answer. But nothing indicates that the transition between the organic and the living can ever be really investigated. It may perhaps never become possible to estimate what the probability was of a living system appearing on earth. If the genetic code is universal, it is probably because every organism that has succeeded in living up till now is descended from one single ancestor. But, it is impossible to measure the probability of an event that occurred only once. It is to be feared that the subject may become bogged down in a slough of theories that can never be verified. The origin of life might well become a new center of abstract quarrels, with schools and theories concerned, not with scientific predictions, but with metaphysics.[33]

Jacob is aware of the fact that the model of the text with which he begins and to which he refers is determined and transformable, and that, therefore, what is at issue is not whether or not one is referring to text but how one is to determine this textuality. You have read the last lines of his book: "But science is enclosed in its own explanatory system and cannot escape from it. Today the world is messages, codes, and information. Tomorrow what analysis will break down our objects to reconstitute them in a new space? What new Russian doll will emerge?"[34]

It is perhaps presuming a lot about this resemblance to what we know today to say that this will still be a "Russian doll," something bearing enough of a resemblance, however "new" it may be, to a Russian doll. Note that a Russian doll that would "emerge," as he says, is itself already rather new and rather monstrous compared to what we know. He wants it to come out of a box in which it is enclosed by a series of nested boxes that are predictable in their overall structure, and yet he wants it to emerge, discontinuously, that is to say, to come out all at once, but from the sea. On the previous page he had not ruled out "slipping in a supplement" to genetic programs. Read pp. 322–23.

33. Ibid., pp. 305–6 [pp. 326–27].
34. Ibid., p. 324 [p. 345].

With the accumulation of knowledge, man has become the first product of evolution capable of controlling evolution. Not only the evolution of others, by encouraging species of interest to him and eliminating bothersome ones, but also his own evolution. Perhaps one day it will become possible to intervene in the execution of the genetic program, or even in its structure, to correct some faults and slip in supplementary instructions. Perhaps it will also be possible to produce at will, and in as many copies as required, exact duplicates of individuals, a politician, for instance, an artist, a beauty queen or an athlete. There is nothing to prevent immediate application to human beings of the selection processes used for race-horses, laboratory mice, or milk cows. But it seems desirable to know first the genetic factors involved in such complex qualities as originality, beauty, or physical endurance. And above all, agreement has to be reached about the criteria for the choice. But that is no longer the concern of biology alone.[35]

Is there any concern of biology alone? We will return to these questions in two weeks. I will direct them toward the notion of biologism, whether it is or is not legitimate to make of the biological a model, to treat, then, not the model in biology but the "bio-logical" model—elsewhere, if elsewhere there is. Following the trail of these questions we will come across texts by Nietzsche, Heidegger, and Freud.[36]

---

35. Ibid., pp. 322–23 [pp. 343–44].
36. In the transcript an arrow here leads from the name "Freud" to two handwritten words: "limping devil."

SEVENTH SESSION[1]

In our exploration of the circular model, or what I called the circulation of the model—though one can also speak here of the circular model insofar as the circle is the model of relations, *circular* relations, therefore, between models—in our exploration of circular possibilities, there is one that I deliberately left in reserve up until now, one that is nonetheless part of the same system of possibilities, the same program. And in such a necessary, such an unavoidable way that, in truth, while leaving it in a sort of reserve, I could not have avoided, at least in principle, already taking it up. What is this circular possibility?

It can be said that, up until now, we have mainly been asking questions about what could serve as a model for the living or, conversely, that for which the living could serve as a model for something else that served as a model for it, such that the exchange of models took place between the living and something else, between two things or two objects, one of which was called the living. It was a question of models as object (living or not), as object of a scientific or philosophical discourse, of scientific or philosophical knowledge, and so on. Models, therefore, for a discourse or for a kind of knowledge. But we can now also ask—this is the other possibility in reserve—what happens when the biological discourse, biological science itself, if you will, is no longer simply questioned as something that involves models or that gets caught up in the circularity of models, but itself becomes,

---

1. In the typescript there is a handwritten addition in the upper-right corner of the page in the form of a list: "A throw of the key [*coup de clé*] / – *Glaskasten* / – thrown key." In the left margin of the first paragraph are the words: "nail / key / enclave // turn of the key / ~~life to~~ / the suicide of the key." [Translators' note:] These words are all references to Nietzsche's 1873 essay "On Truth and Lie in an Extra-moral Sense," as this session will indicate.

as biological science, as scientific discourse on life, a model for other discourses, for example philosophical discourses. What does that mean? It means that, whether surreptitiously or explicitly, the truth of biological science, both its content and its form, become the ultimate reference, the foundation or the measure of other discourses (I say reference, foundation, or measure, but there are other forms of authority for the model — we will have to come back to this). Everything is then organized in terms of biological knowledge, everything becomes an effect of this knowledge, all discourses find in it their last recourse. This is what has often been designated, since the end of the nineteenth century, by the name *biologism*.

You will say that this possibility of biologism was not really kept in such reserve or was not so inapparent in what we have already analyzed. The possibility for biology to become a model for other discourses was already prescribed in the circularity that affected or led to its objective model: its object easily became a model for the very thing that served as a model for it, etc. And more than once we have come to see that it is difficult, and for essential reasons, to limit or delimit the biological field, that this field is its very overflowing, that overflowing is its structure.

And, even more problematically, did I not myself give in to such a biologism by claiming that life was not one model among others since it was defined <by> the very power to reproduce itself [*se reproduire*], that is, to produce itself as a model, or, taken from the other side, that the text as life or life as text were not models among others, which perhaps amounts to making them the ultimate model?

As a result, the question of biologism has, in a certain sense, already been broached and prescribed, acknowledged in its prescription. But we did not treat it explicitly as a relation between objects, object-models, not yet explicitly as a relation between kinds of knowledge and discourses. That is what we are now coming to.

Even though, as it seems to me, the possibility of biologism as a historical possibility is linked to the whole of the history of metaphysics, since the equivalence being-*physis*-life has always been at work there, this historical possibility is differentiated and determined each time in a singular way, and today, I believe, we still belong to one of those determinations, the one that was formed, fixed, and constituted at the end of the nineteenth century in relation to certain advances in biological science. Naturally, since that time many more advances have followed, profoundly transforming what we know about life, as they say, and yet the problematic of biologism does not seem to me to have been radically altered. I take as an indication of the unity

183

of this whole problematic the fact, for example, that discourses like those of Nietzsche and even, from another point of view, of Freud, who have both been accused — for this was an accusation — of biologism, of biologistic scientism, both retain a provocative power or pertinence in the wake of the latest findings of modern bio-genetics. For example, if you consider everything we have said about the text, about the living as a text to be deciphered, as semiotic marking, etc., all of that can find some accommodation, some opening, some capacity, in the Nietzschean or Freudian problematic, regardless of the scientific notions to which Nietzsche and Freud might have adhered in certain cases, and even if, when we look closely at some of these notions, we find certain claims to have become outdated or to have been superseded by more recent findings. It is by assuming this unity, by trusting at least in the appearance of this unity of a historical field, that I am thus going to privilege, as my guiding thread through this question of biologism, the texts <of> Nietzsche and Freud. I have thus just tried to justify

1. the necessity of broaching for its own sake the question of biologism as an effect of the circulation of the model;
2. the necessity of privileging the texts of Nietzsche and of Freud in the treatment of this question.

I now need to explain why I chose as my starting point a particular passage from Heidegger's book on Nietzsche, a passage on the question of Nietzsche's alleged biologism. That will be my task for today.

This is going to be a long detour. A long detour following the path [*démarche*] or the *Holzweg* of Heidegger, the detour being here perhaps not so much a methodical digression of discourse but, or as well, and perhaps first of all, the concept of the relation life-death (life death).[2]

And this detour will perhaps give you a clearer and thus more reassuring picture of my own path [*démarche*] in the course of this seminar. Having started out from life death, from the life death of Nietzsche, in our initial problematization, we have had to follow a loop or a ring (passing through the modern science of life) whose knot, whose solder, leads us today back to Nietzsche. Starting from the life death of Nietzsche, we are going to describe another loop-ring (the Heideggerian one), whose solder, whose knot,

---

2. In the typescript a short paragraph has been crossed out: "in the third chapter of his *Nietzsche, The Will to Power as Knowledge*, Heidegger treats what he called — and that is the title of this sub-chapter — 'Nietzsches angeblicher Biologismus, Nietzsche's Alleged Biologism.'"

will lead us back to Nietzsche's life-death, and then another loop-ring (the Freudian), and then it will be springtime.³

How was the preceding loop supposed to lead us back to Nietzsche? Well, each time I made use of an argument of the following kind: insofar as biological knowledge and knowledge in general, as well as the value of truth or of objectivity that guides knowledge, are effects or products of life death, and all the models that are used as well—and the model of the text par excellence insofar as it today deconstructs the entire modelology that preceded it—if all that is indeed the case, then the science of life (objective genitive) is a science of life (subjective genitive); and when a science has a subjective genitive relation with its supposed object, when it is the object of its object, which becomes the subject of its subject, a great many consequences follow with regard to the concepts of scientificity, objectivity, truth, and so on. Now each time I made use of an argument of this kind, I was implicitly coming back to, having recourse to, a Nietzschean kind of claim. And the same goes for "everything began already with reproduction." And the same goes for the critique of the opposition, as it is deployed here, between metaphor and concept, model and object, and so on. You know that already, beginning with the first texts of Nietzsche that we read here, the problematic of truth was articulated along the lines of life, the "drive to truth" (*Trieb zur Wahrheit*, says *Le livre du philosophe*)⁴ coming to refer, in the final analysis, to life. All the rhetoricity that engenders the effects of concepts and of truth (analogy, metaphors, metonymies) presupposes anthropomorphism, and this latter is itself still a contrivance of life, of the living-human-being. It would be too simple to speak here of *truth*, in the singular [*la* vérité]. And if *truth* were itself an effect of *life*, it would be too simple to speak of *life*, in the singular [*la* vie]. There are truths, effects of truth, and lives, effects of life. And the difficulty is to think this up to the point, and in such a way, that these propositions—there are truths and lives—are not vulnerable to the philosophico-Socratic question that undoes empiricism: so there are truths and lives, effects of truth and effects of life, but then what is the life of life, the livingness [*vivance*] of life, the truth of life and the truth of truth to which you must be implicitly appealing when you continue to speak of truth or of life, even in the plural, anticipating thereby some kind of semantic unity that would allow one to understand this pluralization? Try, then, to think beyond this objection and

---

3. Derrida made several typewritten, interlinear additions to this paragraph that we have tried to integrate.

4. Nietzsche, *Le livre du philosophe/Das Philosophenbuch*, pp. 174–75 [*KSA* 1: 877].

even to denounce the desire (the philosophical desire) of this objection as the very thing that can be explained by this "there are effects of truth, effects of life." This multiplicity or this internal difference which prevents even the concept of truth or of life from being something other than the effect of that of which it is the concept, this internal difference has as its consequence that life (1) wants truth in order to protect or preserve itself, but (2) flees truth in order to protect or preserve itself. There is thus a truth that conserves or serves life and a truth that threatens it or loses it or kills it; there are thus truths, and as soon as life is what both wants truth and flees truth, there are lives, levels, qualities, different forces of life that are heterogeneous and that are protected, lost, or destroyed, etc. Here is just one indication of this from *Le livre du philosophe* (III). It is the passage defining the origin of the *Trieb zur Wahrheit*. I have chosen this passage (I am wondering whether I should tell you why right away?) because a metaphor—though, for Nietzsche, a metaphor is always only a metaphor and more than a metaphor—because a metaphor or a metaphorical scene seems to me to give the key, the best key, for this strange logic that continues and discontinues life in truth, life in lives, truth in truths, and that explains that life is at a loss in truth and truth in life, even though they go together, conjugate [*coïtent*], inhabit the same place all the while wanting the death of the other and death from the other. This key is a key (but what is a key?) and it is important to hear it, first of all here, as part of a narrative, I mean a strange event, a double and thus remarkable event (which is not an event among others since it opens and closes there), the event of a key given and taken back, taken back definitively, which is to say, without return, which is to say, not even taken back but thrown away, and in such a way that (and here is the truth) it is at the moment it is thrown away, at the moment of this terrible event of a thrown-away key, that one knows that there is a key, that one has lived thanks to a key that had been given.

This given key (of which one can speak only because it was thrown away) is to be found, if it so happens to be found, in the passage that defines, then, the *Trieb zur Wahrheit*, at the beginning of the theoretical introduction to "On Truth and Lie in an Extra-moral Sense" (summer 1873, note the date). Nietzsche there speaks of dissimulation as an instinct of preservation, and of the intellect as a means of preservation and, thus, as the very operator of dissimulation (*Verstellung*, which means at once dissimulation, disguise, and displacement, a changing of places that makes something unrecognizable), which already allows us to describe the throwing away of the key — when it takes place — as an essential dissimulating displacement, a movement in space, a topology of truth, an analysis of truth as topology. Nietzsche writes:

The intellect, as a means of preserving the individual (*als ein Mittel zur Erhaltung des Individuums*), unfolds (*entfaltet*) its main powers (*seine Hauptkräfte*) in dissimulation (*in der Verstellung*); for dissimulation is the means by which the weaker, less robust individuals survive, having been denied the ability to fight for their existence with horns or sharp predator teeth. In man this art of dissimulation reaches its peak: among men, deception, flattery, lying and cheating, backbiting, posturing, living in borrowed splendor, wearing a mask, hiding behind convention, play-acting in front of others and oneself, in short, constantly fluttering around the single flame of vanity, is so much the rule and law that there is hardly anything more incomprehensible (*unbegreiflicher*) than how an honest and pure drive for truth [literally, a sincere and pure truth drive: *ein ehrlicher und reiner Trieb zur Wahrheit*] could have arisen among them.[5]

Dissimulation (*Verstellung*) is not something that simply happens to life or that happens to the intellect as an organ of the living being. Such dissimulation is that by which life (the weakest life, says Nietzsche, "the weakest individuals," but since force is always finite, it is always in some sense weakness), such dissimulation is, thus, that by which life (strong, weak) defends itself, preserves itself: against truth, therefore, but also by means of truth insofar as truth is constructed through dissimulation, is a product of dissimulation. That is why there are truths: those that protect and, as we are going to see, those that kill.

If dissimulation is an operation of the living, a behavior of the living, if everything comes down to it as to a *habitus* of the living, a way of being or of doing for the intellect as an organ of the living, then dissimulation produces effects that must be translated not in terms of true-false but truthful-lying, in an extra-moral sense, of course, as the title of the text indicates. And the role of language in this operation confirms this: in man, says Nietzsche, this art of dissimulation (*Verstellungskunst*) reaches its apex insofar as language, discourse, gives to this being-as-lie or to this mask of the false its greatest "truth," if you will.

Here, then, is the key that opens—and closes—this singular logic, and I dedicate this reading of it to Sarah Kofman, whose *Camera Obscura*, while discussing other texts by Nietzsche,[6] says in a chapter titled "The Keyhole": "We must throw away the key." The key to which I am referring here is

---

5. Nietzsche, "On Truth and Lie in an Extra-moral Sense," p. 254 [*KSA* 1: 876]; *Le livre du philosophe/Das Philosophenbuch*, pp. 172–73.

6. At the bottom of the page of the typescript and in the left margin there is this handwritten insertion: "notably a passage from *The Genealogy of Morals* where Nietzsche also speaks of the chamber of consciousness, though not explicitly of a key."

188 to be found in the passage that follows the one I just read.⁷ What dissimulates is life insofar as it maintains and protects itself. Man, as a living being, is thus himself dissimulating but then also dissimulated from himself: the truth concerning what he is, as a product of life, remains dissimulated from him. Dissimulation is dissimulated in him. Truth is not only dissimulated, it is not only dissimulation; it is the dissimulation of dissimulation. Now, of course, to jump ahead a bit, a lot even, I will have you notice that you can find in Heidegger more than one statement of this sort: truth as veiling and as veiling of the veiling, not un-veiling but veiling and veiling-over. Yet Heidegger does not want to make of this (for reasons he goes to great lengths to justify, of course) an operation of the living, of a living subject or, indeed, of life, or even something describable or referable like an act or, indeed, an event. Now, what interests me here in Nietzsche with this story of the key, to which we are coming, is this narrative aspect that he wishes to hold onto and that implies certain acts, operations, a kind of subjectivity (which is why he sounds psychologistic and speaks of lies rather than of falsehood, of belief or illusion, or else of error rather than of falsehood). Of course, this event is not an event—at least not in the everyday sense of the term—since it is at the origin of the entire logic that allows us to constitute this everyday sense. Of course this operation is not, for the same reason, that of some (empirical or transcendental) subjectivity. And then, one might find that this story of the key (⁸a key is not something natural, and to speak, as Nietzsche will, of nature throwing away the key is without any rigor beyond the metaphorical: but the nature in question—here, life, *physis*—is precisely not natural; a nature that dissimulates is not natural, and even less so a nature that dissimulates dissimulation; this is a nature before or beyond the opposition nature/artifice, nature/technics, and so on. And as for the metaphoricity of this narrative, everything *Le livre du philosophe* says about metaphoricity dictates that we not make light of it. Here, then, is the passage of the thrown-away key. It follows the one I translated just a moment ago:

189 Men are deeply immersed in illusions and dreams; their eye glides only along the surface of things and sees "forms"; their feeling nowhere leads to the truth, but is content to receive stimuli and, as it were, play blind games

---

7. Sarah Kofman, *Camera Obscura: Of Ideology*, trans. Will Straw (Ithaca, NY: Cornell University Press, 1999), p. 29 [*Camera Obscura: De l'idéologie* (Paris: Éditions Galilée, 1973), p. 48].

8. This parenthesis does not close in the typescript and the sentence is incomplete.

on the back of things (*gleichsam ein tastendes Spiel auf dem Rücken der Dinge zu spielen*). In addition man, in his dreams at night, allows himself to be lied to all his life, and his moral sense never tries to prevent this, although men are said to have stopped snoring by sheer strength of will. What does man really know about himself? Indeed, would he ever be able to perceive himself completely, as if he were laid out in an illuminated glass case (*erleuchteten Glaskasten*)? Does nature not conceal most things from him . . ."[9]

To conceal, here, is *verschweigt*, which means not to dissimulate what one could show, what one could allow to be seen, but to hide what one could say: in other words, to silence, *verschweigen*. Nature hides in the order of saying or at least in the order of signaling; it hides not by veiling but by not saying or rather by not signifying or not writing, that is to say, by writing — writing something else; that is why the hiding here presupposes an operation of ciphering or de-ciphering, and it is why it is a question of veracity and of lies — in the extra-moral sense — rather than of truth or falsity; truth is first of all an effect of a possible veracity, a possible veridicity, and, because of the dissimulation that constitutes it, because of lies, of cryptology or of cryptography, of apocryphy; and this begins already with the relation of the living body to itself. "Does nature not conceal most things from him, even his own body, in order to detain and lock him up . . ."[10] Be careful with this word *einzuschliessen*: nature has locked us up, with a double turn of the key; nature, a maternal figure of sorts, has locked us up. Ponge, in *The Sun Placed in the Abyss*—a paternal figure here (law and sower), which at the end of its trajectory or its course becomes at midday a redheaded whore—Ponge says at a certain point that the sun has put its seals on nature ("the seals by the sun are affixed on nature. Henceforth, no one can either enter or get out. The juridical verdict is expected. That is where we now stand. That is also why we cannot adore it. And so, rather than complaining, we should thank it for having made itself visible.")[11] Earlier, the text speaks of the possibility of "locking up with a double turn"[12] significations in language. I return to the quotation from Nietzsche: "Does nature not conceal most things

---

9. Nietzsche, "On Truth and Lie in an Extra-moral Sense," p. 254 [*KSA* 1: 876–77]; *Le livre du philosophe/Das Philosophenbuch*, pp. 172–75.

10. Ibid., p. 254 [*KSA* 1: 877]; *Le livre du philosophe/Das Philosophenbuch*, 174–75.

11. Francis Ponge, *The Sun Placed in the Abyss and Other Texts*, trans. Serge Gavronsky (New York: Sun, 1977), p. 62; "Le soleil placé en abyme," in *Pièces* (Paris: Gallimard, 1961), p. 153.

12. [Translators' note:] Ponge, *Sun Placed in the Abyss*, p. 45; the French here is *boucler à double tour*, which Gavronsky translates as "meanings that double back in themselves."

from him, even his own body, in order to detain and lock him up within a proud deceitful consciousness, removed from the coils of the intestines, the rapid flow of the blood stream, the intricate vibration of the fibers?"[13] The last word of this sentence, in the German syntax, is *einzuschliessen*: to lock up. And the next sentence begins, "*Sie warf den Schlüssel weg*":

> Nature has thrown away the key, and woe betide the disastrous curiosity (*verhängnisvollen Neubegier*) which could one day peer out and down through a crack (*Spalte*) in the chamber of consciousness (*Bewusstseinszimmer*) and suspect that man, in the indifference of his ignorance, rests on the pitiless, the greedy, the insatiable, the murderous, as if he were hanging in his dreams from the back of a tiger. Given this constellation, where on earth does the drive for truth come from?[14]

This question is not suggesting that the truth drive cannot appear. On the contrary, Nietzsche will go on to explain how it begins to appear in places where it seems impossible. It seems impossible or, rather than impossible, prohibited, since its impossibility <stems from> this event, this quasi-event of the key's having been thrown away by nature. Hence nature prohibits truth by enclosing us, or rather by enclosing our body, as well as what there is to be seen or known. But a key being a key, it can lock only that which can be opened: before the key there is no truth and no desire or drive for truth. And a key that could not be lost or irreversibly thrown away would not be a key. A key, in order to be a key, must be separable from the room, from the door, from the mechanism it makes turn in order to open and lock. A key must be able to open and lock, but also, to be a key, it must be able to be lost or thrown away, separated from the lock. In other words, as soon as there is a key, there appears the possibility of the key's being given away; but since the possibility of its being given away implies the possibility of its being taken back, the key is always only on loan. A sort of contract forges the key; it is nothing outside of, or before, this strange contract or this strange alliance. One thus cannot say that the truth drive would have been released or even made possible had the key not been thrown away. If the being-able-to-be-thrown-away constructs the structure and the place, the taking-place, of the key, the truth drive is born of the key as that which can be thrown away or taken back even before being constructed or given. But since this key is always double in its capacity and its capacity-to-be—dou-

---

13. "On Truth and Lie in an Extra-moral Sense," p. 254 [*KSA* 1: 877]; *Le livre du philosophe/Das Philosophenbuch*, 174–75.

14. Ibid.

ble in its capacity to open and/or lock, be given away and/or taken back, thrown away (thrown away always by the one who gave it: nature, even if it seems to be the recipient who throws it away)—since the key is always double, is its own double, the key and its double, the truth drive is double, both authorized and prohibited by the "key" event. I insist on the translation of *Trieb* by drive [*pulsion*]. The French translation has "*instinct*" here: that is not wrong and we must not lose sight of the fact that the *Wahrheitstrieb* is natural: it is not a cultural, accidental, symbolic desire, etc. But at the same time, the natural is not all that natural; the natural is here that of a nature that is in itself perverse enough to trick itself and play with the key on its own. The key takes place, but it is not the place where the alternative open/locked gets played out. So that if giving the key amounts to allowing the truth to be seen, and throwing it away amounts to prohibiting it definitively, the key, even insofar as it opens, is the medium, the symbol, the instrument of law and, thus, of prohibition. The absolute transgression consists not in opening what must remain locked, in using the key when it would be prohibited, in making a copy, a double, of the key, in forging another key, in stealing the key. The absolute transgression consists in bypassing the "key" system, bypassing the alternative of the law, the alternative opening/closing, the alternative of the turn of the key. The absolute transgression is to put one's eye to the crack, to do without a key. That is what is terrible. "Woe betide fateful curiosity," says Nietzsche. It is terrible and one risks one's life, for it is then no longer a matter of doing what is prohibited, of opening with a key what was locked with a key, thus contravening the prohibition from within its system (prohibition/transgression), but of transgressing the system itself. Obviously, the transgression of the system re-inscribes transgression within the system; and this analogy is important. But it is, all the same, not the same thing. Why? Because,[15] I would say—to venture an interpretation that goes beyond a commentary authorized by what this brief passage of Nietzsche's literally says—by peering through the crack, by looking at the body (inside the body and the unconscious: I emphasize unconscious here because the room in question, locked with a key, a key that was then immediately thrown away by nature or by life, is the *Bewusstseinszimmer*. Nietzsche later says <of> consciousness: Woe to the one who looks through the crack. Nietzsche says, "woe betide the disastrous curiosity which could one day peer out and down through a crack

---

15. The sentence is incomplete in the typescript and the parenthesis that opens further down does not close.

in the chamber of consciousness."[16] Hence the lock with a key is nothing other than the chamber itself, consciousness itself; that is what locks us up, and contrary to what you, like me, might have been tempted to imagine at first, it is not a matter of peering through the crack *into* a dark room or chamber that we would have to remain outside of once the key has been thrown away, locked up outside, as it were, but rather of looking outside, locked up as we are in consciousness. The body and the unconscious are the outside. I would say, then, venturing my interpretation, that the most serious, the most terrible risk one can run—and the most fateful, necessary in the sense of fateful, *"verhängnisvoll"*—is not only what we might see of the unconscious and of the body, however terrifying that might be, the most terrifying thing is the very act of looking without a lock and key through a crack that was already there in nature. That there exists before any lock and any instituted opening-closing, before any key, whether given away or taken back, a crack—a crack that is thus neither natural nor accidental (technical, instituted)—that the possibility of this crack allows one to see only on the condition that one first sees the crack, that the possibility of this crack (*Spalte*—this gap, this fissure, this hiatus) is what later allows the installation of locks and keys, because for there to be locks and keys one must be able to make openings that are, no doubt, violent, though they are made possible by the structure of a wall that can be cracked, that, therefore, the so-called "natural" structure of the wall must have a crack through which to see—that is what frightens, fascinates and frightens, and makes of the gaze a voyeur exposed to the worst. That is what at once engenders and paralyzes the *Wahrheitstrieb*, between the eye and the crack, the crack (*Spalte*) as or in *physis*.

Before going any further with the reading of this passage, let me plug in here, without commenting on them, Heidegger's readings of an aphorism (number 109) from *The Gay Science* and of a passage from *The Will to Power*. The aphorism from *The Gay Science* says: "*Der Gesammt-Charakter der Welt ist dagegen in alle Ewigkeit Chaos.*"[17] In the course of his interpretation of Nietzschean chaos—an interpretation that is central to the chapter <of his *Nietzsche*> on the eternal return, and one that we will soon take up on its own account—Heidegger recalls that chaos, *khaos*, *khainō*, means *bâille-ment*,

---

16. "On Truth and Lie in an Extra-moral Sense," p. 254 [*KSA* 1: 877]; *Le livre du philosophe/Das Philosophenbuch*, 174–75.

17. Friedrich Nietzsche, *The Gay Science*, trans. Walter Kaufmann (New York: Random House, 1974), p. 168: "The total character of the world, however, is in all eternity chaos" (fragment 109) [*KSA* 3: 468].

yawning, cracking open, gaping open (*das Gähnende*), what splits in two (*das Auseinanderklaffende*). "We conceive of *khaos*," says Heidegger, "in most intimate connection with an original interpretation (*Auslegung*) of the essence (*Wesen*) of *alētheia* as the self-opening abyss (*als den sich öffnenden Abgrund*) (cf. Hesiod, *Theogony*)."¹⁸

We will return shortly to what dictates this interpretation of Nietzsche's chaos by Heidegger.

The second passage that I wanted to graft, as it were, onto this eye cracked open, this eye slit (because the eye is thought on the basis of the slit, in the slit, as the slit), as the place of fascination for truth, is a passage from *The Will to Power*, which I read as it is quoted by Heidegger in the middle of the interpretative commentary he gives of it (in *The Will to Power as Knowledge*, v. 3, p. 132; v. 1, pp. 626–27 of the German text). Read this excerpt from Heidegger's *Nietzsche*:

> The princes of Europe should indeed consider carefully whether they can do without our support. We immoralists—we are today the only power that needs no allies in order to achieve victory; thus we are by far the strongest of the strong. We do not even need to tell lies; what other power can dispense with that? A powerful seduction (*Verführung*) fights on our behalf, perhaps the most powerful there is—the seduction of truth.— "Truth"?¹⁹ Who has put this word in my mouth? But I repudiate it; I disdain this proud word; no, we do not need even this; we would come to power and victory even without truth. The spell (*Zauber*) that fights on our behalf, the

194

---

18. Heidegger, *Nietzsche*, v. 2, p. 91 [v. 1, p. 350; *GA* 6.1: 312]. Heidegger's *Nietzsche* was originally published in German in two volumes (Pfullingen: Günther Neske Verlag, 1961) and then subsequently in Heidegger's *Gesamtausgabe*, ed. Brigitte Schillbach (Frankfurt am Main: Vittorio Klostermann, 1966), vols. 6.1 and 6.2. The two volumes were translated into French by Pierre Klossowski and published in two corresponding volumes, *Nietzsche* (Paris: Éditions Gallimard, 1971). The English version of this work, also titled *Nietzsche*, edited by David Farrell Krell (San Francisco: Harper & Row, 1979–87), was published in four separate volumes, each with its own subtitle: (1) *The Will to Power as Art*, trans. David Farrell Krell, 1979; (2) *The Eternal Recurrence of the Same*, trans. David Farrell Krell, 1984; (3) *The Will to Power as Knowledge and as Metaphysics*, trans. Joan Stambaugh, David Farrell Krell, Frank A. Capuzzi, 1987; (4) *Nihilism*, trans. Frank A. Capuzzi, 1982. All subsequent references to Heidegger's *Nietzsche* will be, first, to the volume and page number of the English edition, then to the volume and page number of the original German edition, the one to which Derrida refers throughout, and, finally, to the volume and page number of the *Gesamtausgabe*, abbreviated *GA*.

19. On his photocopy of the passage cited and inserted into the typescript, Derrida adds in the margins quotation marks around the word "truth."

eye of Venus that charms and blinds even our opponents, is *the magic of the extreme*,[20] the seduction that everything extreme exercises; we immoralists — we are *the ones at the outermost point (die Äussersten)*.[21]

Let's leave all these lines of inquiry open and return to the key. If, in the course of this fabulous event, this non-natural and violent event, non-natural in the derived sense of the word nature, nature threw away the key, or rather gave it as thrown-away, leaving us with the fear of chaos, of the crack, the truth drive is at once elicited and prohibited, elicited as prohibited. And truth gets divided right from the start into a truth that threatens, or even kills, and a truth that protects, preserves, spares. This internal division of truth, of the value of truth, is not, however, an opposition (truth that spares, truth that threatens, or truth that at once threatens [*menace*] and spares [*ménage*]). Insofar as this division is thought in terms of differences of forces, there will be truths more or less received, desired, believed according to the vital forces at war. And what is then called "truth" — objective, universal, the object of a consensus, and so on — is but an effect and a moment of this dissimulation as war, seduction, ruse, and so on. This is the moment when, out of fatigue, boredom, or necessity, in order to replenish its forces or, better, to trick the enemy, the living being decides to make peace, to draw up a contract, to establish a consensus. This happens through the institution of language; it even explains the institution of language, the legislation of language, which is commanded by dissimulation but produces peace treaties or, I would say instead, armistices under the name of "truth." Dissimulation thus dissimulates itself beneath the truth, so that one can say, without playing on words — or simply by explaining the play on words as a possibility of these reversals of force, these ruses and inversions of power: dissimulation (the truth of last resort) dissimulates itself beneath the truth, or else truth is the dissimulation of dissimulation, or else the truth of dissimulation is truth, or else the truth of truth is dissimulation, or else the dissimulation of truth is the truth of dissimulation. The truth drive is thus itself the symptom of this fatigue, this boredom, or this supplementary ruse that leads one to seek peace and consensus and that presides over the instituting of language. From that point on, after the institution of language, the

---

20. On the photocopy of the passage cited and inserted into the transcript, a handwritten line links the words in italics to the marginal annotation: "Magic of the extremes?"
21. Heidegger, *Nietzsche*, v. 3, p. 132 [v. 1, pp. 626–27; *GA* 6.1: 565]; for the passage from *The Will to Power* being quoted by Heidegger, see *KSA* 12: 10[94], p. 510. On the photocopy of the passage cited and inserted into the transcript, the German words in parentheses have been handwritten in the margins.

war between the living will never come to an end; forces are still going to confront one another, but one will now have at one's disposal a regulatory fiction, which is none other than the opposition or the distinction between veracity and lying. The possibility of such a fiction, such a simulacrum of war, is the origin of truth, the origin of the effect of truth. But in order for dissimulation to dissimulate itself, that is, not only dissimulate but dissimulate *itself* in the truth, and in order for truth to continue to produce itself and thus to reproduce itself as such (the truth of truth as consensus is a reproduction that is identical to itself), it is necessary that this origin of truth, this dissimulation as the origin of truth, dissimulate itself absolutely to the agents themselves, to the living subjects, etc. That is to say, it is necessary that it be forgotten. This forgetting—dissimulation of dissimulation—is not one psychological category among others; it is the process of truth, of the dissimulation of dissimulation. And if the story of the thrown-away key, the fabulous narrative of this mythical event, truer than the true, if the story of the throwing away of the key by it (life, nature) is the very mainspring of this dissimulation, of this displacement (for you know that, when one speaks here of dissimulation, this too can be a translation of *Verstellung*, that is, "displacement," "change of place": one is also naming a strange phoronomy and topophory or crypto-topography: I will call this from now on *cryptopography*), if the story of the key, as cryptopography, does not take place in a space of truth or falsity, in a true or false space, but is the origin of the taking-place of truth or of untruth, well, then, this cryptopography must itself be closed (enclosed, as the word indicates) and thus forgotten. It is when the throwing away of the key is forgotten that truth as consensus reigns, as well as the opposition true/false, and all the oppositions or distinctions that are conditioned thereby, including that of life and death, the opposition of all values. One must forget the key, such is the condition of truth. Such is also the condition of the key, of its oppositional functioning (its turning alternation between opening/closing). So it is that when there are keys, when they work and we have them at our disposal, when they turn in their locks, that is when we have most forgotten that the origin and condition of every key is the throwing away of the key and its being-given-away-taken-back, the forgetting of the key. And the key—as the forgetting of the key—is always reproducible. There is always one more key [*une clé de plus*]. One more key when the key's no more [*Plus de clé*]. The key is replaceable, the loss of one elicits another, a copy, a double, as if prepared in advance. And when one cannot open a door to see, one can still open a mailbox, that is to say, a place where vision is delegated or delayed, which does not fundamentally change things since it began by being lost.

Here is a passage from the *Philosophenbuch* that follows the throwing away of the key and that will sum up more clearly what I have just said. (Read *Philosophenbuch*, pp. 174–77.)

> To the extent that the individual wants to maintain himself against other individuals, in the natural state of things he has used the intellect mostly for dissimulation alone; but since man, out of necessity as well as boredom, wants to live in a society or herd, he needs a peace settlement and he tries to make at least the most brutal *bellum omnium contra omnes* vanish from his world. This peace settlement entails something that looks like the first step towards attaining that mysterious drive for truth. At this point what is henceforth to be called "truth" is fixed, i.e., a universally valid and binding designation of things is invented and the legislation of language supplies the first laws of truth. For it is here that the contrast between truth and lie first comes into being. The liar uses the valid designations, the words, in order to make the unreal appear as real: he says, for example, "I am rich," when the correct designation of this condition would be "poor." He misuses the firm conventions by arbitrarily exchanging or even reversing the names. If he does this in a selfish and incidentally harmful way society will no longer trust him and he will be excluded as a result. What men shun in this case is not so much being deceived, but rather being harmed by the deception. At this level too they do not really hate the deception, but the bad, hostile consequences of certain kinds of deception. Only in a similarly restricted sense does man want the truth. He desires the pleasant, life-preserving consequences of truth; he is indifferent to pure knowledge without consequences, and even hostile to harmful and destructive truths. Moreover: how about those conventions of language? Are they perhaps products of knowledge, of the sense of truth: are designations and things congruent? Is language the adequate expression of all realities?
>
> Only through forgetfulness can man ever come to believe that he is in possession of a truth in the degree just described. If he is not content with truth in the form of tautology, i.e., with empty shells, he will for ever be trading truths for illusions.[22]

You see—or you do not see because this can no longer be seen—how death and prohibition play a part in this cryptopography of truth. The *socius* is constituted through a contract of truth that is a ruse or a simulacrum of dissimulation. It is thus constituted upon a truth that is an untruth. And this is done in order to live, that is, in order to avoid the truth that kills, but that kills insofar as it is untruth. Henceforth the *socius* is constituted by a

---

22. Nietzsche, "On Truth and Lie in an Extra-moral Sense," pp. 254–55 [*KSA* 1: 877–78]; *Le livre du philosophe/Das Philosophenbuch*, pp. 174–77.

transgression of truth that institutes truth as untruth. But the transgression of the *socius* also consists in transgressing truth and untruth as an effect of dissimulation, etc. At the end of *Le livre du philosophe*, among the *Entwürfe*, we find this under the title "Truth"[23]: "Without untruth there can be neither society nor culture. The tragic conflict. Everything that is good and beautiful depends on illusion: truth kills (*Wahrheit tötet*)—indeed, it kills itself (*ja tötet sich selbst*) (insofar as it recognizes that its foundation is error (*dass ihr Fundament der Irrtum ist*))."[24] If one were to translate this "without un" (without untruth, neither, nor), one might say: society and culture live off untruth, off illusion, because the truth kills. In other words, the truth off which they live is untruth, but the truth of this untruth is still or already an untruth, a suicide truth, since it is acknowledged, in its truth of truth, as an error or an illusion. And the following paragraph—which I leave you to read (fragment 177)[25]—analyzes this prohibition or this madness that inhabits the truth, the belief in truth. Rather than continuing to read these texts, let me append two conclusions or two accounts:

1. Truth as a ruse of life, a play of the forces of life. It is always living nature—*physis*, if you will—that serves as the final recourse, as that to which all these contrivances of truth and this scene of the key refer. The force of the living, or at least the greatest force of the living, is the last resort.
2. And yet (but is this contradictory?) the truth is suicide in its structure. It is suicide. It is life death, as truth without truth of the truth.

Having reached this point, I am going to leap ahead. I am going to leave here these early texts of Nietzsche (we could have also read, from the same point of view, *The Birth of Tragedy*) in order to begin the second detour, the second detour announced earlier, namely, the Heideggerian detour. To do this, I will leap ahead toward later texts of Nietzsche that support Heidegger's treatment of the question of Nietzsche's alleged biologism. I could not make this leap earlier; in order to make it significant and problematic, it was necessary to clarify the two preceding propositions, namely, <(1)> the

---

23. In quotation marks in Nietzsche's original text.
24. Nietzsche, *Unpublished Writings from the Period of Unfashionable Observations*, p. 190 [*KSA* 7: 29[7], p. 623]; *Le livre du philosophe/Das Philosophenbuch*, fragment 176, pp. 202–3.
25. Nietzsche, "On Truth and Lie in an Extra-moral Sense," pp. 255–56 [*KSA* 1: 877–78]; *Le livre du philosophe/Das Philosophenbuch*, fragment 177, pp. 202–5.

force of life as the final recourse, (2) the suicide structure of truth as an effect of life. Of these two later texts of Nietzsche, one of them is not quoted by Heidegger, if I am not mistaken, though he could have quoted it since it belongs to the set of texts he treats and analyzes, while the other he does quote.

The one that Heidegger does not quote is the following, which is included among the fragments of *The Will to Power* (1887) (you can find the [French] translation in volume 1 of the Gallimard edition, p. 215). It says this:

> "The value of life" [in quotation marks . . .].—Life is a unique case; one must justify *all* existence and not only life—the justifying principle is one that explains life, too.
> Life is only a *means* to something; it is the expression of forms of the growth of power.[26]

Life would thus not be the final recourse, neither the origin nor the end, only a means in view of something that is here named "growth of power," a growth of power that itself refers, therefore, to a will to power that is no longer in its essential or ultimate form *life*, the force of life.

The other fragment is taken from *The Gay Science* (1881–82, ten years, therefore, after *Das Philosophenbuch*), and it is quoted by Heidegger in the chapter on *chaos* that I mentioned earlier. Heidegger starts out from an at least apparent contradiction between two propositions of Nietzsche's, one from *The Gay Science* and another from *The Will to Power*. In this chapter Heidegger enumerates ten points, the first of which is this, which I will quote in order to conclude—and we will start here next time. Let me simply point out that the question of biologism is treated by Heidegger in two essential places in his book,[27] the first, "Summary Presentation of the Thought: Beings in Their Totality as Life and Force; the World as Chaos" (v. 2, pp. 82–97),[28] and the second, "Nietzsche's Alleged Biologism" (v. 3, pp. 39–47);[29] you should, of course, read everything around this to get a sense of the context.

---

26. Nietzsche, *WP*, fragment 706, p. 375 [*KSA* 12: 9[13], pp. 344–45]. *La Volonté de puissance*, v.1, p. 215.

27. [Translators' note:] Derrida says "book" here, in the singular, though he will speak at the beginning of the next session of "two volumes," since, as noted above (see n. 18), Heidegger's *Nietzsche* was originally published in two volumes in German and in two corresponding volumes in French translation.

28. Heidegger, *Nietzsche*, v. 2, pp. 82–97 [v. 1, pp. 339–56; *GA* 6.1: 302–18].

29. Ibid., v. 3, pp. 39–47 [v. 1, pp. 517–27; *GA* 6.1: 465–74].

Here, then, to conclude, is the passage indicated above, v. 2, p. 84, in the chapter on chaos (p. 341 in the original [German]):

What stands in view? We reply: *The world in its collective character* (in ihrem Gesamtcharakter). What all pertains to that? The whole of inanimate and animate existence (*das Ganze des Leblosen und des Lebendigen*), whereby "animate" encompasses not only plants and animals but human beings as well. Inanimate and animate things are not juxtaposed [*nebeneinandergeschoben*: the idea of being next to and able to replace one another], or laminated one on top of the other (*aufeinandergeschichtet*), as two separate regions (*wie zwei Bezirke*). Rather, they are represented as interwoven in one vast nexus of Becoming (*verschlungenen Werdenzusammenhang*). Is the unity of that nexus "living" or "lifeless"? Nietzsche writes (XII, number 112): "Our whole world is the *ashes* [*Asche* is underscored] of countless *living* creatures: and even if the living seems so minuscule in comparison to the whole, it is nonetheless the case that *everything* [*alles* is underscored] has already been transposed into life—and so it goes." Apparently opposed to this is a thought expressed in *The Gay Science* (number 109): "Let us beware of saying that death is the opposite (*entgegengesetzt sei*) of life; the living creature is simply a kind of dead creature, and a very rare kind."[30]

---

30. Ibid., v. 2, p. 84 [v. 1, pp. 341–42; *GA* 6.1: 304–5]; XII, 112 = *KSA* 9: 11[84], pp. 472–73; *Gay Science* 109 = *KSA* 3: 468.

EIGHT SESSION[1]

Cause ("Nietzsche")

So: biologism. The question of Nietzsche's biologism, the meaning of his alleged biologism. You no doubt have a sense that this is not just any question, one question among others, a regional question. First of all because it is a question about regionality, a question of knowing whether the living is a region of being, and then of knowing whether one can or must organize a discourse in conformity with the science of objects belonging to such a region, and so on. And when this question is treated by Heidegger, as a reader or interpreter of Nietzsche, it ends up drawing toward it the entire system or the entire course [*démarche*] of Heidegger's interpretation of Nietzsche, which is also to say, a determination of Western metaphysics, of the relation between science and philosophy, of the question of being, and so on and so forth. Which means that the difficulty or one of the difficulties that we will have to treat will be that of our own reading of Heidegger, the interpretative sectioning out — one that is, therefore, in a certain way, violent — that we will have to perform on his text, not only on the two hefty volumes entitled *Nietzsche*,[2] but on other texts concerning Nietzsche or concerning life and death, and finally, therefore, on the entire corpus, if something of the sort were to exist, of Heidegger and of Nietzsche. I can only point out these difficulties here, unable to provide a genuinely satisfying response. Instead of beginning with an endless series of protocols, I am going to come at the entire edifice at its easiest and most obvious place, thereby risking arbitrariness, empiricism, or deception. If we are in agreement, based on my previous justifications, that biologism is what we must

---

1. For bibliographical information regarding the subsequent publication of this session, see the editorial note, p. xiiing.

2. [Translators' note:] See n. 18 in the previous chapter for the full bibliographical reference to Heidegger's *Nietzsche*.

now treat, the most obvious places are volumes 2 and 3 [chapters 2 and 3 of volume 1 in the French translation] of Heidegger's work on Nietzsche, volumes devoted to *the eternal recurrence of the same* and *the will to power as knowledge*, and particularly the following chapters, which I noted last time, namely, the one on chaos (v. 2, pp. 82–97; pp. 339–56 [in the German]),[3] the one on "Nietzsche's Alleged Biology" (v. 3, pp. 39–47; pp. 517–27 [in the German]),[4] and, finally, the one on "Nietzsche's 'Biological' Interpretation of Knowledge" (v. 3, pp. 101–10; pp. 590–602 [in the German]).[5] The risks of my choice are limited by the fact that we there find each time the same interpretation at work, the same system of reading gathering and summing itself up in a powerful way in each of these places, gathering within it the unity of Nietzsche's thought understood in relation to the consummated unity, the unity being consummated, of Western metaphysics, Nietzsche being precisely the peak, the crest, at the summit of this consummation.[6]

And it is precisely this singular *unity*—inasmuch as it is presumed, posited, thought (and there is thought for him only on this condition) by Heidegger, and insofar as it supports the unity of his book, the unity of his interpretation concerning the unity of something, some gathered whole, some gathering, like Western metaphysics—that ultimately provides the unity of Nietzsche's thought. It is precisely this unity, this presumed unity, that, while eliminating the arbitrariness or the empiricism of my point of departure, of my coming at this book in these particular places, will provide me today with the best traction, the strongest hold, the surest and the most economical hold, on the engine of this enormous machine.

How so? It is this unity, first of all, that allows us here to put back into a rigorous relation the question of the *biological* and the question of the *biographical*, such as we had treated them at the beginning of this seminar, and, as a result, to ask ourselves once again about the name and signature of Nietzsche, about what happens when Nietzsche says or writes I, Nietzsche, the undersigned, *ecce homo*, and so on. How does Heidegger take account of the biographical, of the auto-biographical, and of the signature of the proper name? And how does the way he comes to decide this problem, implicitly or explicitly, end up deciding, in its turn, the whole of his interpretation, and especially of his interpretation of what he calls Nietzsche's "alleged biologism"? In other words,

---

3. Heidegger, *Nietzsche*, v. 2, pp. 82–97 [v. 1, pp. 339–56; *GA* 6.1: 302–18].
4. Ibid., v. 3, pp. 39–47 [v. 1, pp. 517–27; *GA* 6.1: 465–74].
5. Ibid., v. 3, pp. 101–10 [v. 1, pp. 590–602; *GA* 6.1: 532–42].
6. In the middle of the left margin of the typescript, there is the following handwritten addition: "Ecce Homo."

if we are able to make out behind Heidegger's reading of Nietzsche the general premises of a reading of Western metaphysics that strongly supports that reading, the question then becomes this: in what way does this interpretation of Western metaphysics as a whole, or taken as a whole, entail a decision with regard to the unity or the unicity [*unicité*] of thought, which itself entails a decision with regard to the biographical, the proper name, the auto-biographical, and the signature?

The question, in this form, is not very old, and it is not easy.

Let me try to point out, by means of a summary, unrefined, simplifying statement that I hope[7] to show is nonetheless not false, Heidegger's proposition on this subject: there is a unity to Nietzsche's thought (even if it is not that of a system in the traditional sense), and this unity stems from its unicity (the underlying thesis, explicitly stated, is this: every great thinker has but one thought, a unique thought). This unicity was neither constituted nor threatened, neither gathered up nor compromised, by the name or names, by the life (normal or mad) of Friedrich Nietzsche; this singular unity, this unity-unicity, stems from the unity of Western metaphysics, which is there gathered at its summit. As a result of this, the biographical, the auto-biographical, the scene or the forces of the proper name, of proper names, of the signature, of signatures, and so on, are going to regain the inessential status or place that has always been theirs in the history of metaphysics, and this indicates, in short, the necessity of our questioning here.

That's the simplified version. Let us now read Heidegger more closely and try to accredit his interpretation with the greatest coherence possible. And this time, right now, I will allow myself to use classical norms of reading by taking up this book by its beginning, and even earlier than its beginning, the beginning of its preface. This preface was, of course, written after the fact. The book *Nietzsche*, as you know, corresponds to a series of courses given from 1936 to 1940 at the University of Freiburg-im-Breisgau and to some *Abhandlungen* (I do not know why Pierre Klossowski translates this by "digressions"), essays or exposés, dating from 1940 to 1946. We must, of course, pay the greatest attention to these dates, especially if we want to, if we have to, put this interpretation, taken as a whole and in its details, in relation to the historico-political situation and, within it, the institutional, university situation in which the series of lectures and essays was produced. The preface, written in 1961, amounts to two pages. Its main intention, as

---

7. The word "hope" is crossed out and the interlineal, handwritten addition right above appears to read "I am preparing."

is typical, is to justify the publication of this collection by referring to its unity, to the unity of its totality. Heidegger even says there, in the middle: "Considered [*nachgedacht*, reflected on] as a whole [a totality, *als Ganzes*], the publication aims to provide a view of the path of thought I followed from 1930 to the 'Letter on Humanism' (1947)."[8]

The unity of this publication and of this teaching is thus also the unity of Heidegger's entire path of thought over more than fifteen years and at a decisive moment. Which is to say that the unity of this interpretation of Nietzsche, the unity of Western metaphysics to which it is referred, and the unity of Heidegger's path of thought, are indissociable as premises, presuppositions, or as the effect of the whole that we are now going to take up.

Now if I begin by what is given as the beginning of this publication, namely, the first words, the first sentence of this preface, what do I find?

Well, to put it elliptically at first, I find two things.

Why two and why, precisely, two things? And why do these two things have a, precisely, literal relationship with the name of Nietzsche and even with his name in quotation marks?

What happens when a proper name is put in quotation marks? Heidegger does not ask himself this question, and my hypothesis is in fact that his entire enterprise, which is nonetheless titled simply *Nietzsche*, is undertaken—gathered in all its forces—in such a way as to restrain, indeed to cancel out, the force of this question.

One finds two things, I said, concerning Nietzsche's name.

Why two things? Why two and why precisely two things?

I first find—let's take things from this side angle, which is not so much to the side, which is even the "essential" thing, it seems to me—two things if I read first of all, being French, on the side of the Klossowski translation, the only one we have at the moment, and then on the side of what is called the original text.

The translation hits you, it is very provocative, it provokes you to think, even if it is, purposefully or not, the contrary of what Heidegger wanted to be thought.

Let me read the first sentence of the Klossowski translation. I'll even write it on the board:

"'Niet sche' [Gallimard's printer left a typo, a space at the perfectly calculated center 4/4 of Nietzsche's name]—the name of the thinker stands as the title for the *cause* of his thought [*la cause de sa pensée*]." The following paragraph explains or justifies, up to a certain point, Klossowski's choice in

---

8. Heidegger, *Nietzsche*, v. 1, p. xl [v. 1, p. 10; *GA* 6.1: xii].

translating [into French] a certain [German] word by *"cause."* I read: "The *cause*, the litigious case [*cause*: trial, juridical debate] is in itself ex-pli-cation (*Aus-einander-setzung*: with, etc. . . .), taking of a position of one party in relation to the other. To let our thought be penetrated by this cause, to prepare it for this cause — that is the content of the present publication."[9]

For anyone who thus opens this book — without knowing the German text — and who thus reads the first line: "'Niet sche' — the name of the thinker stands as the title for the *cause* of his thought," such a reader today might say, "hey, that's pretty hip [*in*]." The name would be the cause of the thought. The thought of Nietzsche would be the effect of the name Nietzsche. Here's something new and rather singular. In short, and in any case, this is going to be a book on the name of Nietzsche and on the relations between the name and the thought of Nietzsche. Someone so in the know, or so little in the know, might even, given the fact that the name has been accidentally cut in two, expect some kind of analysis of the splitting up of the signifier, indeed of all the forms of the signifier, or indeed of the semantic elements linked to the Slavic (Polish) origin of his name, which would then get quickly linked to what Nietzsche says about his name, or what he says about the negativity or rather negating force of his thinking, and then, if one were to get carried away to the point of delirium [*délire*], all this would then be put into relation with the name or names of the only two cities where, in 1887, he said he could think, *Venise* and *Nice*, in a letter that Heidegger in fact quotes at the beginning of the book (a letter to Peter Gast of 15 September 1887), one will say, "okay, I get it, he wants Nice, *il veut nise*, he wants Nietzsche, *il veut Nietzsche*, the will to power is the will to Nietzsche." Obviously, this works only in French and the delirium ends as soon as one recalls, at least with regard to the names of cities, that, in German, *Venise* is Venedig, and *Nice* Nizza.

But if the French reader were to go on reading a bit, he or she might then wonder what this means: "'Niet sche' — the name of the thinker stands as the title for the *cause* of his thought." Limited to the French text, the reader gets clarification in the paragraph that follows, which tells the reader: "you should not hear *cause* in opposition to effect, cause as causality, as the efficient or material or final or formal cause of thought, but as *causa* (a legal debate, a juridical litigation, an opposition between parties, not to be confused with the parts of the name)." Note that this perspective can still be seductive and intoxicating for a French reader of today: the name as the debate of a thought, the name of Nietzsche as the debate or the stakes

9. Ibid., v. 1, p. xxxix [v. 1, p. 9; *GA* 6.1: xi].

of the thought of Nietzsche, the name of Nietzsche as war, as the litigious case of his thought,[10] that is what remains not at all traditional and, when questioned with the help of new problematics, can be very stimulating and productive.

But since the rest of Heidegger's text in translation does not really seem to pursue this path, our intrepid French reader of 1975, too much in the know or not enough in the know (this always amounts to the same thing), decides to look into things more closely and to check what is called the original text, to see what Klossowski translates by "the name of the thinker stands as the title for the cause of his thought."

So what does he see?

Something else. The other thing, the thing other than the cause. He or she reads the German: "'Nietzsche'—*der Name des Denkers steht als Titel für* die Sache *seines Denkens*."

"'Niet sche'—the name of the thinker provides the title for [acts as the title for] *the thing* [la chose] of his thinking."

In general, what gets translated into French as *cause* is *Ursache*, and it is because of this proximity that Klossowski permits himself to translate *Sache* by *cause*. But, usually, *Sache* means *chose*, thing, not in the sense of a sensible or available thing (*Ding*) but a thing in question, an affair, a thing under consideration, something in litigation. In this sense of *Sache* (thing in question), *causa, cause* (in the sense of a case in litigation, a thing being debated), "*cause*" is a good translation. And as such it poses not only the thing in question but the question of the thing (*die Frage nach dem Ding*), in particular the question of knowing how the relation between the two semantic determinations of cause operates, that is, cause as part of the couple cause/effect and cause as the object of litigation, as well as how the relation between the cause and the thing (as *Ding* or as *Sache*) operates. In any case, the strange translation of *Sache* by *cause* is supported by what follows, when Heidegger adds: *die Sache, der Streitfall*, the thing, the litigious case is in itself, "*ist in sich selbst, Aus-einander-setzung*."[11]

All the same, when Heidegger says "the name of the thinker stands as the title for the cause of his thought," it is quite certain that he does not mean that the name is the cause of the effect "thought" and that the genitive (of his thought) here designates the thing *as his thought*. It means—and everything that follows will confirm this—that the name of Nietzsche as the title of this book is not a proper name of an individual or of a signatory

---

10. An insertion in the left margin reads: "the Thing."
11. Heidegger, *Nietzsche*, v. 1, p. xxxix [v. 1, p. 9; *GA* 6.1: xi].

but the name of a thought, a thought that is one thought; and it is only on the basis of this thing in question—his thought—that we will eventually be able to read or understand the title, namely, the name. Nietzsche is, for Heidegger here, nothing other than this thought, his thought. And were we to pause on the syntax of the genitive in this first sentence, we should be able to note this surprising circulation, namely, that the name as thing or cause of his thought does not at all mean, as Klossowski ran the risk of having it be understood, that the name is before the thought, the thought of Nietzsche, his thought, like a cause that comes before an effect, or even that the thing of his thought—the name—is determinable before the thought. On the contrary (subjective genitive): the name as the thing of thought means that it is incumbent upon thought to think the name and that one will think or understand or read or gather only on the basis of *his* thought. It is only in thinking this thought that we will think the possessive and thus the proper name. The *his* of his thought (*seines Denkens*) will come to have meaning—and thus the proper name will have meaning—only on the basis of the thought of the thought of the signatory or of the bearer of the name. We will know who Nietzsche is and what his proper name says only on the basis of his thought—and not through some more or less sophisticated biographical notice.

Starting here, there are, it seems to me, two paths. One would consist in exploring anew this problematic of the proper name, at the risk of seeing this name broken into pieces or dissolved into masks or simulacra or else constituted only well beyond the "life" of the thinker, drawing toward it the entire future of the world (historical, political, and so on . . .), indeed even the eternal return. This path would complicate in a singular fashion the problem of the bio-graphical or the auto-biographical, but it would in no way do away with it, no more than it would do away with all the problems that are today flagged as "psychoanalytic." This is the path that I had at least tried to point out when we read together certain pages from *Ecce Homo*.[12]

The other path would come down to determining the essentiality of the name on the basis of the thing of the thought, on the basis of the thought, which would ultimately be defined as a content; it would come down to dropping the singular proper name, the biographical, the psychological as so many inessential diversions. For by having misgivings about biographism, psychologism, or even psychoanalyticism, one would be taking aim at various kinds of reductive empiricism that end up dissimulating something that

---

12. All the words after "path" in this sentence are crossed out and are replaced by the interlineal addition: "that I will indicate in a certain reading of" *Ecce Homo*.

presents itself as thought. And that is in fact, along this other path, what Heidegger does. But the question, or one of the questions, is then to know whether he is not resorting here to some classical philosophical or metaphysical gesture at the very moment an appeal is being made to a certain other of metaphysics, with Heidegger situating Nietzsche at the limit, at the summit, of this consummation. It is a classical gesture that consists, in the end, in dissociating the thing of life or of the proper name and the thing of thought, or at least being able to access the former only by means of the latter. Whence this *first effect*: the beginning of Heidegger's lectures dissociates in a very conventional way an absolutely conventional biography of Nietzsche from the questions, the great questions, with which this great philosopher wrestled with all his might. Already in the form of this first lecture, which conforms to an old pedagogical model still in use in the institution, we see this dissociation appear.[13] Heidegger begins with a few brief words on the life and work of Nietzsche for the sake of the students who are preparing for their exam, but he then denigrates biographism and opposes to it thought, the great thought that is about to be discussed. Another way of recalling that "Nietzsche," the title of these lectures or of this book, concerns not Nietzsche, the man or the finite bearer of this name, but the great adventure of thought that traversed him and defined him through this traversal. Read v. 1, pp. 7–8:

> At the outset we should mention briefly the most important aspects of Nietzsche's life, the origins of the plans and preliminary drafts, and the later publication of these materials after Nietzsche's death.
> In a Protestant pastor's house in the year 1844 Nietzsche was born. As a student of classical philology in Leipzig in 1865 he came to know Schopenhauer's major work, *The World as Will and Representation*. During his last semester in Leipzig (1868–69), in November, he came into personal contact with Richard Wagner. Apart from the world of the Greeks, which remained decisive for the whole of Nietzsche's life, although in the last years of his wakeful thinking it had to yield some ground to the world of Rome, Schopenhauer and Wagner were the earliest intellectually determinative forces. In the spring of 1869, Nietzsche, not yet twenty-five years of age and not yet finished with his doctoral studies, received an appointment at Basel as associate professor of classical philology. There he came into amicable contact with Jacob Burckhardt and with the Church historian Franz Overbeck. The question as to whether or not a real friendship evolved between Nietzsche and Burckhardt has a significance that exceeds the merely biographical sphere, but discussion of it does not belong here. He also met

13. There is here a large closing bracket and a note in the left margin: "stop here."

Bachofen, but their dealings with one another never went beyond reserved collegiality. Ten years later, in 1879, Nietzsche resigned his professorship. Another ten years later, in January, 1889, he suffered a total mental collapse, and on August 25, 1900, he died.

During the Basel years Nietzsche's inner disengagement from Schopenhauer and Wagner came to completion. But only in the years 1880 to 1883 did Nietzsche find himself, that is to say, find himself as a thinker: he found his fundamental position within the totality of beings, and thereby the determinative source of his thought.[14]

After this, turning to what he calls "Nietzsche's philosophy proper" (*die eigentliche Philosophie Nietzsches*), Heidegger notes that this philosophy "did not assume a final form and was not itself published in any book,"[15] and criticizing the complete critical edition that was then being prepared, he notes the limitations inherent both in what he calls the principle of completeness (*Vollständigkeit*)—which encourages publishing everything and has its origins, he says, in nineteenth-century publication practices—and in this biographism and psychologism, which are, as it were, the perversion of our times, their monstrosity. Criticizing this editorial undertaking, he writes, I quote, "by the manner of its biographical, psychological commentary and its similarly thorough research of all 'data' on Nietzsche's 'life,' and of the views of his contemporaries as well, it is a product (*Ausgeburt*) of the psychological-biological addiction of our times (*der psychologisch-biologischen Sucht unserer Zeit*)."[16] And Heidegger continues:

> Only in the actual presentation of the authentic "Works" (*des eigentlichen "Werkes"*) (1881–89) will this edition have an impact on the future, granted the editors succeed in their task. That task and its fulfillment are not a part of what we have just criticized; moreover, the task can be carried out without all that. But we can never succeed in arriving at Nietzsche's philosophy proper if we have not in our questioning conceived of Nietzsche as the end of Western metaphysics and proceeded to the entirely different question of the truth of Being.[17]

To pose the question of the truth of being (beyond ontology, of course), to determine the place of Nietzsche as the end of Western metaphysics—that is the precondition for then, potentially, gaining access to the name or the

---

14. Heidegger, *Nietzsche*, v. 1, pp. 7–8 [v. 1, pp. 15–16; *GA* 6.1: 5–6].
15. Ibid., v. 1, pp. 8–9 [v. 1, p. 17; *GA* 6.1: 6].
16. Ibid., v. 1, p. 10 [v. 1, p. 18; *GA* 6.1: 8].
17. Ibid., v. 1, p. 10 [v. 1, pp. 18–19; *GA* 6.1: 8].

biography of Nietzsche and, especially, to his textual corpus. For knowing "who Nietzsche was."

Before questioning and casting doubt on—as I am in fact going to do—the very principle of this schema, it is necessary to be attentive to its necessity, to everything that can justify it, in general as well as in the historico-political situation in which this schema is put to work. Here, first, is the general justification: it is true that easy reliance on psychology and biography in the style in which it is most often done, and in which it was done especially back then, turns around the systematic content of a thought, its internal necessity or specificity. This is a classical schema on which I will not dwell. Then there is the historico-political justification: at the time he was writing, teaching his *Nietzsche*, Heidegger had begun to distance himself from Nazism; he had at any rate resigned his position as rector, and without saying anything in his course that might go against the regime or even anything that might go directly and explicitly against the use that was being made of Nietzsche by Nazism (so many ambiguous precautions and silences, to be sure), Heidegger is nonetheless criticizing openly the edition that the regime was sponsoring, an edition with which Heidegger had initially been associated and from which he withdrew once he saw that it was an operation of falsification in which, notably, Nietzsche's sister, Elisabeth Förster Nietzsche, was participating, someone whose Nazi and anti-Semitic sentiments are notorious, as you know. Now, whether he actually spoke these words at the time or added them later, the fact is that, after distancing himself from this editorial enterprise and criticizing the biographism within it, he writes:

> For a knowledge of Nietzsche's biography the presentation by his sister, Elisabeth Förster-Nietzsche, *The Life of Friedrich Nietzsche* (published between 1895 and 1904), remains important. As with all biographical works, however, use of this publication requires great caution.
> We will refrain from further suggestions and from discussion of the enormous and varied secondary literature surrounding Nietzsche, since none of it can aid the endeavor of this lecture course.[18]

We must also see that the most frequent target of Heidegger's criticism, here and elsewhere, is what he calls "the philosophy of life," the kind of philosophy that also interprets Nietzsche as a "philosopher of life," a criticism that, of course, was aimed especially at the Nazism of the times. Heidegger is in fact also, and at the same time, taking aim at a classical university

---

18. Ibid., v. 1, p. 10 [v. 1, p. 19; *GA* 6.1: 8].

tradition—a pre-Nazi tradition, if you will—that made of Nietzsche a "poet-philosopher" or a "philosopher of life," a philosopher without rigor who was denounced from on high by "chairs of philosophy in Germany."[19] Heidegger denounces this tradition just as much as its (Nazi) reversal, which celebrates Nietzsche as the philosopher of life who would have done away with abstractions. In both cases, it is a "philosophy of life" that is being denounced or praised. Philosophy of life is, for Heidegger, an absurdity and something he always rejected, as early as *Sein und Zeit*.

It is crucial first to recognize this critique of psycho-biographism in order to understand later on Heidegger's critique of "Nietzsche's Alleged Biologism," his effort to shield Nietzsche from a biologist interpretation or the accusation of biologism. We just saw this critique of biographism at work with regard to the name of Nietzsche, as a response, if you will, to the question "what is called Nietzsche?" Here it is again, responding this time to the question "Who is Nietzsche?" It comes right at the opening (again the first words) of the third volume, *The Will to Power as Knowledge and as Metaphysics*, in the first chapter, entitled "Nietzsche as the Thinker of the Consummation of Metaphysics" (*Vollendung der Metaphysik*), v. 3, p. 3; p. 473 [in the German]. I quote:

> Who Nietzsche *is* and above all who he *will be* we shall know as soon as we are able to think the thought that he *geprägt* [stamped, forged, imprinted] in this concatenation of words (*Wortgefüge*): *der Wille zur Macht*. Nietzsche is that thinker who trod the *path* of thought to "the will to power" (*der den Gedanken-Gang zum "Willen zur Macht" gegangen ist*). We shall never experience who Nietzsche is through a historical report (*historischen Bericht*) about his life history (*Lebensgeschichte*), nor through a presentation (*Darstellung*) of the contents of his writings. Neither do we, nor should we, want to know who Nietzsche is, if we have in mind only the personality, the historical figure, and the psychological object and its products. But was not the . . .[20]

Heidegger is here going to raise an objection to what he is saying and then dismiss it. Before getting there, let me make a remark so as not to simplify things, especially not to simplify or facilitate the question I will pose regarding this Heideggerian approach [*démarche*]. Here it is. Despite Heidegger's subsequent efforts to reduce the name of Nietzsche, or the "who is Nietzsche?," to the unity of Western metaphysics, indeed to the unicity of a limit-situation at the summit of the consummation of this metaphysics,

---

19. Ibid., v. 1, p. 5 [v. 1, pp. 13–14; *GA* 6.1: 3].
20. Ibid., v. 3, p. 3 [v. 1, p. 473; *GA* 6.1: 425]; Derrida's emphasis on *path*.

despite the ultimately classical character of this approach, one has to acknowledge the following. Posing the question "who is X?" about a thinker was at that time a rare thing, and it still is. It was not rare, and it is not rare today, if by "who is X?" what is meant is nothing more than the trivially biographical question, the question of the man behind the work, which leads to depictions such as "the life of Hegel" or "the life of Descartes," carefully separated from, or interwoven with, a sort of doxography. But to ask "who is Nietzsche?" in another sense, all the while saying that one is not going to fall into the genre of the biographies of great thinkers, to ask about the name of Nietzsche, to make of the name of Nietzsche the title of a book that is not going to erase purely and simply the proper name by treating the great thought, that is what was not very common, and it still is not. That is what had to be underscored, I believe, even if Heidegger's way of answering this question seems to me to raise today—and I insist on the *today*—*other* questions.

The objection that Heidegger feigns to address to himself after having dismissed psycho-biography is the following: "But was not the last thing that Nietzsche himself completed for publication the piece that is entitled *Ecce Homo*," which, as his "last will," enjoins us to become interested in him? "Is this not" [Heidegger then says, mimicking the objection of a naïve interlocutor] "the apotheosis of uninhibited self-presentation and boundless self-mirroring?" Is it not also "the harbinger of erupting madness"?[21] To this, Heidegger responds that *Ecce Homo* is not an autobiography, it is not a question there "of the person of 'Herr Nietzsche'" "but of the history of the era of modern times, of the end of the West."[22] It is here that things get complicated: one can easily grant Heidegger that *Ecce Homo* is neither an autobiography in the common sense of the term nor the history of Mr. Nietzsche. But when, instead of transforming the concept of autobiography, Heidegger leaves that concept intact and opposes to it nothing other than the destiny of the West, with Nietzsche being none other than the "bearer" (*Träger*) of that destiny,[23] then one may wonder whether he himself escapes this in fact rather classical opposition between empirical biography (psycho-biological, historical, and so on) and an essential thought that corresponds to a historial decision that goes beyond any empirical individual or individuals. One may wonder what reason there is for this Heideggerian discourse and for everything it represents to proceed in this way.

21. Ibid.
22. Ibid., v. 3, p. x [v. 1, p. 473; *GA* 6.1: 425–26].
23. Ibid., v. 3, p. 3 [v. 1, p. 474; *GA* 6.1: 426].

For example, it is remarkable that Heidegger, on the one hand, intends to use this schema to save Nietzsche from his own singular destiny, which remained ambiguous and led to uses of his thought that went against what Heidegger calls his "innermost will (*seinen innersten Willen*)."[24] It is a matter of gaining access to what is innermost to his will in order to distinguish it or even oppose it to the ambiguity, to the duplicity of the empirical figure Nietzsche and to the ambiguity of his immediate posterity, and I insist on *immediate* here because Heidegger thinks that the more distant future, that toward which one must work, will restore this innermost will. And yet, on the other hand, wanting to save him in this way from ambiguity, Heidegger is going to orient his entire interpretation of the essential and singular thought of Nietzsche toward demonstrating the following: this thought did not go beyond the consummation of metaphysics. It is still a great metaphysics, and if it began to go beyond, it did so only barely, remaining on the sharpest crest of the limit, that is to say, in full ambiguity, in full "*Zweideutigkeit*." Heidegger's relation is one of constant ambivalence: at the moment he saves Nietzsche, he damns him. At the moment he says that his thought is "unique," he does everything to show that it in fact repeats the most powerful schema of metaphysics. In rescuing, in claiming to rescue Nietzsche from a certain misappropriation (the one, for example, to which he was being subjected in the prevailing Nazi climate), he uses categories that can support such a misappropriation, namely, the opposition between "essential thinkers"[25] and inessential thinkers, the authentic and the inauthentic, the essential thinker being defined as the thinker who has been "chosen," elected, marked, I would even say signed (*gezeichnet*) by — by what? by no one, by the history of the truth of being. Chosen just enough for that, and yet condemned by the same destiny to fulfill — and to do no more than that, I would say — the consummation of metaphysics, he is the one who was ultimately unable to come to a decision, the sole decision, regarding the predominance of beings and the sovereignty of being, a decision that he was able only to prepare without being able to evaluate its scope and without being able to master it.

In the two or three pages I am now going to read, we will pay close attention to, among other things, the play of essentiality and unicity, and the ambivalence of Heidegger's gesture when he claims to recognize the unicity and the essentiality of Nietzsche's thought, this thought from which we are

---

24. Ibid.
25. Ibid., v. 3, p. 4 [v. 1, p. 475; *GA* 6.1: 427].

able to get to the one who *will be* Nietzsche. (I read pp. 4–6 of volume 3 of *Nietzsche*; v. 1, p. 475 and following of the German text.)

> Nietzsche belongs among the essential thinkers. With the term *thinker* we name those exceptional human beings who are destined to think one single thought, a thought that is always "about" *beings in their totality*.[26] Each thinker thinks only one *single* thought. It needs neither renown nor impact in order to gain dominance. In contrast, writers and researchers, as opposed to a thinker, "have" lots and lots of thoughts, that is, ideas that can be converted into much-prized "reality" and that are also evaluated solely in accord with this conversion-capability.
>
> But the single thought of a thinker is one around which, unexpectedly, unnoticed in the stillest stillness, all beings turn. Thinkers are the founders of that which never becomes visible in images, which can never be historiologically related or technologically calculated, yet which rules without recourse to power. Thinkers are always one-sided, namely, on the sole side assigned to them in the very beginnings of the history of thinking by a simple saying. The saying comes from one of the oldest thinkers of the West, Periander of Corinth, who is accounted one of the "seven sages." The saying goes, "*Meleta to pan.*" "Take into care beings in their totality."
>
> Among thinkers, those are essential whose sole thought thinks in the direction of a single, supreme decision, whether by preparing for this decision or by decisively bringing it about. The abused and almost exhausted word *decision* is especially preferred today, now that everything has long since been decided or at least thought to be decided. Yet even the well-nigh incredible misuse of the word *decision* cannot prevent us from granting to the word that meaning by which it is related to the most intimate scission and the most extreme distinction. The latter is the distinction between beings in their totality—including gods and men, and world and earth—and Being, whose dominion first enables or denies every being whatsoever to be *the* being that it can be.
>
> The highest decision that can be made and that becomes the ground of all history is that between the predominance of beings and the sovereignty of Being. Whenever and however beings in their totality are thought expressly,

---

26. [Translators' note:] What is being translated here as "beings in their totality" is Heidegger's "*das Seiende im Ganzen.*" This phrase is most commonly translated into English, and that is the case in Heidegger's *Nietzsche* volumes, as "beings as a whole." But since Derrida puts so much emphasis on the notion of "totality" in Heidegger's interpretation of Nietzsche, we have translated the phrase throughout—and changed the Heidegger quotations accordingly—as "beings in their totality." It should be noted that Klossowski's French translation of *Nietzsche*, which Derrida cites and refers to throughout the seminar, has "*l'étant dans sa totalité.*"

thinking stands within the dangerous zone of this decision. The decision is never first made and executed by a human being. Rather, its direction and perdurance decide about man and, in a different way, about the god.

Nietzsche is an essential thinker because he thinks ahead in a decisive sense, not evading the decision. He prepares its arrival, without, however, measuring and mastering it in its concealed breadth.

For this is the other factor that distinguishes the thinker: only through his knowledge does he know to what extent he can *not* know essential things. However, such knowing about not-knowing, as not-knowing, must not be confused with what is acknowledged in the sciences as the limit of cognition and the bounds of factual knowledge. The latter takes into account the fact that the human conceptual faculty is finite. Ordinary factual knowledge stops where it does not know what is factually still knowable; the essential knowing of the thinker begins by knowing something unknowable. The scientific researcher inquires in order to reach useful answers; the thinker inquires in order to ground a *Fragwürdigkeit* [the character of what is *worthy of questioning*][27], the *questionableness* or *problematic* of beings in their totality. The researcher always operates on the foundation of what has already been decided: the fact that there are such things as nature, history, art, and that such things can be made the subject of consideration. For the thinker there is no such thing; he stands within the decision concerning what *is* in general, what beings are.

Nietzsche stands within a decision, as do all Western thinkers before him. With them, he affirms the predominance of beings over against Being, without knowing what is involved in such an affirmation. Yet at the same time Nietzsche is that Western thinker who unconditionally and ultimately brings about this predominance of beings and thus confronts the most unrelenting acuteness[28] of the decision (*die härteste Schärfe der Entscheidung*). This is evident in the fact that Nietzsche anticipates the consummation of the modern age with his unique thought of the will to power.[29]

The development that follows, which defines Nietzsche as "the *last metaphysician* of the West,"[30] the one who thought what will have had to be thought, whose reign will continue even if the name of Nietzsche disap-

---

27. This bracketed insertion is that of the French translator, Pierre Klossowski.
28. An arrow leads from the expression "unrelenting acuteness [*crête la plus aiguë*]" to a marginal addition that reads: "cutting edge."
29. Heidegger, *Nietzsche*, v. 3, pp. 4–6 [v. 1, pp. 475–77; *GA* 6.1: 427–29]. The German words in parentheses are written by hand in the margin of the photocopy of this passage that accompanies the session.
30. Ibid., v. 3, p. 8 [v. 1, p. 480; *GA* 6.1: 431].

pears, this development explicitly opposes an "authentic" (*echt*) questioning to an "inauthentic" (*unecht*) questioning.³¹

It was necessary to set up this schema of Heidegger's interpretation of the *biographein* of Nietzsche in order to get to his interpretation of the biological in Nietzsche, of Nietzsche's "alleged biologism." Here too it will be a matter of saving, in the most ambiguous way, the unique character of a thought from the ambiguity of a life and a work. What we have just seen to be the delimitation of the biographical and of the proper name defines the general space of interpretation within which the interpretation of the biological takes place. I did not say, but now it is time to point it out, that before the first words of the preface, "Niet sche," before even the beginning of the book, there is an exergue, which this time I am not going to forget. And this exergue, borrowed by Heidegger from *The Gay Science*, begins by the word "life," by the word "life" which thus turns out to be the title, the first word, of the book, before any decision between bio-graphy and bio-logy. The passage from *The Gay Science* reads: "Life (*Das Leben* . . .) . . . more mysterious (*geheimnisvoller*) since the day the great liberator (*der grosse Befreier:* the great liberator, thought) came over me—the thought that life should be an experiment of knowers [literally: the thought that life could (*dürfe*) be the experiment of the knower (*des Erkennenden*)]."³²

One of the first intriguing things about this exergue is that Heidegger does not quote the entire paragraph and, in not quoting it completely, he does not simply break off before the end but puts ellipsis marks within the quotation in order to indicate that he is leaving out some words. Now among the words he leaves out and that we are going to reinsert, there is one that Klossowski, in turn, at least if the German text to which I am referring is not in error (it is the Schlechta edition, which is questionable in many ways but perhaps not for a substitution of words of this sort), replaces, strangely, by another. Here is the text, fragment 324 of *The Gay Science*. It is titled "In media vita!" and it begins in this way:

> *In media vita.*—No! (*Nein!*), life has not disappointed me [or disillusioned me: *enttäuscht*]. On the contrary, I find it truer [*wahrer*, which Klossowski curiously translates by "richer," even though nothing in the text justifies that. Now it turns out that *wahrer*, "truer," is one of the words that Heidegger is going to let slip into the ellipsis, as well as the adjective *begehrenswerther* (desirable, worthy of being desired), in order to keep only the third adjective (*geheimnissvoller*: mysterious)—I now return to the quotation],

---

31. Ibid., v. 3, pp. 8–9 [v. 1, pp. 479–81; *GA* 6.1: 432].
32. Ibid., v. 1, p. xxxix [v. 1, p. 7; *GA* 6.1: x].

truer [Klossowski says "richer"] more desirable and more mysterious every year—ever since the day when the great liberator came to me: the idea that life could be an experiment of the seeker for knowledge [Klossowski has "an experiment of knowledge," but it is in fact an experiment of the knower: *des Erkennenden*; and this is where Heidegger's exergue ends]—and not a duty, not a calamity, not trickery. —And knowledge itself: let it be something else for others; for example, a bed to rest on, or the way to such a bed, or a diversion, or a form of leisure—for me it is a world of dangers and victories in which heroic feelings, too, find places to dance and play. "*Life as a means to knowledge*" [underscored and in quotation marks: "*Das Leben ein Mittel der Erkenntniss*": a proverbial rallying cry]—with this principle in one's heart one can live not only boldly but even gaily, and laugh gaily, too. And who knows how to laugh anyway and live well if he does not first know a good deal about war and victory?[33]

Life as an experiment of knowledge, as a means of knowledge, these are statements that, even if they remain very ambiguous and, in the end, difficult to interpret, mysterious, in the end, just like the title *In media vita*, which makes of life a medium [*milieu*], in the sense both of a middle-place between two things and an elementary milieu in relation to which and in which the experiment of knowledge is situated, an experiment that can itself not only be situated in life but can depend on life, can hold itself beyond life as its end, can define life starting from its end, and so on.[34] The relation life/knowledge is not really defined other than as a mystery in this text. But we can readily see why Heidegger places it in exergue. From the outset it seems to complicate a simplistic, biologistic reading of Nietzsche, whether it be understood as serving the model of biological science or as celebrating life or the living as the ultimate end or as the determination of beings as a totality [*l'étant en totalité*] or of beings par excellence as *life*. The choice of this exergue is itself enough to confirm that the question of life and of "alleged biologism" is at the active center of Heidegger's *Nietzsche*.

I wanted to note a second thing about this exergue. I said that "*Das Leben*" was the first word of the exergue, and that's true, it's the first word of the Nietzsche quotation. But the quotation itself is preceded by a short sentence from Heidegger that introduces the exergue, something that is rarely done. It reads: "*Die sein Denken bestimmende Erfahrung nennt* Nietzsche [the

---

33. Nietzsche, *Gay Science*, fragment 324, p. 255 [*KSA* 3: 552–53]. Derrida is working with the French translation, *Le Gai Savoir. Fragments posthumes (1881–1882)*, trans. Pierre Klossowski (Paris: Gallimard, 1967).

34. The sentence is not complete in the French typescript.

italics on *Nietzsche* disappear in the French translation] *selbst. . . ,*" which can be translated this way: "The experience that determines his thinking, Nietzsche names it himself."³⁵ One can thus say this: it is Nietzsche himself who names (Heidegger indeed says *names*) that which determines his thinking, his experience of thinking; and if, as Heidegger wants to show right after, the name of the thinker here gives the title to the thing of his thought, then the exergue as a whole (Heidegger's sentence plus the Nietzsche passage) means this: Nietzsche names himself, he names that on the basis of which one can name him. And by saying that "the name of Nietzsche is his thought," one is simply naming Nietzsche as he names himself, as he calls himself in his autonymy or auto-nomy; one is subjecting one's reading to Nietzsche's law, to its circular autonomy, being true to the way he himself wanted to be read and called; one is calling him as he calls himself, as he wants one to call him, and he calls himself on the basis of what is called thinking, his thinking. And I wonder up to what point the German syntax of Heidegger's sentence would not in fact support this reading: "*Die sein Denken bestimmende Erfahrung nennt* Nietzsche *selbst*": the experience determining his thought names *Nietzsche* himself, the italics marking the double place of the name, the double play of the name.³⁶

What is Nietzsche called — what does Nietzsche call himself? [*Comment Nietzsche s'appelle-t-il?*] That, in any case, is what is at stake in this question of the *bios*, before any biographical or biological determination.

To this question, Heidegger intends to provide an answer, *one* answer, a single answer. I am insisting here on the one, on the unicity. By maintaining that an essential thinker (an extremely problematic notion, of course) is rich only because he is poor and thinks only one thing, Heidegger must thus be implying, at this stage of the reading, that *Nietzsche in the end has only one name*, that he gives only one name to the experience determining his thought, that he thus has only one name and is called by name only *one single time*.³⁷ His name happens only once and he has only one name. It happens only once, even if the place of this event is a sharp limit from which one can see on both sides. And this "single time" of the single, unique thought [*pensée unique*] is ultimately the name of the unity of Western metaphysics,

---

35. Heidegger, *Nietzsche*, v. 1, p. xxxix [v. 1, p. 7; *GA* 6.1: x].

36. [Translators' note:] Because the nominative and accusative case endings are in this instance (the feminine noun *Erfahrung*) identical, the passage could mean either that *Nietzsche* names the experience determining his thought or that the experience names *Nietzsche*.

37. Next to this expression in the left margin is the word "Ereignis."

which comes to an end and which gathers or assembles itself, resembles itself, in this name.

But who said that one bears only one name? And thus—or perhaps first of all—that there is *a* Western metaphysics? And what if this presupposition regarding the unicity of the name (and thus of the resembling or assembling, gathering unity of this *one* Western metaphysics) were the effect of this desire for a single, unique name?[38] And what if that which Nietzsche (under many names, because, after all, he is the one, the only one, along with Kierkegaard, among all Western thinkers to have multiplied his names, his identities, his signatures, his nominal masks), what if that which Nietzsche called for, without calling himself a single time unique, were this festival of names, this multiplicity of names which disturbs that whole schema and that whole desire? You no doubt noticed in the long passage I read earlier that Heidegger wanted at all costs to save Nietzsche from the ambiguity surrounding his person. And what if it were this rescue operation, or that in the name of which this rescue operation, itself very ambivalent, was carried out, that had to be—in the names (plural) of the nietzsches[39]—called into question?

Perhaps, in reading Heidegger, the reading of Nietzsche by Heidegger, it will be a question of casting suspicion not so much upon the content of this interpretation as upon this presupposition—which itself perhaps belongs to something like metaphysics, in the singular, whence a strange circle—according to which there must be *one* interpretation, indivisibly one, gathered up around a thought that unifies a single, unique text and that ultimately names in a single, unique name being, the experience of thinking, and from that place, the patronymic proper name of a signatory. This unity-unicity, which support each other through the value of *name*—that is perhaps the thing that is the cause of concern [*en cause*], the *Streitfall*, the war or the *Auseinandersetzung*, this time between, let's say, *the nietzsches and Martin Heidegger* or so-called Western metaphysics, in the singular, which, from Aristotle up to at least Bergson, has, in one way or another, repeated that to think and to speak is to think and to speak something that is one, that is a single thing, and that to think-speak something (some cause) that is not one is not to think-speak.[40]

---

38. Insertion indicated in the left margin: "I <illegible word> unique."
39. As such in the typescript.
40. Derrida's typescript here reads: "and that not to think-speak something (some cause) that is not one is not to think-speak."

Now the *legein* of this logic, which would have it that to speak-think is essentially, for the essential thinker, to think-speak the one-unique, the *legein* of this logic, if it was ever put into question by the nietzsches (this plural is beginning to sound like the name of a carnival family or a family of tightrope walkers, and it takes the feast of which both Nietzsche and Heidegger speak in the direction of the carnival, the circus of the feast or the feast of the circus—though not of the circle) . . . Let me read here, in counterpoint, what Heidegger says of the feast in *Nietzsche*, v. 1 pp. 5–6; pp. 15–16 of the French translation:

> These common judgments about Nietzsche are in error. The error will be recognized only when a confrontation with him is at the same time conjoined to a confrontation in the realm of the grounding question of philosophy. At the outset, however, we ought to introduce some words of Nietzsche's that stem from the time of his work on "will to power": "For many, abstract thinking is toil; for me, on good days, it is feast and frenzy" (XIV, 24).
>
> Abstract thinking a feast? The highest form of human existence? Indeed. But at the same time we must observe how Nietzsche views the essence of the feast, in such a way that he can think of it only on the basis of his fundamental conception of all being, will to power. "The feast implies: pride, exuberance, frivolity; mockery of all earnestness and respectability; a divine affirmation of oneself, out of animal plenitude and perfection—all obvious states to which the Christian may not honestly say Yes. *The feast is paganism par excellence*" (WM 916). For that reason, we might add, the feast of thinking never takes place in Christianity. That is to say, there is no Christian philosophy. There is no true philosophy that could be determined anywhere else than from within itself. For the same reason there is no pagan philosophy, inasmuch as anything "pagan" is always still something Christian—the counter-Christian. The Greek poets and thinkers can hardly be designated as "pagan."
>
> Feasts require long and painstaking preparation. This semester we want to prepare ourselves for the feast, even if we do not make it as far as the celebration, even if we only catch a glimpse of the preliminary festivities (*Vorfeier*) at the feast of thinking—experiencing what meditative thought (*Besinnung*) is and what it means *to be at home* in genuine questioning.[41]

So, were the *legein* of this logic (of this logos)—the *legein* that would have it that to speak-think is, for the essential thinker, to speak the one-unique, a

---

41. Heidegger, *Nietzsche*, v. 1, pp. 5–6 [v. 1, pp. 14–15; *GA* 6.1: 4| XIV, 24 = *KSA* 11: 34[130], p. 463; *Der Wille zur Macht* (*WM*) 916 = *KSA* 12: 10[165], p. 553.

single unique thought—were this *legein* to be put into question, broken up into pieces or into plural masks by the feast of the nietzsches, it would indeed be exempted from all biologism, though less from the *bios* than from the *logism*. And this style of autobiography, insofar as it would *blow up* [faire sauter] (in all the senses of the expression) the unity of the name and of the signature, would indeed be that which threatens *both* biologism *and* the Heideggerian critique of biologism insofar as it operates, as we will see, in the name of essential thought.

Next time, then, we will get to this critique by Heidegger of Nietzsche's alleged biologism and to this ambiguous rescue operation undertaken by Heidegger, who provides a net for the tightrope walker (who is on a very thin wire) but only so as to ensure that the other, having taken no risks, falls into the net already dead. None of that happens in *Zarathustra*, nor in Basel or Nice, but in Freiburg im Breisgau, over the course of a winter semester, sometime between 1936 and 1940, while preparations were underway for the feast in "*Heimischsein im echten Fragen* [being at home in genuine questioning]."[42]

---

42. Heidegger, *Nietzsche*, v. 1, p. 6 [v. 1, p. 15; *GA* 6.1: 4].

NINTH SESSION[1]

Of Interpretation

You will recall the two sentences—I might also say the two samplings—with which, two weeks ago now, I began Heidegger's reading of Nietzsche, at least with regard to the question of life death and biologism. Let me quote them again quickly. One is taken by Heidegger from the notes of *The Will to Power* (Heidegger, v. 2, p. 84; v. 1, pp. 341–42 of the German):

> Nietzsche writes (XII, number 112): "Our whole world is the *ashes* of countless *living* creatures [*ashes* and *living* underscored]: and even if the living seems so minuscule in comparison to the whole, it is nonetheless the case that *everything* [*alles* is underscored] has already been transposed into life (*ist alles schon einmal in Leben umgesetzt*)—and so it goes."

And immediately after quoting this Heidegger continues:

> Apparently opposed to this (*entgegenzustehen*) is a thought expressed in *The Gay Science* (number 109): "Let us beware of saying that death is the opposite of life; the living creature is simply a kind of dead creature, and a very rare kind."[2]

Before following Heidegger in his interpretation of these two passages and reconstituting the overall trajectory in which he inscribes them, and from which I, a bit arbitrarily, just now extracted them, let me say just a couple of words right on the fringes of this text and without following Heidegger here.

---

1. At the top of this page in the typescript, at the center and to the right, the words "Of Interpretation" are circled and followed by an arrow that leads to "chaos," which is also circled and followed by "2nd question: *Totality* ("Nietzsche")." "Totality" is underscored twice. For bibliographical information regarding the subsequent publication of this session, see the editorial note, p. xiiin9.

2. Heidegger, *Nietzsche*, v. 2, p. 84 [v. 1, pp. 341–42; *GA* 6.1: 304–5].

In the first of the two thoughts cited, there is announced—how to put it?—a paradoxy that we must not forget with regard to the value of *totality*, a disrespect, in the end, for the security of what is being thought under the category of totality. We must not forget this, and even less so when reading Heidegger insofar as he, when making of Nietzsche a metaphysician, the last metaphysician, defines the metaphysical as the thinking of beings as a totality, a thinking riveted to a thought of beings as a totality, closed off to the question of the being of beings. Now whatever the complexity of these questions, one can already see, in reading this single statement, that Nietzsche does not trust any thought of totality when he says that "even if the living seems so minuscule in comparison to the whole, it is nonetheless the case that *everything* has already been transposed into life": if the living is smaller than a whole that nonetheless was wholly and will be wholly converted into life, if the living is thus both more and less than the whole that it is, and if this, then, must be said at the same time of the dead, is it not the case that this thought of life death cannot be subjected in any way to a univocal signification of totality, a univocal signification of the relationship whole/non-whole, and that, as a result, the thought of eternal return that, of course, traverses this statement is not a thought of totality? Now what will Heidegger put forward as one of the most certain, most repeated, and most decisive results of his reading? This, for example, and I quote:

> For one thing, we have circumscribed the field in which the thought of return belongs and which the thought as such concerns: we have surveyed this field [*feldmässig*: like a field] of beings in their totality (*das Seiende im Ganzen*) and determined it as the interlacing unity of the living and the lifeless (*die in sich verschlungene Einheit des Lebendigen und Leblosen*). For another, we have shown how in its foundations the totality of beings—as the unity of living and lifeless—is structured and articulated: its constitution (*Verfassung*) is the character of force and the finitude of the totality (at one with infinity) that is implied in the character of force—which is to say, the immeasurability of the "phenomenal effects" [*Wirkungserscheinungen*, "phenomenal effects," and not, as the French translation has it, "phenomena and their effects"].[3]

We will see later what is to be understood by *Verfassung* (constitution), as opposed to modality: once Heidegger thinks he has demonstrated that the Will to Power is this constitution of beings (*quid, quidditas, essentia*), as he explains elsewhere, he will then need to demonstrate the *quo-modo*, the

---

3. Ibid., v. 2, pp. 96–97 [v. 1, p. 355; *GA* 6.1: 317].

how, the modality, *eo quod, existentia*, eternal return as the modality of being, and he will then have demonstrated that this discourse operates metaphysically in accordance with the opposition between, for example, *quid* and *quod, essentia* and *existentia* (see v. 2, p. 163).[4] Then, if Will to Power is indeed (we are still on the same page), in[5] the constitution of beings and of being,[6] the principle of knowledge and the material principle of eternal return, then we will indeed have here a grand metaphysics.[7]

Let me clarify: in order to analyze what he calls Nietzsche's *metaphysische Grundstellung* (his fundamental metaphysical position), <Heidegger>[8] must here consider the response that Nietzsche, according to Heidegger, gives to the question of beings as totality. This response is double: the totality of beings is Will to Power, the totality of beings is eternal return. What is the relation between these two responses? Are they compatible, complementary, juxtaposed, incompatible? Well, Heidegger's ploy here, which will allow him to identify metaphysics in Nietzsche's response, is to focus not so much on the content of the response or the double response as on the relation between the two responses, a relation in which he identifies, precisely, a metaphysical schema. What is this relation? It is the relation between, precisely, two determinations of the verb *to be*, being as *quidditas* or *essentia* and being as a modality of existence. It is because this schema has gone unrecognized that we have erred up until now when faced with the enigma of this double response by Nietzsche and failed before the relation between the eternal return and the Will to Power. The Will to Power responds to the question of beings in their *Verfassung*, their essential structure; the eternal return responds to the question of beings in their *Weise*, their mode of being, and one must understand the reciprocal belonging together of these two responses, which form two moments (*Momente*: factors) in the beingness of beings (*Seiendheit des Seienden*). As a result, it appears that Nietzsche's philosophy is indeed the end of metaphysics: it returns in its own way to the beginning of Greek thought (the question of beings, as a totality, a response in accordance

228

---

4. Ibid., v. 2, p. 163 [v. 1, p. 425; *GA* 6.1: 381].
5. The word "in" is crossed out.
6. The word "being" is crossed out and two or three illegible words are written beneath it.
7. There is in the typescript a handwritten insertion mark, repeated in the left margin, with the note: "p. 2 bis." A page composed of just one paragraph is to be found between pages 2 and 3 of T1. At the top of that page we find the notation "2 bis (addition)." That paragraph has been inserted here.
8. Derrida writes "N," for "Nietzsche," when it is clearly Heidegger that he means.

with *Verfassung* and *Weise*) and it closes the ring (*Ring*). Limit: closure (soldering? What is happening here? the serpent, the ring? . . .)

For the moment, then, we see Heidegger analyzing the eternal return as, I quote again, "the determination of beings in their totality."[9]

Now, if the first of these two statements quoted by Heidegger ("even if the living seems so minuscule in comparison to the whole, it is nonetheless the case that *everything* has already been transposed into life"), if this statement — of the eternal return — is at odds with a thinking of totality, if it resists a thinking of totality or of any opposition whatsoever between the whole and the non-whole, then it is perhaps all too hasty, and for this reason alone, to make of Nietzsche a metaphysician, if the metaphysician is, for Heidegger, a thinker who adheres to a thinking of beings as a totality. Perhaps Nietzsche is no longer even a thinker of beings if there is an essential link between beings as such and totality. Moreover, is it not noteworthy that it is life-death, which — far from being just one of the determinations of beings and thus far from reducing the question of being to a determination of beings — that it is thus life death, in the name of life death, that the value of totality comes to lose its privileged position once the whole becomes, in accordance with the eternal return, both more and less than itself? What, then, of life death if they no longer belong to a thinking of totality?

That is, in a very preliminary fashion, a question that could be asked here at the outset. Second remark, which is just as preliminary. Heidegger, quoting the two thoughts I just mentioned, puts them together because of their at least apparent contradiction. Having quoted the first, he says: "Apparently opposed to this (*entgegenzustehen*) [what seems to run counter to this] is a thought expressed in *The Gay Science*."[10] Now, even if this is merely a feigned or provisional objection, it is vitiated or can be dismissed in its very principle as soon as opposition and contradiction are no longer laws — or rather proscriptive laws — for thought. Why are they no longer laws? Well, at the very least because life and death, as that on the basis of which we think the rest, are not opposed, or at least their opposition, that opposition, does not allow them to be thought: "Let us beware of saying that death is the opposite (*entgegengesetzt*) of life; the living creature is simply a kind of dead creature, and a very rare kind."[11] At the same time, the relation between genus and species, governed by the thought of totality, is itself dislocated here. When one value that is opposed to another in its everyday mean-

---

9. Heidegger, *Nietzsche*, v. 2, p. 106 [v. 1, p. 365; *GA* 6.1: 326].
10. Ibid., v. 2, p. 84 [v. 1, p. 342; *GA* 6.1: 305].
11. Ibid.

ing, life to death, for example, is found to be a species of the opposing genus or the genus of a greater whole, a part of its opposite, then the opposition is no longer valid, and neither is the juxtaposition, so that what we have instead is a strange inclusion without any possible totalization, one whose logic can no longer be that of a metaphysics, so long at least as metaphysics aims to determine a totality by privileging present beings, beingness, without posing the question of the being of beingness. And what if it were with the words *life death* and everything these words bring along with them in their non-totalizable and non-oppositional logic that Nietzsche was, in fact, breaking free from the constraint of *beings as a totality*?

Third preliminary remark: Heidegger takes this last sentence ("Let us beware . . .") from a long aphorism (109) of *The Gay Science* from which he will subsequently, in the course of this chapter, pull out two or three other sentences, leaving out many things, leaving lots of blanks, therefore, that we will perhaps have to fill in on our own. As a result, our reading of Heidegger will often turn around the interpretation of this important aphorism. Let me just read it for a first time here. (Read *The Gay Science*, pp. 167–69):

> *Let us beware.*—Let us beware of thinking that the world is a living being. Where should it expand? On what should it feed? How could it grow and multiply? We have some notion of the nature of the organic; and we should not reinterpret the exceedingly derivative, late, rare, accidental, that we perceive only on the crust of the earth and make of it something essential, universal, and eternal, which is what those people do who call the universe an organism. This nauseates me. Let us even beware of believing that the universe is a machine; it is certainly not constructed for one purpose, and calling it a "machine" does it far too much honor.
>
> Let us beware of positing generally and everywhere anything as elegant as the cyclical movements of our neighboring stars; even a glance into the Milky Way raises doubts whether there are not far coarser and more contradictory movements there, as well as stars with eternally linear paths, etc. The astral order in which we live is an exception; this order and the relative duration that depends on it have again made possible an exception of exceptions: the formation of the organic. The total character of the world, however, is in all eternity chaos—in the sense not of a lack of necessity but of a lack of order, arrangement, form, beauty, wisdom, and whatever other names there are for our aesthetic anthropomorphisms. Judged from the point of view of our reason, unsuccessful attempts are by all odds the rule, the exceptions are not the secret aim, and the whole music box repeats its tune eternally, a tune that can never be called a melody—and ultimately even the phrase "unsuccessful attempt" is too anthropomorphic

and reproachful. But how could we reproach or praise the universe? Let us beware of attributing to it heartlessness and unreason or their opposites: it is neither perfect nor beautiful, nor noble, nor does it wish to become any of these things; it does not by any means strive to imitate man. None of our aesthetic and moral judgments apply to it. Nor does it have any instinct for self-preservation or any other instinct; and it does not observe any laws either. Let us beware of saying that there are laws in nature. There are only necessities: there is no one who commands, no one who obeys, no one who trespasses. Once you know that there are no purposes, you also know that there is no accident; for it is only beside a world of purposes that the word "accident" has meaning. Let us beware of saying that death is opposed to life. The living is merely a type of what is dead, and a very rare type.

Let us beware of thinking that the world eternally creates new things. There are no eternally enduring substances; matter is as much an error as the god of the Eleatics. But when shall we ever be done with our caution and care? When will all these shades of God cease to darken our paths? When will we have a nature that is altogether undeified! When will we human beings be allowed to begin to *naturalize* ourselves by means of the pure, newly discovered, newly redeemed nature?[12]

We are now going to see how Heidegger will do all he can — and not without some difficulty, it seems to me — to make of this thought a metaphysical thought (of the totality of beings) and even a thought of humanization that, despite all appearances, never put humanization in doubt. All of this takes place, in the end, through an interpretation of midday and the instant in *Zarathustra*. According to this Heideggerian interpretation of midday and of the instant, a circle is put in place that ends up drawing Nietzsche's thought of the eternal Return, despite the will to dehumanization (*Entmenschung*: deanthropologization, rather), toward an extreme anthropologization (*Vermenschung*). And Nietzsche remains or would remain in this circle for not having asked the question "what is man?" in relation to the question "what is the totality of beings?," in other words, for not having freed himself and freed his question from a metaphysical position within the totality of beings. "However, the latter question [of knowing the totality of beings and thus man] embraces," says Heidegger, p. 365 [in German], v. 2, p. 105, "a more original question, one which neither Nietzsche nor philosophy prior to him unfolded or was able to unfold."[13]

---

12. Nietzsche, *Gay Science*, fragment 109, pp. 167–69 [*KSA* 3: 467–69]; the last three sentences are cited in Heidegger's *Nietzsche*, v. 2, p. 94 [v. 1, p. 276; *GA* 6.1: 314].

13. Heidegger, *Nietzsche*, v. 2, p. 105 [v. 1, p. 365; *GA* 6.1: 326].

In addition to all the difficulties we might have pulling together such a reading (I mean the reading of Nietzsche by Heidegger) in a course that is as short and schematic as this one, there is the essential difficulty of the limit, and of Heidegger's way of playing with the limit with respect to Nietzsche. He places him on a border, a peak, says Klossowski's translation. Which means that at *every instant* he plays a game of *fort/da* with him, throwing him back into metaphysics, taking him back beyond metaphysics, *fort/da*, or else affirming in him a certain beyond of metaphysics (*fort* this time positively valued) and then taking him back into metaphysics (*da*). He does this at every instant, I just said, and the instant, moreover, is going to play the role of this limit, on the edge of which, as we are going to see, everything takes place, looking on both sides, as in the *topos* of Zarathustra with regard to the eternal return (the gateway, where one can look on both sides). And then I spoke of the game of the *fort/da*: well, everything is in fact going to get played out in relation to the game (of the aeon of Heraclitus, a child playing at draughts), in relation to the *fort* and the *da*, in which we can already see announced a certain scene from *Beyond the Pleasure Principle*, a scene that awaits us after the Easter break. So, to conclude these protocols of the game, if the child plays *fort/da* with something like its mother (but we will perhaps have to complicate this schema), and if, in addition, one brings to light, as I have tried to do elsewhere, Nietzsche's maternal desire, and if, finally, one is to take into account what has been said earlier about the logic of (she) the living [*la vivante*], then to say that Nietzsche is at once the mother and the father of Nietzsche is perhaps to say something very trivial in the end. No doubt. But what interests me in this triviality is that it at least lets it be thought that the so very enigmatic schema of the *fort/da*, of the game, of the relation to father/mother, is not an example, a particular case, an offshoot of the great questions stirred up by Heidegger's *Nietzsche* but that which in fact also includes them. And then, in addition to the link in general and in principle that we will try to spell out between these problems and the beyond of the pleasure principle, it so happens, let me at least note for its anecdotal value, that Freud names in passing, a bit metaphorically, exoterically, the "eternal return of the same" in chapter 3 of *Beyond*.[14] It is true that he is talking there about neuroses of destiny, men, for example, whose friendships all end in betrayal by their friend or men who spend their whole lives putting on a pedestal people they will soon knock down off that pedestal and deprive of all authority; or else lovers whose love affairs

232

---

14. Derrida is referring here to Freud's *Beyond the Pleasure Principle*. See the eleventh session, p. 219n3, for the full bibliographical reference.

with women always go through the same stages and so come to the same result. It is, says Freud, the "eternal return of the same."

All right. Having finished these preliminaries, let me take up Heidegger's reading at the point where his interpretation of the eternal return encounters the question of life. This comes at the moment he is examining four unpublished notes from the month of August 1881 and the first sketch of the plan related to the eternal Return, the eternal return as "the fundamental conception of the work <*Zarathustra*>," as *Ecce Homo* puts it.[15] Let me read this first plan, just as Heidegger quotes it (v. 2, pp. 74–75; p. 330 [in German]):[16]

The Return of the Same.

Plan.

1. Incorporation of the fundamental errors.
2. Incorporation of the passions.
3. Incorporation of knowledge and of the knowledge that can renounce. (Passion of insight.)
4. The Innocent. The individual as experiment. The amelioration of life, degradation, enervation — transition.
5. The new *burden: the eternal return of the same*. Infinite importance of our knowing, erring, our habits, ways of life, for everything to come.

What will we do with the *rest* of our lives — we who have spent the greater part of them in the most essential uncertainty? We shall *teach the teaching* — that is the most potent means of *incorporating* it in ourselves. Our kind of beatitude, as teacher of the greatest teaching.

Early August, 1881, in Sils-Maria, 6,000 feet above sea level and much higher above all human things![17]

What does Heidegger say about this? Attentive here to the centrality of the "*Einverleibung*" and to the fact that it cannot be separated (as a schema for the ingestion of food, and so on) from the operation of teaching, in which the mode of teaching is just as important as the content, he remarks that the effect of a cut (the rest of our lives, and so on) is balanced by the effect of a transition (*Übergang*): the doctrine of the return, however new it may be, remains as if stretched between the two extremes of a transition.

---

15. Nietzsche, *Ecce Homo*, p. 295 [KSA 6: 335].

16. In the typescript there is this handwritten note: "T.I."

17. Quoted in Heidegger, *Nietzsche*, v. 2, pp. 74–75 [v. 1, p. 330; *GA* 6.1: 294]; *KSA* 9: 11[141], p. 494.

But in the two brief pages of his commentary, Heidegger's reading remains itself rather ambiguous, itself suspended between two gestures. Or rather, what remains definitively suspended is an operation that would take into account the *singularity* of Nietzsche's notes, notably with regard to the incorporating (the *Leiben* of the *Einverleibung*), with regard to this strange "*rest* of our lives" and to this teaching in which the manner matters more than the content. However, what is not going to remain suspended is an operation that defines this entire plan as a *Grundstellung* with regard to beings as a totality, which will then carry over into the general interpretation of Nietzsche's thought as a metaphysical position. To put it another way, if you will, there are two types of statements in these two pages: (1)[18] statements that acknowledge that all of this is very singular and that we do not have a schema for digesting it in turn. These statements acknowledging rupture and heterogeneity remain suspended *around* another type of statement, a traditionalizing kind of statement that makes Nietzsche fall back in line: a metaphysical position regarding beings as a totality, which, in sum, can give rise to a teaching of metaphysics within the tradition. And it is obviously this traditionalizing statement that is then going to dominate Heidegger's entire interpretative machine. I speak here of statements of heterogeneity suspended *around* a statement of homogeneity for this supplementary reason, namely, that the commentary on this first plan consists of three paragraphs,[19] the first and the third acknowledging the heterogeneous, while the second, the mediate one, leads back to homogeneity and will subsequently be found in the dominant position.

The first paragraph acknowledges the cut, the incision (Heidegger speaks of the *Skizzierung* [sketching] of an *Einschnitt* [incision])[20] in life, between what has been lived and what remains, what remains to be lived, which is not in any way homogeneous with what has been lived. What remains does not resemble. Here is another point of originality according to Heidegger: the place occupied by *Einverleibung* in this plan, which here signifies that what is taking place with regard to the body proper [*corps propre*] in this new incorporation must produce an effect first of all, or even only, on the doctor (*Lehrer*), on the teacher, on the body of the new teacher. Simply by translating this as "a new kind of beatitude" (*Seligkeit*),[21]

---

18. This numbering does not continue.
19. It is the French translator who introduces the third paragraph; the original German and the English translation have only two.
20. Heidegger, *Nietzsche*, v. 2, p. 75 [v. 1, p. 331; *GA* 6.1: 295].
21. Ibid., v. 2, p. 76 [v. 1, p. 331; *GA* 6.1: 295].

Heidegger is already somewhat retraditionalizing this thought. Now, in speaking of traditionalization, I do not mean to say that Nietzsche and the doctrine of the eternal return are not traditional in any way; I too think that <this doctrine> is deeply rooted in the tradition, that it is a thinking of the tradition. Yet the question regarding the novelty of the tradition and of the traditional relation to the tradition remains (same thing for Heidegger . . . comment). The third paragraph (I am skipping the second for the moment) also acknowledges the absolute singularity of the plan and of the motif of incorporation, which is right at its center. It acknowledges that we do not have a "schema" for mastering this plan or finding the right place for it. It is necessary to find a schema that is "proper" (*eigene*) to it, that is proper to this absolutely singular book project, singular in its content, in its mode of action or inaction, its mode of operation or non-operation, in the fact that the thinking that is taught there is less important than the mode of teaching, the body of the teacher, and so on. "The plan sketched here is nothing other than the germ of the plan for the coming work, *Thus Spoke Zarathustra*." It is "not," notes Heidegger, "a sketch toward a 'theoretical,' prosaic elaboration of the thought of return."[22]

And yet, all the while acknowledging these unprecedented singularities and the fact that we do not have at our disposal any schema to take them in, Heidegger has in the meantime, along the way, laid out in the second paragraph the net of the most powerful schema in which to receive, and first of all to make fall, Nietzsche or the thought of the eternal return. That is the schema according to which this entire project is a metaphysical *Grundstellung* with regard to beings as a totality, which thus reinscribes the project into the history of philosophy, and thus also of a certain teaching in which the content is more important than the mode of teaching, or in which the place of the teaching body no longer has the strange singularity or even the form of the written text that the third paragraph nonetheless acknowledges. Now, you know that it is the net of this schema that is stretched out in the form of Heidegger's very book and that dominates its entire operation. Here, then, is the second paragraph. (Read Heidegger, v. 2, p. 76):

> We know from *Thus Spoke Zarathustra* how essential the question of the "incorporation" of the thought is; we know that Zarathustra first becomes a convalescent after he has incorporated the weightiest elements of the thought. If we pursue the meaning of this word we arrive at the notion of "eating," of devouring and digesting. Whatever is incorporated makes the

---

22. Ibid., v. 2, p. 76 [v. 1, p. 332; *GA* 6.1: 296].

body—and our embodiment—steadfast and secure. It is also something we have finished with and which determines us in the future. It is the juice that feeds our energies. To incorporate the thought here means to think the thought of the eternal return in such a way that right from the start it becomes our fundamental stance toward beings in their totality, pervading every single thought as such and from the outset. Only when the thought of the return has become the basic posture of our thinking as a whole has it been appropriated—and taken into the body—as its essence demands.[23]

Heidegger then turns to the second plan, which seems to him to reverse the order of the principal thoughts and begins with the eternal return. This time it is a question of the "play of life" (*das Spiel des Lebens*). Here it is:

1. The mightiest insight.
2. Opinions (*Meinungen*) and errors transform mankind and grant it its drives (*Triebe*), or: the incorporated errors (*einverleibten Irrtümer*).
3. Necessity and innocence.
4. The play of life.[24]

Here again, Heidegger's reading operation consists not so much in interpreting each element as metaphysical thinking as in determining the arrangement of the elements in accordance with a metaphysical order, so as then to identify or sketch out the identification of an arrangement, a schematics, if you will, that is metaphysical. How so? He starts out from the third point: necessity and innocence. He notes that the necessity here is not just any necessity but that of beings as a totality. We will come back to this: if necessity (for example in fragment 109 of *The Gay Science*) is indeed that of "the whole of the world as chaos," we now know that this whole as the relation dead/living without any simple totalization is just as much a challenge regarding the present, and thus beings, and totality. To determine, therefore, the necessity of chaos as the totality of beings is perhaps excessive. But that is just one sentence in this page of commentary. Heidegger then turns his attention to the "play of life" in order to note that this "reminds us immediately of a fragment of Heraclitus, to whom Nietzsche *believed* he was most closely akin." (Heidegger underscores *believed* because, according to him, every interpretation of Heraclitus, and in particular Nietzsche's, has to be reconsidered.) In question here is the fragment: "*Aiōn pais esti paidzōn, pesseuōn; paidos hē basilēiē*. Aeon is a child at play, playing at draughts;

---

23. Ibid., v. 2, p. 76 [v. 1, pp. 331–32; *GA* 6.1: 295–96].
24. Ibid., v. 2, p. 77 [v. 1, p. 333; *GA* 6.1: 297]; *KSA* 9: 11[144], pp. 496–97.

sovereignty is the child's." To this translation Heidegger then adds the following, in parentheses, as if he were simply commenting on the last words, *paidos hē basilēiē*: "(*nämlich über das Seiende im Ganzen*: namely, over beings as a totality).''[25] With the word *totality* introduced to comment on the two words "necessity" and "innocence," thanks to an association provided by a fragment of Heraclitus, which is itself rather actively interpreted, the paragraph that follows can then equate *aiōn*, totality, innocence, and life; and since the interpretation of *aiōn* will be a key piece in this game of draughts that the interpretation itself is for showing that the authority of the present is there predominant, the knot is tightly tied. I am going to continue reading because one has to follow here all the micro-advances and, especially, all the little leaps in this process. After closing his parenthesis ("namely, over beings as a totality"), Heidegger continues, in a new paragraph:

> The suggestion is that innocence pervades beings in their totality (*Das Seiende im Ganzen ist durchherrscht von der Un-schuld*). The totality is *aiōn*, a word that can scarcely be translated in an adequate way (*sachgerecht*). It means (*meint*) the totality of the world, but also time [naturally, what looks like leaps here are appeals to other texts of Heidegger that justify this interpretation of *aiōn*; it is still the case that, in a commentary that presents itself as a direct reading of the words "necessity and innocence," it is a rather aggressive move], and, related by time to our "life," it means the course of life itself. We are accustomed to defining the meaning of *aiōn* thus: "Aeon" suggests the "time" of the "cosmos," that is, of nature, which operates in the time which physics measures. One distinguishes time in this sense from the time we "live through." Yet what is named in *aiōn* resists such a distinction. At the same time, we are thinking of *kosmos* too cursorily when we represent it cosmologically.[26]

What is sketched out here is a gesture that is constantly at work in Heidegger and particularly in this book: cosmology does not think the cosmos; that is not its charge. No more than it is the charge of physics to think *physis* or of biology to think *bios*, no more than it is the charge of science in general to think in general the essence of the beings on which it works. Understanding this distinction is indispensable for understanding what is going on in this interpretation. At issue is an interpretation of the relations between science, philosophy, and thinking. Science operates on objects or beings whose essence it is not its prerogative, as science, to determine. The biologist is concerned with biological things, but as for the essence of the

25. Ibid.
26. Ibid., v. 2, p. 77 [v. 1, pp. 333–34; *GA* 6.1: 297].

biological, as for the question "what is the living?," a philosophical question that falls within the province of another logic, the biologist as such has nothing to say. He begins to operate as a biologist only at the moment when he can presuppose an essence of the living, one whose determination is the effect of a properly philosophical question or response. It is with this distinction in the background (we will return to this) that Heidegger can save Nietzsche from the suspicions of "biologism." By determining the essence of the living-being, Nietzsche breaks with biological discourse, with scientific discourse in general; he is speaking as a philosopher.

It is at this juncture—in a commentary on the second plan regarding the eternal return—that Heidegger notes that Nietzsche then uses the word "life" in an "ambiguous" (*zweideutig*) way,[27] in order to designate the totality of beings, on the one hand, and our "existential" situation within the totality of beings, on the other, as if in the first plan he emphasized this existential dimension (our lives, the rest of our lives having to incorporate the doctrine, and so on), while in the second it is rather the metaphysical signification (a position with regard to the totality of beings) that is privileged. Are we dealing here then with a whole that is articulated into a metaphysico-existential system? Heidegger asks himself this, all the while suspecting that this distinction between the metaphysical and the existential—a distinction he nonetheless did everything to highlight—is just as unsatisfactory as that between the theoretical or prosaic content, on the one hand, and the poetic, on the other, a distinction he nonetheless used, in the end, when reading the preceding plan. He then moves on to read the two other plans (dating from the same month), titled "*Midday and Eternity*: Pointers Toward a New Life" and "On the 'Plan for a New Way to Live,'"[28] where it is a question of the dehumanization of nature. I am going to skip this reading, which seems to me to bring nothing new to the schema that has been laid out, except for this: the instant (which is like the semantic soldering between midday and eternity) is there underscored as an indication that eternity is thought in time and that the determinations of time, the highest determinations of time, are the titles chosen to address beings in their totality and the new life at the heart of beings. Those of you who are somewhat familiar with Heidegger's work since *Sein und Zeit* will recognize here an essential lever for his analysis of metaphysics: metaphysics has determined the beingness of beings on the basis of an implicit determination of time that privileges

---

27. Ibid., v. 2, p. 78 [v. 1, p. 334; *GA* 6.1: 297].
28. Ibid., v. 2, pp. 78, 80 [v. 1, pp. 335, 337; *GA* 6.1: 298, 300]; *KSA* 9: 11[195, 197], p. 519.

the present, eternity as present, whence the importance of the reference to *aiōn*, which would be that which allows one to conceive of the totality of beings as present, on the basis of the present. And by privileging, in his turn, the instant in his thinking of the eternal return, Nietzsche would appear to be reproducing this same gesture of metaphysics, the gesture that forms the essence of metaphysics.

It is right after this that we read the chapter toward which we were supposed to be headed and from which I had excerpted the two passages on the living and the non-living. The chapter is titled "Summary Presentation of the Thought" (*Zusammenfassende Darstellung des Gedankens: Das Seiende im Ganzen als Leben, als Kraft; die Welt als Chaos*).[29] After having criticized the editions and the titles given to later notes, editions and titles that are never innocent, and after having acknowledged that Nietzsche in these notes resorts to scientific language, referring to works of physics, chemistry, and biology (an irrefutable fact), Heidegger says that it remains to be seen whether these scientistic interpretations, "even when they are conjured by Nietzsche himself,"[30] can serve as a criterion for an interpretation of the "thought of thoughts" in his philosophy. "Such a question becomes unavoidable the moment we have grasped Nietzsche's philosophy and our confrontation with it—this is to say, with all of Western philosophy—as a matter for this century and the century to come."[31]

It is already clear that with regard to science Heidegger has no intention of trusting what Nietzsche himself might believe, in one place or another, about the relationship of his thought to science, already clear that it is this Heideggerian interpretation of the relationship science/philosophy/thought that is going to orchestrate the entire reading.

Leaving behind this diachronic approach to these texts and plans, Heidegger goes on to propose a synopsis in ten points of unequal importance for what interests us here.[32]

1. The first point concerns the two sentences on the living and the non-living. This point is the least clear and the most held in suspense. Instead of noting, as we have seen could have been done, the non-pertinence of the category of totality—something that would have had disastrous consequences for the whole enterprise; instead of expressing surprise at the fact

---

29. Ibid., v. 2, pp. 82–97 [v. 1, pp. 339–56; *GA* 6.1: 302–18].
30. Ibid., v. 2, p. 83 [v. 1, p. 340; *GA* 6.1: 303].
31. Ibid.
32. In the typescript there is this handwritten addition following this sentence: "→ space of the E<ternal> R<eturn> rather than the E<ternal> R<eturn> itself."

that when it is a question of the *Gesamtcharakter der Welt* Nietzsche makes statements that prohibit simply remaining within a thinking of totality, Heidegger concludes with an enigma and with a suspension regarding that which remains inaccessible to calculative reason. He writes: "From all this we discern one decisive point: by setting the non-living in relief against the living, along the guidelines of any single aspect (*nach einer einzigen Hinsicht der Sachverhalt*), we do not do justice to the state of affairs—the world is more enigmatic than our calculating intellect [*Verstand* and not "reason," *raison*, as the [French] translator says] would like to admit."[33]

2. Second aspect in this synopsis: the pervasive character of the world is force, which Nietzsche will call a few years later will to power and which, Heidegger wants to insist on this point, no physics as such can think as such (v. 2, pp. 86–87),[34] and which belongs neither to the derived opposition static/dynamic nor to the derived signification of *dynamis*.

3. The finiteness of force: the notion of infinite force is incompatible, says Nietzsche, with the notion of force. This finitude is a necessary belief, a taking-for-true linked to the power of thought (thinkability), though Nietzsche, according to Heidegger, does not question, any more than any other philosopher in general has done, whether thinkability should serve as the court of jurisdiction for the essence of beings. (Very debatable: in a certain sense Nietzsche asks nothing but this.)

4. This internal finitude of force has as its consequence that the force of the whole is determined and undergoes neither accretion nor diminution.

5. No equilibrium of force: "'Had an equilibrium of force been achieved at any time, it would have lasted up to now: hence it never entered on the scene' (XII, number 103)."[35] Becoming, then, without birth, evolution, or progress.

6. The effects of this finite force are not infinite or innumerable but incommensurable, incalculable (practically).

7. There is no empty space; space was born only of the empty space that does not exist, says Nietzsche. All is but force. Heidegger here corrects and criticizes Nietzsche's argumentation when it claims, a bit quickly, that space could have been born only out of empty space, which presupposes space in order to give birth to space. But in spite of this *contre-sens*, says Heidegger, Nietzsche's remarks can make sense, given that space is born (*ent-steht*) from the essence of the world and that being can indeed include a void.[36]

---

33. Heidegger, *Nietzsche*, v. 2, p. 85 [v. 1, p. 343; *GA* 6.1: 306].
34. Ibid., v. 2, pp. 86–87 [v. 1, pp. 343–44; *GA* 6.1: 306–7].
35. Ibid., v. 2, p. 88 [v. 1, p. 346; *GA* 6.1: 308]; XII, 103 = *KSA* 9: 11[245], p. 534.
36. Ibid., v. 2, p. 89 [v. 1, p. 347; *GA* 6.1: 310].

8. Beginning with the eighth remark, the interpretative activity seems to me to intensify. The first <seven> points are rather neutral, more or less paraphrastic or repetitive, very close to the letter of certain of Nietzsche's texts. That is going to change in the three following points, which are also, particularly the ninth, developed at much greater length. That is because it is a question of time and, especially, of chaos. The stakes are very high because it is in this interpretation of time and of chaos that one is going to be able to decide that (or whether) Nietzsche, according to Heideggerian criteria, is or is not a metaphysician, that is, a thinker of the totality of beings who never questioned the temporal horizon on the basis of which he determined beings [comment on "beings"] and who, having left intact the vulgar concept of time, thought by way of that concept, according to that concept, the totality of beings, making of chaos a gathered totality of beings, a necessity of totality. I think that in these final points—and especially the one concerning chaos—what I would call the *murkiness* [trouble] of the Heideggerian enterprise with regard to Nietzsche lends itself a bit better than elsewhere to analysis. That is what I am going to try to begin to demonstrate in order to conclude this session.

The eighth point concerns time. Here, for once, for this one and only time, which is perhaps symptomatic, Heidegger does not mince words. He does not try to make as if he is saving when he wants to condemn, to have it be thought that, despite the *contresens* and the naïveté, there is something to be thought behind one or another of Nietzsche's propositions. For once, he rejects as naïve, meager, and impoverished everything Nietzsche says about time. He claims without the slightest equivocation or ambiguity that questions concerning time remained "closed" to Nietzsche. And the condemnation is swift and without appeal. Heidegger recalls a few of Nietzsche's propositions with regard to the real character of time (as opposed to space, which is imaginary), and thus its infinity. As one fragment says (90), "the time in which the universe exercises its force is infinite; that is, force is eternally the same and eternally active." In another fragment cited by Heidegger (103), Nietzsche speaks of "the course of infinite time" and, elsewhere, of "the eternal hourglass of existence." And he says somewhere else: "To the actual course of things an *actual* time must also correspond" (XII, 59).[37]

It goes without saying that what Nietzsche says, means, and seeks to say about infinite time cannot but be an absolutely indispensable part of the

---

37. Ibid., v. 2, p. 90 [v. 1, p. 348; *GA* 6.1: 310]; fragment 90 = *KSA* 9: 11[202], p. 523; fragment 103 = *KSA* 9: 11[245], p. 534; *KSA* 3: *Gay Science* 341, p. 570; XII, 59 = *KSA* 9: 11[184], p. 513.

doctrine of the eternal return. One thus cannot both take seriously, that is, attempt to save as a great thought—even if it is still metaphysical—the doctrine of the eternal return and at the same time maintain that what Nietzsche claims with regard to time is impoverished, horribly impoverished. And yet that is exactly what Heidegger does. For once, all of a sudden, he does not even try to complicate things; he forecloses: all this is impoverished, closed off to the most profound question. And with a violently simplifying gesture, he juxtaposes these last fragments with statements from 1873, excerpts from the essay "On Truth and Lie in an Extra-moral Sense" which he does not even attempt to interpret, and which he simply characterizes as "subjectivist," "representational," and "Schopenhauerian."

Here is the paragraph. (Read and comment, v. 2, p. 90.)

> "To the actual course of things an *actual* time must also correspond" (XII, number 59). Such actual, infinite time Nietzsche grasps as *eternity*. Viewed as a whole, Nietzsche's meditations on space and time are quite meager. The few thoughts concerning time that inch beyond traditional notions are desultory—the most reliable proof of the fact that the question concerning time, as a means of unfolding the guiding question of metaphysics, and the guiding question itself in its more profound origin remained closed to him. In the earlier, immensely important essay, "On Truth and Lie in an Extra-Moral Sense" (summer 1873), Nietzsche, still perfectly in tune with Schopenhauer, writes that we "produce" representations of space and time "in us and out of us with the necessity of a spider spinning its web" (X, 202). Time too is represented subjectively and is even defined "as a property of space" (WM 862).[38]

244

One could attempt here an entire analysis of this Heideggerian foreclosure, an analysis that would also take into account the date of his *Nietzsche*. This is still at a time, close to *Sein und Zeit*, when the question of the meaning of being must, for Heidegger, be developed from within the transcendental horizon of time and so calls for a reinterpretation, against the entire history of metaphysics, of temporality. We know that, without contradicting or criticizing this gesture, Heidegger in some sense interrupted it, displacing the horizon, reducing the privilege of this question of time, "reversing," to say it quickly, the relation being/time into the relation time and being. As a result, Nietzsche—I'm moving very quickly here—by making of time merely a product of representation, or by not pausing at the question of time, would have implicitly *either* cast suspicion upon a gesture of

---

38. Ibid., v. 2, p. 90 [v. 1, p. 348; *GA* 6.1: 310–11]; X, 202 = *KSA* 1: 885; *WM* 862 = *KSA* 11: 25[211], p. 69.

the kind we find in *Sein und Zeit* or else anticipated the interruption of *Sein und Zeit* (only the first part of the book was published), or even the subsequent displacement of the question of time. So many reasons, so many motivations, for Heidegger to close the reading or to say hastily that Nietzsche closed it or remained closed to it. This, at least, is a hypothesis I wanted to submit to you. What is certain is that Heidegger here hastens the verdict in an unjustified way.

9. The ninth point gathers together, or intends to gather together, all the others. It concerns precisely chaos as the total character of the world from all eternity. Chaos would be the systematic concept that gathers together all the previously defined predicates. Heidegger first calls it "the fundamental representation of beings in their totality."[39] This representation would have a double signification: that of a (pseudo-Heraclitean) *"ständig Werdendes"* and that of a necessity without human or divine law, without intentionality, and so on—not disorder, not magma, but a necessity that no human or divine reason, no aim, end, or intention, can succeed in ordering. And that is indeed what the fragment from *The Gay Science* that we read at the beginning says, the one that began, as Heidegger recalls, as an injunction: "Let us beware (*Hüten wir uns*)": let us beware of humanizing or divinizing the necessity of chaos.[40]

I would now like, very quickly, very schematically, to point out the operations or the signs of the operation that Heidegger then undertakes and that seem to me, with regard to this decisive question of *chaos*, illegitimate, or—since it is no longer a question here of justness or of justice, of law—problematic to the extent that they are reductive, that is, enfeebling, incapable of measuring up to the greater force of Nietzsche's text or, at least, reducing this force in order to affirm the greater force of the Heideggerian text. For what we are witnessing here is quite clearly a conflict of forces, an agonistic scene. Here are those signs:

1. Heidegger does not draw any consequences from what he nonetheless says about chaos as *khainō*. (Read and develop v. 2, p. 91): "Chaos, *khaos, khainō* means 'to yawn'; it signifies something that opens wide or gapes. We conceive of *khaos* in most intimate connection with an original interpretation of the essence of *alētheia* as the self-opening abyss (cf. Hesiod,

---

39. Ibid., v. 2, p. 91 [v. 1, p. 349; *GA* 6.1: 311].
40. Though Derrida earlier spoke of ten points in the Heidegger text, he stops here at the ninth.

Theogony)."⁴¹ *Gaping open* should prohibit any totalization of present beings. And yet Heidegger is going to determine chaos as totalization. See what Nietzsche himself says about philosophy as totalization (Thales in *Philosophy in the Tragic Age of the Greeks*).⁴²

2. When Nietzsche says *Being*, Heidegger translates it in brackets in a way that is somewhat laughable because it is so blatant (it is a question of the totality of beings). I read v. 2, p. 92: "'To attribute a feeling of self-preservation to Being [what is meant is beings in their totality]⁴³ is madness! Ascribing the 'strife of pleasure and revulsion' to atoms!' (XII, 101)."⁴⁴

It is not that Being is spoken by Nietzsche in the sense Heidegger gives it, but that Nietzsche perhaps intimates the difference between *Sein* and *das Seiende im Ganzen*, taken in a non-metaphysical sense.

3. Heidegger is absolutely intent on having Nietzsche "rehumanize" what he dehumanizes (because of totality). He thus juxtaposes various fragments without explicating them in order to reveal a contradiction. (Read v. 2, p. 94):

> "When will all these shades of God cease to darken our paths? When will we have a nature that is altogether undeified! When will we human beings be allowed to begin to *naturalize* ourselves by means of the pure, newly discovered, newly redeemed nature?" (Nietzsche, *The Gay Science*, no. 109)
>
> Yet it is said at the same time, elsewhere: "To 'humanize' the world, that is to say, to feel ourselves increasingly as masters in it—" (*WM* 614; cf. *WM* 616). Yet we would lapse into terrible error if we were to label Nietzsche's guiding representation of the world as chaos with cheap slogans like "naturalism" and "materialism," especially if we were to think that such labels explained his notion once and for all. "Matter" (that is, tracing everything back to some elemental "stuff") is as much an error as "the god of the Eleatics" (that is, tracing it back to something immaterial). The most fundamental point to be made about Nietzsche's notion of chaos is the following: only a thinking that is utterly lacking in stamina will deduce a will to godlessness from the will to a de-deification of beings. On the contrary, truly metaphysical thinking, at the outermost point of de-deification, allowing itself no subterfuge and eschewing all mystification, will uncover that path

---

41. Heidegger, *Nietzsche*, v. 2, p. 91 [v. 1, p. 350; *GA* 6.1: 312].
42. Friedrich Nietzsche, *Philosophy in the Tragic Age of the Greeks*, trans. Marianne Cowan (Chicago: Regnery Gateway, 1962); *KSA* 1: 800–872.
43. The brackets are Heidegger's.
44. Heidegger, *Nietzsche*, v. 2, p. 92 [v. 1, p. 350; *GA* 6.1: 313]; XII, 101 = *KSA* 9: 11[265], p. 543.

on which alone gods will be encountered—if they are to be encountered ever again in the history of mankind.

Meanwhile we want to heed the fact that at the time when the thought of eternal return of the same arises Nietzsche is striving most decisively in his thought to dehumanize and de-deify beings in their totality. His striving is not a mere echo, as one might suppose, of an ostensible "positivistic period" now in abeyance. It has its own, more profound origin. Only in this way is it possible for Nietzsche to be driven directly from such striving to its apparently incongruous opposite, when in his doctrine of will to power he demands the supreme humanization of beings.[45]

4. Finally, and especially, the accusation of "negative theology," which some have not hesitated—out of bad faith—to make against Heidegger, is here leveled by Heidegger against Nietzsche. It assumes that chaos is "the world in its totality" as unsayable . . . (Read and comment v. 2, pp. 94–95):

> In Nietzsche's usage, the word *chaos* indicates a defensive notion in consequence of which nothing can be asserted of beings in their totality. Thus the totality of the world becomes something we fundamentally cannot address, something ineffable—an *arrēton*. What Nietzsche is practicing here with regard to the world totality is a kind of "negative theology," which tries to grasp the Absolute as purely as possible by holding at a distance all "relative" determinations, that is, all those that relate to human beings. Except that Nietzsche's determination of the world as a totality is a negative theology without the Christian God.[46]

Conclusion: A chaos of (hermeneutic) interpretation or an interpretation of chaos? (Read the end and comment.)

> We have elaborated a series of determinations concerning the world totality in Nietzsche's view, reducing them to eight points. All eight are brought home in the principal determination contained in point nine: "The collective character of the world . . . into all eternity is chaos." Must we now take this statement to mean that it is properly incumbent on us to revoke the earlier determinations and to utter no more than "chaos"? Or are all those determinations implied in the concept of chaos, so that they are preserved within this concept and its application to the world totality as the sole determination of that world? Or, on the contrary, do not the determinations and relations pertaining to the essence of chaos (force, finitude, endlessness, Becoming, space, time), as humanizations of Being, also scuttle the concept

---

45. Ibid., v. 2, p. 94 [v. 1, pp. 352–53; *GA* 6.1: 314–15]; *WM* 614 = *KSA* 11: 25[312], p. 92; *WM* 616 = *KSA* 12: 2[108], p. 114.

46. Ibid., v. 2, pp. 94–95 [v. 1, p. 353; *GA* 6.1: 315].

of chaos? In that case we dare not propose any determinations at all; all we can say is *nothing*. Or is "the nothing" perhaps the most human of all humanizations? Our inquiry must push on to these extremes if it is to catch sight of the uniqueness of the present task, the task of determining beings in their totality.[47]

Hence the following chapter: reservations on the subject of humanization.

---

47. Ibid., v. 2, p. 95 [v. 1, pp. 353–54; *GA* 6.1: 316].

TENTH SESSION

Thinking the Division of Labor — and the Contagion of the Proper Name

249   Nietzsche's single [*unique*] name, his single thought, one name, one thought. One thing, one thing, one chaos, one. Of this *one* we said that it was, according to Heidegger, the condition of an essential thought, the essential thought of an essential thinker (for we must assume with Heidegger, who has no doubts about this, that there are essential thoughts and thinkers). As we were also able to see, this implied that when Nietzsche says "I am two," "I know two" (the two: *ich bin beides, ich kenne beides*, or "I am life," "I am death," and so on . . .),[1] he is saying something inessential with regard to the essential unity-unicity of his thought; or, more seriously still, that when Heidegger seems to be saying two things about Nietzsche (for example, that he is right on a limit, at once the great gatherer who completes metaphysics and the one beyond it), he is saying a single thing, that he is saying a single thing when he acknowledges that we do not have at our disposal a schema for receiving and reading this singular thought and when, at the same time, he reduces it to the most powerful, the oldest, the most gathering schema of metaphysics as the thought of the totality of beings.

This unity-unicity must constantly be recalled and gathered up by Heidegger, as if something constantly threatened it, threatened it as that which threatens thought itself. To think and to think this (unique, single) one is the same; thinking would be, in this sense, gathering and thinking the one.

All this happens each time through nomination or naming, the naming of thought and the thought of naming.

250   At the moment Heidegger, after having treated the Eternal Return of the Same, takes up the theme of the will to power, he must thus recall the unicity of Nietzsche's thought. And that the thought of the Eternal Return and the thought of the will to power form a single thought. Now this is so

---

1. Nietzsche, *Ecce Homo*, p. 222 [*KSA* 6: 264].

essentially linked to a thinking of the name and of naming, of an act or a naming decision, that Heidegger's chapter begins this way:

> We call (*Wir nennen*) Nietzsche's thought of will to power his *sole* thought [*seinen* einzigen *Gedanken, einzigen* is underscored]. At the same time we are saying that Nietzsche's other thought, that of eternal recurrence of the same, is of necessity included (*eingeschlossen*) in the thought of will to power. Both thoughts (*Beides*) — will to power and eternal recurrence of the same — say *the same* [*dasselbe* is underscored] and think the *same* fundamental characteristic of beings as a totality. The thought of eternal recurrence of the same is the inner — but not the retrospective — completion (*innere Vollendung*) [Klossowski actually says here "not the supplement," rather than "not the retrospective completion" — *nicht nachträgliche*] of the thought of will to power. Precisely for this reason Nietzsche thought eternal recurrence of the same at an earlier time (*zeitlich früher*) than he did will to power [it is thus this temporal order that Heidegger's course and book followed . . .]. For when he thinks it for the first time, each thinker thinks his sole thought in its completion (*Vollendung*), though not yet in its full unfolding (*Entfaltung*); that is, not yet in the full scope and in the danger that make it something excessive, something that must first be sustained [review translation].²

This value of unicity — whose stakes we have already noted — has to be put in relation to that of authenticity, the authentic (*echt, eigentlich, Eigentlichkeit*). I simply point out this essential relation in Heidegger's thought; I point it out here because I will not have the time this year to analyze this link in what other texts of Heidegger, notably *Sein und Zeit*, describe as the authenticity of Dasein as being-towards-death, or as authentic temporality, this value of authenticity playing (in fact) an essential role in the Heideggerian thinking of death. As well as in all the conceptual oppositions that organize the existential analytic. We would really have to look at these other texts directly, something we cannot do here.

Now, it was in the preceding paragraph (at the end of the preceding chapter, which we read and which opened with the question of "who Nietzsche is" or "above all who he will be") that the authenticity of the question or of the interpretation was in fact said to be dependent on the relation to the unicity of Nietzsche's thought. It is only insofar as we refer ourselves to what is unique or singular in Nietzsche's thought that we will be questioning and interpreting authentically:

---

2. Heidegger, *Nietzsche*, v. 3, p. 10 [v. 1, pp. 481–82; *GA* 6.1: 432–33]; French translation, pp. 375–76.

Whether we incorporate Nietzsche's "philosophy" into our cultural legacy or pass it by is always of no significance (*bedeutungslos*). It will be fatal (*Verhängnisvoll*) if we, lacking the decisiveness (*Entschiedenheit*) required for genuine questioning (*zum echten Fragen*), simply "busy" ourselves (*beschäftigten*) with Nietzsche and take this "busyness" for a thoughtful confrontation (*Auseinandersetzung*) with Nietzsche's unique thought.³

Will to Power would thus be Nietzsche's unique thought, the thought from which or on the basis of which we would have the possibility of gaining access to "who Nietzsche is" and "who Nietzsche will be." One must thus think the thought of the Will to Power. After a few preliminary remarks on editorial problems, Heidegger offers a justification for not proposing a reading of this faux-book titled *The Will to Power* but opening it right at the place where the law and the structure of the Will to Power are set forth. This happens in the third part, the summary of the third part, titled "Principle of a New Valuation"⁴ (*Prinzip einer neuen Wertsetzung*). The subtitle underscores the importance of this value of value: "Attempt at a Revaluation of All Values" (*Versuch einer Umwertung aller Werte*).⁵ Value signifies for Nietzsche, according to Heidegger, a condition of life, a precondition for life to be life. There is life to the extent that there is evaluation. It is starting from the possibility of the evaluation or of the positing of value that life is thought. "Life" is understood sometimes in the sense of everything that is (living), the character of the living in general, sometimes in the sense of "*our* life,"⁶ life as the being of man.

First critique of Nietzsche's alleged biologism: according to Heidegger, Nietzsche does not think the essence of life on the basis of what biology tells him about it, for example the vitalism of the times or Darwinism and the doctrine of "self-preservation" or the "struggle for life."⁷ Life is thought on the basis of its condition, that is, on the basis of that which bears, supports, activates, and gives rise to life. The only thing that has value, or rather, says Heidegger, the only thing that is *value*, is that which "intensifies," as Klossowski translates it, that which enhances (*steigert*) life and — as Heidegger immediately transposes it — the totality of beings. That is the role here of

---

3. Ibid., v. 3, pp. 8–9 [v. 1, p. 481; *GA* 6.1: 432].

4. In the typescript Derrida has typed in the word "position" above the word "institution." [Translators' note:] The French translation of the title reads "The Principle of a New Institution of Value."

5. Heidegger, *Nietzsche*, v. 3, p. 15 [v. 1, pp. 487–88; *GA* 6.1: 438].

6. Ibid., v. 3, p. 15 [v. 1, p. 488; *GA* 6.1: 439].

7. Ibid. The phrase "struggle for life" is in English in Klossowski's French translation.

value or of the positing of value: to ensure life as enhancement (*Steigerung*), the elevation of life. Life is enhancement, and value is the condition for this enhancement; value is life as the enhancement of value, and so on. This enhancement is the essence of life, which means that any simple doctrine of the preservation of life is a doctrine of non-life, of non-value.

But, of course, when we say that the value of life is the condition of an enhancement of life, this can have meaning only if we know what is being enhanced, what life is as enhancement or as the tendency toward enhancement. One must start out from a principle or a foundation, namely, from what the essence of life is, in order to know anything about its enhancement and its being as value. This foundation, that through which something begins, in its essence, is, Heidegger recalls, what the Greeks called *arkhē* and what in Latin is called *principium*.[8] This note, made as if in passing, will then, following a hidden thread, traverse the entire (very long) chapter, all the way up to a sort of reversal or knot that will make of the principle "life" or of this essence of life that is at the origin [*au principe*] of self-enhancement, that will make of this principle of the essence of life, a principiating essence. Let me try to explain this in simpler terms: the principle of life consists in going back to first principles [*se mettre au principe*], that is to say, to the commencement-commandment, to the *archē*, which means at once commencement and commandment (as does *principium*). The essence of life consists in a capacity for commanding, an imperative capacity (a capacity for ordering, *Befehl*), which is coupled with, on another side, a capacity for *Dichten* (for poetizing [*poétifier*], as Klossowski translates it), in the space that is freed up by Kant's theory of the transcendental imagination, which acknowledges in the essence of reason a poetizing (which does not mean poetic) power, this doctrine of the schematism and the transcendental imagination sustaining and revealing the entire modern determination of reason (see v. 3, pp. 95–97),[9] the one in which Fichte, Schelling, and Hegel evolved, though also Nietzsche.

The question concerning the principle of life thus receives, at the end of a trajectory we are going to question, the following response: if Nietzsche does indeed lead everything back to life, to the "biological," he is so far from thinking biologically, biologistically, so far from thinking on the basis of biological life (animal or vegetal), that he determines the essence of the living in the direction (*Richtung*) of being able to command and being-able-to-poetize (*Befehls- und Dichtungshaften*), the capacity to have a perspective

---

8. Ibid., v. 3, p. 18 [v. 1, p. 491; *GA* 6.1: 441].
9. Ibid., v. 3, pp. 95–97 [v. 1, pp. 584–86; *GA* 6.1: 526–27].

and a horizon, which Heidegger translates as a "capacity" for freedom. Accordingly, it is on the basis of or in view of the human (perspective, horizon, commandment, *Dichtung*, representation of beings) that Nietzsche thinks the living. This is another way, of course, of freeing Nietzsche from the accusation of biologism in order then to confine him within the limits of anthropological or humanist metaphysics, Nietzsche's concept of principle being indebted to the Aristotelian-Hegelian tradition and his concept of *Dichtung* to the space of Kantian modernity. Which means that Nietzsche never escapes Platonism in the end.[10] That is where we are headed.

Heidegger begins with the assurance that the essence of life, or the totality of beings, is, for Nietzsche, Will to Power. This assurance is established on the basis of two notes in particular, one from 1888, number 693, which says, "If the innermost essence of being is will to power . . ." (*WP* 693), the other, an earlier one, from 1885, "And do you know what 'the world' is to me? . . . *This world is will to power—and nothing besides!* And you yourselves are also this will to power—and nothing besides!" (*WP* 1067).[11] "World," according to Heidegger, here means the totality of beings, and this is a word that Nietzsche indeed often assimilates to "life." It follows that Nietzsche would then determine life as Will to Power. Beings [*L'étant*] in their totality are "life," the essence of life is Will to Power. With this utterance, this phrase, <this> "*Spruch*" — life is Will to Power — Western metaphysics comes to an end, the Western metaphysics at whose beginning is to be found this "obscure statement": beings in their totality are *physis*.[12] This utterance is not the "*Privatansicht*" (the private view) of a person named "Nietzsche." The thinker who knows how to say, the thinker and sayer (*Denker und Sager*) of this utterance, is "a destiny" ("I am a destiny").[13] Which means, Heidegger translates (*Dies will sagen*): the being-a-thinker of this thinker, like that of every essential Western thinker, consists in "an almost *inhuman*" fidelity to the most hidden history of the West, the history of the (thinking and poetizing) struggle for or around the word (*Wort*) for being [*l'être*] as a totality.[14] In other words, when Nietzsche says, "I, Friedrich Nietzsche, I am a destiny," he would in effect be naming Western metaphysics; he would be a sort of powerful autonymy for this Western metaphysics,

---

10. Ibid., v. 3, p. 122 [v. 1, p. 615; *GA* 6.1: 554].

11. Ibid., v. 3, p. 18 [v. 1, pp. 491–92; *GA* 6.1: 442]; *WP*, fragment 693, p. 369 = *KSA* 13: 14[80], p. 260; *WP*, fragment 1067, p. 550 = *KSA* 11: 38[12], p. 611.

12. Heidegger, *Nietzsche*, v. 3, p. 18 [v. 1, p. 492; *GA* 6.1: 442].

13. Ibid., v. 3, p. 19 [v. 1, p. 492; *GA* 6.1: 442].

14. Ibid.

which would be represented in the name of an essential thinker, a thinker who would be essential only to this extent. Nietzsche is a pseudonym for the destiny of Western metaphysics. Thinking this pseudonymy is the sole condition for understanding the proper name of Nietzsche.

In other words,[15] one must understand the proper name on the basis of the *Spruch* or the *Wort*, the word or the utterance, the poetico-thinking language that says, or that struggles to say, beings as a totality. A name becomes essential only at the moment it is invested, traversed, *borne* [*porté*] by the logos, the word or the utterance that is equal to the totality of beings in their essence. I emphasize here *borne*: it a matter of the bearing [*portée*] of a proper name, the essential bearing of the name of Nietzsche, a bearing that alone gives access to the so-called or alleged bearer; that bearing or scope [*portée*] is that of this word — which is more than a word, more like a master-word, a language — of this *Wort* or *Spruch* that illuminates the essence of the word and of language rather than being itself illuminated by these latter insofar as this *Wort* or *Spruch* (here *physis*) says the totality of beings, gathers them in their historial unicity. Nietzsche does not bear his name; the individual or the empirical subject Nietzsche does not bear his name, and when it is said, through his mouth, "I am Friedrich Nietzsche," or "I, Friedrich Nietzsche, I am a destiny," it is Western metaphysics that speaks and bears the name and says *I*. Not I as a subject, the value of the subject or of egoity being itself a determination or a particular epoch of this history of Western metaphysics. It is difficult to say whether, in doing this, Heidegger erases or inflates the name of Nietzsche. One must not caricature this gesture, and especially not rush to think that Nietzsche would have refused or rejected it. On the one hand, of course, it resembles the classically philosophical (metaphysical) operation that consists in erasing or reducing — as an accident or as an empirical epiphenomenon — the names of "thinkers" in the name of the philosophy, the system, or the more than systematic whole they represent. On the other hand, there is here a powerful analysis of the functioning of the proper name in language. If the proper name is not simply foreign to language, if it is inscribed within it and negotiates with it according to original laws, and if, besides, the essence of something like language can announce itself only on the basis of thoughts-names as singular as *logos, physis, ousia,* and so on, names that are not only concepts but also in some sense strange singularities that take the form of (untranslatable) proper names, then this

---

15. In the left margin of the typescript are these handwritten words: "extraordinary contagion of proper names (proper name of the world), the totality of beings." The word "contagion" is circled.

untranslatability suspends the trivial opposition between proper names and common names or concepts. There is then no longer a relationship of erasure or of reduction to the empirical (a value that itself comes from Western metaphysics) or one of representation between Western metaphysics and the proper name, for example, the name of Friedrich Nietzsche. There is instead, as Heidegger and Nietzsche both in fact say, an enigmatic struggle to take hold of language, of names, a struggle over poetizing sovereignty, and so on. One has to get to the point of saying, of making say, for example, Friedrich Nietzsche : *physis*, or *physis* : Friedrich Nietzsche : destiny, and so on. This would be a way—a still Nietzschean way—of saying "This world is Will to Power—and nothing besides! And you yourselves are this Will to Power." Although Heidegger pays no attention to the second part of this aphorism ("you yourselves are this Will to Power"), we could take what he says about Western metaphysics and the "person 'Nietzsche'" (*eine Privatansicht der Person Nietzsche*) in this direction and tie it all to a problematic of the proper name. The Will to Power is a proper name, *physis* is a proper name, and so on, provided that we displace and reelaborate the obscure concept of proper name. I leave this, for lack of time, merely as a suggestion to be followed.[16]

Once we have said, with Nietzsche, that life or beings as a totality are Will to Power, we can no longer simply think Will to Power on the basis of everyday representations of will or of power, for example, through a psychology of the will or a physics of power. Since the Will to Power is the essence of all beings, one should be able to find it everywhere, in every region of beings, in nature, art, language, history, politics, science, and knowledge in general.

In this series (nature, art, history, politics, science or knowledge), science and knowledge have a privilege that interests Heidegger. He is going to follow this out by claiming that, indeed, "'science' is not simply *one* field of 'cultural' activity among others";[17] it constitutes a fundamental power (*Grundmacht*) in Western man's relation to beings.

What, then, is knowledge as Will to Power for Nietzsche? To know is equivalent to grasping the true; knowledge (*Erkenntnis*) is a sort of *Erfassen des Wahren*, a grasping of the true. We must thus think the relationship between knowledge as Will to Power and truth.

Nietzsche says in a note from 1884, at the moment when, says Heidegger, he is beginning to formulate "consciously" (*bewusst*) the thought of Will to

---

16. In the left margin of the typescript there is the handwritten note: "Return to p. 16."
17. Heidegger, *Nietzsche*, v. 3, p. 20 [v. 1, p. 494; *GA* 6.1: 444].

Power: "'honoring (*Verehrung*) truth is already the *consequence* (*Folge*) of an *illusion*' (WM 602)."¹⁸ Elsewhere, he says that (1888) "'art is *worth more* than truth' (WM 853),"¹⁹ and that "'*Truth is the kind of error* without which a certain kind of living being [namely man] could not live' (1885) (WM 493)."²⁰

Instead of concluding too hastily that this is nihilism — one that makes truth the equivalent of an illusion or an error, at once harmful for the enhancement of life (as opposed to art, which would have greater value) and necessary for living beings, but canceling itself out as soon as it becomes its mere contrary (illusion, error), or canceling itself out in the absurdity of a circle that would dictate that in order to know the nature of the error or the illusion that truth is one would still have to presuppose the value of truth — one must try to penetrate the singular logic or force of this thought. To do so, Heidegger, after having explained yet again his doubts about the editorial organization of the *Nachlass*, proposes jumping right into the middle of the Nietzschean interpretation of knowledge as Will to Power by reading fragment 507 (1887). Here it is: (read Heidegger's *Nietzsche*, v. 3, p. 33). (V)²¹

> As the point of departure for our inquiry we choose number 507 (spring–fall 1887):
> "The *estimation of value* 'I believe that such and such is so' as the *essence* of '*truth*.' In estimations of value are expressed *conditions* of *preservation* and *growth*. All our *organs of knowledge and our senses* are developed only with regard to conditions of preservation and growth. *Trust* in reason and its categories, in dialectic, thus the *value-estimation* of logic, proves only their *usefulness* for life, proved by experience — *not* their 'truth.'
> "That a great deal of *belief* must be present; that *judgments* may be ventured; that doubt concerning all essential values is *lacking* — that is the precondition for every living thing and its life. Therefore, what is necessary is that something *must* be held to be true — *not* that something *is* true.
> "'The *true* and the *apparent* worlds' — I have traced this antithesis back to *value relations*. We have projected the conditions of *our* preservation as *predicates of Being* in general. Because we have to be stable in our beliefs if we are to prosper, we have made the 'true' world a world not of mutability and becoming, but one of *being*."²²

258

---

18. Ibid., v. 3, p. 24 [v. 1, p. 499; *GA* 6.1: 449]; *WM* 602 = *KSA* 11:25[505], p. 146.
19. Ibid., v. 3, p. 25 [v. 1, p. 500; *GA* 6.1: 449]; *WM* 853 = *KSA* 13: 17[3], p. 522.
20. Ibid., v. 3, p. 32 [v. 1, p. 508; *GA* 6.1: 457]; *WM* 493 = *KSA* 11: 34[253], p. 506.
21. Derrida writes the same letter next to the passage on the photocopied page of Heidegger that he is about to quote.
22. Heidegger, *Nietzsche*, v. 3, p. 33 [v. 1, pp. 509–10; *GA* 6.1: 458]; *WM* 507 = *KSA* 12: 9[38], pp. 352–53.

Starting here, from this quotation of Nietzsche by Heidegger, after a movement that, up until now, I have done little more than comment on, or rather paraphrase, there begins an active reading by Heidegger that we must follow closely in order to pinpoint Heidegger's decisive intervention in its specific place and time. It takes place over a few pages, a few lines, but to linger there is not to shut ourselves up in it and to shut the rest of the book, since it in fact reverberates throughout and is represented in Heidegger's entire interpretation of Nietzsche.

The aim — and the conclusion — of this interpretation as it is already explicitly formulated in these few pages is that the overturning introduced by Nietzsche with regard to truth remains a secondary modification within a traditional determination of truth, a determination that governs all of metaphysics and that Nietzsche does not question, which he even needs in order for his statements to have a meaning and a value. In other words, the displacement brought about by Nietzsche does not have a bearing on truth in general or on a particular determination of this truth but on the conditions (the evaluation of the conditions of life, preservation and enhancement) of this truth. That Nietzsche alters absolutely nothing about the determination of truth as correctness (*Richtigkeit*, "conformity to" as formal non-contradiction of the utterance or as conformity to the content of the representation, or else to beings), as adequation or *homoiōsis* — that is what Heidegger is absolutely set on concluding, and he comes back to this with an insistence and a rather strained determination that lead us to wonder first of all this: if Nietzsche really leaves untouched this fundamental and traditional determination, then what exactly does he touch and why does Heidegger say at the same time that this concept of truth "changes peculiarly and inevitably,"[23] or that truth, once characterized as an "estimation," is turned (*abgedreht*) in a "*completely different direction* [this is underscored: in *eine ganz andere Richtung* abgedreht]."[24] There is something strange about this, something that, to tell you the truth — I won't hide it from you — I have difficulty understanding in these few pages where something decisive for the entire interpretation is at stake.

Here, first of all, to take things slowly and to be as clear as possible, are the statements that insist rather heavy-handedly on the fact that Nietzsche's discourse on truth belongs to the most intractable Platonico-Aristotelian determination. Here is a first passage, the most astonishing, in truth, where Heidegger, while noting that Nietzsche writes "truth" in quotation marks

---

23. Ibid., v. 3, p. 35 [v. 1, p. 513; *GA* 6.1: 461].
24. Ibid., v. 3, p. 37 [v. 1, pp. 515–16; *GA* 6.1: 463–64].

in the fragment quoted, does not credit him with wanting to displace the tradition that is "quoted" in this way ("what one calls truth," "what the tradition...," "what you call truth," and so on). The reading Heidegger gives of it is the following: there are quotation marks because Nietzsche is evoking what is commonly thought about truth; he is going to provide an explanation for it, an etiology, an interpretation, but he is not going to modify the content of this tradition. The difference is subtle but everything is at stake. Someone says to you: "I believe that such and such is so, is the essence of 'truth'": How do you understand such an evaluation? Either as Heidegger is set on understanding it, namely, what you call or what is called "truth," the definition of which I will not touch, leaving it totally intact, is an evaluation of the type "I believe that, etc."? Or else, a hypothesis that credits Nietzsche with a more profound alteration: by saying that "truth" in quotation marks is an evaluation of the type "I believe, etc.," I affect the very core of the traditional determination. Heidegger will opt, has to opt, for the first hypothesis, even though he wants — otherwise he would not be interested in Nietzsche — to recognize in him a change of direction, a change of direction that must nonetheless reorient a motive, if you will, that in itself remains untouched. Here, then, first of all, is the passage on the quotation marks (read Heidegger's *Nietzsche*, v. 3, p. 34), W:[25]

> The piece begins, "The *estimation of value* 'I believe that such and such is so' as the *essence* of '*truth*.'" Every word, every underline, each aspect of the writing and the whole word-structure are important here. The introductory remark makes volumes of epistemologies superfluous, if only we can muster the quiet and the stamina and the thoroughness of reflection that such words require in order to be understood.
>
> It is a question of the essential definition of truth. Nietzsche writes the word *truth* in quotation marks. Briefly, this means truth as it is ordinarily understood and as it has long been understood — in the history of Western thought — and as Nietzsche himself also must understand it in advance, without being conscious of this necessity, its scope, or even its ground. The essential definition of truth that since Plato and Aristotle dominates not only the whole of Western thought but the history of Western man in general down to his everyday doings and ordinary opinions and representations runs, briefly: Truth is correctness of representation, and representation means having and bringing before oneself beings, a having that perceives and opines, remembers and plans, hopes and rejects. Representing adjusts itself to beings, assimilates itself to them, and reproduces them.

25. Derrida writes the same letter next to the passage on the photocopied page of Heidegger that he is about to quote.

Truth means the assimilation of representing to *what* beings are and *how* they are [to their quiddity and to their modality].²⁶

This theme is taken up again and it regularly punctuates the remaining three pages in the chapter, as Heidegger recalls the nature of truth as correctness, adequation, or *homoiōsis*. Thus:

1. "Correctness is then understood as the translation of *adaequatio* and *homoiōsis*. For Nietzsche, too, it has been decided in advance and in accordance with the tradition that truth is correctness."²⁷

2. (On the next page): "Accordingly, in the sentence we are clarifying, which says that truth is a *Wertschätzung*, a 'value-estimation,' Nietzsche is basically thinking nothing other than this: Truth is correctness. He seems to have completely forgotten his saying that truth is an illusion."²⁸

Who is forgetting this? And how can Heidegger suspect Nietzsche of having forgotten it? What is the meaning of such a suspicion? (A general problem of hermeneutics: Heidegger does not take into account the general syntax, the narrative made up of simulacra, the trajectory: each time, he believes.)²⁹ Heidegger has just isolated this statement of Nietzsche's that says that the true is an "I hold as true," "I believe," etc., a statement that identifies truth with a holding as true in a judgment. But as soon as Nietzsche takes it upon himself to explain this judgment, Heidegger accuses him of seeing the truth only in this traditional form, Heidegger himself forgetting that by saying that truth is belief in truth Nietzsche is able to call into question even this very core. For if truth is evaluation, is it still the traditional truth? I return to my quotation:

> . . . Nietzsche is basically thinking nothing other than this: Truth is correctness. He seems to have completely forgotten his saying that truth is an illusion. Nietzsche even seems to be in complete agreement with Kant, who once notes explicitly in his *Critique of Pure Reason* that the explanation of truth as the "agreement (*Übereinstimmung*) of knowledge with its object" is "here granted and presupposed."

And then a few lines later:

> The medieval theologians, and Aristotle and Plato too, think about "truth" in the way in which Kant explains its general essence. Nietzsche does not

---

26. Heidegger, *Nietzsche*, v. 3, p. 34 [v. 1, p. 511; *GA* 6.1: 459–60]. The material in brackets is added in the French translation of Klossowski.
27. Ibid., v. 3, p. 35 [v. 1, p. 512; *GA* 6.1: 461].
28. Ibid., v. 3, p. 36 [v. 1, p. 514; *GA* 6.1: 462].
29. In the typescript there is this handwritten note in the left margin: "develop."

just *seem* to be in accord (*in Einklang zu stehen*) with this Western tradition, he *is* in accord (*steht im Einklang*) with it; only for this reason can he, must he, distinguish himself from it.³⁰

One cannot but be surprised by this logic or this rhetoric: it is because he is in accord that he is not in accord and that he needs to be not in accord. In itself, this logic is not necessarily shocking: discord always presupposes some measure of accord, disagreement some measure of agreement, disharmony some measure of harmony. What is more interesting is to see how Heidegger distributes the accord and the disaccord in his reading in order to save Nietzsche's originality up to a certain point but then confine him to the tradition. Once he has insisted on the basic accord (*Einklang*), Heidegger has to note what is "disconcerting" (Klossowski's translation), strange (*befremdlich*) <in> the Nietzschean determination of truth as illusion. (Read v. 3, pp. 35–36, up to the word *beings* [étant]):

> For Nietzsche, too, it has been decided in advance and in accordance with the tradition that truth is correctness.
>
> If this is so, then Nietzsche's first, very strange essential definition appears disconcerting. Nietzsche's saying that truth is an illusion, a kind of error, has as its innermost presupposition, one that is thus never uttered at all, the traditional and never challenged characterization of truth as the correctness of representing. Yet for Nietzsche this concept of truth changes peculiarly and inevitably—hence not at all arbitrarily. The first sentence of number 507 says what this necessary change looks like. Viewed grammatically, the piece begins not with a proposition but with a key word that, simply, clearly, and completely, indicates Nietzsche's position with regard to the traditional concept of truth and serves him as a directive for his own path of thought. According to this word, truth is in its essence an "estimation of value." That phrase means to appraise something as a value and posit it as such. But (according to the statement noted earlier) value signifies a perspectival condition for life-enhancement. Value-estimation is accomplished by life itself, and by man in particular. Truth as value-estimation is something that "life" or man brings about, and that thus belongs to human being. (Why and to what extent that is so still remains a question).
>
> Nietzsche unequivocally characterizes what kind of value-estimation truth is in the words "I believe that such and such is so." This valuation has the character of a "belief." But what does "belief" mean? Belief means to *hold* such and such as *being* thus and thus. "Belief" does not mean assenting to and accepting something that one oneself has *not* seen explicitly as a being or can never grasp as in being with one's own eyes; rather, to believe here

263

---

30. Heidegger, *Nietzsche*, v. 3, pp. 36–37 [v. 1, pp. 514–15; *GA* 6.1: 462–63].

means to hold something that representation encounters as *being* in such and such a way. Believing is holding *for something*, holding it as *in being*. Thus believing here by no means signifies assent to an incomprehensible doctrine inaccessible to reason but proclaimed as true by an authority, nor does it mean trust in a covenant and prophecy. Truth as value-estimation, that is, as holding for something, as holding for something as being in this or that way, stands in an essential connection with beings as such. What is true is what is held in being, as thus and thus in being, what is taken to be in being. *What is true is beings* [l'étant].³¹

(Comment on the word "*beings* [étant]."³² And what if Nietzsche made of the form "beings" the effect of illusion — not becoming but becoming not beings, thus no totality of beings ... comment at length.)

Here is another passage that marks Heidegger's surprise. (Read v. 3, pp. 37–38):

The question is why he nevertheless thinks the essence of truth differently — and in what sense differently. The key word concerning the essence of truth as belief does have as its *pre*supposition the unspoken position that truth is correctness; but it says something else, and that is what is essential for Nietzsche. For this reason, it moves immediately to the foreground by means of the sentence structure and the emphasis.

"*Estimation of value* ... as the *essence of 'truth'*": That means that the essence of truth as correctness (correctness as such) is really a *value-estimation*. Nietzsche's decisive metaphysical insight lies in this interpretation of the essence of correctness (of the traditional, unquestioned concept of truth). This means that the essence of correctness will by no means find its explanation and basis by saying how man, with the representations occurring in his subjective consciousness, can conform to objects that are at hand outside of his soul, how the gap between the subject and the object can be bridged so that something like a "conforming to" becomes possible.

With the characterization of truth as estimation of value, the essential definition of truth is rather turned in a *completely different direction*. We see this from the way in which Nietzsche continues his train of thought: "In estimations of value are expressed *conditions* of *preservation* and *growth*." This sentence initially gives evidence for the characterization of the essence

---

31. Ibid., v. 3, pp. 35–36 [v. 1, pp. 512–14; *GA* 6.1: 461–62].

32. [Translators' note:] The French *étant* (being) is the present participle of the verb *être* (to be, being). When used as a noun with an indefinite article, *un étant*, it means a being or an entity, and when used with a definite article, *l'étant*, it can refer either to a specific being or entity, "the being," or to "beings" in general. It is in this last sense that *l'étant dans sa totalité* is the common French translation of *das Seiende im Ganzen*, that is, "beings as a whole" or "beings in their totality."

of "value" in general that we mentioned at the beginning: first, that it has the character of a "condition" for "life"; secondly, that in "life" not only "preservation" but also and above all "growth" is essential. "Growth" here is simply another name for "enhancement." However, "growth" sounds like merely quantitative extension and could indicate that "enhancement" is ultimately intended only in this quantitative sense of increase—although not in the manner of piecemeal accumulation, since growth points to the autonomous development and unfolding of a living being.

The "value-estimation" that is determined by the essence of truth in the sense of holding-to-be-true, any "estimation of value" whatsoever, is the "expression" of conditions of preservation and growth, as conditions of life. What is appraised and valued as a "value" is such a condition. Nietzsche goes still farther. Not only does "truth" revert to the scope of "conditions of life" with regard to its essence, but the faculties for grasping truth also receive here their sole determination: "All our *organs of knowledge and our senses* are developed only with regard to conditions of preservation and growth." Accordingly, truth and grasping the truth are not merely in the service of "life" according to their use and application; their essence, the manner of their organization, and thus their entire activity are driven and directed by "life."[33]

We have thus said nothing, elucidated nothing, about this concordance/discordance so long as we have not thought what Nietzsche thought about life.

. . . .

(Pause)

What, then, about life for Nietzsche? And for Nietzsche according to Heidegger? <It is> right at the moment this questions emerges, at the moment Heidegger puts the word "life" in quotation marks, the moment it is a question of knowing how and starting from where Nietzsche thinks "life," what is called "life," that Heidegger inserts, that he deems it necessary to insert, his refutation of biologism and of "Nietzsche's alleged biologism" (*Nietzsches angeblicher Biologismus*).[34] If this refutation comes before anything else, it is because its stakes are decisive, once again, for the entire undertaking. For it has to consolidate the whole set of relations between science and philosophy, between philosophy and thinking (beyond metaphysics). Let me give you right away, before returning to Heidegger's text, what seems to me to be the schema (a schema that has at once great force, great necessity, and a certain vulnerability) that supports Heidegger's discourse at this point. Since this schema is everywhere at work in his thought, since it

---

33. Heidegger, *Nietzsche*, v. 3, pp. 37–38 [v. 1, pp. 515–16; *GA* 6.1: 463–64].
34. Ibid., v. 3, pp. 39–47 [v. 1, pp. 517–27; *GA* 6.1: 465–74].

conditions everything he says about science, technology, and metaphysics, and since it is also a question of the relations between philosophy and a certain concept of science, what we are venturing on this topic cannot be restricted, despite appearances, to the dual relation Nietzsche Heidegger and even less to one or another of their texts.

Taken in its most general form, this schema is the following—and I believe that at the very moment Heidegger claims, while reading Nietzsche, to be taking a step beyond metaphysics or starting from a step beyond metaphysics, this schema, at this very moment, is the most traditionally metaphysical (which does not, to my eyes, totally disqualify it, but rather gives it a force[35] that is, in a certain sense, inexhaustible), the most Hegelian even, I would say, with respect to the relations between science and philosophy. This relation is the following and it presupposes that science—what is called science, that is to say, what philosophy calls science and what, following philosophy, one usually calls science, and even scientists call science—this relation presupposes that science conforms to what philosophy says it is, namely, a determinate knowledge of a certain type of being. Sciences are specific, they are concerned with a determinate type of being (or of object, as one might say along with Kant or Husserl, the object being a determination of beings). The sciences are thus regional; they are concerned with only one region of objectivity or of beings. But they can begin as sciences, as the determinate knowledge of one type of beings, only at the moment <when> the meaning or the essence of the beings they treat has been thought. There can be physics as such only if one has access to and delimits the meaning of what a physical thing is, what the physicality of the physical is; there can be history as such only if one is able to recognize the historicity of the historical as such, only if one has at least some prior sense that allows one to distinguish in principle the historical from the non-historical, from the extra-historical, and so on. Now this access to the meaning of the regional-being, to the physicality of the physical, the historicity of the historical, and so on, cannot be, as such and according to the schema I am laying out, accessible to science or to the scientist as such, in what is proper to their scientific activity. It is not physics that tells us what physicality is, it is not history or mathematics that tells us what the historicity or the mathematicity of the object is. At the moment when the properly scientific work of physics, mathematics, or history begins, the scientific work as such, the scientist must, in order to put himself or herself forward as a physicist, mathematician, or historian, be assured as to the meaning of the beings or the

---

35. In the typescript the word "resource" has been handwritten above "force."

ontic region or the region of objectivity in which he or she is working. The scientist is concerned with beings or with objects but thinks neither the beingness or determinate objectivity of those objects — and that is the condition of the scientist's efficacy — nor, a fortiori, beingness or objectivity. It is philosophy (or metaphysics) that poses the question of knowing what physical beings are as such and, a fortiori, beings as a totality. It is philosophy that distributes and assigns to the regional sciences the meaning of their field. It can, of course, sometimes happen that scientists will pose such questions about the meaning of the determinate field or about the totality of fields, but at that point they are doing this not as scientists but rather as philosophers, and there is no possible confusion or transition between one type of question and the other; we are dealing here with an absolute leap.

What is presupposed by this schema, this very powerful, very traditional schema, which I have obviously rigidified and simplified? What is presupposed is that there are things like science, that all sciences are species of something like Science, that there is, therefore, a general scientificity of science distributed equally among the regional sciences, that science is concerned with things that are determinable as beings, that beings (or objective beings) are the general form of what is at issue in science. It is obviously difficult to deny that this is what science does: for who would dare say that science is not concerned with things that are (that is, with beings), who would dare say that it does not carve out its field of objects by anticipating the meaning of the objects in that field, and so on? And then, we might go on to say, if there appeared, under the name of science, questions or activities of thought that were no longer concerned with determinable beings as beings, well, then, that would simply no longer be science.

To take things at the most schematic level, where the lever is most laid bare, you can see that this powerful systematics presupposes that scientific knowledge or truth has an object proper to it and that this object is given in the form of beings. Without that, the entire schema collapses.

Without returning to what was said five or six sessions ago about the transformation of the status of knowledge, of science, of the relation to the object and to the referent as a result of the textualization of the scientific object, without returning to all that, even though this is where the problem lies, and it is tied to what we are saying today, I will simply note the following: if what Nietzsche calls "life," if Nietzsche resorts to science to speak of what he calls "life" at the very moment he in fact suspects what is called "the real world" of being posited by life, for life, as a world of beings, if he suspects the form "beings" of being itself an effect of "life," if, then, beings, beingness, and the being of beingness are but effects of "life,"

268

which itself, then, would be neither a being nor the totality of beings, then the philosophical schema I just sketched out would not just take a hit; it would actually be the principal target of Nietzsche's discourse, the principal thing being accused. That would not necessarily mean that Nietzsche gives in to biologism, but that the mistake of this *–ism*, which consists in examining every being on the basis of the science of a regional authority (psychologism, sociologism, historicism, physiologism, biologism), this mistake can no longer be attributed to him once the juridical code charged with attributing it has itself been deconstructed. This code presupposes a distribution of regions, of tasks, a division of the field and of labor; it presupposes strict boundaries between regions, an order and a hierarchy in the power of questioning or constituting. It presupposes that the biologist does biology when he or she is doing biology, that the sociologist does sociology when he or she is doing sociology, and that the philosopher is the one who, in the final analysis, identifies the field in its totality and the specificity of the objects. But what if—as we now see—the "biologist" were no longer simply a biologist; what if in his or her work as a so-called biologist he or she had to do history, linguistics, semantics, chemistry, physics, the science of institutions, even literature? What if the mathematician were the only one able to speak of the foundations or non-foundations, of the epistemology or the history, of mathematics? What if "beings" were no longer this general form that circulates among the specialized fields in order to give unity to the encyclopedia and assign the various tasks, forbidding us, in the end, from breaking with the principle of the division of labor and with the philosophical order that is there to oversee it, the philosopher being there to allocate this division of labor and remaining himself the only one, in the end, to escape it, though in so doing he serves everything that has an interest in maintaining it?

The paradox here—and this is what is interesting about Heidegger's operation—is that, on the one hand, Heidegger deconstructs the metaphysical onto-logy that supports this schema, and yet he subjects the reading of Nietzsche to it and does not want to credit Nietzsche with this deconstruction. He saves Nietzsche from biologism only in order to make of him a great metaphysician, or else to make of "biologism" the effect of metaphysics. This explains—and it is with this quotation that I am going to conclude my preliminary and schematic questions in order to enter into the chapter on Nietzsche's alleged biologism—this explains, then, why Heidegger finds the interpretation he himself proposes to be "disconcerting," "strange" (*befremdlich*, once again). I am reading from the middle of this chapter (v. 3, p. 46; p. 526 in Heidegger's original).

As strange (*befremdlich*) as it may sound [resonate: *klingen*] at first, the truth of the following assertion can be founded by sufficient reflection (*Besinnung*): when Nietzsche thinks beings as a totality—and prior to that Being—as "life," and when he defines man in particular as "*Raubtier*" [predator, beast of prey], he is not thinking biologically. Rather, he grounds this apparently merely biological worldview *metaphysically*.[36]

How did we get to this strangeness (*Befremdlichkeit*)?

Heidegger does not deny that Nietzsche's thought is very "biological," even biologizing. If *bios* means life, the course of life, closer in Greek to the biographical than to the biological, it is nonetheless clear that biology, Heidegger says, means "the study of life in the sense of plants and animals"[37] (a trivial definition that Heidegger, at this point, does not seem too concerned with) and that a thinker such as Nietzsche gives all kinds of signs of biologism whenever he speaks, in particular with regard to man, of "discipline and breeding (*Zucht und Züchtung*)," of a "beast of prey," of the "splendid *blond beast* lustfully roving after prey and victory."[38] Heidegger thus accumulates indications of a properly biologistic—or at the very least biological, biologizing—thinking in Nietzsche, indications of his "metaphysics of life,"[39] including the passage with which we began this seminar, namely, that fragment from *The Will to Power* in which Nietzsche says, "'Being'—we have no other representation of this than as '*living*.'—How can anything dead 'be'?"[40] I am not going to comment on this again.

And yet, despite all these indications, Heidegger claims to be showing that this "biologistic" interpretation of Nietzsche is the principal obstacle (*Haupthindernis*) to penetrating his thought. Although Heidegger, at this point in his itinerary, associates biologism and the metaphysics of life as two species of the same *contre-sens* or the same obstacle to penetrating Nietzsche's thought, I think we will be able to say at the end of the day that he saves Nietzsche from biologism only in order to confine him to a metaphysics of life.

But let us see how that happens.

If "biology" means (*heisst*) the science or the doctrine of life or, better, says Heidegger, of the living (*Lebendigen*: see Hegel and Jacob), it covers all the phenomena, processes, and laws drawn from the various domains

---

36. Heidegger, *Nietzsche*, v. 3, p. 46 [v. 1, p. 526; *GA* 6.1: 473].
37. Ibid., v. 3, p. 39 [v. 1, p. 517; *GA* 6.1: 465].
38. Ibid.; see *KSA* 12: 7[64], p. 318, and the *Genealogy of Morals*, 1, in *KSA* 5: p. 275.
39. Heidegger, *Nietzsche*, v. 3, p. 41 [v. 1, p. 519; *GA* 6.1: 467].
40. Ibid., v. 3, p. 40 [v. 1, p. 518; *GA* 6.1: 466].

of life in general, namely, the vegetal, the animal, the human. Botany and zoology, anatomy, physiology, and psychology are sectors of biology, sometimes subordinated to general biology. All biology, beginning with general biology, presupposes a prior concept of the essence of the living that would define the unity of the domain, the field, or the region. Now—and this is the argument that is decisive for Heidegger's entire reading and that, as I was saying earlier, is the metaphysical argument par excellence, the charter of philosophy as such—this domain of essence (*Wesensbereich*) in which science operates, the essentiality of this domain, could never, in any case whatsoever, be posited or founded by science.

> The *Wesensbereich* [the essential realm] in which biology moves can itself never be posited and grounded (*gesetzt und begründet*) by biology as a science, but can always only be presupposed (*vorausgesetzt*), adopted, and confirmed. This is true of every science.

And Heidegger goes on:

> Every science rests upon propositions about the area of beings within which its every investigation abides and operates. These propositions (*Sätze*) about beings—about what they are—propositions that posit and delimit the area, are metaphysical propositions. Not only can they not be demonstrated by the concepts and proofs of the respective sciences, they cannot even be thought appropriately in this way at all.[41]

The same holds, then, not only for biology, which as such is not able to decide what the living is but is only able to concern itself with, to busy itself with, in the end, that which only the metaphysician as such (even if this is, in fact, an individual who also does biology) thinks and delimits as living. This goes for every science (Heidegger gives other examples of this), and what gets reproduced each time is the general structure of the relations between science and metaphysics.

This relation is, at bottom, one of absolute exteriority and heterogeneity. There is no continuity between the types of questions in each, even if they are posed by the same individual in what seems to be the same course of research or discourse. From scientific questions to metaphysical questions, there is a leap, says Heidegger. There is no transition or reciprocal transformation; the passage (*Übergang*) is a leap between the two. It is thus from the outside, from an absolute outside, that metaphysics assigns to science its domain of research and distributes, organizes, maps out the general field

---

41. Ibid., v. 3, pp. 41–42 [v. 1, p. 520; *GA* 6.1: 468].

of science into determinate domains, with borders that are essential, in the end, and cannot, in principle, be crossed. Naturally, Heidegger would protest, and he does in fact protest, explicitly, against such a translation when he specifies that it is not a question of a *Massregelung*, of a regulation of the sciences under the jurisdiction of philosophy. On the contrary, it is out of respect for the dignity of science, which is thereby acknowledged to have a hidden, higher knowledge (that of metaphysics), that we recall this relation to metaphysics, which is in a relation neither of mastery (technical or scientific) nor of juxtaposition with science. And, obviously, the heterogeneity of the two types (the scientific and the metaphysical) would alone prohibit such a coordinated relation between the two.

It remains the case that this type of argument (no mastery because the completely other is at stake, because there is no contact or continuous transition, and so on) is the typical argument for justifying all hierarchies, including the most violent.

There is indeed here a sort of war whose social, historical stakes are very concrete. Heidegger wants to head off "the danger of often unnoticeable transgressions of various fields,"[42] as if the real ill stemmed from this kind of illegitimate invasion, this transgression (*Überschreitung*) by which a science no longer knows its limits, neither its limits as a determinate science nor its limits as science, that is, as science in general. I would like to make you aware of all the — how should we call them? — connotations (but these are not connotations, on the contrary, they are essential propositions that actually found the values that appear elsewhere as connotations) that are marked out in this paragraph where Heidegger denounces, warns, and frets when speaking of the presumptuousness of science, or rather of scientism, of its transgressive arrogance in a modernity that no longer knows how to question itself as to its provenance and its metaphysical belonging. Here it is (read and comment: v. 3, p. 44; German pp. 523–24):

> The more secure the sciences become within the scope of their affairs, the more stubbornly do they evade metaphysical reflection on the specific field, and the greater becomes the danger of often unnoticeable transgressions of that field and confusions resulting therefrom. The zenith of intellectual confusion is attained, however, when the opinion crops up that metaphysical propositions and views about reality could be grounded by "scientific insights," whereas scientific insights are, after all, only possible on the basis of a different, higher, and stricter knowledge concerning reality as such. The idea of a "scientifically founded worldview" is a characteristic offshoot

---

42. Ibid., v. 3, p. 44 [v. 1, p. 523; *GA* 6.1: 471].

of the intellectual confusion in the public mind that emerged more and more strikingly in the last third of the nineteenth century and attained remarkable success in those half-educated circles that indulged in popular science.[43]

When Nietzsche speaks of life, when he determines, according to Heidegger, the totality of beings as life, he is thus, by definition, not borrowing his concepts from a regional science called biology. His approach has nothing to do with biologism either as an exceeding or an imperialist transgression of a region or as the scientific naïveté that ignores its metaphysical foundations and believes it is able to secure its own foundation from within itself. Nietzsche thinks in a metaphysical way both life and the conditions of life as the totality of beings. It is in this way that he brings to its ultimate fruition that which had been held in reserve ever since the initial determination of being as *physis*.

That alone would be enough for us to think that if a regional science such as biology has a particular relation of affinity with *physis* as a name of being since the dawn of Western metaphysics, then this very logic of the relations between metaphysics and regional sciences gets complicated at precisely this point. But I do not want to insist on this; these are schemas that we have previously defined on the subject of the living that cannot be an object like any other for science in the traditional sense, that is to say, in the philosophical sense, of science. And that is indeed why Heidegger is in all these texts relentless in going after the arrogance of this science, or indeed of this philosophy of life.

We are now going, rather arbitrarily, unjustifiably, to abandon Heidegger at this point. I would have wanted to pursue along this path a more complicated and detailed analysis, beginning with what is said further on about chaos (which Nietzsche, according to Heidegger, does not think "in the primordial Greek sense":[44] what is decisive is the relation to the totality of beings, etc.) and about all the other themes of this third volume. My initial intention was also to read with you other texts by Heidegger on being-towards-death, on the existential analytic of Dasein, and so on. But taking some comfort in the thought that at least the principle (even if a bit complicated) of my reading has been conveyed, at least schematically, I think it is preferable that in the few sessions remaining after the Easter break we begin to follow the trajectory of the third loop I announced: Nietzsche and the Freud of *Jenseits*.

43. Ibid., v. 3, p. 44 [v. 1, pp. 523–24; *GA* 6.1: 471].
44. Ibid., v. 3, p. 77 [v. 1, p. 562; *GA* 6.1: 506].

ELEVENTH SESSION[1]

The Escalade — of the Devil in Person[2]

Already in the first session of this seminar — perhaps you will remember this, or, if not remember, perhaps you will have seen what follows from it — I justified the title of the seminar and advanced the proposition of another logic by linking the question of life death [*la vie la mort*] to the question of positing (*Setzung*), of positionality, of oppositional (oppositional or juxtapositional) logic. I am not going to return to this. I also suggested, in a word, that the logic of the beyond, of the step (not) beyond, would therefore be not in a relation of opposition but in another relation with that which it goes beyond [*franchit*] or breaks free from [*s'affranchit*] transgressively. This is the case for *Beyond Good and Evil* and *Beyond the Pleasure Principle*.[3] In coming to Freud's book for the third loop announced earlier, I must clarify, precisely, that the selective, discriminating reading I am going to give will attempt to make appear the essentially non-positional, non-thetic structure

---

1. In the typescript there is this handwritten addition at the top of the page, just to the right of the title: "photo. p. 5, 19." For bibliographical information regarding the subsequent publication of this session, see the editorial note, pp. xiii–xivnn10–12.

2. "The Escalade" is a civic celebration of the city of Geneva. It commemorates the failed attempt of a Savoyard army to scale (*escalader*) the walls of Geneva on the night of December 11–12, 1602. The Genevans celebrate their independence on this day down to the present. Later in this session Derrida will cite Rousseau on a certain diabolical theatrical production during the celebration of "The Escalade."

3. Sigmund Freud, *Beyond the Pleasure Principle*, ed. & trans. James Strachey, in collaboration with Anna Freud, assisted by Alix Strachey and Alan Tyson, in v. 18 of *The Standard Edition of the Complete Psychological Works of Sigmund Freud* (London: Hogarth Press and Institute of Psychoanalysis, 1959), ["Jenseits des Lustprinzips," in v. 13 of *Gesammelte Werke* (London: Imago, 1952)]. In what follows all references to Freud will be, first, to the *Standard Edition*, abbreviated *SE*, followed by the volume and page number, and then to the *Gesammelte Werke*, abbreviated *GW*, followed by the volume and page number.

275

of this text, to make appear—against so many other readings—the essential impossibility of settling on a single thesis, on a conclusion of a scientific or philosophical kind, on a theoretical conclusion in general, an impossibility that leads this text toward a sort of fictional drift, a fictional—I am not saying literary—drift that we will try to question as such in its relation to the theoretical thesis in general, to theoretical decidability, and to the logic of lifedeath [*lavielamort*], since it is obviously not by chance that this indefinitely suspended drift takes place with regard to lifedeath [*la viela mort*],[4] with regard to the enigmatic death drive [*pulsion de mort*] that appears, as you know, in *Jenseits*. Will we get there in three or four sessions? Certainly not. To save time and to make my intentions clearer, I should refer you first of all to a few of my previously published essays, more and less recent, notably "Freud and the Scene of Writing" (*Writing and Difference*) and "Le facteur de la vérité" (*Poétique* 21), and to certain passages from *Glas* on fetishism.[5]

Some additional preliminaries: the trajectory of these three winding loops was supposed to lead back each time to—in order to depart again from—Nietzsche. Nothing is easier in this case. So I will be brief on this topic. To take the shortest path, let me recall, for example, what was said of the child and of the game (which we will again find in *Jenseits*). Let me recall once again what Freud said of his relation to Nietzsche (as well as, in fact, to philosophy) in a striking gesture of denegation. I have cited this elsewhere, but let me recall it very quickly here.[6] This is from the *Selbstdarstellung*, "An Autobiographical Study": "Nietzsche, another philosopher whose guesses and intuitions often agree in the most astonishing way with the laborious findings of psychoanalysis, was for a long time avoided (*gemieden*) by me on that very account; I was less concerned with the question of priority than

---

4. As such in the typescript.
5. "Freud and the Scene of Writing," in *Writing and Difference*, trans. Alan Bass (Chicago: University of Chicago Press), pp. 196–231 ["Freud et la scène de l'écriture," in *L'écriture et la différence* (Paris: Éditions du Seuil, 1967), pp. 293–340]; "Le facteur de la vérité," in *The Post Card: From Socrates to Freud and Beyond*, trans. Alan Bass (Chicago: University of Chicago Press, 1987), pp. 411–96 ["Le facteur de la vérité," in *La carte postale, de Socrate à Freud et au-delà* (Paris: Flammarion, 1980), pp. 439–524; first published in *Poétique*, no. 21 (1975): 96–147]; *Glas*, trans. John P. Leavey Jr. and Richard Rand (Lincoln: University of Nebraska Press, 1986) [*Glas* (Paris: Éditions Galilée, 1974)].
6. In "To Speculate—On 'Freud'" (in *The Post Card*), where Derrida takes back up and develops this reading of *Beyond the Pleasure Principle*, there is a note that reads: "For example in *Qual Quelle* (in *Margins of Philosophy*, p. 306)."

with keeping my mind unembarrassed."⁷ The value of avoidance, the word "avoid," to avoid for the very reason of proximity, is all the more interesting (besides all the facile things that could be said about the already well known impossibility of avoiding what one wants to avoid or says one is avoiding), all the more interesting in that it appears a bit earlier in the same passage, this time with regard to philosophy in general. And what he says about his own avoidance with regard to philosophy will lead us directly to *Beyond*, and you will see why in just a moment.⁸ In the *Selbstdarstellung*, in any case, a few lines before the ones I just read, he writes the following about what he calls his latest "speculative" works (those that surround, precisely, the publication of *Jenseits*, both before and after 1919–20)—and pay particular attention to the word "speculative," which we will want to look at closely in the course of this reading:

> The attempt [he is talking here about metapsychology] remained no more than a torso; after writing two or three papers—"Instincts and their Vicissitudes" [1915c], "Repression" [1915d], "The Unconscious" [1915e], "Mourning and Melancholia" [1917e]⁹ ["*Triebe und Triebschicksale*" – "*Die Verdrängung*" – "*Das Unbewusste*" – "*Trauer und Melancholie*"], etc.—I broke off, wisely perhaps, since the time for theoretical predications of this kind had not yet come. In my latest speculative works I have set about the task of dissecting our psychical apparatus on the basis of the analytic view of pathological facts and have divided it into an *ego*, an *id*, and a *super-ego*. ("*Das Ich und das Es*," 1922.) The super-ego is the heir of the Oedipus complex and represents the ethical standards of mankind.
>
> I should not like to create an impression that during this last period of my work I have turned my back upon patient observation and have abandoned myself entirely to speculation.¹⁰ I have on the contrary always remained in the closest touch with the analytic material and have never ceased working at detailed points of clinical or technical importance. Even when I have moved away from observation, I have carefully *avoided* any contact with philosophy proper. This avoidance has been greatly facilitated by constitutional incapacity. I was always open to the ideas of G. T. Fechner and have followed that thinker upon many important points. The large

---

7. *SE* 20: 60 [*GW* 14: 86]. In the quotation Derrida circled the word "laborious." [Translators' note:] Derrida is using—and modifying—Marie Bonaparte's French translation of the essay, in *Ma vie et la psychanalyse, suivi de Psychanalyse et médecine* (Paris: Éditions Gallimard, 1949), p. 74.

8. In the left margin of the typescript there is a handwritten addition, perhaps the number "1," circled.

9. In the left margin of the typescript is the handwritten addition: "TR."

10. In the typescript the word "speculation" is circled by hand.

extent to which psychoanalysis coincides with the philosophy of Schopenhauer—not only did he assert the dominance of the emotions and the supreme importance of sexuality but he was even aware of the mechanism of repression—is not to be traced to my acquaintance with his teaching. I read Schopenhauer very late in my life. Nietzsche, another philosopher . . .[11]

A few remarks on this passage in its relation to *Jenseits*.

1. First of all, Schopenhauer. He is thus one of the two philosophers, along with Nietzsche, to whom Freud feels very close, but to whom he *owes* nothing, to whom psychoanalysis, psychoanalytic theory, *owes* nothing.[12] This absence of debt, which is underscored repeatedly, does not prevent Freud from having sought to avoid—to avoid at once philosophers and philosophy.[13] He protected himself against philosophy, and we will return to this self-protection that sometimes takes the form of a denegation. For the moment, let me simply note that the reference to Schopenhauer, whether it be one of negation or denegation, appears at the center of *Jenseits* (like the reference to Nietzsche), and it is linked to one of the most important propositions (I am not saying theses) of *Jenseits*. It comes at the moment when the dualism of pulsional life is being acknowledged, in chapter 6 to be precise. Freud writes (pay attention here to the form, to the modality of these statements):

> We may pause for a moment over this pre-eminently dualistic view of pulsional life. According to E. Hering's theory, two kinds of processes are constantly at work in living substance, operating in contrary directions (*entgegengesetzter Richtung*), one constructive or assimilatory and the other destructive or dissimilatory (*ab-bauend*).[14]

Abbauend: that is the word that catechistical French Heideggerians have recently taken the liberty of translating by *dé-construction*, as if everything

---

11. *SE* 20: 59–60 [*GW* 14: 85–86]; Derrida's emphasis on *avoided*.

12. In the left margin of the typescript are the handwritten words "counterfeit money," and below these an arrow pointing in two directions: ← →. This reference to Schopenhauer gets developed in "To Speculate—On 'Freud'": "No more than to Nietzsche, nothing is *due* to Schopenhauer. As such, psychoanalytic theory *owes* him *nothing*. It has no more inherited from him than one can inherit conceptual simulacra, in other words counterfeit money, bills issued without any guarantee of value." (*Post Card*, p. 266 [p. 284])

13. In the left margin of the typescript is a handwritten addition, perhaps the word "property."

14. *SE* 18: 49 [*GW* 13: 53]. In the typescript the German word is circled by hand and is linked by another line to a notation in the left margin, itself also circled, which reads: "on the board."

were already everywhere and they were already at the front of the parade; it is true that they do not have a monopoly on the belated [*après-coup*] discovery and then reappropriation in the form of the always-already of the word, if not the concept, deconstruction, since, on the other side, *so to speak*, we see the word "deconstruction" falling from the sky into Marx's text; and then—and this one is even better—the expression "*aufgelöst werden können*," from *The German Ideology*, an expression that has traditionally and faithfully been translated in the past by *resolved* or *dissolved*, has now all of a sudden been translated, in a recent issue of *Dialectiques*,¹⁵ without further ado and without any explanation, by "can be deconstructed," an operation in which the theoretical naïveté does not overcome the insidiousness of the amalgam since the sentence taken as a whole, after the appropriation of the word "deconstruction," lets it be understood that this word is still behind the times. Let me read this new translation, which will find its rightful place, I hope, in the annals of Franco-German scholarship:

> it [this new materialist conception of history] does not explain practice from the idea but explains the formation of ideas from material practice, and accordingly it comes to the conclusion that all forms and products of consciousness cannot be deconstructed [says the translator for "*aufgelöst werden können*"]¹⁶ by mental criticism, by resolution into "self-consciousness" or transformation into "apparitions," "specters," whimsies," etc., but only by the practical subversion [this to translate "*durch den praktischen Umsturz*": the traditional translation—that of the Éditions Sociales—of this term by *reversal* has been replaced by *subversion*, at once more "hip [*in*],"¹⁷ more modern, flirting with leftism and dispensing with the thorny problem of the "reversal" and, a trick that is a bit too tricky to swallow whole, a translation that lets it be understood that deconstruction is still too theoretical and is not yet the equivalent of a "practical subversion," by which one dispenses with something else, that is, with reading] by the practical subversion of the actual social relations which gave rise to this idealistic humbug.¹⁸

---

15. In the typescript the title is followed by an insertion mark, which is repeated in the left margin and followed by: "10–11, p. 68." The essay in question is Georges Labica's "Histoire/idéologie," published in *Dialectiques*, no. 10–11 (Autumn 1975): 67–92; the passage to which Derrida refers is on p. 68.

16. In the left margin of the typescript there is a handwritten addition that appears to be "before [*devant*] the dream."

17. "In" in English in the original.

18. Marx, *German Ideology*, p. 61 [p. 38].

The translation then, without the slightest compunction, refers in a footnote to the Éditions Sociales, without even specifying, as the fastidious academic is wont to do: translation slightly modified.

Having paid this homage to militant zeal (to all forms of militant zeal), I pick up Freud's text at the point where I left it:[19]

> According to E. Hering's theory, two kinds of processes are constantly at work in living substance, operating in contrary directions, one constructive or assimilatory and the other destructive or dissimilatory (*ab-bauend*: disassimilation). May we venture to recognize in these two directions taken by the vital processes the activity of our two pulsional impulses (*Triebregungen*), the life drive and the death drive? There is something else, at any rate, that we cannot remain blind to [another gesture of self-protection: one should avoid, one would wish to avoid, to conceal from oneself, something, then, that one cannot avoid recognizing. What is it?]. We have unwittingly steered our course into the harbor of Schopenhauer's philosophy. For him death is [and Freud then quotes] "*das eigentliche Resultat*," that is, "the proper result and to that extent the aim (*Zweck*) of life," while the sexual drive is the embodiment (*Verkörperung*) of the will to live (*Willens zum Leben*).[20]

Then there is a new paragraph, which begins: "Let us make a bold attempt at another step forward." (Follow the steps in *Jenseits*.)

Death as the "proper result" and, thus, as the aim of life—this is not only a statement of Schopenhauer's, it is also at least consistent with, if not literally coinciding with, certain statements of Nietzsche that we tried to interpret regarding life as a very rare kind of what is dead (*The Gay Science* 109), regarding life as a "particular case" and a "means to something else" (*The Will to Power*), this something other than life being necessarily linked to death, regarding the absence (in the end) of the instinct for self-preservation, etc. I am not going to go back over all of that. The Schopenhauerian "harbor" is thus, at this level of generality and at this distance, Nietzschean as well. That's the first point.

2. Second remark. Nietzsche is not named here, but as I already noted in a previous session, the expression, in quotation marks, "eternal return of the same," appears in chapter 3 of *Beyond*,[21] in a passage where, in order to demonstrate the existence within psychical life of an irresistible tendency

---

19. In the typescript there is a handwritten addition of four words in the left margin, perhaps: "*addition / deconstruction / not opposition.*"

20. *SE* 18: 49–50 [*GW* 13: 53].

21. *SE* 18: 22 [*GW* 13: 21]; see above, p. 183.

to reproduction, to repetition, a tendency that no longer takes into account the pleasure principle,²² placing itself above it even, Freud evokes what are called neuroses of destiny and their demonic aspect. The figure of the demon, of the demonic or the diabolical, plays an important role, as you know, in *Beyond*, and we will have to follow its passage, its step, its gait [*démarche*]. This text has a diabolical gait, continuously proceeding without advancing, miming a walk, always taking a further step without ever getting a step further. A limping devil, I would say, to make reference to the fact that as soon as <that> which is opposed to the pleasure principle is taken into consideration, Freud speaks of the "demonic," and the last words of the essay are a literary reference suggesting that, "as the Book tells us," "it is no sin to limp." Since this figure of the diabolical is one of the points of passage, one of the places of passage, between *Jenseits* and "Das Unheimliche," an essay that is more or less contemporary with it (you know all the theoretical links that unite these two texts), I felt the urge to provide here as an exergue to this reading of *Beyond* a short note from Rousseau's *Letter to d'Alembert* which I recently came upon somewhat by accident. I am not yet quite sure what we will be able to do with it, but it is clear in any case that the allusion made there to the appearance of the devil in person, on the stage, a stage where he was simply being represented as an actor or as a character (which one is a little unclear), this appearance of the devil in person, in addition to his representation, this appearance of the original devil, as it were, in addition to his representative, this appearance of the very thing represented as a supplement to his representative, this appearance no doubt disturbs the comforting order of (theatrical) representation not by erasing or reducing but actually by increasing the effects of doubling, of the stand-in,²³ the effects of a duplicity without original, which is what diabolicity in fact is. The original brings no comfort; it produces, on the contrary, fright, says Rousseau, *Unheimlichkeit*, Freud would no doubt say. Here, then, is one of the two logics of repetition (for there are two logics of repetition and both of them are at work in, and vie for, I would say, the Beyond of the Pleasure

---

22. Here and almost everywhere in these sessions Derrida writes "PP" for "pleasure principle [*principe de plaisir*]" and "PR" for "reality principle [*principe de réalité*]." We have assumed that Derrida would have pronounced these terms in full up until the end of the session when he makes an explicit play on the homophony between "PP" and "Pépé" (Grandfather) and "PR" and "Père" (Father). From this point on he would have continued to use this invention, on which his analysis in "To Speculate—On 'Freud'" will draw extensively.

23. In the typescript the word "*revenant*" is handwritten in the left margin.

Principle), here is one of the two logics of repetition or of reproduction between which we will have to move. Here is the passage from Rousseau (note 4, p. 220 in the Garnier edition; the note comes right after the word "devil"):

> I read, when I was young, a Tragedy, which was part of the Escalade, in which the Devil was actually one of the Actors. I have been told that when this play was once performed, this character, as he came on stage, appeared double, as if the original had been jealous that they had had the audacity to imitate him, and instantly everybody, seized by fright, took flight, thus *ending* the performance. This tale is burlesque and will appear much more so in Paris than in Geneva; however, whatever suppositions we may indulge in, in this double apparition will be found a theatrical effect and a really terrifying one. I can imagine only one Sight simpler and more terrible yet, that is the hand emerging from the wall and writing unknown words at the feast of Balthazar. The very idea makes one shudder. It seems to me that our lyric Poets are far from these sublime inventions; to no avail they make a great fuss with scenery for the purpose of horrifying. Even on the stage, not everything should be said to the eyes, but the imagination must also be excited.[24]

3. Third remark on the passage from the *Selbstdarstellung*. The avoidance (of Schopenhauer, of Nietzsche, of philosophy), such avoidance must not, it seems to me, be interpreted too straightforwardly. On the one hand, if there is such a persistent avoidance of both philosophy and what Freud calls, with a word that we will have to follow very closely, "speculation,"[25] if there is such a persistent avoidance, it is, of course, because there is temptation, tendency, inclination. And Freud recognizes this because he notes a bit earlier that with the works of the past few years (and among them *Beyond*) he has, I quote, "given free rein to the inclination, which I kept down for so long, to speculation."[26] One must, therefore, if we are to believe him, admit (1) a constitutional incapacity for philosophizing; (2) an inclination to speculation; (3) an avoidance of philosophy; and (4) a non-avoidance of what he calls speculation, which is thus neither philosophy nor simple scientific experimentation or traditional clinical work. We must thus try to find out whether, beyond the more or less motivated behavior of avoidance or of

---

24. Jean-Jacques Rousseau, *Letter to d'Alembert, and Writings for the Theater*, in *The Collected Writings of Rousseau*, v. 10, trans. and ed. Allan Bloom, Charles Butterworth, and Christopher Kelly (Hanover, NH: University Press of New England, 2004), p. 340; Derrida's emphasis. In the left margin of the typescript there is this handwritten notation: "Who is Freud's devil?"

25. This word is circled in the typescript.

26. *SE* 20: 57 [*GW* 14: 84].

denegation, speculation does not come to have, in *Beyond*, for example, a singularity that I will even hesitate to call, and you will see why, theoretical or something with a theoretical status and that distinguishes it from both classical philosophical logic and classical scientific logic, whether that logic be pure, a priori, or empirical.

All right. Let me end here these preliminary remarks. We could have extended them indefinitely, of course, beginning especially with the *Selbstdarstellung* and with what links the new position of the question of death in psychoanalysis to Freud's autobiographical point of view. He himself in fact associates what he calls the works of the second period of his life (which include *Beyond*) with the rhythm of his own biography and, in a singular fashion, as he writes, with the time "when a grave illness warns [him] of the approaching end."[27] (He writes this in 1925, but the illness in question had manifested itself several years earlier.) One could thus legitimately, once again, intertwine in what would be, to be sure, an unusual style, questions of life death as they are treated by Freud with questions about his autobiography or his auto-graphy or his auto-thanatography. I am not going to do that here for lack of time. Given our time constraints, an "internal" reading of *Beyond* seems to me more urgent. So much, then, for the question of biography. As for the question of biology and of biologism, which better than any other question picks up on what we have been saying up to now in this final loop, you will very quickly see it take shape once again and become imperative in a straightforward reading of the text.

Which I thus open right now, without any further precautions and as naively as possible.

The first page of the first chapter includes (1) a reminder of the present state of analytic theory and everything that has been learned from it. Analytic theory exists — performative utterance. The first page includes (2) the taking of a position with regard to philosophy, a position of non-position, of neutrality or indifference. The first page includes or rather implies (3), under the word "speculative," a concept of reflection that comes neither from philosophy or metaphysics nor from experimental science, even if psychoanalytic, that is, coming from psychoanalytic experience. The first sentence — the first two sentences — of the essay are already very difficult. Let me read them and retranslate them as we go:[28]

---

27. *SE* 20: 55 [*GW* 14: 82].

28. Derrida cites and modifies throughout the French translation of *Beyond the Pleasure Principle* by Samuel Jankélévitch, "Au-delà du principe du plaisir," in *Essais de psychanalyse* (Paris: Payot, 1927), pp. 10–81.

In the theory of psychoanalysis [which is thus already constituted, with twenty years of existence and results, an institution that allows one to say "we," etc.] we assume *unbedenklich* [without hesitation, without scruple, without reflection] that the course taken by mental events is automatically [this last word is left out of the French translation] regulated by the "*Lustprinzip*" [which is usually translated as "pleasure principle," which is appropriate, but one must not forget that *Lust* also means "*jouissance*" and "desire," as well as concupiscent desire, as Laplanche says in *Life and Death in Psychoanalysis*,[29] a book that often proves useful in more than one way]. We believe, that is to say, that the course of those events is invariably set in motion by an unpleasurable tension [full of unpleasure: *unlustvolle Spannung*], and that it takes a direction such that its final outcome coincides with a lowering of that tension — that is, with an avoidance (*Vermeidung*) of unpleasure (*Unlust*) or a production of pleasure.[30]

Note that this reminder is neither a confirmation nor yet a putting into question. I would say that it will in fact never become such — neither a confirmation nor a simple putting into question or putting into doubt. Nevertheless, Freud presents this state of analytic theory as an assumption that might be a bit rash (we assume *unbedenklich* — without any qualms, without any reservations, without any doubts — the authority of the pleasure principle), as an assumption that is perhaps too assured with regard to the authority of the pleasure principle and as a belief — "we believe" — with regard to what this pleasure principle consists in: when he says the pleasure principle — "that is to say," "*das heisst*," an attempt to bring about a lowering of tension — he specifies, "we believe." This "we believe" leaves suspended not only the status of this law, that is, of this relation or this relation of relation between quantities, but more fundamentally, as we will see, the qualitative essence of pleasure: the pursuit of pleasure, the preference for pleasure, the substitution of pleasure for non-pleasure, the fact that pleasure depends on a diminution of tension — all that presupposes that we know what pleasure is but it does not tell us what it is. It is with regard to the ultimate meaning of pleasure and of unpleasure that philosophy will soon be evoked.

Freud calls this definition of the pleasure principle *economic*. It is formulated from an economic point of view — that is to say, here, essentially

---

29. Jean Laplanche, *Life and Death in Psychoanalysis*, trans. Jeffrey Mehlman (Baltimore: Johns Hopkins University Press, 1985), p. 120 [*Vie et mort en psychanalyse* (Paris: Flammarion, 1970), p. 205].

30. *SE* 18: 7 [*GW* 13: 3]; Derrida's emphasis.

quantitative—and metapsychology is a description of the psychical processes, a description that takes into account this economic point of view as well as the topographical and dynamic points of view (concerning pulsional forces and their relations).

Having recalled this, Freud declares a sort of amiable indifference, a kindly independence with regard to all philosophies of pleasure. It is of no concern, he says, it is of absolutely no interest to us to know whether, in saying this about the pleasure principle, we have come closer to, or even become identified with, some time-honored philosophical system. We are aiming for neither priority nor originality. We are only formulating *speculative* hypotheses in order to explain and describe the facts we observe on a daily basis. And Freud adds that psychoanalysis would be very grateful to philosophy if it were to tell it the meaning (*Bedeutung*) of these feelings of pleasure and unpleasure which act so imperatively upon us. What does all this mean?

First, as regards the speculative: the speculative is not the philosophical. It is a matter of speculative *hypotheses* that are not formed a priori, neither in a pure a priori nor in a descriptive a priori. The speculation, which is not philosophical in its origin and which expects nothing in the end from philosophy[31] (because when Freud says that he would readily express his gratitude to philosophy were it to tell him what pleasure and unpleasure mean, we can detect a bit of irony, for the implication is that the philosopher, even when he talks about pleasure—and more than one, as you know, have done so—does not know what he is talking about, does not say what he is talking about, presupposes that we all know what this is, but this presupposition remains dogmatic, and we will later see the root of this, namely, the fact that there is such a thing as an unconscious pleasure, a pleasure that is given in the experience—which is understood by philosophy to be conscious experience—of unpleasure).[32] This speculation is thus foreign to philosophy or to metaphysics; it is not, for example, the speculative in Hegel. But neither is this speculative an empirical description, that goes without saying, nor even a knowledge of laws derived by induction from observable facts. That has never been called speculation. And yet we are also not dealing here with a pure a priori theory that would precede any so-called empirical content. What, then, about this concept of speculation and why does it come on the scene right at the moment when it is a question of life

---

31. This sentence is incomplete in the transcript.
32. We here close the parenthesis opened above.

230 ‡ ELEVENTH SESSION

287 death, of pleasure-unpleasure, and of repetition?[33] That is the question that will continue to guide us, in a more or less explicit way, and that I would like to put into relation with the singular structure of this text, which does not correspond to any known model of text, neither philosophical nor scientific, but also not literary, poetic, or mythological.

The end of the first chapter, a very short introductory chapter, confirms, very curiously, the value of belief in the authority of the pleasure principle, after an initial series of concerns, indeed, of possible objections. And yet, despite this first confirmation, which indicates that, in the end, nothing has yet been shaken, despite this, Freud speaks of the need "to produce new material and raise new questions (*neue Fragestellungen*),"[34] not only new questions born of new material, not only new contents of questions, but new problematics, new modalities of questioning. I am skipping right away to the end of the first chapter, that is to say, to the first time things come to a standstill, the moment when, despite the return to the point of departure, in a sort of paralysis, where the pleasure principle remains unshaken, Freud announces that, *therefore*, new *Fragestellungen* are necessary. I quote this ending before rereading the rest of this first chapter in order to make you attentive to the strange composition of this approach [*démarche*].

> The reaction [to external danger] can then be directed in a correct manner by the pleasure principle or the reality principle by which the former is modified [and in fact the first chapter will have shown that the reality principle is not opposed, as is believed, to the pleasure principle, but instead modifies it, puts it in *différance*, with an *a*]. This does not seem to necessitate any far-reaching limitation of the pleasure principle. Nevertheless the investigation of the mental reaction to external danger is precisely in a position to produce new material and new *Fragestellungen* in relation to our present problem.[35]

288 Let us now return to the rest of this first chapter, which is very short but already extremely complex.

First moment. Having acknowledged that this feeling of pleasure-unpleasure, about which, in short, no one has yet said anything, not the researcher in psychology, not the philosopher, not the psychoanalyst, having

---

33. In the left margin of the typescript are several handwritten words: "speculation that precedes the speculative <illegible words> and <illegible word>." A second note appears at the bottom right of the page: "Why is F<reud> attracted in such a <illegible word> way to speculation," followed by an arrow.

34. *SE* 18: 11 [*GW* 13: 8].

35. *SE* 18: 11 [*GW* 13: 8].

acknowledged that this feeling called *Lust/Unlust* is one of the most obscure and inaccessible, and that we nonetheless cannot "avoid" (yet again) "contact with it," it seems best to try out the most open hypothesis, the "least rigid" (*lockerste*), Freud even says. What is this least rigid hypothesis? One must pay close attention to Freud's rhetoric here. To his rhetoric, which is also to say, to the scene, the gestures, the movements, to the selective, discriminating, active strategy of an approach that is not governed by some reassuring idea of science or philosophy. For example, here, having admitted to being at a total loss when it comes to knowing what pleasure-unpleasure is, and faced with having to choose the least rigid hypothesis or assumption, Freud decided, "we decided (*wir haben uns entschlossen*)," to establish — according to the economic point of view, therefore — a first relation. A relation between two quantities, then;[36] on the one hand, the quantity of something whose essence we do not know (<nor> even, which is even more enigmatic, the appearance and the quality, because what is going to be revealed is the fact that there are pleasures, pleasures of a neurotic nature, that are felt or experienced in the experience of unpleasure, that is, pleasures that are lived as unpleasures), a relation, then, between two quantities, on the one hand, the quantity of pleasure or of unpleasure and, on the other, a quantity of energy, of unbound energy (*nicht gebundenen*), as Freud specifies in a parenthesis, that is all part of psychical life. With this appeal to the notion of energy (bound or unbound), we touch on one of the most difficult points of *Beyond*. In chapter 4, Freud says that with this notion of free or bound energy he is referring to a distinction established by Breuer, one that, in fact, he and Breuer had both already used in their studies on hysteria (1895), especially in their explanations of conversion hysteria. Freud recalls here that Breuer distinguished between quiescent or bound energy and mobile, freely circulating energy. But he then adds, exercising caution, that it would be advisable given the current state of our knowledge to refrain from any definitive affirmation on this subject. In fact, the source common to both Breuer and Freud is the distinction made by Helmholtz between free energy and bound energy, which is based on the Carnot-Clausius principle of the degradation of energy. Helmholtz distinguishes between an energy that can be transformed freely and used for different kinds of work and one that manifests itself only in the form of heat. The constant internal energy is the sum of free energy and bound energy, the first having the tendency to decrease and the second, bound energy, to increase. Laplanche, in the

---

36. In the typescript there is an insertion mark, repeated in the left margin, followed by: "(≠ essences <illegible words>."

book I mentioned earlier, suggests that Freud has in fact very freely interpreted—with "irreverence," says Laplanche—the claims of Helmholtz and of Breuer by interpreting the qualification "free" in the sense of freely mobile rather than free to be used.[37]

Let us leave aside, at least for the moment, this tricky question of borrowing an energetic model. Once this borrowing has been made, the introduction of the term *energetic* into the relation proposed by Freud gets rather complicated. This relation is, in its principle, the following: unpleasure corresponds to an increase, pleasure to a decrease, in the quantity of (free) energy. But this relation—and the complication is immediately pointed out by Freud—is neither a "simple correlation (*einfaches Verhältnis*)" between two forces (that of feelings and that of the changes in energy to which they are related) nor a direct proportionality. Already this non-simplicity and this indirectness in the relation, right on the threshold of the most open, most preliminary hypothesis, guarantee a very strange field for speculation. In addition, an appeal is made, and it is a decisive one, to a consideration of time in the establishing of this relation. It is probable, says Freud, that the "decisive factor (*das entscheidende Moment*)" is the measure of increase or decrease "in time," "in a given period of time."[38]

In the passage from the *Selbstdarstellung* that I cited earlier,[39] before the names Schopenhauer and Nietzsche, it is the name of Fechner that is immediately advanced, and this time without any declaration of avoidance: "I was always open to the ideas of G. T. Fechner and have followed that thinker upon many important points."[40] Here in *Beyond*, Fechner is called upon right away to bolster the hypothesis. In 1873, he had formulated the psycho-physical law according to which every psycho-physical movement is accompanied by pleasure when it approaches complete stability, by unpleasure when it approaches complete instability. These two poles or these two limits are the only two qualitative thresholds that allow one to speak of pleasure or unpleasure. In Freud's long quotation from Fechner that then follows, there is a sort of parenthetical remark that does not get taken up and will not be used later on, or so it seems to me, and that is the recognition, in passing, of a certain "aesthetic indifference (*ästhetische Indifferenz*)"[41] be-

---

37. See Jean Laplanche, *Life and Death in Psychoanalysis*, p. 102 [p. 205].
38. *SE* 18: 8 [*GW* 13: 4].
39. See above, pp. 221–22.
40. *SE* 20: 59 [*GW* 14: 86].
41. *SE* 18: 9 [*GW* 13: 5].

tween the two thresholds,[42] which we will no doubt have to speak of again. In any case, Freud argues immediately thereafter that the psychical apparatus represents a "special case" of Fechner's principle, and he concludes from this that the pleasure principle can be deduced from the principle of constancy, which was itself, in circular fashion, inferred from the facts that forced the pleasure principle upon us, namely, that the psychical apparatus endeavors to keep the quantity of excitation present within it as low as possible or at least to keep it constant.

So there it is, the pleasure principle well established and confirmed in its authority. I am often using the word authority here, for reasons that will appear later on.[43]

Freud then makes, or pretends to make, a first objection. If it is the case that the pleasure principle is absolutely dominant, where would unpleasure, whose experience can hardly be disputed, come from? We suffer, this experience says to us.

(Pause) Is that so certain? What do we know about this? What does this mean? And what if the experience of suffering produced pleasure elsewhere? Etc. Let us leave these questions aside for now. Freud pretends to address this commonsense objection to himself. If the pleasure principle is all-powerful, where does the experience of unpleasure come from, an experience that seems to contradict in such a flagrant way the omnipotence [*la toute-puissance*] of the pleasure principle? Here is the first response: we are talking about a principle of pleasure, that is, a tendency. What is principal in this principle is the tendency, and it is this tendency that organizes everything. But this tendency can also, and Fechner recognizes this, encounter external obstacles that prevent it from reaching its ends without, however, calling it into question as a tendency toward pleasure, toward the desire for pleasure, as the organizing tendency of the psychical processes. This obstacle, "a familiar one which occurs with regularity,"[44] says Freud, can have its source in the external world. When a simple, direct, and reckless affirmation of the pleasure principle puts the organism in danger — for pleasure can lead to death in certain cases — "the drive for self-preservation (*Selbsterhaltungstriebe des Ichs*)" forces the pleasure principle not to disappear but temporarily to cede its place to the reality principle. There is no

---

42. In the typescript the word "thresholds" is crossed out by hand and replaced by the interlineal insertion "limits."

43. In the left margin of the typescript there is the handwritten word "*Herrschaft* [dominion or mastery]."

44. *SE* 18: 10 [*GW* 13: 6].

renunciation of pleasure, only a detour in order to defer (*Aufschub*), a *différance* of satisfaction. Freud speaks here of "long detours (*auf dem langen Umwege*)"⁴⁵ with a view to pleasure. In this case, the pleasure principle submits temporarily to the reality principle, which is in fact in its service. It is like a master who cautiously submits to his slave, to the work of a slave who is in contact with reality.⁴⁶ There is thus no opposition between the pleasure principle and the reality principle, as is sometimes believed. It is one and the same principle at work in *différant* exercises or manifestations, the absolute master being the pleasure principle.

But as for this logic of the differing, deferring [*différant*] detour, which is not questioned in its own right here by Freud and which can — possibly, this is a hypothesis — account for the interminable detour of this very text, as for this logic of the detour, of the *Umweg*, what does it mean?

Since pure pleasure and pure reality are ideal limits — each, in fact, as destructive and deadly as the other as ideal limit — the relation of detour or of *différance* between the two is, I would say, the effectivity [*effectivité*] of the process, of the psychical process as a living process. It is the common — differing, deferring [*différante*] — root of the two. But it is an effectivity that is necessarily impure, structurally destined for compromise.⁴⁷ So that, already, by whatever end you take this structure in three terms (pleasure principle, reality principle, *Différance*) that make only one, that make only one because the reality principle and the *Umweg* are simply effects or modifications of the pleasure principle, by whatever end [*bout*] you take this structure in one-three terms, it is death, I am indeed saying in the end [*au bout*], a death that has no opposite, that is not different, in the sense of an opposition, from the pleasure principle, the reality principle, or this diverting, detouring différance [*différance détournante*], but is inscribed in the very functioning of this structure. Freud does not say this, he does not say it here, or anywhere else, in fact, in this form. But my reading hypothesis — with this text and a few others — is to draw out between the pleasure principle and that which appears as, and indeed is, *its other* (namely, for example, the death drive) a structure of alterity without opposition, without opposition in the final analysis, which will make death's belonging to pleasure — a belonging that

---

45. *SE* 18: 10 [*GW* 13: 6]; translated by Strachey as "the long indirect road."

46. In the left margin of the typescript there is an insertion mark followed by a word that could be, if one follows the corresponding passage in "To Speculate — On 'Freud'" (*Post Card*, p. 282 [p. 301]), "lieutenant."

47. In the typescript there is an insertion mark here and in the left margin the handwritten words: "speculative transaction."

is without interiority—at once more continuous, immanent, and natural, but also, from the point of view of a logic of opposition, of position, of thesis, more scandalous. Out of this *différance*, no thesis can be made. And my "hypothesis"—you can see now in what way[48] I am using this word—is that the speculative structure, in the way it imposes itself on Freud, finds its place and its necessity in this logic.

How, then, is death at the end of this structure, that is, at all of its ends (the three interlaced that make just one)? Well, each time that one of the terms, one of the pseudo-terms or pseudopodes of the structure, goes right to the end of itself [*au bout de lui-même*], holding onto its extreme purity, without negotiating a compromise with the other two, that is to say, with one of the others through the mediation of the third, it is death. If the reality principle becomes autonomous and functions all by itself, it cuts itself off from all pleasure and all desire (*Lust*), from all self-relation, all auto-affection, or all auto-eroticism, from all that without which pleasure or desire can no longer even appear to themselves.[49] It is death, a death that holds on at both ends, that is to say, to a reality principle functioning all on its own, without pleasure, as well as to a reality principle which, delegated in its structure to the service of the pleasure principle, would bring death to that service, being still in its service, out of an economic zeal for pleasure. This would already be a pleasure that, in safeguarding itself too much, in protecting itself, in accumulating itself in its reserve, would come to asphyxiate itself.

But conversely (if we can say this, for this second hypothesis is not the converse of the first), if we go to the end of this compromise that the *Umweg* is—pure[50] *différance* as it were—this too is death: no pleasure would ever present itself. Death is inscribed in *différance* as well as in the reality principle, which is but another name for it, just as pleasure and reality are but other names for it.

---

48. In the typescript there is here an insertion mark and in the left margin a few handwritten words: "thesis <illegible word> death sentence [*l'arrêt de mort*] (in action [*en acte*]) / of *différance*." See *Post Card*, "The thesis would be the death sentence (*arrêt de mort*) of *différance*" (p. 285 [p. 305]).

49. In the left margin are several handwritten words, the first of them heavily underscored: "*sprain* [entorse] / deadly / strain / toy." See *Post Card*, "it is death, the mortal sprain, which puts an end to the strain of calculation" (p. 285 [p. 305]).

50. In the typescript the word "pure" is circled and in the left margin there are the handwritten words: "*différance* that is pure [différance pure] ≠ pure *différance* [*pure* différance]."

Finally, conversely (if we can say this, for this third hypothesis is not the converse of the preceding one or ones), if the pleasure principle is immediately unleashed, without protecting itself from the obstacles of the external world or from dangers in general, or even while following its law, its tendency, which leads to the lowest level of excitation—that too is death. At this stage of Freud's text, that is the only hypothesis explicitly considered by Freud. That is, if there is a specificity to the "sexual drives," it consists, precisely, in their wild, uneducable, or barely educable character ("so much harder to educate," "*schwerer erziehbaren Sexualtriebe*"), which gives them a tendency not to submit to the reality principle but only to the pleasure principle. But what does this mean when the reality principle is nothing other than the pleasure principle? What else but that the sexual is the force that of itself resists being bound, that resists its own preservation, resists that which protects it from itself. The sexual drives endanger, they spontaneously expose or expose themselves to danger; they are the exposure, not, however, by opposing the reality principle, which is not their other, their opposite, but by turning against themselves or opposing themselves, themselves, in some sense, as others. They expose themselves to death by abolishing a barrier or a safeguard that is, however, nothing but their own modification, just as the RP is the modified PP (just as, I would say, the *Père* [father] is the modified *Pépé* [grandfather]).[51] Now that is a principle, or rather a very general functioning of principles, that can then be modified, differentiated. It is one of its modifications that Freud evokes in these few lines devoted to the pleasure principle in the first chapter. He has just spoken of the *Umweg* of the reality principle, and he adds: "The pleasure principle long persists, however, as the method of working employed by the sexual drives, which are so hard to 'educate,' and, starting from those drives, or in the ego itself, it often succeeds in overcoming the reality principle, to the detriment of the organism as a whole."[52]

Up until now—but we are only just beginning—the laws and the logic of this structure in one or three-in-one term (the same in *différance*), these laws and this logic, which are already extremely complicated, can be explained, in some sense, without having to appeal to a specific structural process [*instance*] that would go by the name of *repression*.

Is the intervention of repression—something as enigmatic, in the end, as repression—an effect that can be explained on the basis of the structure we

---

51. In the typescript the words in parentheses are underscored and an illegible word is handwritten in the left margin, perhaps "comment."
52. *SE* 18: 10 [*GW* 13: 6].

have just evoked or is it something that transforms this structure, affects it in a structural, global way, or even constitutes it in its very possibility?

The scope of this question obviously cannot be overestimated, since it is a question, in sum, of the irreducible specificity of something like psychoanalysis, a specificity that, if it were demonstrated, would be represented nowhere else, neither in what is called experience in the broad sense nor in science in the traditional sense, nor in philosophy. Neither in science as science or else as objective knowledge insofar as it is a question here of the qualitative evaluation of an affect that is, how shall I put it, subjective, where something like a subject is irreducibly implicated. Nor <in> philosophy, <in> the philosophical or the everyday concept of experience, since in both of these one either presupposes a knowledge or pre-knowledge of what pleasure is or else implies that the ultimate criterion for something like pleasure is the conscious or perceptual experience of pleasure. A pleasure that would not be experienced as such would thus make no sense at all; a pleasure in the experience of unpleasure would here be considered either a semantic absurdity that merits no further consideration or an imaginary speculative madness that does not even allow a discourse to become organized or communicated. Hence any philosophy that speaks of the subject, of subjective affect, would be phenomenological in its essence. What we have here, then, is the very possibility of a speculation that would be neither philosophical or phenomenological nor scientific in a traditional sense (a devil of a speculation for philosophy or for science) but one that would nonetheless open onto another science or another fiction, and this speculative possibility, insofar as it admits that a pleasure can be lived as unpleasure, this speculative possibility, which here finds its very resource, presupposes something like repression. Repression itself is thinkable, in its specificity, only in this speculative hypothesis, and we can write about it, I would say, only speculatively, provided that we understand the concept of speculation in this sense.[53]

Let us, then, in order to conclude, see how the recourse to repression intervenes already in this first chapter, which develops completely from within

---

53. In the left margin of the typescript there are several handwritten words: "*différance*, (neither science/nor philosophy/nor concept), which does not mean that all desire <illegible word> Rep<ression> <illegible word>." We might be able to see here the first draft of what Derrida adds at this point in "To Speculate—On 'Freud'": "As soon as it—and it alone—is principially capable of giving rise to this concept of speculation and to this concept of repression, the graphics of *différance* belongs neither to science nor to philosophy in their classical limits" (*Post Card*, p. 288 [p. 308]).

the hypothesis of certain psychoanalytic gains, namely, within the hypothesis of an analytic theory that never doubts the authority, in the last analysis, of the pleasure principle.

The substitution or, rather, the relay of the reality principle explains, Freud remarks, only a small number of our experiences of unpleasure, and these are, moreover, the least intense. There is thus "another *source (eine andere* Quelle)"[54] of the discharge of unpleasure, of what delivers or gives unpleasure (an *Unlustentbindung*: a delivery as in a giving birth, a giving birth to unpleasure (comment)). That is because, in the constitution of the ego, in the synthesis of the personality, certain drives or certain partial drives show themselves to be incompatible with others in terms of their goal (*Ziel*) or their tendencies (but what is to be made of this incompatibility? —that is a question that Freud does not even touch on here). These drives or partial drives are split off by the process that is called, precisely, repression; they do not participate in the synthesis of the ego, and they remain at a very archaic level of psychical organization and are more or less deprived of satisfaction. But since it can happen that these drives obtain satisfaction by paths that are either direct or indirect or substitutive (by *Umwegen* or *Ersatzbefriedigung*), this is then felt *by the ego* as unpleasure (by the ego and not by the organism, as the [French] translation says). It is there that repression, with its topographical differentiation, with its structuring of agencies that it constructs and instructs, shatters the traditional logic implicit in all philosophy and makes it so that a pleasure can be felt—by the ego—as unpleasure. As Freud then says immediately thereafter: "The details of the process by which repression turns a possibility of pleasure into a source of unpleasure are not yet clearly understood or cannot be clearly represented [describable: *darstellbar*]; but there is no doubt that all neurotic unpleasure is of that kind—pleasure that cannot be felt as such."[55] The German phrase is less paradoxical and, ultimately, less startling than its French translation. Freud speaks of "pleasure that cannot be felt as such," "*Lust, die nicht als solche empfunden werden kann.*" Jankélévitch's translation says, "a pleasure that is not felt as such." But since, in the end, they say the same thing, namely, that there is pleasure lived as unpleasure, I prefer the French translation, even if it is unfaithful to the letter of the text. It is faithful to this paradox of repression whereby there can be pleasure, a possibility of pleasure, lived as unpleasure, *qua* unpleasure, so that experience, the "as such" of experience,

---

54. Ibid., *SE* 18: 10 [*GW* 13: 6]; Derrida's emphasis; translated by Strachey as "another occasion."

55. *SE* 18: 11 [*GW* 13: 7].

is no longer the measure or the criterion of something that presented itself, up to this point, as essentially qualitative, as a value of experience. Obviously, if one keeps the "cannot be experienced as such," the paradox is less evident: it is then a question of a possibility of pleasure that is not realized, rather than an actual pleasure that is not lived as such. And yet this second possibility, as we will see, is more in line with the Freudian radicalization of this logic—which is not yet at full term. Indeed, as long as—and this is the case here—pleasures and the experience of unpleasure are located in different agencies [*instances*], and so long as what is pleasure in one place is lived as unpleasure in another, the topographical differentiation introduces an element of systematic coherence and classical rationality. It is not pleasure that is lived as unpleasure or the reverse. But, as we will see, with the problematic of primary narcissism and masochism, which are indispensable parts of this system of *Beyond*, one will have to follow out this paradox to the very end and not settle for the easy way out that topography provides.

At this juncture—where I am going to stop for today (at the end of the first chapter)—not only has the authority of the pleasure principle not been refuted but Freud declares that there are other sources of unpleasure that need to be inventoried and that they, no more than the previous ones, do not compromise this authority. The following two chapters continue this exploration, and it is only in chapter 4 that, announcing this time a "pure speculation," Freud will entertain the possibility of a function of the psychical apparatus that, without being opposed to the pleasure principle, would be no less independent and even more primitive than the *tendency* (tendency/function . . .) to seek pleasure and avoid unpleasure: how will this lead to granting the hypothesis of drives in the "service" of which the pleasure principle would work?[56] How is this reconcilable with so many Freudian affirmations, before and after *Beyond*, according to which "our unconscious is just as inaccessible to the idea of our own death, just as murderously inclined towards strangers, just as divided (that is, ambivalent) towards those we love, as was primeval man."[57] Or else, read "Thoughts for the Times on War and Death" (1915), v. 14, p. 296.

> What, we ask, is the attitude of our unconscious towards the problem of death? The answer must be: almost exactly the same as that of primeval

---

56. In the left margin of the typescript there is a long line leading to a handwritten note: "F<reud> will regret / the pure speculation / that he <several illegible words>."

57. *SE* 14: 299 [*GW* 10: 354]; from "Thoughts for the Times on War and Death." The French translation to which Derrida refers is "Considérations actuelles sur la guerre et sur la mort," in *Essais de psychanalyse*, p. 263.

man. In this respect, as in many others, the man of prehistoric times survives unchanged in our unconscious. Our unconscious, then, does not believe in its own death; it behaves as if it were immortal. What we call our "unconscious"—the deepest strata of our minds, made up of instinctual impulses—knows nothing that is negative, and no negation; in it contradictories coincide. For that reason it does not know its own death, for to that we can give only a negative content.[58]

Or else, "Inhibitions, Symptoms, and Anxiety," v. 20, pp. 129–30:

But the unconscious seems to contain nothing that could give any content to our concept of the annihilation of life. Castration can be pictured on the basis of the daily experience of the feces being separated from the body or on the basis of losing the mother's breast at weaning. But nothing resembling death can ever have been experienced; or if it has, as in fainting, it has left no observable traces behind. I am therefore inclined to adhere to the view that the fear of death should be regarded as analogous to the fear of castration and that the situation to which the ego is reacting is one of being abandoned by the protecting super-ego—the powers of destiny—so that it has no longer any safeguard against all the dangers that surround it.[59]

We will come back to all of this.[60]

---

58. *SE* 14: 296 [*GW* 10: 350].
59. *SE* 20: 129–30 [*GW* 14: 160]. The French translation to which Derrida refers is *Inhibition, symptôme et angoisse*, trans. Michel Tort (Paris: PUF, 1965), p. 53.
60. At the bottom of this final page of the typescript of this session is the number "192."

TWELFTH SESSION[1]

Freud's Leg(acies)[2]

By the end of the first chapter of *Beyond* nothing has yet contradicted or contravened the authority of the pleasure principle. Freud thus announces the need for new "positionings of the question," the need for new problematics. Now, in trying to remain attentive to the original modality of the "speculative," to the singular proceeding [*démarche*] of this text, of this textual form that advances without advancing and without ever positing or settling anything (I am not going to return to this), one is all the more struck by the fact that the next chapter, chapter 2, while rather rich in content, indeed rich in new content, while apparently taking several steps forward, does not gain an inch of ground and does not provide any decision or end result with regard to the question that concerns us here, namely, that of the authority of the pleasure principle. I say that we are all the more struck because this is no doubt one of the most celebrated chapters of *Beyond*, the chapter that — in the exoteric space, and probably beyond the exoteric space, of psychoanalysis — one recalls being the most important or one of the most important of the essay. Notably because of the story of the wooden spool and the *fort/da* of the child. And since, in this exoteric space, one immediately connects the repetition compulsion (*Wiederholungszwang*) to the death drive, and since there is indeed a repetition compulsion in this scene of the spool, it is believed that this story can be tied to the demonstration of a death drive. But that is to forget or not to have read the fact that Freud retains *nothing* of this story of the *fort/da* in his demonstration and claims to be able to explain it still on the basis of the pleasure principle.

---

1. For bibliographical information regarding the subsequent publication of this session, see the editorial note, pp. xiii–xiv nn 10–12.

2. In the typescript, at the top of this first page of this session, there are several handwritten notes in different colors: "Fortsein," "F<reud>'s legacy [*legs*]," "Auto-bio-thanato-hetero-graphic," "fortsein ." In the left margin there is the single word "zeal."

If[3] one extracts, first, the skeletal structure, the argumentative schema, of this chapter, one notices that what is repeated here (because it is necessary to identify the repetitive process not only in the content, the examples, the material analyzed or described by Freud, but already or still in the writing, in Freud's *dé-marche*),[4] what is most obviously repeated here, is Freud's gesture of rejecting, leaving aside, renouncing everything that seems to call into question the pleasure principle, which he notes each time is not sufficient, that it is necessary to go further, to look elsewhere, etc. Sticking, then, to the bare bones of the argument, I note that after some argumentation regarding the example of traumatic neurosis, Freud writes: "I propose to leave the dark and dismal subject of the traumatic neurosis."[5] Then, after having argued at length about the *fort/da* of the wooden spool and the child's game, Freud concludes: "No certain decision (*keine sichere Entscheidung*) can be reached from the analysis of a single case like this."[6] And then, after a second wave of argumentation on the topic, Freud concludes: "Nor shall we be helped in our hesitation between these two views by further considering children's play."[7] And finally—and these are the last words of the chapter—after evoking games and artistic imitation, and once again an aesthetics guided by the economic point of view, Freud concludes: "They [these cases and situations] are of no use [they yield nothing, *leisten sie nichts*] for *our* purposes, since they presuppose the existence and dominance [the mastery, *Herrschaft*: I want to emphasize this . . .] of the pleasure principle; they give no evidence of the operation of tendencies *beyond* the pleasure principle, that is, of tendencies more primitive (*ursprünglicher*) than it and independent of it."[8] Keep in mind this language of mastery, servitude, and independence; it will become more and more significant for us, for a whole host of reasons.

That is the end of the chapter. We have not advanced a single step along the path of inquiry. It repeats itself, and it bears repeating [*Ça se répète*]. And yet in this repetitive walking in place, the repetition insists. If these determinate repetitions, these contents, species, or specifications of repetition or of reproduction, are not enough to dethrone the PP [pronounce it *Pépé*], at least the repetition-form, that is, repetitiveness, re-productivity, will have

---

3. In the typescript, a line links the beginning of this paragraph to a handwritten note in the left margin: "<two illegible words> which the *fort/da* of the spool <several illegible words> of the PP."
4. In the left margin of the typescript there is the handwritten word: "Fort."
5. *SE* 18: 14 [*GW* 13: 11].
6. *SE* 18: 16 [*GW* 13: 13].
7. *SE* 18: 16 [*GW* 13: 14].
8. *SE* 18: 17 [*GW* 13: 15].

begun to insist, to work, as if silently, a bit like at the end of the book when Freud will say (pretty much on the last page) that the death drives seem to work in silence, accomplish their unseen subterranean work, putting into their service the master himself, namely, the PP. What I mean is that, in the form—which we should no longer simply call form, since there is no longer a content or a thesis—in the *démarche* of the Freudian text, this is how it happens [*ça se passe comme ça*], even before it is ever a question of the death drive in person. So that the de-monstration (I would say, without overdoing a somewhat facile play on words), the de-monstration that proves without showing [*montrer*], without bringing any conclusion forward, the de-monstration without thesis, the de-monstration that transforms, that transforms itself into its own process rather than advancing some new conclusion, the de-monstration that bends and that bends even the very form of its discourse and the process of its text, along with the frames and the norms of ordinary discourse, that demonstration is the text—Freud's way of proceeding [*démarche*], rather than the meaning or the signified of the text, that which it seems to want to say.

Let us return now briefly to the apparent content of this second chapter.

As part of the new material called for at the end of the preceding chapter, material that seemed to resist analytic explanation, there are traumatic—so-called traumatic—neuroses, of which the war that had just ended provided many examples. Explaining them as the result of organic lesions of the nervous system had proven insufficient. The same disorder (subjective ailment, as in melancholia, motor symptoms, enfeeblement of psychical functions) can appear without any mechanical violence. Freud then distinguishes fear (*Furcht*), which is provoked by the presence of a *determinate* object of danger, from anxiety, which is related to an unknown, indeterminate danger, and which, as preparation for danger, can actually protect against trauma and is linked to repression. The latter, anxiety, is either the effect of trauma, or, as Freud will later say in "Inhibitions, Symptoms, and Anxiety" about Little Hans, that which produces repression, in opposition, he then says, to what had been said earlier, namely, that repression produces anxiety (the affect of anxiety in phobia has as its origin not the process of repression but the repressing itself). Freud distinguishes, then, among fear before a known danger, anxiety before an indeterminate danger, and then fright (*Schreck*), which anxiety protects us against and which itself produces trauma since it is provoked by an *unknown* danger, by the irruption of a danger for which one was not prepared.

Now what do we observe in the case of traumatic neuroses, that is, in the case of frights that lead to so-called traumatic neuroses? One observes, for example, that dreams—the most trustworthy means, says Freud, of investigating deep psychical processes—reproduce, have the tendency to reproduce, the traumatic accident, just as with hysterics, who, as Freud and Breuer had said as early as 1893, "suffer mainly from reminiscences,"⁹ though we are here talking not about memories but about oneric reproduction. It is here that Freud makes a curious pirouette: since it is agreed, or assuming we agree, that the predominant tendency of the dream is wish-fulfillment, then it is difficult to understand what a dream that reproduces a situation of extreme unpleasure could possibly be. One would then have to admit, he says, either that the function of the dream has, in such cases, undergone a serious alteration that diverts it from its purpose, or else that there are masochistic tendencies. Now at this point in the text, Freud sets aside or drops these two hypotheses (that of an alteration of the function of the dream and that of masochistic tendencies), though he will take them up later. In chapter 4 he will admit that certain dreams are an exception to the rule that dreams are wish-fulfillments. And in chapter 6, he will acknowledge not only the part played by masochism but even, contrary to an earlier definition of masochism, the possibility of a primary, originary masochism.

But for the moment, he drops these two hypotheses, or, rather than letting them drop, he leaves them up in the air—for reasons that, rhetorically, from the point of view of the development of the argumentation, appear obscure. "At this point I propose [he says somewhat arbitrarily, I put forward the proposition: *Ich mache nun den Vorschlag*] to leave the dark and dismal subject of traumatic neurosis and pass on to examine the method of working employed by the psychical apparatus in one of its earliest *normal* activities—I mean in children's play."¹⁰ Here is what justifies this gesture: first, the return to normality, exploring in depth certain normal processes. (We will take up again later the question of traumatic neuroses once the question of bound or unbound energy has allowed us to establish a more hospitable, more pertinent theoretical space; and we will take back up the question of masochism once the question of agencies [*instances*], of narcissism and of the ego, etc., has been more fully developed.)¹¹ For the moment, then, let us explore normality as far as possible, in order to see if something escapes, in the end, the authority of the pleasure principle. And, especially,

---

9. *SE* 18: 13 [*GW* 13: 10].

10. *SE* 18: 14 [*GW* 13: 11]. In the left margin of the typescript there is this handwritten note: "he is in a hurry to get there, since he's all worked up, but why if this brings him nothing."

11. We are here closing the parenthesis that was opened above.

let us study this normality for what is, precisely, most originary about it, that is, what is earliest, what is first, namely, childhood. Does the normal activity of the originary, namely, of what serves here as its model, the child, obey the pleasure principle, sometimes perhaps through its offspring, the reality principle? So we have the example of the child because of this normal originality, and the example of child's play because that is the normal or typical activity associated with children, and perhaps also because the pleasure principle is there apparently free of the reality principle and so appears there in its purest state of mastery.

What are we to say about the famous, all too famous analysis that follows?

First, this: it is the first occurrence in this book of an autobiographical, indeed a domestic element. It is neither merely anecdotal nor insignificant. It is a question of an experience of which Freud was not only the concerned witness but which took place in his family (though he does not say so directly in the text); and as for the child in question, he was his . . . grandfather (PP). From this experience that he more than observed, that he participated in, he retained certain elements, selected, as he him<self> says, certain details, those related to the economic point of view, a point of view that can be translated—by playing a bit, though not in a gratuitous way—as the *oikos* point of view, the domestico-familial and even domestico-funereal point of view, and you are soon going to see why. Let me read first of all the following, where this economic selectivity is confirmed:

> These theories [regarding children's play, theories he considered to be still insufficient] attempt to discover the motives which lead children to play, but they fail to bring into the foreground the *economic* motive, the consideration of the yield of pleasure involved. Without wishing to include the whole field covered by these phenomena, I have been able, through a chance opportunity [the chance[12] of the autobiographical event] which presented itself, to throw some light upon the first [comment . . .] game played by a little boy of one and a half and invented by himself (*selbstgeschaffene Spiel*) [comment . . .]. It was more than a mere fleeting observation, for I lived under the same roof as the child and his parents for some weeks, and it was some time before I discovered the meaning of the puzzling activity which he constantly repeated.[13]

Freud insists here on the repetition (*das andauernd wiederholte Tun*). It is the repetition that is the problem, and it is the repetition between pleasure

---

12. In the typescript there is an arrow leading from the word "chance" to the beginning of the following paragraph.
13. *SE* 18: 14 [*GW* 13: 11].

and unpleasure, the repetition of a pleasure and an unpleasure, that will slowly lead us to the hypothesis of a drive that is more originary than the pleasure principle and independent of it.

Now, overlay [*repliez*] what the grandfather says about the repetition of the grandson, the oldest of his grandsons, Ernst; overlay what he says his grandson does (we are about to look at this in detail) with all the earnestness befitting an eldest grandson named Ernst (*The Importance of Being Earnest*, Wilde would say); overlay what he says his grandson does while playing so earnestly; and overlay all of this onto what Freud himself does in saying this, and in writing *Beyond*, in playing so earnestly at writing beyond. He — the grandson but also the grandfather — repeats compulsively without this ever leading to anything, an operation that consists in putting at a distance, or in making as if he were putting at a distance, pleasure, the object of pleasure, the wooden spool representing the mother (or, as we will see, a certain object representing the father — who is also Freud's son-in-law), in order to bring it back untiringly, or else, as well, in making as if he were putting at a distance the pleasure principle in order constantly to bring it back and to conclude: it retains all its authority.¹⁴ One can, down to the smallest detail, map the description of the *fort/da* onto the description of the earnest speculative game of Freud writing beyond. One can see in the description of the earnest game of Ernst, the eldest grandson of grandfather Freud, not a theoretical argument that would allow one to conclude that there is a repetition compulsion or a death drive or a limit to the pleasure principle — you know that he does not do this — but an auto-biography of Freud, not¹⁵ simply an auto-biography of Freud writing his life but a living description of his own writing, of his way of writing what he writes, especially in *Beyond*, the fascination this story of the spool holds for readers stemming perhaps less from its demonstrative value than from its value as a repetition *en abyme* of what Freud does in *Beyond*, this value of a repetition *en abyme* of Freud's writing having itself a relation of structural mimesis with the relation between the pleasure principle and the death drive, this latter not being opposed to the former but hollowing it out, *en abyme*, originarily, at the origin of the origin.

---

14. In the typescript there is an insertion mark that is repeated in the left margin, followed by the handwritten words: "Still there [*Toujours là*]?" The word "*là*" is underlined twice.

15. In the typescript there is an insertion mark and, in the left margin, an illegible word that the corresponding passage in "To Speculate — On 'Freud'" (*Post Card*, p. 303 [p. 324]) suggests is "simply" ("Not simply an autobiography . . .").

There is still something else, still many other things, to say about this abyssal-auto-biographical structure, but I will leave them for later, after we will have begun to read the description of the *fort/da* of Ernst, the son of Freud's daughter Sophie, whose death will soon appear in a strange footnote written after the fact.

In the description he gives of the child's game, Freud insists on the normal character of this child, who is, all in all, paradigmatic: he is not particularly precocious, he is on good terms with everyone, particularly with his mother; he is obedient, he does not cry at night (and, especially, he does not cry over his mother's absences). BUT—he had an annoying habit, and the funny thing is to see how, all of a sudden, Freud interprets this annoying habit by saying, "I eventually realized that it was a game." But at this point it would be best for me to read and comment as we go along. So:

> The child was not at all precocious in his intellectual development. At the age of one and a half he could say only a few comprehensible words; he could also make use of a number of sounds which expressed a meaning intelligible to those around him. He was, however, on good terms with his parents and their one servant-girl, and tributes were paid to his being a "good boy" [easy, reasonable, "*anständig*"]. He did not disturb his parents at night, he conscientiously obeyed orders not to touch certain things or go into certain rooms, and above all (*vor allem anderen*) he never cried when his mother left him for a few hours. At the same time, he was greatly attached to his mother, who had not only fed him herself but had also looked after him without any outside help.[16]

Let me interrupt for a moment my reading of this picture, still without any blemishes, still without "but"; the "but" is going to make its appearance right after. What is good about this child—his normality, his calmness, his absence of fear, of tears, etc., his strength in bearing the absence of his beloved mother—suggests that all this has been propped up, constructed, dominated by a system of rules and compensations, by an economy that is going to become apparent in a moment in the form of a "bad habit" that makes it possible to accept what the "good habits" of "this good little boy (*dieses brave Kind*)" must have cost him. Naturally, in this apparently banal description of this child, Freud has very actively selected, put in place, the elements that would be useful for the *mise en scène* and the reading of the scene to follow, namely, the originary normality in relation to the good breast, his apparent ability to master the distancing of the good breast, the economic principle according to which this unpleasant experience of the

---

16. *SE* 18: 14 [*GW* 13: 11–12].

distancing of the breast requires, is going to require, compensation by another supplementary pleasure, the good habit having to be paid for by a bad habit, etc.... What is this bad habit? Let me pick up my reading of this most famous passage. I am going to read it all the way through to the note at the bottom of the page, to the first of two footnotes in this chapter, notes that, once again, appear to me to be most decisive.

> This good little boy (*Dieses brave Kind*), however, had an occasional disturbing habit of taking any small objects he could get hold of and throwing them away from him into a corner, under the bed, and so on, so that the *Zusammensuchen* [gathering up, looking for in order to gather up] of his toys (*seines Spielzeuges*) was often no small work (*oft keine leichte Arbeit war*).[17]

Let me note already that the work — for the parents but also for the child who delegates this work to his parents, who expects it of his parents — this work is that of a gathering up, a looking for in view of a gathering up: *Zusammensuchen*. Freud calls this "work," hard work. And yet he characterizes as a game the dispersion that sends all these objects flying; it is not yet a question of the spool, where the example is one of the child doing the throwing and the gathering up all by himself, the child who is holding the string and is making do without his parents. Before the spool, there is not only a multiplicity of objects that make up the set of the *Spielzeug* (his collection of toys) but also a multiplicity of agents: a child who throws, scatters, parents who pick up, gather together, put away, and straighten up. Note the expression "Spielzeug" (*so dass das Zusammensuchen seines Spielzeuges oft keine leichte Arbeit war* . . .): it is a collective, a set, the unity of a scatterable multiplicity that must be, precisely, gathered back up through the work of the parents. It is the collective unity of a[18] play set that can be, in every sense of this word, dislocated: it can change locations and it can be dismantled-dispersed. Do not forget that the word used to designate the collection as a whole is *Zeug*, which means contraption, tool, thingy, and, according to the

---

17. *SE* 18: 14 [*GW* 13: 12].

18. On the back of page 8 of T1 there is a four-line handwritten note with many words crossed out: "I will not open this curtain on all the other words <illegible word> (curtains, canvases, screens, veils, hymens, umbrellas) <which I elsewhere> today <three illegible words> this affair (<six or seven illegible words crossed out>." In the corresponding passage in "To Speculate — On 'Freud'": "I myself will not open this curtain — I leave this to you — onto all the others, the words and things (curtains, canvases, veils, hymens, umbrellas, etc.) with which I have concerned myself for so long. One could attempt to relate all these fabrics to one another, according to the same law" (*Post Card*, pp. 308–9 [p. 330]).

same semantic connection in German as in French or English, the masculine sex, the penis. Obviously, Freud does not say it, but it is easy to read the scene in this way: by scattering his objects, his collection of toys, the child throws away not only his mother (as will appear to be the case later on, according to Freud), and even his father, but also and first of all, in a relation of substitution for the maternal breast, his own penis, and, as we will see in the first note I just mentioned, himself: it is the object, himself, the breast, the mother, the penis, etc., that he throws and scatters in a movement that is called a game, a game he plays while his parents work to put things back together. I continue my translation:

> As he did this [throwing away all these objects] he gave vent to a loud, long-drawn-out "o-o-o-o," accompanied by an expression of interest and satisfaction. His mother and the writer of the present account [that is, the father of the mother, the Pépé] were agreed[19] in thinking that this was not a mere interjection but represented the German word "fort" ["gone"]. I eventually realized that it was a game, *dass das ein Spiel sei*, and that the only use he made of any of his toys [*seine Spielsachen:* same commentary as earlier] was to play "gone" with them (*mit ihnen "fortsein" zu spielen*).[20]

Here, Freud's intervention, which seems straightforward enough, deserves a closer look.[21] He says: "I eventually realized that it was a game." But what does he call a game, as opposed to work, which consists in gathering together? Well, paradoxically, the game consists in not playing with his toys except (that is, "the only use he made" of his toys, the only way he used, *benütze*, his toys, were as a tool, making of his playthings, *Spielsachen*, something useful) in order to play "*Fortsein*" with them: thus the game consists here in not playing with his toys but in making them useful for another function, namely, to be "gone."[22] To be gone in view of what, in view of whom — that is what will soon become apparent. I continue:

> The child had a wooden spool (*Holzspule*) with a piece of string (*Bindfaden*) tied round it. It never occurred to him (*Es fiel ihm nie ein*) to pull it along the floor behind him, for instance, and play at its being a carriage. What he did was to hold the spool by the string and very skilfully throw it overboard

---

19. In the typescript the word *concordants*, translated here as "agree," is circled and a question mark is written in the margin.
20. *SE* 18: 14–15 [*GW* 13: 12].
21. In the typescript there is an insertion mark, which is repeated in the left margin, followed by this handwritten notation: "O.A. (language?) (to be developed)."
22. In the left margin of the typescript are the handwritten words: "what's the use? [*à quoi ça sert?*]"

[*par-dessus bord*], over the edge [*le bord*] of his curtained crib, so that it disappeared into it, at the same time uttering his *bedeutungsvolles* "o-o-o-o." He then pulled the spool out of the crib again by the string and hailed its appearance (*Erscheinen*) with a joyful "*da*" ["here"]. This, then, was the complete game (*das komplette Spiel*) — disappearance and return (*Verschwinden und Wiederkommen*).²³ As a rule one only witnessed its first act, which was repeated (*wiederholt*) untiringly as a game in itself, though there is no doubt that the greater pleasure was attached to the second act.²⁴

After this last word, there is a note, which I will read in a moment. A few remarks on this passage.

1. Freud²⁵ seems surprised by the fact that the child never had the idea to pull the spool [*bobine*] along behind him and play at its being a carriage. Freud's problem is this: why does he not play at its being a carriage, which would be normal, pulling the thing behind him? That is Freud's problem, who would have apparently preferred to play at its being a carriage and who is surprised that the idea never occurred to Ernst. To play at its being a carriage is never to throw the thing away; it is to hold it continually at the same distance, to make it move at the same time as oneself. It is also, you will note, never to see it except by turning around; it is never to have it in front of oneself, like Eurydice or like the analyst, hearing it rather than seeing it, naturally. Freud finds Ernst's choice to be strange, but you have to admit that Freud's desire is no less strange when you consider that all this is taking place in a crib and that it has only ever taken place in a crib with curtains. One has to wonder how Ernst would have gone about playing at the spool being a carriage by pulling it behind him in a curtained crib. In order to have the spool — or the vehicle or thingamajig — behind oneself in a crib, one has to have ideas.²⁶ Follow the thread on Freud's side. What

---

23. In the left margin of the typescript there is a handwritten addition that appears to be an abbreviation: "l. P."

24. *SE* 18: 15 [*GW* 13: 12–13]. Derrida is here modifying the French translation by Samuel Jankélévitch. But when he cites this passage again in "To Speculate — On 'Freud,'" he restores Jankélévitch's formulation, "*par-dessus le bord de son lit* [over the edge of his crib]," instead of translating it, as he does here, by "*par-dessus bord* [overboard], *le bord* [over the edge]." See Derrida, *Post Card*, p. 313 [p. 334]; see note 26 below.

25. In the left margin of the typescript are two handwritten additions in two different colors. The first is: "complete Return (*Wiederkommen*)"; the second: "F<reud> wanted to play with <several illegible words>."

26. In "To Speculate — On 'Freud,'" Derrida, in the wake of his own revised translation (see note 24 above), replaces this commentary with the following passage: "In-

is surprising, then, is not that Ernst never had these ideas but that the Pépé considers them the most natural.

Because, after all, this crib was not a couch. Not yet.

2. What Freud calls the complete game is thus the game in its two phases—disappearance, reappearance, absence/presence, plus repetition, return, the re- of reappearance. And he insists on the fact that pleasure, the greatest quantity of pleasure, is occasioned by the re-appearance, the second phase. Which, on the one hand, makes it possible to foresee how this operation, taken as a whole, is going to be placed under the authority of the pleasure principle, which, far from being simply foiled [*déjoué*] by repetition, itself seeks a certain repetition of appearing, of presence, of re-presentation, of a repetition that is, as we are going to see, mastered, masterable, able to validate and confirm symbolic mastery, so that already it seems possible to say not only that the mastery of the pleasure principle is confirmed but that it consists of mastery, of mastery in general (*Herrschaft*). So that it is already possible, perhaps, to foresee that what will come not to contradict or oppose the pleasure principle but to undermine it or hollow it out *en abyme* from something originary that is more originary than it and independent of it, that this more originary, independent thing that goes under the name of the death drive or the repetition compulsion will not be another master or a counter-mastery but something other than mastery, a non-mastery that will not be in a dialectical relation (for example of master-slave, with death becoming, as Hegel says, the true master, etc.).

I am indeed saying the pleasure principle as mastery in general because, at this juncture, when Freud says "the complete game," he is no longer concerned with a particular object, the spool or that for which it plays the role of a substitute: it is now a question of the disappearance-re-appearance of the object in general; it is this disappearance-reappearance, the repetition

311

---

stead of playing on the floor (*am Boden*), he insisted on putting the bed into the game, into play, on playing with the thing over the bed, but also in the bed. Not in the bed as the place where the child would be, for contrary to what the text and the translation have often led many to believe, (and one would have to ask why), he is not in the bed at the moment when he throws the spool, it appears. He throws it from outside the bed over its edge, over the veils or curtains that surround its edge (*Rand*), from the other side, which quite simply might be into the sheets. And in any event, it is from 'out of the bed' (*zog . . . aus dem Bett heraus*) that he pulls back the vehicle in order to make it come back: *da*. The bed, then, is *fort*, which perhaps contravenes all desire; but perhaps not *fort* enough for the (grand)father who might have wished that Ernst had played more seriously on the floor (*am Boden*) without bothering himself with the bed" (*Post Card*, p. 315 [p. 336]).

of the couple presence-absence in relation to an object, that constitutes the complete game and that gives the greatest pleasure. This is so true that it is no longer even a question of the object in general as object, that is, as something determined in front of or behind oneself, but of the object — when pushed to the extreme — as oneself, the disappearance-reappearance of oneself, of oneself as object, of one's own mug [*bobine*], one's face, that is, of one's visibility as "*bobine*," as one says in French, of one's own *bobine* at the end of a *Bindfaden*, which one hangs onto by a string.²⁷ That is exactly what gets borne out . . .²⁸

3. therefore, in the note. The note is occasioned by the expression "the greater pleasure." Let me read it; it reveals that the child plays *fort/da* not only with an object, with the spool, the bobbin, the *bobine*, but with *his* bobine, his face, with himself as object in and without the mirror. Let me read:

> A further observation subsequently confirmed this interpretation fully. One day the child's mother had been away (*abwesend*) for several hours and on her return was met with the words "Baby o-o-o-o [always four in Freud's transcription]!" which was at first incomprehensible. It soon turned out, however, that during this long period of solitude the child had found a method of making *himself* disappear (*sich selbst verschwinden zu lassen*). He had discovered (*entdeckt*) his reflection in a full-length mirror which did not quite reach to the ground (*Standspiegel*), so that by crouching down he could make his mirror-image "gone [*fort*]."²⁹

To whom was this given to be seen?

The child thus plays at being fortified [*se faire fort*] by his own disappearance, by his "*fort*" in the absence of his mother. Double pleasure [*jouissance*]: he identifies with the mother since he disappears like her, and he makes her come back by making himself come back, for the³⁰ pleasure [*jouissance*] is here coupled; it has to do with the fact that he makes himself disappear, which is a way of mastering himself symbolically, of playing with his death or his absence, but also that he is able to make himself reappear, when he

---

27. [Translators' note:] Derrida is here playing on the fact that the German *Spule*, translated into English by "spool," is translated into French by *bobine*, which also means in common parlance "face" or "mug."

28. In the left margin of the typescript is this handwritten addition: "O.A. (language) and <illegible word> (language)."

29. *SE* 18: 15n1 [*GW* 13: 13n1].

30. In the typescript there is here an arrow leading to a handwritten addition of several words, which could be "next to [*auprès de*] SP."

wants to, like his mother who is held at the end of the string. He affects [*s'affecte*] himself spontaneously with his presence-absence in the absence-presence of his mother, etc. I won't dwell on this.³¹

Let us pause for a moment here, with this first note.

Because all this is only just beginning.

If the earnest game of *fort/da* is that of the absence-represence or the re-presented absence of oneself, of the one who plays as his own object, with his own object, with his own, the abyssal analogy that I proposed earlier between, on the one hand, that which — the object that — Freud analyzes, writes, describes, questions, namely, the content of *Jenseits*, and, on the other, writing, gesture, the scene of writing, the abyssal mirroring [*le rapporté abyssal*] is here confirmed. In writing this, Freud writes and writes that he is writing; in describing this, he describes this that he describes [*il décrit ce qu'il décrit*], that is, what he describes and the fact that he describes. Just as Ernst, in calling back to himself the object (mother, penis, or whatever it may be), recalls himself in the mirror, so too Freud, in describing or recalling this or that, calls himself back — and so does his text. And in an absolutely formal or general way, the scene of the *fort/da*, whatever its exemplary content, is always in the process of describing in advance its own description. The writing of a *fort/da* is always itself a *fort/da*, and it is in this *abyme* that we will need to look for both the pleasure principle and the death drive. In an absolutely formal and general way, I was saying: indeed, as soon as these objects can be substituted for one another symbolically, the formal structure of the scene appears, a scene where it is a question no longer simply of the distancing that makes this or that absent and then the bringing near that reappropriates this or that by making it present, but of the distancing of that which distances itself and of the presentation and re-presentation of presence: no longer of the absent/present but of the absence and the presence of the present, of the distancing of the distant, and the closeness of the close, a distancing that is itself not distant, no more than the closeness of a close object or subject, of something that is close, is close. The *fort* is no more distant than the *da* is close; the *fort* is no more there than the *da* is here. See Heidegger and Blanchot. Let's cut things off here.

So not only does Freud (re)call himself (back) [*se rappelle lui-même*], like Ernst in the looking glass, but his writing, his speculative operation, (re)calls itself (back) in the looking glass, specularly, for specularity is not, especially not, as is often believed, simply reappropriating, no more than the *da* is.

---

31. In the typescript a handwritten addition follows this paragraph: "The great speculator <two or three illegible words>."

He (re)recalls himself (back): what does that mean? He describes what he is doing, of course, without doing it on purpose, no doubt, but everything that I describe here, in its necessity, does not refer, especially not, to a deliberate, conscious calculation: that is why it is interesting and necessary. Freud does not calculate any more than his grandson does.

He *himself* (re)calls [Il *se* rappelle]. Who and what? Who?—him of course, but we cannot know who he is without knowing what, that is, what he recalls. He recalls (this) that he cannot recall. Here is where we have to appeal once again to the autobiographical. In a major way. This text is autobiographical, and in a way that differs from what anyone has said up until now.³² Autobiographical, though that does not mean that we know what the autobiographical is and that we are here providing an example of it. Nor does it mean that, once it begins recounting the life of the author, it does not have any value beyond that, that it has no truth value, as we say, no scientific or philosophical value. No, we are in a domain where the opposite is in fact the case, where the inscription, as they say, of the subject in his text is also the condition for the pertinence and efficacy of a text, thus for the fact that it has value (albeit not of truth in the traditional sense) beyond what is called an empirical subjectivity (assuming that something of the sort exists once this subjectivity begins speaking, writing, and substituting one object for another). But here—as elsewhere—the autobiographical is not some preexisting space in which Freud is going to recount a story, one of the stories that took place in his life. What he recounts is the autobiographical; the *fort/da* here in question is a particular autobiographical story that describes, recounts what the autobiographical in general is, and says to us: every auto-bio-graphy is a *fort/da*, for example this one, the *fort/da* of Ernst, of his grandfather, and of the book *Beyond*, etc.³³

And I would say—elliptically, for lack of time—that the logic of Beyond, of the word "Beyond" (*Jenseits* in general) is the logic of the *fort/da* inasmuch as closeness there distances itself *en abyme* (*Entfernung*). The death drive is there, in the pleasure principle, setting the *fort/da* in motion.³⁴

But it is now necessary, in order to be more concrete, for me to specify the exemplary auto-biographical content of this *fort/da*.

---

32. In the left margin of the typescript there is a handwritten addition, which could be "not/step [*pas*] auto-analytical, auto-biographical of F<reud> who is not the author."

33. In the typescript there is a handwritten addition in the left margin, "auto-thanato-graphical."

34. In the typescript a handwritten notation seems to modify this phrase in the following way: "which is put in motion by a *fort/da* [*qui s'agit d'un* fort/da]."

Freud himself recalls [*se rappelle*]. In a trivial sense, first of all, he recalls, he remembers—conscious memory—a memory that he recounts: a scene that happened to another, to two others, but others who are his daughter and grandson (the eldest, do not forget: the first grandson).[35] But of this scene, of which he says at several points that he is an "observer," he is a particularly invested, involved, and present observer. The whole thing is taking place under a roof that is pretty much his own. On what grounds—before moving on to the greatest formal generality that I indicated earlier—can we say that, in recounting, in recalling what happened to the subject Ernst, he is himself recalling, recalling that this happened to him? In many respects—at least three, which come down to just one.

1. Ernst recalls [*rappelle*], first of all—if we can say this—his mother; he reminds one of his mother. Who happens to be Freud's daughter, Sophie. Already at the time Ernst was doing this, Freud could identify with him, could recall his daughter to himself, or else, through an identification with the grandson (at once rather common and—we will have more than one proof of this later on—particularly spectacular in Freud),[36] recall Sophie as his mother. I say: already at the time the scene took place. This goes a fortiori for the moment when Freud wants to write it and recall it to himself [*de se la rappeler*]. For we now have to introduce the second note I spoke of earlier. It was written after the fact and recalls that Sophie is dead, that the mother recalled by the child died shortly thereafter. Let me first read the note: "When this child was five and three-quarters, his mother died. Now that she was really 'gone' ('o-o-o' [three this time]), the little boy showed no signs of grief. It is true that (*Allerdings*) in the interval a second child had been born and had roused him to violent jealousy."[37]

Jealousy between two children for sole possession of the mother: this remark is all the more interesting (from the point of view of Freud's autobiography and his relation, in particular, to his daughter, Sophie) given that this note comes, in the main text, right at the moment when Freud entertains the hypothesis that the throwing, indeed the throwing away, the rejection, of a toy could also signify hostility, for example, toward the father whom the child wants to go away. It happens at the moment when Freud, still dissatisfied and uncertain about the interpretation of the *fort/da* (p. 16,

---

35. In the left margin of the typescript is a handwritten addition of three words, which could be "but having come, *he*."

36. In the left margin of the typescript is this handwritten addition: "*Conjoint* [conjoined, spouse] F.S."

37. *SE* 18: 16n1 [*GW* 13: 14n1].

compensation, activity/passivity), puts forth another interpretation that he will also leave suspended.³⁸ I read:

> But still another interpretation (*Deutung*) may be attempted. Throwing away the object so that it was "gone" might satisfy an impulse of the child's, which was suppressed in his actual life, to revenge himself on his mother for going away from him. In that case it would have a defiant meaning: "All right, then, go away! I don't need you. I'm sending you away myself." A year later, the same boy whom I had observed at his first game used to take a toy, if he was angry with it, and throw it on the floor, exclaiming: "Go to the fwont (*Geh in K(r)ieg*)!" He had heard at that time that his absent father was "at the front"; he showed, moreover, not the slightest desire to see his father [no more, might we say, than his PP?]; on the contrary he made it quite clear that he had no desire to be disturbed in his sole possession (*Alleinbesitz*) of his mother.³⁹

"No desire," perhaps no more than Freud, than Freud in general (you know the autobiographical tale of his "Oedipus"), no more than Freud insofar as he identifies with his grandson (at once in general, for if the son becomes the father of his father then the identification grandson/grandfather could not be easier, and in particular, as we will see later).

So Sophie died in the interim and Freud (work of mourning, look at "Mourning and Melancholia") can now have the desire to recall her to himself [*de se la rappeler*].

It has not been uncommon—you will find this in Jones—to associate, in the crudest form of psycho-biography, the problematic of the death drive and *Beyond* with the death of this daughter of Freud's. She died in 1920, the same year *Beyond* was published. Freud knew that the two things would be linked. In June of 1920, he had read a summary of *Beyond* at the Vienna Society. The article was completed before the summer holidays, and Freud later asked Eitingon to testify to the fact that when the article was half finished Sophie was still in perfect health.⁴⁰ "Many people will shake their heads over it."⁴¹ Jones, in recalling this curious request for testimony and Freud's insistence on the subject, does not exclude the possibility that

---

38. In the left margin of the typescript are several handwritten additions that are only partially decipherable: "2ⁿᵈ part / ½ of the complete game / <eight or nine illegible words> / 7 years / seven days," then "rejection (Sigmund)" and then, circled, "4 + 3 / 000."

39. *SE* 18: 16 [*GW* 13: 14].

40. This sentence is crossed out by hand in the typescript.

41. Ernest Jones, *The Life and Work of Sigmund Freud* (London: Hogarth Press, 1953), v. 3, p. 40.

this was an internal denial. The fact is that whatever the reality may be, so to speak, and with regard to dates, Freud at least admits through his request and his insistence that the autobiographical thread here has some meaning, and that is what interests us. Without this meaning, the meaning of this thread, the insistence itself would have been useless and absurd. And he would not even have had to write to Eitingon that he had an "unruffled conscience" in the matter. Sometime later, in 1923–24, a biographer of Freud, F. Wittels (*S. F.: His Personality, His Teaching, and His School*, N.Y., 1924),⁴² suggests a relationship between the death of Sophie and the theory of the death drive. Freud writes this to him (18 December 1923):

> That always seemed interesting to me. I certainly would have stressed the connection between the death of the daughter [of *a* daughter] and the concepts of *Beyond* [i.e., *Jenseits (des Lustprinzips)* — footnote of Ernest Jones] in any analytic study on someone else. Yet still it is wrong. *Beyond* was written in 1919, when my daughter was young and blooming; she died in 1920. In September of 1919 I left the manuscript of the little book with some friends in Berlin [Eitingon and Abraham] for their perusal, it lacked then only the part on mortality or immortality of the protozoa. *Probability is not always the truth.*⁴³

But what truth are we talking about here? Where is the truth when it comes to a *fort/da* that constructs even the concept of truth?

2. I said that, in at least three respects, Freud himself recalls in recalling to himself [*en se rappelant*] his daughter or his grandson. Second, then, the identification is in every sense (in the *fort/da*) an identification with the grandson, a structural identification that is exemplified in a privileged way in the case of Freud, as a subsequent event comes to show, and which will confirm that auto-bio-graphy is in every *fort/da* an auto-thanato-graphy, which is also to say, a hetero-graphy. What happens in June 1923, the year in which Freud writes to Wittels what I just quoted? First of all, his cancer of the mouth is diagnosed as malignant and fatal. Already in 1918 he thought he was going to die (in February 1918, as he had always believed, as you know), and this pained him on account of his mother. He writes: "My Mother will be eighty-three this year and is no longer very strong. I sometimes think I shall feel a little freer when she dies, for the idea that she might have to be told that I have died is a terrifying thought."⁴⁴ There was also the war, fear of losing his sons — you know all that and I am not going

---

42. Fritz Wittels, *Sigmund Freud: His Personality, His Teaching, and His School*, trans. Eden Paul and Cedar Paul (London: G. Allen and Unwin), 1924.

43. Jones, *Life and Work of Sigmund Freud*, v. 3, pp. 40–41.

44. Ibid., v. 2, p. 196.

to return to it. So, in 1923, what happens? He knows that he will not survive his illness, and he writes that "the working through of mourning [but which one?] is going on in the depths."⁴⁵ Now, that very same year there was an event that tolled as if for Freud's own death, and he experienced it as such. This is the time when he talks of suicide, when he asks Deutsch to help him "disappear from the world with decency,"⁴⁶ when he worries about what his own death would do to his mother, etc. This event is the death, this time, of his grandson, Sophie's other son, Ernst's brother (Heinerle, Heinz-Rudolf). Freud loved him more than any other, considered him the most intelligent boy he had ever known. "He had had his tonsils removed about the time of Freud's first operation on his mouth." (Read Jones) "And when the two patients first met after their experiences he asked his grandfather with great interest: 'I can already eat crusts. Can you too?'"⁴⁷ He died of miliary tuberculosis when he was four and a half years old. This was the only time Freud was seen to cry. And he said to Jones that this loss had affected him differently from any of the others, that it killed something inside him. Two years later he would say to Marie Bonaparte that he had been unable to become attached to anyone or anything since that death. And that this blow had struck him more than his own cancer and that he was suffering from depression for the first time in his life. Three years later, as Jones recounts, Freud writes to Binswanger after the death of Binswanger's oldest son and tells him that Heinerle had "stood to him for all children and grandchildren."⁴⁸ I will not comment on this declaration, which confirms so completely everything I have been trying to say. And especially the fact that Freud lived this death of his entire descendancy as his own death—that too is conveyed in these words written to Binswanger, which suggest that he died in his grandson: "It is the secret of my indifference—people call it courage—toward the danger to my own life."⁴⁹

Fort/da, work of mourning on oneself as a great scene of descendancy, of filiation, etc. . . . of legacy [*de legs*].

3. There is yet a third thread [*fil*],⁵⁰ if we can say this, in this work of identification, introjection or incorporation, in this self-relation as grandson

---

45. Ibid., v. 3, p. 91.
46. Ibid., v. 3, p. 90.
47. Ibid., v. 3, pp. 91–92.
48. Ibid., v. 3, p. 92.
49. Ibid.
50. In the typescript the word "third" is crossed out and this interlineal addition handwritten above it: "there is <illegible word>."

or younger brother of the grandson—the story of Julius. Julius, Freud's brother—like Heinz in relation to Ernst—died at eight months of age, when Freud was nineteen months old, the age of Ernst's *fort/da*.

> Before the newcomer's birth [Julius, says Jones] the infant Freud had had sole access to his mother's love and milk, and he had to learn from the experience how strong the jealousy of a young child can be. In a letter to Fliess (1897) he admits the evil wishes he had against his rival and adds that their fulfillment in his death had aroused self-reproaches, a tendency which had remained ever since.[51]

If this guilt is displaced onto the one whose death he lived as his own, namely, the younger brother of Ernst, you can see the whole network of identifications, at once grief-stricken, murderous, jealous, and infinitely guilty, that supports this scene. Legacy and jealousy are not accidents or modifications of the structure of the *fort/da*; they construct it and are an essential part of it—that is what I wanted to suggest. And legacy and jealousy construct not only the *fort/da* but the *fort/da* as a scene of auto-bio-thanato-heterographical writing; and the scene of writing does not in the end recount an event, a content that would be called the autobiothanatoheterographical *fort/da*; this content is already a scene of writing, it is structurally a scene of writing.[52]

320

---

51. Jones, *Life and Work of Sigmund Freud*, v. 1, pp. 7–8.
52. At the bottom of the last page of the typescript are several handwritten lines, in two different colors, some of which have been crossed out. In the center is the word "supplement"; on the right an arrow leads from the word "scene" in the last line of the text to the following notation: "*marche, pas* [does not, work/walk] / at the end of F<reud> and the s<cene of writing>." On the left, in pencil: "Beyond / already gives up on it / and does not advance <illegible word> / does not advance, like a step [*pas*] / that does not [*pas*] advance <illegible word>." There are four more lines that are illegible or crossed out.

THIRTEENTH SESSION[1]

Sidestep Detour

Thesis, Hypothesis, Prosthesis

---

321   Progress beyond the pleasure principle, which was barred in the first two chapters of the book, seems to become possible in the third. But this progress is not of the order of a gain, of a thesis or a demonstration. As I have already said, and this will be confirmed again today, in this book there is never progress of this kind. But in chapter 3, there is progress to the point of entertaining a hypothesis. Freud entertains, finally, the hypothesis not yet of a death drive but of a repetition compulsion. He is going to examine this hypothesis—as a hypothesis—and ask to what function, *according to this hypothesis*, the repetition compulsion would correspond. The word *function* is very important here, as is the distinction between tendency and function, as we will come to see a bit later.

So the hypothesis is entertained at the end of chapter 3, the conclusion of which I am now going to read. Freud has just mentioned the hypothesis, the assumption (*Annahme*), of a repetition compulsion that is more originary, more elementary, more pulsional (*triebhafter*) than the pleasure principle that it tends to eclipse, and he writes:

> But if a compulsion to repeat *does* operate in the mind, we should be glad to know [the French translation says, conveying perfectly well the connotation: "we would be curious to know"; and Freud in fact will return to this curiosity and to the fact that everything has been said, written, and surmised, attempted, out of curiosity, "just to see"; he will come back to this
322   again] something about it, to learn what function it corresponds to, under what conditions it can come on the scene [*hervortreten*: one must insist on the letter of this word, not squash it, as in the French translation by *manifester* (to appear), because the operation of the repetition compulsion can take place even if it or the death drive does not appear, come on the scene

---

1. For bibliographical information regarding the subsequent publication of this session, see the editorial note, pp. xiii–xivnn10–12.

as such, in person] and what its relation is to the pleasure principle—to which, after all, we have hitherto ascribed dominance [predominance: *Herrschaft*] over the course of the processes of excitation in mental life.²

How did this hypothesis—a provisional hypothesis—finds its way into this chapter?

As I have announced—and in order to save time—I am not going to analyze this chapter, which you will have read. Let me simply note, very algebraically, the points of progression that I should have underscored or would have wanted to underscore.

1. It is at the moment of the failure of a purely interpretative psychoanalysis, where the patient's becoming conscious of the *Deutung* produces no therapeutic effect, it is at the moment when this practical or therapeutic failure of an interpretative psychoanalysis requires finding another way, a real transformation of the situation, that we come to what Freud thus calls transference (*Übertragung*) <and> that the question gets revived. It is through transference that one will have attempted to reduce the "resistances" (*Widerstände*) of the patient who has not responded by simply becoming conscious of the *Deutung*. But transference is itself a resistance. It is in the course of an analysis of the "transference neurosis" that succeeds the prior neurosis that we observe this tendency to reproduce (*Reproduktion*: it is the problem of reproduction that we have been following from the beginning of this seminar imposing itself here in a new way—*wiedererleben*). I leave you to read or reread what Freud says about repression—repression not by the unconscious but by the ego (which includes unconscious elements).

2. I would have³ wanted to comment on the series of examples given to illustrate the repetition compulsion that manifests itself here (a tendency to relive unpleasant events: everything is centered on the "narcissistic scar"—Freud speaks here of "his own observations" and not merely those of Marcinowski⁴—the "narcissistic scar" of the jealousy caused by the birth of a new child, the matrix for all jealousies and experiences of infidelity in general, everything happening as if this narcissistic scar were not simply one example among others; recall what we said the last time).

---

2. *SE* 18: 23 [*GW* 13: 22].

3. In the left margin of the typescript is the handwritten addition: "the narc<issistic> wound."

4. *SE* 18: 20 [*GW* 13: 19]. The reference here is to German neurologist Johannes (Jaroslaw) Marcinowski (1868–1935).

3. I would have⁵ wanted to insist on the *demonic*, the word and then also the value associated with it, which appears in this chapter and several times elsewhere, a value that would be of interest to us on more than one account (its link to *das Unheimliche*, the logic of duplicity without an original, the essential link to so-called fantastic or fantasy literature and to the literary as such, along with the place of the mythical and the literary in this text).

4. And that is the fourth point⁶ to which I would have wanted to draw your attention, the rather lengthy reference to a literary work that, better than any other (see *Das Unheimliche*),⁷ can support the hypothesis of the repetition compulsion, namely Tasso's *Jerusalem Delivered*, in which Tancred, after having unwittingly killed his beloved Clorinda, whom he did not recognize in the armor of an enemy knight, kills her a *second time* when, her soul having taken refuge in a tree, he cuts the tree in two and blood streams out and the voice of Clorinda can be heard lamenting the harm that her beloved has once again inflicted upon her. I would have wanted to read at great length the account Freud gives of this poem.⁸ Each time it is a man (a suit of armor or a tree) that Tancred kills without knowing what he is doing, etc. Even at the moment, then, that Freud allows for the hypothesis of the repetition compulsion (more originary than the pleasure principle), he underscores that it appears so intimately tied to the search for the pleasure principle that it is very difficult to tell them apart.

All right, then, let me leave this third chapter, all too quickly. Once this hypothesis has been accepted, the speculation really goes into full swing. It is unleashed, freed, as such. And when I say freed or unleashed as such I also mean that the unleashing or the unbinding will necessarily have to be treated there and that the hypothesis—the speculative hypothesis—of the repetition compulsion and of the death drive does not proceed without, is not freed without, this reference to unleashing itself, a reference to the very principle of unleashing, that is, to the free, unleashed, unbound energy of the primary process.⁹

---

5. In the left margin of the typescript is the handwritten addition: "the demon."

6. In the left margin of the typescript is a handwritten addition that begins: "the lit\<erary\> \<illegible word\> / is imported."

7. See Freud, "The 'Uncanny,'" *SE* 17: 219–53 ["Das Unheimliche," *GW* 12: 229–68].

8. *SE* 18: 22 [*GW* 13: 21].

9. In the left margin of the typescript is a handwritten addition that is difficult to read but that, following the corresponding passage in "To Speculate—on 'Freud,'" could be "de-stricturation": "Its unobstructed discourse is a treatise on unleashing, on detaching, on unbinding. On destricturation." (*Post Card*, p. 343 [p. 365]).

Speculation unleashed, therefore, as unleashing, beyond a pleasure principle whose mastery, as we will see, is a structure of binding, of leashing or of linking [*enchaînement*], at once linking and linked [*enchaînante et enchaînée*].

We will have to read in its entirety the short paragraph of chapter 4 that thus marks the re-beginning, the freed beginning, of the passage to Beyond:

> What follows is speculation (*Spekulation*), often far-reaching (*weitausholende*) speculation [second time], which the reader will consider or dismiss according to his individual predilection [in a certain sense, he is not trying to convince anyone of a truth, or even to circumvent the power and the investments, or indeed even the associations, that each individual may have. This speculative comment almost has the value or status of what is given in analysis or in the "literary" field: you can do with this what you want or what you can, it is no longer my concern,[10] there is no law here, especially no scientific law. And yet inasmuch as this absence of thesis is proper to both science and literature—there is no thesis in science or in literature—we are here also very close to the specificity of the scientific and of the literary as such]. It is further an attempt to follow out an idea consistently, out of curiosity (*aus Neugierde*) to see where it will lead.[11]

The whole first part of chapter 4 is a sort of *topology* whose setting into place is indispensable, just as a map is or would be for scouting out some place or set of places (here the psychical apparatus), places that would clearly delimit a battlefield, I would almost say a *front*, the structure of a capital front, both in the strategico-military sense and in the physiological or physiognomical sense (once again the *bobine*, the fore-head), the front on which the pleasure principle can, according to Freud's own image, be put out of action (*ausser Kraft*),[12] the front where the authority, mastery, predominance (the greatest force) of the pleasure principle might be found, the first to be put to rout. We are talking, then, about the place of the master's defeat, the defeat of the mastery (*Herrschaft*) of the pleasure principle. Why do I call this a front?

If I begin—as I usually do—by laying out the rhetorical and demonstrative nervure of this first part of the chapter, which identifies a topographmy, I note that, once again (according to the *dé-marche* that . . .),[13] over the course of seven long pages, the description of this topography will not get

---

10. In the left margin of the typescript is a handwritten addition: "But it concerns you."
11. *SE* 18: 24 [*GW* 13: 23].
12. *SE* 18: 29 [*GW* 13: 29].
13. As such in the typescript.

to where it wants to go, namely, to the limit of the pleasure principle. Indeed, p. 18, p. 29 of the original text, seven pages after the beginning of the chapter, Freud's provisional assessment is that this is all still insufficient: "I have an impression that these last considerations have brought us to a better understanding of the dominance of the pleasure principle; but no light has yet been thrown on the cases that contradict that dominance. *Gehen wir darum einen Schritt weiter:* Let us therefore go a step further."[14]

What is, then, or what was, then, this topological description that was so indispensable to the intelligibility of the pleasure principle but insufficient for providing an account of its defeat? Let me recall it very quickly. In metapsychological terms, consciousness is a system (*Cs.*, *Bw* in German) that provides perceptions of excitations coming from outside and feelings of pleasure/unpleasure coming from within. It is thus a system *Pcpt.-Cs.* (Perception-Consciousness) (*W.Bw.* in German) that has a position in space (*räumliche Stellung*) and that thus has limits. The limit must lie between inside and outside, turned toward the external world and yet able to receive feelings from within. Freud comments that this brings nothing new and merely adopts the views of cerebral anatomy (we are not very far from the fore-front, the forehead [*front*]) with the theory that locates the "seat" (*Sitz*) of Consciousness in the outermost, enveloping layer of the central organ, the cerebral cortex.

In this system Perception-Consciousness, then, there must be something other than Perception-Consciousness; there must be, as in the other systems, enduring traces (*Dauerspuren*) and memory remnants (*Erinnerungsreste*). We know, in fact, that the most intense and the most enduring of these traces, in all the systems and in general, are those provided by processes that never became conscious. There can be no enduring traces in the system Consciousness, for if there were, this system would quickly be limited in its capacity to receive impressions. It has to be the case, then—and this is a description whose schema orients the entire problematic of the mystic writing pad, which I encourage you to look at[15]—that the processes of excitation in the system *Cs.* leave no lasting traces, can leave traces only in another system, and that, as Freud says, consciousness must arise there where the memory trace ends, or more precisely, in the place (*an Stelle*) of the memory trace (*Erinnerungsspur*). It follows that the originality of this system Perception-

---

14. *SE* 18: 29 [*GW* 13: 29].

15. See Derrida's "Freud and the Scene of Writing," in *Writing and Difference*, 196–231 ["Freud et la scène de l'écriture," in *L'écriture et la différence*, 293–340], where Derrida addresses Freud's "Note on the Mystic Writing-Pad" (1925).

Consciousness lies in the fact that it, unlike any other system, is never modified in a lasting way by what excites it precisely because of its exposure to the external world. If one begins with the hypothesis (put forth by Freud as far back as his "Project,"[16] more than twenty years earlier) that a lasting trace presupposes a breaching (*Bahnung*) and a resistance that is overcome, one must conclude that in the system Perception-Consciousness there is no trace because there is no resistance. It is here that we find the first reference to Breuer's distinction (which we have already mentioned)[17] between bound cathectic energy (*gebunden*) <and> mobile or free cathectic energy in the psychical system. Here, in the system Perception-Consciousness, there would be neither trace nor resistance and thus a free circulation of energy, without any obstacle, tension, or pressure. But Freud interrupts this line of argument: in the current state of "speculation," he says, using this word once again, it is best to leave things undetermined, though we have already detected a certain relationship between the emergence of consciousness, the seat of the system Perception-Consciousness, and the particularities of the excitatory processes.

From this point on, still in the topographical description that constitutes the first part of chapter 4, Freud's discourse becomes more and more obscure and elliptical. He himself knows this, and he acknowledges it: "I know that these remarks must sound very obscure (*dunkel klingen*), but I must limit myself to these hints."[18] Freud here speaks of the image (we will come back later to this problem of metaphor) of the living "vesicle" (that is, the bubble, the "*bulle*," rather than the ball, the "*boule*," as *Bläschen* is usually translated in French) and the cortical layer that must protect itself from the violence of excitations coming from the external world so as to dampen them, filter them, limit their quantity of energy, and gather information, as if by feelers or antennas that draw back as soon as the information has been received. (I refer you for all of this once again, as well as for the paragraph that begins a critique of Kant's transcendental aesthetic, which, for Freud, remains at the level of an abstract representation of time linked to the system Perception-Consciousness, while the unconscious psychical processes would be "*zeitlos*" (in quotation marks), making it impossible to apply the category of time to them; I refer you for all of this to the problematic of the mystic writing

---

16. Derrida is referring here to Freud's 1895 "Project for a Scientific Psychology," *SE* 1: 295–397 [*Entwurf einer Psychologie, GW Nachtragsband, Texte aus den Jahren 1885 bis 1938*, pp. 387–477].

17. See above, p. 231.

18. *SE* 18: 28 [*GW* 13: 28].

pad.)[19] So the living vesicle protects itself against external aggressions, but it has no way of protecting itself on the other front, the other front line, since it is at the limit of inside and outside. It has no way of protecting itself against that which comes from within, that is, for example, against feelings of pleasure or unpleasure. These latter thus win out in every case over that which comes from the outside. But it follows that the organism is also oriented in such a way as to be able to oppose every internal excitation that could lead to an increase in unpleasure, which is the main enemy and the one before which we are most vulnerable. Freud thus reaffirms here, in this place of the topographical description of the vesicle—of the system Perception-Consciousness—that everything here is governed by the pleasure principle. And he even finds here an explanation for the pathological phenomena of *projection*, which, in order to implement an even simpler, more efficient system of protection, would consist in treating excitations that have their origin on the inside as if they came from the outside.

Thus, up until now, the authority of the pleasure principle remains uncontested. This entire topology is designed so that this principle might reign over the territory, over the field of the psychical system *Pcpt.-Cs*. End of the first part of the chapter: it is thus necessary to take a further step.

The topology of the living vesicle has at least reshaped a definition of trauma: there is trauma when, at the limit, on the front, the protective shield is broken, and the entire system of defense, its entire economy of energy, is defeated, put to rout. It is at this moment, says Freud, that the pleasure principle is the first to be "put out of action" (*ausser Kraft gesetzt*). What was once in command of operations is no longer able to master the situation when it is submerged, flooded (*Überschwemmung*: an image of a sudden liquid surge) by great quantities of excitations that overflow [*débordent*] the psychical apparatus. The apparatus, panic-stricken, no longer seeks pleasure, it would seem, but attempts to bind (*binden*) these large quantities of excitation and gain mastery over (*bewältigen*) the excitation. To do this, the psychical apparatus carries out, in the region that has been invaded, a counter-insurgency [*contre-investissement*], a counter- or anti-cathexis (*Gegenbesetzung*) of energy, at the cost of a psychical impoverishment in other regions. These energetico-military metaphors (for instance, a withdrawing of forces from one front in order to send them in all haste to shore up another that has just been breached) are called by Freud *Vorbilder* (models, prototypes, paradigms), and he says that they are essential for propping up the metapsychology. Recourse to these metaphors becomes all the more nec-

---

19. See above, p. 264n15.

essary inasmuch as Freud, at the moment he proposes the law according to which a system is more capable of *"binden,"* of binding or of banding energies, when its own charge, in a state of rest, is great, at the very moment he speaks of quantities of binding, banding, or counter-banding in a counter-investment, he does not know—and he asserts that we do not know—what we are talking about, what is bound or unbound in this way. We know nothing, he says, about the nature of the excitatory process that takes place within the psychical process. This content, this nature of the excitatory process, is an unknown factor, a "large unknown factor," "a large X," he says.[20] It is obviously in place of this X, this thing X, that the *"Vorbilder"* come, that is, models, images, and metaphors borrowed from some other field.

Freud has thus returned—he had abandoned this in the first chapter—to the example of trauma, and even to an explanation for trauma, which, he admits, is not that far from the old, naïve theory of shock. It is just that, here, the shock is no longer localizable as a lesion inflicted directly on the molecular or histological structure but as a rupture of the protective shield described in this new topology, when the apparatus is no longer prepared (for example, through anxiety) to bind the quantities of energy that flow in. When the intensity of the trauma is too great, when there is too great an inequality of energies, too great a surge of energy, the pleasure principle can no longer function normally. And the dream, for example, instead of bringing about hallucination, the hallucinatory fulfillment of wishes, begins to re-produce the traumatic situation. "We may assume (*annehmen*)," Freud then says,

> that dreams are here helping to carry out another task, which must be accomplished [solved] before the dominance of the pleasure principle can even begin.... [Freud continues] They thus afford us a view of a function of the mental apparatus which, though it does not contradict the pleasure principle (*ohne dem Lustprinzip zu widersprechen*), is nevertheless independent of it and seems to be more primitive than the purpose of gaining pleasure and avoiding unpleasure.[21]

This is the first exception to the law that says that the dream is the fulfillment of a wish. This law was able to govern the function of dreams only after the pleasure principle had asserted its dominance, its mastery. As if this mastery were, then, an effect, the effect of a history, of a certain history or a certain

---

20. *SE* 18: 31 [*GW* 13: 31].
21. *SE* 18: 32 [*GW* 13: 32].

original genesis, a relatively late effect, already a victory over a terrain that does not belong to it in advance. Victory of the binding over the unbinding, of the banding over the counter-banding, or even of the counter-banding over the absolute disbanding of the ranks.[22]

This hypothesis has just been accepted—as a hypothesis—on the basis of the example of traumatic neuroses and the collapse of the front in the face of external aggressions. Chapter 5 extends the scope of the hypothesis by considering excitations whose origin is internal, those that come from the drives and their representatives, that is, from the most important but also, Freud notes, the most obscure object of psychoanalysis. The first important affirmation—and we are here entering into the richest and most active phase of this text—concerns the character of these nervous processes coming from internal sources (drives and their representatives), namely, that they are not *bound*. Freud relies here upon everything that had been learned from psychoanalysis up until that time, everything about dreams, about the processes of transference, about displacement and condensation, in order to show that if this happened in the conscious or preconscious systems or on conscious or preconscious material, it would not work and it would yield only invalid results, etc. He recalls that (in the *Traumdeutung*)[23] he had given to these unconscious processes the name of "primary process" (*Primärvorgang*). The primary process thus corresponds to a free, non-bound, non-tonic cathexis and the secondary process to the binding or leashing [*l'enchaînement*] of energy. The task of the higher strata of the psychical apparatus thus consists in binding, in leashing pulsional excitations coming from the inside. Hence—and this is what is most important, it seems to me—the pleasure principle (or its modification, the reality principle) can affirm its mastery (*Herrschaft*) only to the extent that, and only from the moment when, this leashing or binding has been able to operate, has been successful, the moment when the primary process is bound, dominated. That does not mean that there was not, before this moment, any attempt to master or bind the excitation; it means simply that the psychical apparatus attempts to bind its excitations to some extent (a rather loose formulation) prior to the pleasure principle and in disregard of it. But without opposing it. When this fails, what gets produced are disturbances "analo-

---

22. In the typescript the word "disbanding" has been crossed out and the word "*l'abande*," perhaps, added between the lines. At the end of the sentence there is a handwritten addition that could be "or the disbanding." For this series of terms, see *Glas*, for example, 11–12bi [18bi], 22–23b [30b], 66bi [77bi], 83ai [97ai], and 133b [151b].

23. See Freud, *Interpretation of Dreams*, SE 4–5 [GW 2–3].

gous" (*analoge*) to traumatic neuroses and traumas of an external origin. The obscurity here stems from the fact that, before the assured, affirmed mastery of the pleasure principle, there is already a tendency toward binding and mastery, a tendency that announces the pleasure principle and sometimes collaborates with it. There is here a zone, of sorts, between the pure Primary Process (a "myth," says the *Traumdeutung*) and the pure secondary process.[24] And this indecision resides in the concept of repetition, in the logic of repetition that sets this whole text in motion. Let me indicate very schematically the oscillation: sometimes, in a traditional way, the repetition repeats something that precedes it; the repetition comes afterward, after an originary that is foreign to the repetition, which is thus secondary, derived. Sometimes, however, according to a non-traditional logic of repetition, repetition is originary and induces—through a propagation without limit—not only a deconstruction of the entire traditional philosophy or onto-logic of repetition but, first of all (and we are now coming back to what I said when we first took up this book),[25] a deconstruction of the whole psychical construction, of everything that props up the drives and their representatives, everything that ensures the integrity of the psychical organization under the *Herrschaft* of the pleasure principle. Secondly, and as a result, repetition sometimes collaborates with mastery and thus with the pleasure principle, and sometimes, more originary than the pleasure principle, it undermines it, threatens it, sometimes even seeking, as we will soon see, a non-bindable pleasure that resembles, as one bubble resembles another, a horrendous unpleasure.

Only by taking account of these two logics of repetition, which do not oppose one another any more than they simply repeat one another (or, if they repeat one another, it is by repeating this duplicity that inhabits the structure of all repetition), only by taking account of this double band of repetition (which is not thematized by Freud) can we understand the passage that immediately follows.

Freud says that the repetition compulsion—in the child and in the first stages of analytic treatment—has a pulsional character (which is not necessarily in opposition to the pleasure principle), but also, when it seems to oppose the pleasure principle, a *demonic* character. Sometimes, then, repetition serves pleasure and ensures mastery, sometimes the contrary. Freud comes back to the example of children's play: its normally repetitive character reinforces mastery, yields the pleasure linked to identification, to recognition

---

24. See Derrida, "Freud and the Scene of Writing," in *Writing and Difference*, p. 226 [p. 334].
25. See the beginning of the eleventh session, p. 219ff.

of the same, of the identical (I would say idealization, see Husserl). In this case, the case of childhood, repetition produces pleasure, while in the adult, Freud notes, novelty is the condition of pleasure (the example of narrative: interesting: the child would never tire of . . .). But when the adult (in analysis, for example, and in the form of transference) compulsively reproduces a situation from childhood, he or she goes beyond the pleasure principle (*hinaussetzt*). He or she behaves in an infantile fashion and shows that the repressed memory traces coming from the child's first psychical experiences continue to exist in an unbound, unleashed state, incompatible with the secondary processes. The repetition compulsion, which in transference or in transference neurosis is a first condition of analysis, can become an obstacle when it hinders the resolution of the transference and detachment from the analyst. There is something demonic in this, and when one is fearful of analysis it is often because one senses this relation to a demonic element that would have been better off left alone.[26]

As you will have noticed, the question of death has not yet come up. This double logic of repetition, with its undecidable relation to pleasure (but what, given all this, is pleasure?), has not required any discussion of death.

At the moment Freud begins asking about the relationship between the drives and repetition, he advances a hypothesis about the very nature of the drives and, perhaps even more generally, all organic life. This attribute (*Charakter*), which is inscribed in every drive and perhaps in all organic life, is indicated through a trace (*Spur*) in everything we have followed up until now. What is this attribute? Freud says:

> It seems, then, that a drive (*Trieb*) is an urge (*Drang*) inherent in organic life to restore (*Wiederherstellung*) an earlier state of things which the living entity has been obliged to abandon under the pressure of external disturbing forces; that is, it is a kind of organic elasticity, or, to put it another way, the expression of the inertia inherent in organic life.[27]

The external, which here comes to disrupt this tendency and produce, in some sense, the whole history of the evolution of a life that has done more than merely repeat itself and regress, is the world, the system of earth and sun, and so on. I am going to skip over the part of the demonstration where Freud says he is not afraid of being criticized for the "profound," even

---

26. In the left margin of the typescript is a handwritten addition of several words, two of which could be "mvt," an abbreviation of the word "movement": "mvt maintains the mvt."

27. *SE* 18: 36 [*GW* 13: 38]. There is here in the typescript an insertion mark that is repeated in the left margin along with the words: "differs / Force = writing." These last two words are circled.

"mystical" character of this meditation; I skip over it in order to come to the determination of the *Umweg* (of the detour in the *démarche*) that follows. We already encountered, as early as the first chapter, the value associated with the *Umweg* in the relations between the pleasure principle and the reality principle. Here, the meaning of the *Umweg*, in its most general sense, in its widest scope, comes to overflow its determination in the first chapter and provides its most general foundation [*assise*]: the *Umweg* would be not only *différance* or delay in view of pleasure or preservation (the reality principle in the service of the pleasure principle) but also detour in view of death or of a return to the inorganic state. As a result, the *Umweg* of the first chapter would be but an internal and secondary modification of the absolute or unconditioned *Umweg*; it would be in the service of the general *Umweg*, that is, of the sidestep of the detour [*du pas de détour*] that leads back always to death. It is this double determination of difference that I had in the past assigned to the word *différance* with an *a*.[28]

But all this obviously is not self-evident. The end of life, its goal and its end point, is this return to the inorganic, so that life and the evolution of life are but a detour (*Umweg*) of the inorganic toward itself, toward the inorganic, a race to death. So that death (the end toward which life tends) is inscribed as an internal law and not as an accident of life (recall the law of supplementarity, the analysis of Jacob, etc.). It is life that is like an accident of death, inasmuch as life dies "for internal reasons (*aus inneren Gründen*)"[29] (relations of type, of genre, recall Nietzsche from earlier).[30] I say that the question is not so simple because Freud must then explain the existence of conservative drives, which he acknowledges can be found in all living beings, drives that also motivate the recourse to repetitive processes. Why this conservative detour if the tendency to death is so internal and so general? Faced with this risk of contradiction, what option does Freud have and what is his response? (1) To make of the conservative drives or of the detour in its conservative form a *partial* process, partial drives (*Partialtriebe*), and, (2) referring to the clearly indispensable distinction between inside and outside, to determine the meaning or the necessity or the finality of these conservative, partial drives as a movement that tends to ensure that

---

28. See Derrida, "Différance," in *Margins of Philosophy*, pp. 1–27 [pp. 1–29].

29. *SE* 18: 46 [*GW* 13: 49].

30. In the typescript there is an insertion mark repeated in the left margin, followed by: "here: / life = / accident / death = inter. / <elsewhere: mvt?> / does not prescribe death." Below are several illegible additions in different colors: "life forms an angle/ <illegible word>," "partial?," "The proper = life death, <illegible word>."

the path toward death responds to *immanent*, internal possibilities. In other words, to die of its own death. The organism conserves itself, spares itself, protects itself, etc., in order to protect itself not against death but against a death that would not be its own. It protects itself (whence the detour or the sidestep of the detour or the sidestepping of the detour) against that which could steal its death from it, cause a death to come to it from the outside. The drive of the proper, as an internal drive, would here be stronger than both life and death, which are not opposed to one another. It is right at this point, at the moment Freud says, "What we are left with is the fact that (*Es erübrigt, dass*) the organism wishes to die only in its own fashion," that it would be necessary to bring together — though I cannot do it for lack of time — what Heidegger says about being-towards-death (*Sein zum Tode*), which, quite beyond all the metaphysical categories of subject, consciousness, person, etc., must have a relation to its own, to its own death, as the condition of its authenticity (*Eigentlichkeit*), with what Freud says about the *Todestrieb, Todesziel, Umwege zum Tode*, and, literally, about the "*eigenen Todesweg des Organismus.*"[31] It is indeed a matter, beyond all oppositions, of an economy of death, of a law of the proper (*oikos*) as that which governs the detour and seeks its proper event (*Ereignis*), its propriation, rather than life and/or death. The lengthening or shortening of the detour would be in the service of this economic law of the self as proper, this economic law of auto-affection. It is necessary above all to affect oneself with one's own death, to make it so that death is the auto-affection of life or life the auto-affection of death. All *différance* resides in the desire of this *auto* insofar as it differs from itself and defers itself in its wholly other.[32]

This value of safeguarding (you know how Heidegger treats this same topic) is gathered up in all its polysemy or polymetaphoricity — in particular in its strategico-military metaphor — at the moment Freud defines the conservative drives of life, the guardians of life, as sentinels of death or myrmidons of death (*Trabanten*):

> Thus these guardians of life [the sentinels of life, *Lebenswächter*, those that watch over life, that oversee it, that keep it, that keep watch over it, that guard it, that mount guard over it, the sentinels of life that the drives are] were originally (*ursprünglich*) the myrmidons of death (*Trabanten des Todes*: satellites de mort).[33]

---

31. *SE* 18: 39 [*GW* 13: 41].

32. In the left margin of the typescript are two handwritten additions, the first of which could be "Da-sein," and the second: "no proper *name*."

33. *SE* 18: 39 [*GW* 13: 41].

Satellites or myrmidons, like an agent in the more or less obscure and clandestine service of an absolute power, or a body whose movement obeys the revolution of another more powerful body. What safeguards life is in the sphere of influence [*mouvance*] of what safeguards death, for it is as much a question here of safeguarding death as exposing to death. It is a question of safeguarding death inasmuch as one must here save the death that is proper, that of the living to die in its own way, at its own rhythm. It is always necessary to safeguard (from) death or to safeguard (from) life [*il faut toujours garder de la mort ou garder de la vie*], such is the syntax or the logic of this strange vigilance. This changing of the guard, of the sign of the guard, the sentinel of life becoming, or rather having been, having to become, what it will have been, namely, a myrmidon or satellite of death, this changing of the sign, this vacillation, can be found in an even more overt form in *Das Unheimliche*. It is by means of this strange logic that, in the rest of the chapter, Freud speaks of sexuality or of sexual difference, which, having come on the scene rather late in the history of life, will nonetheless have existed from the origin and exhibits an activity, a work of opposition (*Gegenarbeit*), against the "interplay [*jeu*]" of the ego's conservative drives.

End of chapter 5, the *"treibende Moment"* (the "driving factor"), quotation from part 1 of Goethe's *Faust*: Mephistopheles says, *"ungebändigt immer vorwärts dringt."*[34]

One might this time, at the end of chapter 5, consider the hypothesis confirmed: there does indeed exist a beyond of the pleasure principle and, as the logic of the repetition compulsion demonstrates, a death drive.

Yet once again—as I recalled earlier—Freud says he is not satisfied. The beginning of chapter 6 acknowledges this. Still no satisfaction. The conclusion of the preceding chapter does not satisfy us, it is bound not to satisfy us, says Freud (*wird uns ... nicht befriedigen*). What is unsatisfactory, at the point we have now reached, can be summed up in the form of the following hypothesis: two groups of drives, on the one hand, the ego-drives, which would obey a logic of regressive and deadly repetition,[35] and which seek to return, from the first breath of life, to an inanimate state, and, on the other hand, the sexual drives, which, all the while reproducing primitive states, would seek through the fusion of two germ-cells to pass on life and immortalize it, to lend it an appearance of immortality.

---

34. *SE* 18: 42 [*GW* 13: 45]. [Translators' note:] Translated by Strachey as "presses ever forward unsubdued" (*SE* 18: 42n1).

35. In the left margin of the typescript is the handwritten word "conservation."

Freud then begins questioning, from what he calls a "scientific" point of view, that which acted as the principal axiom of the previous chapter, namely, this value of the inside, of death as an internal, immanent necessity of life. And what if, he asks, this value of the immanence of death in life were but the object of a comforting belief, that is, what if it were an illusion designed to help us "bear the burden of existence (*um die Schwere des Daseins zu ertragen*),"[36] as we say, or as the poet says? What if this death that is immanent in life were, precisely, a poem, the creation, the doing, of the comforting poet within us? Such a belief is not originary; look at primitive peoples, says Freud (not childhood, this time, as the index of originality, but "primitive" culture): they believe so little in natural death that they attribute it always to the aggressivity of an enemy.[37]

Here is where we come to the detour through biology, through the genetics of the times, the only part of the essay, says Freud, that had not been written at the time of his daughter's death, or at least at the time of the first signs of her impending death. It would be very interesting to read these few pages in light of Jacob's book and what we emphasized there with regard to death as immanent or not, sexuality (whether belated or not), protozoa (whether immortal or not), etc. We would see that in their theoretical schemas they remain astonishingly contemporary, and that the, so to speak, new contents of scientific knowledge (empirical discoveries, if you will), those since 1920, have not changed the slightest theoretical element in the positing of problems, in the types of questions, in the kinds of answers or non-answers. The genetic model that most interests Freud (I say "model" here to pick up the thread of our earlier problematic and because Freud actually speaks here of an "unexpected analogy," *unerwartete Analogie*,[38] of a "striking similarity" or bizarre kinship, *auffällige Ähnlichkeit*,[39] and of a "significant correspondence," *bedeutsame Übereinstimmung*),[40] the genetic model that most interests Freud is that of Weismann (his work of 1906–14),[41] which distinguishes in the morphology of the living substance between

---

36. *SE* 18: 45 [*GW* 13: 47].

37. In the left margin of the typescript is a handwritten addition of five or six illegible words. Beneath, there is "p. 19," circled. See *Post Card*, p. 363 [p. 386], for the corresponding passage.

38. *SE* 18: 46 [*GW* 13: 48].

39. *SE* 18: 49 [*GW* 13: 53].

40. *SE* 18: 46 [*GW* 13: 49]. In the left margin of the typescript there is the handwritten addition: "sympathy," followed by two illegible words that have been crossed out.

41. The Weismann works Freud is referring to actually date from 1882, 1884, and 1892. Derrida appears to have gotten the dates 1906 and 1914 from a note on the fol-

the *soma*, the body considered apart from its sexual and hereditary substance (which is always condemned to death), and the immortal germ-plasm. After having shown the limitations of this analogy (Weismann restricts this duality to multicellular organisms, the only organisms for which death would be natural, while protozoa would be "potentially immortal"),[42] Freud deems this analogy to be still valid, at least in its dualistic schema, which mirrors the distinction between death drives/life drives. It is at this point that he speaks—and I alluded to this in the beginning—of the harbor of Schopenhauer's philosophy, according to which death would be "*das eigentliche Resultat*" of life and the sexual drive the embodiment of the will to live.

Still dissatisfied with his *démarche*, and yet at the same time pleased, as he says, with the scientific analogy, Freud proposes, once again, that we make a bold attempt (*Versuchen wir kühn*) at "an additional step forward, *einen Schritt weiter zu gehen*."[43]

Freud takes up the biological model but then redirects it slightly toward a politico-psychoanalytic metaphor: a vital association of cells that supports the life of the organism as a cellular State that continues to live in spite of the death of one or another of its subjects; a natural contract according to which copulation serves the end of reproduction and the rejuvenation of the other cells. One can thus transfer and compare (*übertragen*)[44] the psychoanalytic theory of libido to these bio-political cells and say that the two drives present in each cell neutralize in part their death drive by taking other cells as their object, keeping them alive, and going so far as to sacrifice themselves, if need be. To this altruistic heroism of certain cells, which all of a sudden begin to look like private second class soldiers from the war of 1914, on the Austrian side, of course, soldiers susceptible to traumatic neuroses, to these decorated cells right on the front line there are, opposed to them, the other kind of cells, the "narcissistic" ones, which keep all their libido for themselves, not wanting to transfer the least amount of it onto some object, keeping it in reserve for some momentous constructive activity (for example art or science). And Freud at this point does not exclude the possibility that malignant tumors—which are cells that suddenly develop

---

lowing page of *Beyond* where Freud refers to works of Hartmann (1906) and Lipschütz (1914).

42. *SE* 18: 46 [*GW* 13: 49].

43. *SE* 18: 50 [*GW* 13: 53]. In the typescript is this handwritten addition: "*Tjrs le pas* [always the step/not]."

44. In the left margin of the typescript is a handwritten addition of two words, which appear to be "analytic mvt."

on their own in an uncontrollable fashion [*déchaînée*]—are "narcissistic" cells in this sense, cells that withdraw from the front and find refuge beneath it, beneath what faces front, a hypothesis that must be heard coming, of course, from Freud's mouth.

It is this concept of narcissism that is now going to free up a new "additional step," two pages after the first one (the one that consisted in the appeal to the Weismannian model) had left us, as Freud says, "groping in the dark," *piétinant* [in French], making no headway.[45] This new additional step is psychoanalysis's discovery of a libido turned toward the ego, which becomes a sexual object and even the most important of all sexual objects. Freud refers here to the introduction of/to narcissism (1914). If such a libido exists, the opposition between a (deadly) ego-drive and a sexual drive of self-preservation or procreation is no longer valid or at least no longer has a qualitative value; its value is, at most, only topographical. The risk of this innovation is the risk of monism, the Jungian risk: every drive is sexual-libidinous. Freud's resistance to this monism is here one of principle. "Our views have from the very first been *dualistic*, and today they are even more definitely dualistic than before,"[46] he says, even while admitting that, given the current state of research, it is not possible to demonstrate the existence of non-libidinal drives. The only remaining way to account for the existence of a death drive would be through the sadistic element, which had been discovered long before, at a time when psychoanalysis was not yet aware of the difficulty we are now considering, a sadistic component that would thus be a death drive detached from the ego and turned toward the object, and masochism, a partial component that complements sadism insofar as it turns sadism back toward the ego and thereby rediscovers, regressively, an originary deadly tendency within the ego. This hypothesis is sharpened by the correction that Freud had recently brought to masochism, which he now thinks could be originary, something he had earlier contested.[47]

After a new *effort* to find in the exercise of the instincts of self-preservation (for example, in protozoa) an illustration of this law governing the tendency to reduce, keep constant,[48] or remove internal tension (the Nirvana prin-

---

45. *SE* 18: 51 [*GW* 13: 54].

46. *SE* 18: 53 [*GW* 13: 57].

47. In the left margin of the typescript is this handwritten addition: "again [*encore*] / (*fort/da*) / 7 years? / <one hundred years?>."

48. Starting here and until the end of the session, our transcription is based on T2, that is, the carbon copy of the original typescript, whose five last pages are missing in the archives. These pages from T2 have almost no handwritten additions.

ciple), the principal reason, in fact, for believing in the existence of death drives—which nothing has thus yet proven—after having evoked the notion that sexuality may well have arrived late and "by chance," a chance that would have then become established because of the advantages it offered, after having thus evoked the late, secondary, and derived character of the life drives, Freud nonetheless reproduces the observation of a relative failure: even if sexuality is late, secondary, the result of chance, it was able to arise and, especially, to become established only to the extent that some presexual life drive preceded it, virtually animated it, determined its end. So it seems that the life drive is indeed always and indissociably coupled with the death drive. We now have—and this is the only progress that has been made—a hypothesis with two unknowns. We have not taken a single step forward since the beginning.

It is precisely here, in this place of paralysis, that we find the famous reference to the myth of the *Symposium*—which I will refrain from commenting on because it is too well known. I simply want to underscore that this recourse to myth occurs right at the place where the speculative fails at becoming either science or philosophy, where it runs aground right on the limit, the place where it would be a matter of going beyond not only one limit or another but the very idea of the limit as a front between two opposed terms, as a line of distinction between two identities (for example life/death). And I also wish to underscore, with regard to the textual *dé-marche* of this passage of *Beyond*, that Freud also abandons the help offered by this myth (which itself played an analogous role in Plato's text) and seems once again to throw up his hands: "*Ich glaube, es ist hier die Stelle, abzubrechen*":[49] I think this is the place to break things off, to cut things short, to end the session, etc.

What he nonetheless adds immediately thereafter, and which is like a "critical commentary," a "critical reflection" (that is his phrase: *kritische Besinnung*), on what is happening, on what has just happened, on the status of his discourse and his essay, this post-script to this penultimate chapter, is of great interest. Freud puts himself onstage, in the scene [*en scène*]. He tries to define his place—or even his non-place, his absence, a certain nonposition—with regard to what is happening here, with regard to this discourse, these hypotheses, these advances, retreats, missteps [*faux-pas*], false *sorties*, etc. What he thus says, putting himself on the scene or removing himself [*se dé-mettant*] from it, is very significant for us, which does not mean that we believe in it or do not believe in it, but it is very significant for us insofar as we think that the question of the status of this text (*Beyond*

---

49. *SE* 18: 58 [*GW* 13: 63].

the Pleasure Principle) and of the discourse that is developed within it, of the place of Freud, of his relation to psychoanalysis as science, as practice, as mythology, as philosophy, as literature, as speculation, etc., that this question concerning the nature, the event, and the status of such a text or of its scene is anterior and even preliminary to any debate that might be had over the so-called theses that one would want to find in it, theses that one would be hard-pressed, as I have tried to show, to find there in it. These questions have—to my knowledge—never been posed, they have never worried those who, especially from within the analytic movement, from 1920 up to today, have been engaged in a pitched battle around this text and the theses they believe it contains, some taking them seriously and developing their entire discourse upon the seriousness of *Beyond* (the most spectacular case in this respect being that of Lacan), others taking them more lightly, or, if you prefer, more heavily, shrugging their shoulders at this flight into mysticism or this very unserious game on the part of the master. But on neither of these two sides has the singularity of the scene of writing—and of the text—and of what that implies concerning the context of psychoanalysis ever been subjected to questioning. At the very most, one has gone so far as to note all the mythological ornaments that here embellish Freud's prose. That is why I am insisting on what I call the textual (autobioheterothanatographical) *dé-marche* and, particularly, on what Freud says in this sort of post-script to the penultimate chapter.

What does he say? He says: One might ask to what extent I am convinced by the hypotheses that I have just expounded. To this I will answer... What is he going to answer? The syntax of the answer is curious: I am no more convinced by them than I am trying to get others to believe in them. That is what he answers. He does not say that he believes in them, but neither does he say that he does not believe in them. This *démarche* would be just as strange for a scientist convinced of the truth of a demonstration as it would be for a philosopher advancing a thesis, and even for a poet or a priest who is always looking to gain the other's adherence, to draw the other in, to touch the other. Here, the relation to the other—which exists, of course—is completely other: as if one were seeking to reach the other only through a game being played for oneself, narcissistically. So he does not believe in them any more than he tries to make others believe in them. But he is also not saying that he does not believe in them. He clarifies his statement (*Richtiger*, he says, "more precisely"): "I do not know how far I believe in them: *Ich weiss nicht, wie weit ich an sie glaube.*"[50]

---

50. *SE* 18: 59 [*GW* 13: 64].

This suspensive attitude, this *epochē* that brackets—as in a phenomenology that would have to be invoked here beyond the real limits or beyond the interdictions and the slogans—this *epochē* that brackets or withholds judgment, conclusions, and, precisely, as in phenomenology, theses, is also determined by Freud as a suspension of affect, of the affective moment or factor that accompanies all *Überzeugung* and all *Glaube*, all conviction and all belief. And yet, if the affect of conclusion is indeed suspended, it is difficult to say that affect is absent from the investigation, even if the investigation is carried out simply to see, out of curiosity. Once that affect of conclusion (conviction or belief) is suspended, "it is surely possible," says Freud, "to throw oneself [to give oneself up to—it is a strong phrase: *sich hingeben*] into a path of thought, a line of thought (*Gedankengang*), and to follow it wherever it leads out of simple scientific curiosity, or, if one prefers (*wenn man will*), as an *advocatus diaboli*, who is not on that account himself sold [by written contract] to the devil (*sich darum nicht dem Teufel selbst verschreibt*)."⁵¹ This recurrence here of the devil, yet again, deserves our attention. It is strange to see a suspensive *démarche*, one that is being attributed to simple curiosity or else to scientific curiosity, compared to a diabolical operation, or, more precisely, because all this is even more diabolical, more double, to playing the devil's advocate. Why would curiosity be on the side of the devil? What about the devil in science or in psychoanalysis? But also, one has to be careful here; the devil's advocate is not the devil; it is more cunning than the devil. It is what represents the devil in court, what feigns to take the side of the devil, but is not itself the devil and does not believe in the devil. Or at least, even if it believes in him, it manages to take the devil's side or to put the devil on its side without putting itself on the side of the devil, without giving itself over, or selling itself, or promising itself, to the devil, without any contract with the devil. No promissory note to the devil (*nicht dem Teufel sich verschreiben*). One would here have to read next to this all the devils of psychoanalysis, especially the one with which the painter Christoph Haitzmann had contracted that double pact, in red and in black (in blood and in ink), that devil with double breasts and a double sealed pact [*double seing*], treated in "A Seventeenth-Century Demonological Neurosis."⁵²

In this post-script, which I here abandon to its diabolical supplement, one can also identify, under the rubric of critical reflection on the operation in process, two essential motifs on the final page.

51. Ibid.
52. *SE* 19: 72–105 [*GW* 13: 315–53].

1. One of these, which I have often noted elsewhere, concerns the metaphoricity of Freud's language. The limit of psychoanalytic discourse, especially in this essay, has to do, he says, with the fact that we have to work with scientific terminology, which, far from immediately conferring the value of scientificity upon psychoanalysis, makes this latter bear the weight of the whole *Bildersprache*, the language of images that limits science, and, in particular, psychology and so-called depth psychology. For the moment, we need these images, not merely in order to talk about psychical processes but even in order to represent them to ourselves (comment). Freud's hope: to move on not to a proper language but to another science, psycho-chemistry, to another system of images (images more familiar and thus simpler) (comment).

So much, then, for the rhetoric that keeps us subjected to a specific science.

2. Second motif, second limitation, that of biological models, hence the provisional biologism of psychoanalysis. The drawback here is that biology is a science with unlimited possibilities from which we can expect at any moment the most extraordinary revelations, so that everything we borrow from it one day can become obsolete the next and thus cause the whole edifice of our hypotheses to collapse in an instant. Like a house of cards, says the French translation, which is interesting because it underscores once again the game-like character of this speculation. There is no house of cards in the German text, but there is a "*künstlicher Bau von Hypothesen*," which is just as interesting: an artificial, artistic construction of hypotheses that would be "blown away (*umgeblasen wird*)" by new biological discoveries.⁵³

Faced with all these risks, all these uncertainties, all these suspensions, Freud assumes both the throw of the dice [*coup de dés*] and his desire [*désir*]. He does this in the last words of the chapter, which sound like a response to every disgruntled objection, a sort of: "Screw you all, I myself am rather pleased with this, the beyond of pleasure, that's my pleasure [*tel est mon bon plaisir*]; the hypothesis of the death drive — that's what I like, that's what interests me."⁵⁴ Here is what I translated in that way: "If so, it may be asked why I have embarked upon such a line of thought as the present one, and in particular why I have decided to make it public. Well — I cannot deny that some of the analogies (*Analogien*), correlations, and connections which it contains seemed to me to deserve consideration (*mir der Beachtung würdig*

---

53. *SE* 18: 60 [*GW* 13: 65].

54. [Translators' note:] Derrida is working here with a formulation commonly attributed to French monarchs: "tel est notre plaisir" or "tel est notre bon plaisir," "such is our pleasure" or "such is our good pleasure," that is, "such is our desire."

erschienen sind)."⁵⁵ These are the last words of the chapter, of its postscript, as it were. They could have been the last words of the book.

And yet they are not quite the last. There is still a chapter, the seventh, the last one. It is by far the shortest and it resembles a postscript to the entire book. First of all, because everything seems over when it opens, and then because it resembles, in its brevity, a sort of exit line [*chute*]. It is even shorter than the first chapter, which is already very short. For anyone also interested in this aspect of the composition of the work, it is noteworthy that the chapters get progressively longer: first five pages, then twice seven pages, then twice a dozen pages, then twenty, and then, all of sudden, the last chapter, three short pages. They form a free, detachable appendix, a play appendix [*appendice de jeu*], a supplemental postscript at play, all the more detachable insofar as it seems to add nothing, in terms of content, to the body of the essay as a whole. Yet another round [*coup*] of *fort/da*, for nothing, a final assessment in the form of a comet's tail, all the more detachable, even useless, insofar as it begins by declaring — once again — that everything remains unresolved (*noch ungelöst*), that the problem of the relations between the repetition compulsion and the mastery of the pleasure principle is still unresolved, and it concludes, limping, with a poetic reference to limping, which is no sin, and a reference to the interest there is in knowing when to abandon unfruitful paths. It is as if this short and useless chapter were a sort of atrophied member or clubfoot that remarks, by its very existence, the limping it inflicts upon the composition.

Does nothing really happen with this clubfoot or this shortened member? Does nothing about it work or walk [*marche*]? In chapter 5, Freud gave an example, to which I did not draw attention at the time, wanting to keep it for the end, an example of the repetition compulsion or of reproduction from the biological realm: at issue there is, I would say, the prosthesis, the operation by which a living being can replace a lost member by another, a process that can go on and on: "So too the power of reproduction extends far up into the animal kingdom, the power that replaces (*ersetzt, Ersatz:* prosthesis) a lost organ by growing afresh (*Neubildung*) a precisely similar one."⁵⁶

Prosthesis, then. Freud was beginning to know, to have a sense of, what it means always to have a prosthesis or to speak of prostheses whenever one opens one's mouth. I say this not because of his cigars but because of the terribly narcissistic cells that constantly had to be replaced, right up until his death, by an ever more palatial, plastic palate [*palais*], one that the PP had

345

---

55. *SE* 18: 60 [*GW* 13: 66].
56. *SE* 18: 37 [*GW* 13: 39].

difficulty accommodating. But the discourse of the prosthesis had begun much earlier, always already.

Does nothing then happen in this little prosthesis of a last chapter? Does it lead to nothing? Does it come to nothing? Perhaps not. We will read it next time, word by word, during the first part of the session, so as to open the discussion that will follow and close this seminar.

FOURTEENTH SESSION[1]

Tightenings

I will not come back to what has been said about the singularity of this seventh and final chapter of *Beyond*. After all the exhausting fits and starts, all the moments of indecision, the back and forths, the further steps and the steps no further [*les pas de plus et les plus de pas*], everything that characterizes the *démarche*, the de-ambulations, of this scene of writing, let me simply recall that at the opening of this last little chapter that has the air of a postscript, yet another postscript, everything is still, according to Freud's own words, unresolved, "*noch ungelöst.*"

What kind of irresolution, what kind of in-solution, what in-solvency, are we talking about here? I am indeed saying *insolvency*.

Insolvency or irresolution: these words perhaps resonate not only in the register of a theoretical problem to be resolved, a difficult question to be resolved—one that would be, perhaps, in the end, insoluble or insolvent—but also perhaps in the lexical register of speculation, where they would indicate some investment that speculates to the point of no longer being able to pay back what it owes, contracting debts to the point of insolvency, taking on obligations that no one can any longer fulfill, making every debtor (and first of all the theoretician who promises more than he can deliver) insolvent, a bankrupt speculator, the death drive or the repetition compulsion drawing him, sucking him into the abyss of the pleasure principle and adding always more abyss, a supplement of abyss, beneath his

---

1. There are handwritten annotations on the first page of the typescript that differ somewhat between T1 and T2. On the top right of T1 is the word "*serrements.*" To the left, two words: "*stricture / serrure.*" On T2, there are, in addition to the words from T1, these words at the center of the page: "the pleasure principle reigned over the plan," where "of" and "over" are circled; on the right, "Tightenings [*Des Serrements*]." For bibliographical information regarding the subsequent publication of this session, see the editorial note, pp. xiii–xivnn10–12.

347

every step, so that the obligation[2] to treat a question becomes like a debt, or even a culpability of which he will never again be absolved and for which no reconciliation will ever be possible. The theoretician-psychoanalyst responsible for *Beyond the Pleasure Principle* will never be forgiven. A crime, an offense, a violence has taken place. An unpayable debt has been contracted. Unpayable, perhaps, because what was violated and transgressed is perhaps an economy (not the economic in general), an economy whose principle of equivalence and thus of currency, and thus of signs (signifiers and signifieds), was done violence to, underwent forced entry — here, precisely, speculation — which makes the debt at once insolvent and void.

Insolvency and irresolution — these words also resonate, perhaps, with the code of what might be called a libi*n*dinal economy, that is, with the *bind* (*binding, double bind,* band, contreband, *binden* in German), a concept or metaphor that, as we saw, plays a major role in this text and in this problematic. A question of binding, then, the binding of energy, a binding that can or cannot be resolved, absolved, that is to say, dissolved, detached, *gelöst*, or that, as we will perhaps see, is bound or that binds itself back up by virtue of having been detached, etc.

Well, it turns out that these three registers of *lösen* (unbinding, dénouement, detachment, separation, or else the resolution of a problem, or the payment of a debt, the acquittal of an obligation, etc.), these three registers are constantly implicated in the text we are reading, which we are also reading as a narrative, an autobioheterothanatographical[3] narrative that, at the moment of the postscript, does not yet know its dénouement, the end of a *liaison* that continues to dominate the scene in the always dominating form — dominating par excellence and in essence — of the pleasure principle. The liaison that Freud cannot get over is *liaison* or binding itself, the principle of binding [*liaison*] that is bound up with the authority, the mastery, of the pleasure principle.

What is now going to happen? Are we going to learn the dénouement? No, of course not. But is nothing going to happen? No, of course not.

At the moment when (first paragraph of this chapter) this last leg begins (brief, truncated, as if interrupted), we are holding on by a hypothesis — as

---

2. In the typescript there is an insertion mark that is picked up in the left margin with the handwritten addition of two words: "contract / oath [*serment*]."

3. In the typescript it appears that Derrida wanted to add here a few words between the lines and place them before this neologism. But an arrow indicates that he subsequently decided to place them afterward. We can read here only "inter-," the remainder being illegible because of an ink stain on the typescript.

one would say by a thread—and the irresolution spoken of is itself hanging on this hypothesis. The argument has the following form: even if it were true (even following our hypothesis . . .),[4] the essential part of what we are looking for remains—would remain—unresolved.

So what exactly does this first paragraph say, a paragraph that begins by *If* (*Wenn*) and ends with the acknowledgment of *Unlösigkeit*, if not *Unlösbarkeit*. "*If* it is really the case that seeking to restore an earlier state of things is such a universal characteristic of drives, we need not be surprised that so many processes take place in mental life independently of the pleasure principle."[5] That is the intermediate stage in the argumentation: if our hypothesis were sound, we should not be surprised that so many processes are independent of the pleasure principle. It is in fact not totally clear why—and this will come back later—we should not be surprised once pleasure has also been defined as a drop in tension and a discharge. In any case, for the moment, we should not be surprised, says Freud, by this independence with respect to the pleasure principle. But the entire problem stems from the fact that this notion of independence remains highly indeterminate. Independence is not a relation; it is even rather a non-relation. And to say that certain processes are independent of the pleasure principle is to say nothing of these relations with the pleasure principle. What is going to remain *ungelöst* is precisely the question of this relation. *Ungelöst* also characterizes this non-relation or this indeterminacy of the relation between the pulsional processes of repetition and the pleasure principle. Freud says of these manifestations of the repetition drives:

> These are matters over which the pleasure principle has as yet no power (*Macht*); but it does not follow that any of them are necessarily opposed to it (*im Gegensatz zu ihm zu stehen*), and we have still [our task, *Aufgabe*, is still] to solve the problem of determining (*bestimmen*) the relation of the pulsional processes of repetition to the dominance of the pleasure principle.[6]

The *Herrschaft* of the pleasure principle is a power, a force, a holding sway, a mastery. It reigns over the so-called psychical domain—and it is indeed necessary to call this a domain. As soon as it begins to reign over

---

4. In the margins of the typescript there is a typewritten sentence preceded by the handwritten notation "p. 8": "Our hypothesis: irresolution, speculation, bottomless debt, unbinding or interminable binding, this irresolution is not simply on the side of the theoretical (comment) but in the thing itself, if there were such a thing, or actually in the scene of writing that binds them, unbinds them, etc." See below, p. 293n25.
5. *SE* 18: 62 [*GW* 13: 67]; Derrida's emphasis.
6. *SE* 18: 62 [*GW* 13: 67].

psychical life, both conscious and unconscious, to reign, therefore, over every living subjectivity, the meaning of such mastery has no regional limit. What I mean is that in speaking here of mastery we are not speaking metaphorically. It is perhaps, on the contrary, only on the basis of the mastery of something that is here called (hypothetically) the pleasure principle over the subject (that is, the psychical, and thus living, conscious and unconscious, subject), only on the basis of this mastery over the subject, that any mastery whatsoever can then be defined in a figurative or derivative way, for example, the ordinary meaning of mastery (in the sense of technique, expertise, or politics, or the struggle between consciousnesses). All these masteries presuppose a subject or a consciousness. If there first reigns over this subject or this consciousness the mastery (of the pleasure principle), it is to that mastery that one would first have to refer in order to look for any kind of proper meaning. It remains to be seen whether it really is a proper meaning that we would be dealing with here. And whether we are not still very ill-equipped to insist on a proper meaning in this region. We are going to confirm this later, in the process of expropriation that defines the structure of the pleasure principle. But, especially, we already acknowledged last time that we are in a region where the search for the proper, the law of laws, a law without law, exceeded all oppositions, and those of life and death par excellence, putting itself *en abyme*, and that the death drive, the self-destruction drive, had to be, precisely, one of *self*-destruction, of dying one's own death, a death coming from within; if the proper still produces itself as autothanatography, then it diverges enough from itself that we no longer know very well what we are talking about when we talk about the proper, the law of the proper, economy, etc.

What I have just said here about the figure of mastery and the inversion of meaning that has to be carried out with regard to it, from the figurative to the proper, from the regional to the non-regional, can and must be said about all notions, all concepts, all figures, whether they are directly dependent on this figure or not. For example, all those figures that come up in this chapter in decisive places, first among these being the figure of service (*Dienste*, when Freud says, for example, that certain processes operate *in the service* of the pleasure principle, or, conversely, that the pleasure principle is *in the service*, *im Dienste*, of the death drives), or else the values of tendency and of function. Take *functioning*, for example. The idea of function must be all the more rigorously subjected to this reevaluation insofar as it could initially be taken for a technological, machinic figure (a figure of machinic regularity) that is then transported into the psycho-biological domain. And you are aware of the almost unlimited scope of this functionalist vocabulary today, which is most often used in a dogmatic, pre-critical way. The idea of function—of psychical function—plays, indeed, a decisive role in this chapter. Freud distinguishes it from tendency.

Starting out from the "metaphor," if that's what you want to call it, of the psychical apparatus, Freud recalls one of its most important (decisive: *wichtigsten*) functions (*Funktion*) and, especially, one of its oldest, most primitive (in other words, quasi-congenital, essential, inseparable) functions, namely, that of *Binden*, the operation of banding, the structure, as I would say, of binding, strapping, tying, or chaining up. Okay, but what exactly? Well, what is just as primitive as this binding function, namely, pulsional forces, pulsional excitations (the X about which we know absolutely nothing before it is bound and represented by representatives). This so very early and decisive function consists, therefore, in *binding* and in replacing, for binding is immediately supplementing-substituting [*suppléer*], replacing (*ersetzen*, putting in place a prosthesis). It is in the same statement, describing one and the same operation, one and the same function, that Freud says that this function consists in binding (*binden*) the primary processes and replacing[7] (*ersetzen*) those primary processes that have mastery (*herrschenden*) in pulsional life with secondary processes (displacement, replacement of mastery, therefore). This replacement transforms the freely mobile cathectic energy into immobile cathectic energy (tonic: the value of tonicity, which is regularly associated with the effect of binding and which thus signifies at once elasticity and tension, very much legitimates the translation of *binden* by *bander* [in French]).[8] This early and decisive function of *binden* —this absolutely general function in the psychical apparatus—can be accompanied or not by unpleasure, a fact that is, says Freud at this point, of little importance to him. What is important to him is that this function is not opposed to the pleasure principle—on the contrary. And since we are reading Freud with one hand, and, through an analogous vocabulary, Hegel with the other, the Hegel of, for example, the master-slave dialectic, well then, note the word Freud uses to say that the function of *binden* does not end up contradicting the pleasure principle—on the contrary. He says: "this does not imply that

---

7. In the typescript this word is circled by hand and in the left margin there is this handwritten addition: "stricture = / supplementary detachment." These words are underlined several times and an arrow points toward the bottom of the page.
8. Above the word "*bander*" is the handwritten addition "*Porte-bande*." On Derrida's use of the words "band," "banding," "contra-banding," and so on, in *Glas*, see above, p. 268n22.

the pleasure principle has been suspended,"⁹ *aufgehoben*: one could almost say relieved [*relevé*] of its function.¹⁰ And he then adds: the *Umsetzung*, the displacement-replacement brought about by the binding, by the *binden*, emerges, takes place (*geschieht*), rather, *im Dienste des Lustprinzips*, in the service of the pleasure principle. Binding works for the pleasure principle. But then how does banding work in the service of the pleasure principle? There are, here, two predicates, two descriptive elements and two times. The *Bindung* is a "preparatory act (*vorbereitender Akt*)" in anticipation of the pleasure principle. As such, then, it is not yet the pleasure principle; it paves the way for the mastery of the pleasure principle. It introduces (*einleitet*) the master and then, in a second time, during the second phase of the same function, it confirms, affirms, "assures," says the translation, the mastery of the pleasure principle: "the binding is a preparatory act which introduces and assures (*einleitet und sichert*) the mastery of the pleasure principle."¹¹

The *Aufhebung* just named thus leaves open the question of whether, according to the hypothesis whereby the pleasure principle would come to be this time (it is not yet) *aufgehoben*, the *relève* or sublation will or will not be of a conventional Hegelian type, which could mean many different things but not its simple defeat or suppression. And this, once again, is not just one question of translation or rhetoric among others, or even one example of the difficulty we have had since Hegel (and no doubt before him) of translating *Aufhebung*!¹² If the pleasure principle is a decisive, early, and general function of the psychical apparatus, what I said earlier about the concept of mastery holds here for that of the *relève*: we are not going to grasp what is happening with the pleasure principle on the basis of what

---

9. [Translators' note:] Derrida has here modified the French translation to read: "*mais le principe de plaisir ne se trouve pas par là relevé*."

10. *SE* 18: 62 [*GW* 13: 67]. In the left margin of the typescript is the handwritten addition: "Heidegger? / cf. *Identity and Difference*."

11. *SE* 18: 62 [*GW* 13: 67].

12. In the typescript the exclamation point is circled and linked by an arrow to a handwritten addition of several words in the left margin: "Nancy, *auflösen aufheben*, p. 46 <illegible word>." For this reference to Jean-Luc Nancy, see *Post Card*, p. 395n5 [p. 422n2]: "On this entire problematic, today, the reading of Jean-Luc Nancy's admirable book, *La remarque spéculative (un bon mot de Hegel)* (Paris: Galilée, 1973), seems imperative to me. The relation between *Aufheben* and *Auflösen* in Hegel is precisely what is analyzed there, pp. 45ff." As for the translation of the Hegelian *Aufhebung*, Derrida proposed the French "*la relève*"; see "The Pit and the Pyramid: Introduction to Hegel's Semiology," in *Margins of Philosophy*, trans. Alan Bass (Chicago: University of Chicago Press, 1982), p. 88, and "Différance," *Margins of Philosophy*, p. 19.

we understand by the word *Aufhebung*. It is rather the entire interpretation of the *Aufhebung* that is going to be determined in return by what we say about the functioning of the pleasure principle, and about the psychical apparatus, *Bindung* in particular.

If the function of *Bindung* is not yet accompanied by pleasure or unpleasure, if it prepares the authority of the pleasure principle, where is the pre- of this preparation to be located and what does it mean? If the function is so general that it exceeds and precedes, in any case, the pleasure principle, how are we to conceive the relation between the function and the pleasure principle?[13] Freud sharpens the distinction he had earlier suggested (I noted it in passing) between tendency and function (*Tendenz/Funktion*). The relation of service (*Dienst*) is precisely the relation between tendency and function. There is an absolutely general function, a principle of functioning of the psychical apparatus, which is to render the psychical apparatus unexcitable (*erregungslos*), impassive, free of excitation, or at least to keep the amount of excitation within it constant and as low as possible (sleep . . .).[14] This general function to reduce excitation would be part of this *Streben*, part of this most general urge [*poussée*] of the living to return to the quiescence of the inorganic world. This finality, the finality of this return to the lowest possible state of excitation, to the inorganic, to non-movement, would thus be the most general function. And so the pleasure principle would be not a function but a tendency (*Tendenz*) in the *service* (*Dienst*) of this function.

(Nirvana) Function
↑
PP
↑
Binding function[15]

For example, the most intense pleasure we can attain, says Freud, sexual pleasure, coincides with the — it must be said — solution/resolution, the dissolution (*Erlöschen*, from the same root as the word *ungelöst*, which we commented on earlier) of this highly intensified excitation: one would thus say that the irresolution of the text or of the scene that we are reading is that of a *Bindung* that extends, unresolved, to an extreme degree, without conclusion,

---

13. In the left margin of the typescript is the handwritten addition "SAS," followed by "CAPS" or "CARS," both words or acronyms circled by hand.

14. In the left margin of the typescript is this handwritten addition: "paraphrase <for> the tr<anslation>."

15. These arrows were added by hand on the typescript.

without solution, without actually doing the deed [*passage à l'acte*], without orgasm, a scene that holds itself constantly at the limit, on the highest of high tension lines, at the limit of the beyond of the pleasure principle, which is also to say that it does not go beyond, since the best way of going beyond is to go by this way, the beyond of pleasure being the end of pleasure. And when one wants a pleasure without end, well, that is also the end of pleasure; one takes no pleasure so as not to lose it, so as not to go beyond in the "solution." All right, let me break that off here.

So pleasure would be a tendency in the service of this function to return to the inanimate. Let us not forget that this function[16] is also the function of a trajectory, and of a trajectory of return, and thus of the annulment of its own process, its own progress. The pleasure principle would thus be a tendency in the service of this function. It would come to serve the process of return. Why seek pleasure? Well, so as to return to the inanimate, to the discharge that produces this drop [*chute*] in excitation. It rises and it extends only to come back down; it gets charged only to discharge. Hence the function of *Bindung* would be a function preparatory to the exercise of this tendency, itself in the service of the general function. "The binding (*Bindung*) of pulsional excitations would be a preliminary function (*vorbereitende Funktion*) designed to prepare [*zurichten*, to ready] the excitation for its final resolution (*endgültige Erledigung*) in the pleasure of discharge (*Abfuhrlust*)."[17]

Pleasure, the tendency to pleasure, the mastery of the pleasure principle, are thus caught between two limits of non-pleasure, and between two functionings, two functions that are themselves without pleasure, the *Bindung* and the discharge, the preparation and the end, desire, if you will, and its ultimate fulfillment. No [*pas*] pleasure before, no [*pas*] pleasure after. Over what, then, over what time, does the pleasure principle reign—the pleasure principle whose *pas*, whose threshold, would nonetheless be so difficult to cross, a step [*pas*] so difficult to take [*dont le pas serait pourtant si difficile à franchir*]? Is not pleasure, between these two limits, a master whose sole operation consists always in producing itself only by limiting itself, only in the limitation of itself?

Our pains are not yet at an end. The concept and the place of pleasure appear more and more enigmatic. We asked at the beginning, do we even know what pleasure is? Do not philosophers, does not everyday language,

---

16. Here begins the transcription of a page, numbered 7, which is transcribed from T2 because it is missing in T1.

17. *SE* 18: 62 [*GW* 13: 68].

and does not even Freud himself make as if everyone knows what this strange limit is, this ungraspable limit between two limits, a this-side and a beyond that reduce the passage-between to nothing?

No pleasure, but then also, if it is pleasure that ceaselessly limits itself, negotiates with itself, contracts with itself in order to prepare itself, produce itself, resolve itself, disappear, reemerge, limit itself in order to produce itself, resolve itself, disappear, to serve the general function of which it is a tendency, there is nothing but pleasure. How is that possible?

The following paragraph brings the enigma or the paradox to its point of climax, since what will appear there is, it seems to me, something like this: the pleasure principle is[18] a sort of enemy of pleasure,[19] a sort of counter-pleasure, a contra-band band that comes to limit pleasure in order to make it possible, that limits and runs counter to the possibility of it in order to make it possible. A movement of bandaging [*bandage*] that I will call strictural, which limits so as to reproduce, is impotent so as to make potent, and so on. And everything takes place, then, between differences in quantity. Not a general but a strictural economy. What does Freud in fact say?

He basically says that the pleasure principle increases (in mastery) as the quantity of possible pleasure decreases. The primary processes, says Freud, are distinguished from the secondary ones by two features: on the one hand, they are, of course, prior, more originary (they are even the only originary processes), and, on the other hand, they are capable of giving rise to the most intense feelings, "much more intense (*weit intensivere Empfindungen*)" than the secondary processes. Much more intense in both directions, on the side of pleasure as well as of unpleasure. If, now, binding is the violent replacement of the primary by the secondary, thereby assuring the mastery of the pleasure principle, we get a very paradoxical result, that is, as Freud modestly puts it, "at bottom a not very simple result (*im Grunde nicht einfachen Ergebnis*),"[20] namely, that it is by limiting the capacity for intensity, by limiting the possible intensity of pleasure—as well as unpleasure—that the pleasure principle establishes its mastery. Its mastery is the result of a weakening, of a loss of intensity, a decrease in the force of unpleasure—as well as pleasure. One cannot master the one (and thus weaken it) without mastering (and thus weakening) the other. If the pleasure principle assures

---

18. The transcription of page 7 from T2 ends here.
19. In the left margin of the transcript is the handwritten addition "Socrates," which is circled by hand.
20. *SE* 18: 63 [*GW* 13: 68].

its mastery, it assures it first of all *over* pleasure.²¹ It is the prince of pleasure, the prince whose pleasure is the subjected subject, a subject that has been enchained, bound, weakened.²² Pleasure loses at this game, by assuring its own mastery. But does it not lose each and every time [*à tous les coups*] by winning each and every time? It wins each and every time to the extent that, as I suggested earlier, it is there before being there, it prepares itself, limits itself only to discharge itself, fulfill itself; it negates itself only to produce itself, it is beyond itself and pervades everything. (Hegelian *Aufhebung*.) But it loses each and every time in that, if it did not submit to binding, if it did not get linked up in the secondary process and did not submit to the pleasure principle, then its unleashed intensity would be threatening.²³ Death threat: (no) more [*plus de*] pleasure principle, thus (no) more modifying *différance* in the reality principle. Binding—the binding stricture—thus produces pleasure by limiting it. It is played out between two infinites. It wagers and it speculates on the surplus value of pleasure that the restriction of pleasure will be worth, this surplus value having to take the form not of a sharp increase but of a regulation, a tendency to constancy. Yet the master, namely, the pleasure principle, is not the master, the subject, or the author of this speculation. It is pleasure or, rather, desire that here speculates on the effects of stricture, that attempts by binding or by letting itself be bound, by making room, by giving way, precisely, to the mastery of the pleasure principle, thus limiting the quantity of pleasure, to increase it under the best possible conditions. It is the X (excitation giving rise to pleasure or unpleasure) that speculates; it is a speculative organization that calculates the proper subterfuge of its *Aufhebung*: it limits itself so as to increase, but if it limits itself, it does not increase, and if it limits itself absolutely, it disappears. But, conversely—if we can still say this—if it does not limit itself, if, for example, it absolutely frees something that is as close as possible to the primary process (a theoretical fiction), if, therefore, it does not limit itself at all, it limits itself absolutely (absolute discharge, death, etc.).

It is in this impossible logic that, finally, perhaps, the irresolution would be found. This irresolution (between the solution, i.e., non-binding, non-stricture, dis-banding [*débandade*], and the non-solution, i.e., binding, stric-

---

21. In the typescript this word is circled and underlined. There is also in the left margin this handwritten notation: "playing at two different games, hedging one's bets [*joue sur 2 tableaux*]."

22. There is here in the transcript the interlineal addition "semi."

23. In the left margin of the typescript are four words, among them, perhaps, "gl<as>" and "stricture."

ture,[24] *Bindung*) is the speculative stricture. It is not to be found on the side of the researcher or the psychoanalytic theoretician, on the side of Freud questioning the relations between the repetition compulsion and the pleasure principle. Or at least, it is not on that side because it is first of all on the side of the "thing-itself," which is not a thing but this *causa*, the process of this insolvent stricture of desire. Our own hypothesis: irresolution, speculation, bottomless debt, interminable unbinding or binding — all this irresolution is not simply on the theoretical side . . . but in the thing itself, if there were such a thing, in the scene of writing, in fact, that binds, unbinds them, etc.[25] In this process, there is no longer any opposition between pleasure and non-pleasure, life and death, this side and the beyond. We have just seen how the strictural logic (a non-dialectical, non-oppositional logic that nonetheless produces dialectical or oppositional effects, of the type master-slave, master-enchained-by-the-slave, that is to say, by himself, dying because he is afraid of death, etc.),[26] how the strictural logic is in some sense without lack, without negativity, or at least without oppositional negativity, without desire that comes from lack, without "without," if you will. There is, if you like, only pleasure that of itself limits itself, or only pain that of itself limits itself, with all the differences of force or intensity that make it so that, for example, in a particular system, a particular whole (not necessarily a subject or an individual, and even less an "ego"), a forceful stricture (a broad concept that includes all the concepts of repression — originary or secondary — as well as suppression) gives rise to "(no) more" pleasure and pain than a less powerful stricture would in another system. And the force of stricture — the capacity to be bound [*se lier*] — is also in relation with *what* is to be bound, the bindable quantity.[27] Which means, among

358

---

24. In the typescript there are two interlineal additions in this sentence: the word "lock [*serrure*]" is written above "non-stricture" and, in the following line, above "stricture." In the left margin is the handwritten word "*Glas*." For Derrida's use of the neologisms "stricture" and "striction" (constriction), see *Glas*, for example, pp. 99–100a [115a], 109bi [125bi], 142bi [162bi], 149bi [169bi], 184bi [207bi], 202b [227b], 244a [272a] and 249bi [276–77bi].

25. In the typescript there is an insertion mark that is repeated in the left margin with the following notation: "p. 2 margin," which is circled by hand. This refers to the preceding sentence typed in the left margin of page 2 of the typescript under the notation "p. 8." See above, p. 285n4.

26. In the left margin of the typescript are four handwritten words: "without castration / without *pas*."

27. In the typescript this last word is crossed out by hand and replaced by a handwritten interlinear addition, which may be "power [*puissance*]."

other things, that very free systems can and, I would even say, must be slightly eroticized, hedonized. But can one say eroticized or hedonized when the stricture in question is no longer directly or only of the order of sexual pleasure or sexuality? What Freud invites us to think here is[28] the beyond of sexuality silently at work in sexuality. The pleasure principle works in the service of sexuality, but just as well in the service of non-sexuality. Its mastery is no more sexual than non-sexual. And it would be necessary to treat mastery in general in a way that is analogous to what I sketched out last week on the subject of the proper, on the value of the proper that is beyond the opposition life/death as soon as a living being wants to die properly, in its own, proper, and immanent way. Well, there would be, bound to stricture, a value of mastery that would be neither of life nor of death, nor of consciousness (Hegel, or the struggle between consciousnesses), etc., neither sexual nor non-sexual. Where is mastery to be located? Where is the desire for mastery in this other sense? I would have liked to develop this problematic, particularly by picking up the thread of a concept and of a word that appeared in the course of the description of the grandson's *fort/da*. That is the concept of a *Bemächtigungstrieb*: a drive for mastery, a drive for power, or a drive to have power over [*pulsion d'emprise*], this last being perhaps best since it better underscores[29] the relation to the other (even in the power over oneself, mastery of the drive by itself).[30] *Bemächtigungstrieb* is a word, a concept, that has never occupied the forefront of the scene in Freud but that appears very early on (as early as *Three Essays on the Theory of Sexuality*, 1905) and then intermittently thereafter. To save time, let me simply refer you to the article by Laplanche and Pontalis[31] which examines the principal references to this notion and the evolution of it, *Beyond* marking, precisely, an important stage in this evolution, as is particularly clear in the passages related to sadism that I read last week. Look especially at

---

28. In the typescript there is here an interlineal addition of two words: "to bind." In the left margin is the handwritten addition of three or four words, two of which might be "in secret."

29. In the typescript a line drawn in pencil here leads to a handwritten addition in the left margin of three illegible words, which are circled. The first of these may be "*eigen*."

30. An arrow here leads to a notation in the margin: "mastery / of the drive / which itself <unreadable word>."

31. Jean Laplanche and Jean-Bertrand Pontalis, "Fantasme originaire, fantasme des origines, origine du fantasme," *Les Temps Modernes*, no. 215 (1964): 1833–68 ["Originary Phantasm, Phantasms of Origins, Origins of the Phantasm" (revised and abbreviated translation), *International Journal of Psychoanalysis*, no. 49 (1968): 1–18].

what is said there on p. 58³² about the oral organization of the libido, which, in *Liebesbemächtigung* ("erotic mastery [*emprise d'amour*]"),³³ tends toward the destruction of the object, while later, in what is called the genital phase, when procreation becomes the principal objective of love, the sadistic tendency urges one to lay hold of (*bewältigen*: to master, to dominate through force or violence) the sexual object and to dominate it to the extent necessary to complete the sexual act. *Bewältigung* is in fact a word or a concept that Laplanche and Pontalis associate, precisely, with *Bemächtigung*, and they are right to do so, it seems to me. It would be necessary to systematize the logic of this concept which is at play well beyond, as you see, all sorts of classical conceptual oppositions. This is also one of the places — it is all too obvious — where the relation to the Nietzschean will to power would have to be examined.

If it is thus the case that speculation remains necessarily unresolved because it always plays at a double game, band against band, losing to win and winning to lose, one should not be surprised that this goes so poorly; it goes poorly, and it has to go poorly, for it to go well. It very well limps along.³⁴ The allusion to limping that concludes the chapter must be understood not only as an illustration that reflects Freud's theoretical *démarche* (its explicit meaning) but also as the very form of the "thing." On the last page, which I am going to read in order to conclude quickly, there are three other motifs that I would emphasize if I had the time:

1. The fact that it ends with a quotation from a poet³⁵ (no traditional theoretical suture but a scene of citational writing: already commented on). No thesis but a prosthetic grafting, etc.

---

32. In the typescript there is an insertion mark and this interlineal addition: "p. 68 tr." [Translators' note:] This corresponds to page 54 in the English translation of *Beyond*.
33. *SE* 18: 54 [*GW* 13: 58].
34. In the typescript there is here an insertion mark that is repeated in the left margin with a handwritten addition, perhaps: "reread Z<arathustra> / to limping." Further down, we read: "not a sin." Between these two additions and in a different color is "Glas," which is circled by hand.
35. In the typescript a long arrow links the beginning of this paragraph to a handwritten addition in the bottom margin that could be: "quotation is *limping* [boiteuse] after <boitement?>."

2. The subterranean, silent workings of the death drives, which do not oppose, do not contradict, which say no more than they say against the pleasure principle, though they are in fact the mistresses [*maîtresses*][36] of the master [*maître*].

3. The question of the absolute magnitude of the charge, the cathexis, or of its modifications, the question of knowing whether the "feeling of tension (*Spannungsempfindung*)" is related to the absolute magnitude, to the level of investment, or to its variations over time, to the modification or alteration (*Änderung*) of quantities of investment in the series of pleasures or unpleasures. This question is very important. I will conclude with it. Let me read the last page first.[37] (Read pp. 63–64):

> Here might be the starting-point for fresh investigations. Our consciousness communicates to us feelings from within not only of pleasure and unpleasure but also of a peculiar tension which in its turn can be either pleasurable or unpleasurable. Should the difference between these feelings enable us to distinguish between bound and unbound processes of energy? Or is the feeling of tension to be related to the absolute magnitude, or perhaps to the level, of the cathexis, while the pleasure and unpleasure series indicates a change in the magnitude of the cathexis *within a given unit of time?* Another striking fact is that the life drives have so much more contact with our internal perception—emerging as breakers of the peace and constantly producing tensions whose release is felt as pleasure—while the death drives seem to do their work unobtrusively. The pleasure principle seems actually to serve the death drives. It is true that it keeps watch over stimuli from without, which are regarded as dangers by both kinds of drives; but it is more especially on guard against increases of stimulation from within, which would make the task of living more difficult. This in turn raises a host of other questions to which we can at present find no answer. We must be patient and await fresh methods and occasions of research. We must be ready, too, to abandon a path that we have followed for a time, if it seems to be leading to no good end. Only believers, who demand that science shall be a substitute for the catechism they have given up, will blame an investigator for developing or even transforming his views. We may take comfort, too, for the slow advances of our scientific knowledge in the words of the poet:

---

36. In the typescript the word "mistresses [*maîtresses*]" is circled by hand, and in the left margin there are these handwritten additions: "for fear of the other" and "has the *power*."

37. In the left margin of the transcript, next to this paragraph, is the handwritten word "inaugurated."

Was man nicht erfliegen kann, muss man erhinken.
. . . .
Die Schrift sagt, es ist keine Sünde zu hinken.

("What we cannot reach flying we must reach limping. . . . The Book tells us it is no sin to limp.")

Rückert, *Maqâmât* of al-Hariri[38]

So let me go back and simply say a word about the question of the absolute value of the charge or the cathexis and the question of knowing whether the feeling of tension (and thus of tonicity, of binding, of linking, of stricture) is linked to the absolute quantity of the cathexis or to the modification of the cathexis over time, this modification over time being at the origin of the experience pleasure/unpleasure. In this hypothesis, the ultimate concept or value would be that of a certain *rhythmos* that would have to be considered completely apart from all philosophy.[39] I tried to suggest this elsewhere (<in> DS[40] and in *Glas* with regard to Freud).[41] With regard to this hypothesis, let me simply, in order to conclude, and in order at least to give the appearance of paying my debt or fulfilling my contract,[42] of closing the loop, as I had announced, return briefly to Nietzsche, who writes in *The Will to Power*—and I read him here in translation since I did not have the time to find the original text: (Read *WP* 552-553-554[43] and beyond.)[44]

---

38. *SE* 18: 63–64 [*GW* 13: 68–69].

39. In the left margin of the typescript is a handwritten addition, perhaps "Fortsein."

40. This is probably an abbreviation of "The Double Session," in *Dissemination*, trans. Barbara Johnson (Chicago: University of Chicago Press, 1981), pp. 173–285 ["La double séance," in *La dissémination* (Paris: Éditions du Seuil, 1972), pp. 201–86].

41. See *Glas*, p. 154b [p. 174bi].

42. In the typescript there is an insertion mark and in the left margin this handwritten addition: "commitment / oath [*serment*]."

43. In the typescript the number "550" is handwritten above "552." [Translators' note:] These numbers correspond to the fragment numbers of the French edition of Nietzsche's *La volonté de puissance*, v. 2, trans. Geneviève Bianquis (Paris: Gallimard, 1948), pp. 370–71; none of these fragments appear in the English edition of *The Will to Power*.

44. In the large margin at the bottom of this last page of the typescript are several handwritten notations: "return to Nietzsche (recall the title / of the seminar) / Cut / <four illegible words> / <an illegible word> intemporal / mastery lever – quantity / <two illegible words>."

550

My first solution: tragic *pleasure* in watching what is highest and best sink (because one considers it too limited in relation to the Whole); but this is only a mystic way of approaching the superior "good."

My second solution: supreme good and supreme evil are identical.

1884–1885 (XIV, 2nd part, §168, lines 7–8)[45]

552

If we were to ask ourselves the crazy and impudent question of knowing whether it is pleasure or pain that prevails in this world, we would be indulging in complete philosophical dilettantism. One is better off leaving this question to women and dreamy poets. It may be that there is on a nearby star so much happiness and pleasure that it alone is able to offset ten times over "all the misery of the human condition"; what do we know? But also, we want to be the heirs of Christian meditation and sagacity and not condemn life *in itself*; if one no longer knows how to make a moral use of life, for the "salvation of the soul," one should at least leave it its aesthetic value, whether one be the artist or the spectator of it. If one were to eliminate all pain, the world would be unaesthetic in every sense of this word; and perhaps pleasure is but a form and rhythmic mode of pain! I mean, perhaps pain is of the very essence of existence.

IX 1885 – VI 1886 (XIII, §227)[46]

553

We can see just how much we are accustomed to living with a feeling of *well-being* from the fact that pain is felt *much more acutely* than any pleasure taken by itself.

A. 1883 (XIII, §665)[47]

554

Pleasure is a sort of rhythm in the succession of minor pains and in their relative *degree*, an excitation that results from rapid variations of intensity, as when one irritates a nerve, a muscle, but with a generally ascending curve; tension is here just as necessary as release. A tickling.

---

45. *KSA* 11: 27[67], p. 292. [Translators' note:] This fragment is cited in Georges Bataille, *On Nietzsche*, trans. Stuart Kendall (Albany: State University of New York Press, 2015), p. 169.

46. *KSA* 11: 39[16], p. 626.

47. *KSA* 10: 7[83], p. 271.

Pain is the feeling of being faced with an impediment; but since power becomes aware of itself only through impediments, pain is an *integral part of every activity* (every activity is directed against something it must overcome). The will to power thus *aspires* to find resistances, pain. There is a will to suffer at the root of all organic life. (As opposed to "happiness" taken as an "end.")

III–XII 1884 (XIII, §661)[48]

---

48. *KSA* 11: 26[275], p. 222.

INDEX OF PROPER NAMES[1]

Abraham, Karl, 257
Al-Hariri of Basra, 297
Aristotle, 21–23, 40, 76, 88–89, 102, 104, 174, 202, 206–8
Avery, Oswald, 113

Bachelard, Gaston, 69, 74
Badiou, Alain, 121
Bergson, Henri, 22, 174
Bernard, Claude, 21–22, 69–76
Binswanger, Ludwig, 258
Blanchot, Maurice, 5, 36–37, 54–56, 253
Bonaparte, Marie, 258
Bourdieu, Pierre, 11
Breuer, Joseph, 231–32, 244, 265
Brillouin, Léon, 122, 127
Buffon, Count George-Louis Leclerc de, 72
Burckhardt, Jacob, 163

Canguilhem, Georges, 20–23, 48, 57, 62, 68–76, 81
Carnot, Sadi, 231
Castil-Blaze (François-Henri-Joseph Blaze), 73
Clausius, Rudolph, 231

Darwin, Charles, 60–65, 100, 200
Descartes, René, 167
Deutsch, Felix, 258

Eitingon, Max, 256–57

Fechner, Gustav Theodor, 221, 232–33
Fétis, François-Joseph, 72
Fichte, Johann Gottlieb, 201
Fliess, Wilhelm, 259
Förster-Nietzsche, Elisabeth, 165
Freud (Halberstadt), Ernst, 246–56, 259
Freud, Julius, 259
Freud, Sigmund, 5, 87, 91, 137, 140, 183–84, 218, 219–97

Gast, Peter, 160
Gödel, Kurt, 114, 115, 134
Goethe, Johann Wolfgang von, 273

Haitzmann, Christoph, 279
Halberstadt, Heiz-Rudolf (Heinerle), 258–59
Halberstadt, Sophie (née Freud), 247, 255–58

---

1. This index of proper names covers only names that appear in Derrida's seminar, not those found in "The General Introduction to the French Edition," the "Editorial Note," the "Translators' Note," or in any of the notes of the editors or translators.

INDEX OF PROPER NAMES

Hegel, Georg Wilhelm Friedrich, 1–6, 21–24, 40, 47–48, 84, 87–89, 97, 167, 201–2, 212, 215, 229, 251, 287–88, 292, 294
Heidegger, Martin, 4, 6, 44, 47, 99, 102, 137, 140, 144, 148–50, 153–54, 156–218, 222, 253, 272
Helmholtz, Hermann von, 231–32
Hemery, Jean-Claude, 51
Heraclitus, 183, 187–88, 194
Hering, Ewald, 222
Hesiod, 149, 194–95
Hitler, Adolph, 44–45
Homer, 51
Husserl, Edmund, 212, 270

Jacob, François, 3, 8–23, 48, 57, 62, 76, 77–99, 101, 104, 106–114, 115, 118–137, 215, 271, 274
Jankélévitch, Samuel, 238
Jones, Ernest, 256–59
Jung, Carl, 276

Kant, Immanuel, 201–2, 208, 212, 265
Kierkegaard, Søren, 27, 174
Klossowski, Pierre, 158–59, 161–62, 171–72, 183, 199–201, 209
Kofman, Sarah, 58, 143

Lacan, Jacques, 278
Laplanche, Jean, 228, 231–32, 294–95
Lederberg, Joseph, 113
Leibniz, Gottfried Wilhelm, 75, 88–89

Marcinowski, Johannes (Jaroslaw), 261
Marx, Karl, 17, 47–48, 99–105, 223
Maxwell, James Clerk, 122
Meysenbug, Malwida von, 41
Monod, Jacques, 9, 89

Nietzsche, Friedrich, 4–6, 23–24, 27–49, 50–54, 56–69, 72, 74, 82, 88, 89, 137, 140–55, 156–76, 177–97, 198–218, 220, 222, 224, 226, 232, 271, 295, 297–99

Oedipus, 50–58, 64, 221, 256
Overbeck, Franz, 163

Periander of Corinth, 169
Plato, 23–24, 202, 206–8, 277
Ponge, Francis, 115, 145
Pontalis, Jean-Bertrand, 294–95
Pythagoras, 51

Rousseau, Jean-Jacques, 225–26
Rückert, Friedrich, 297

Schelling, Friedrich Wilhelm Joseph, 201
Schopenhauer, Arthur, 163–64, 193, 222, 224, 226, 232, 275
Schrödinger, Erwin, 127–28
Socrates, 84, 141
Sophocles, 51
Spinoza, Baruch, 88–89
Szilard, Leo, 122

Tasso, Torquato, 262
Tatum, Edward, 113
Thales, 195

Vialatte, Alexandre, 34–35, 37
Vico, Giambattista, 100

Wagner, Richard, 41, 163–64
Weismann, August, 274–75
Wiener, Norbert, 125
Wilde, Oscar, 246
Wittels, Fritz, 257
Wollmann, Elisabeth, 113
Wollmann, Eugène, 113

Zarathustra, 25, 31–33, 38, 48, 183, 186

www.ingramcontent.com/pod-product-compliance
Lightning Source LLC
Chambersburg PA
CBHW022034290426
44109CB00014B/854